Flyfisher's Guide to™
TEXAS

Titles Available in This Series

Flyfisher's Guide to™
TEXAS

Phil H. Shook

Flyfisher's Guide to™ Series

Wilderness
Adventures
Press, Inc.™

Belgrade, Montana

This book was made with an easy opening, lay flat binding.

Published by Wilderness Adventures Press, Inc.™
45 Buckskin Road
Belgrade, MT 59714
866-400-2012
Website: www.wildadvpress.com
email: books@wildadvpress.com

Printed in the United States of America

ISBN: 978-1-885106-88-9 (1-885106-88-2)

Dedication

To Kitty and Beth and our wonderful years in Texas.

Table of Contents

PRAIRIES and LAKES, REGION 2 — PAGE 68

PINEYWOODS, REGION 3 — PAGE 150

GULF COAST, REGION 4 — PAGE 214

Acknowledgements

Flyfishers and fly tiers, ranchers, fisheries officials, fly shop operators, writers, photographers, biologists and naturalists from across Texas were generous in providing me with their knowledge and insight about Texas waters.

I would like to recognize the following people for their help and support: Barry Austin, Mike Barbee, Greg Berlocher, Triple Bitter, Jack Boettcher, Brooks Bouldin, Larry Bozka, Rod Brashears, Cleve and Rosemary Breedlove, Jesse Breedlove, Ken Brumbaugh, Frank Budd, Fred Bunch, Ivan Calhoun, Jim Butler, Paul Cañada, Brian Camp Jr., John Carlin, Patti Carouthers, Raymond Chapa, Jr., Al Cohen, Jim Cox, Allen Crise, Charlie Cypert, Jim Dailey, Scott Daniel, Jim Darnell, Tim DeBord, Joe DeForke, Claude Dixon, Henk DeWit, Joe Doggett, Charles Ducote, Malcolm Duke, Charles Dukes, Charles Duvic, Susan Ebert, Dan Edwards, Howard Elder, Johnny Elkins, Jack Ellis, Marcos Enriquez, Tim Erdman, Sugar Ferris, Jay Forrest, Jim Foster, Wright and Susanne Friday, Brian Gambill, Bill Gammel, Bruce Gillan, Scott Graham, Duane Hada, Tom and Cindy Hargrave, Kendal Hemphill, Jeffrey Hines, Larry Hodge, Harvey B. Hopps, Mike Huffman, Kevin Hutchison, John Jefferson, Walter Jensen, Jeff Johnson, Ken Jolly, Wilfred Korth, Jinger Knight, Ken Kurzawski, Cruz Lamas, Lorraine Leavell, Steve LeBou, Verne and Judy Lehmberg, Lee Leschper, John Likakis, Jerry Loring, Joey Lin, Brian Lundy, Bob Lusk, Tom Lyons, Dan Lynch, Jeff Mack, Charly McTee, Steve Magnelia, Cary Marcus, Thom Marshall, Rosario Martinez, Ron Mayfield, Mark McDonald, Larry McKinney, Walter McLendon, Bob Miller, Doug Ming, Rusty Mitchum, Jerry Moulden, Billy Munn, Ron Newton, David Nichols, Larry Notley, Earl Nottingham, Dee Ogden, Richard Ott, Andy Packmore, Mark Petrie, Chris Phillips, Doug Pike, Polly Polishuk, Johnny Quiroz II, Ronnie and Sherry Ray, Ed Rizzolo, Ronnie Robison, Joe Robinson, Marcus Rodriguez, Lydia Saldaña, David Sams, John Scarborough, Art Scheck, Jim Schutze, Lindsay Sharpe, Brian Shivers, David Sikes, Lynn Solomon, Scott Sommerlatte, Colby Sorrels, Barkley Souders, Harold Speed, Ron Smith, Russell Smith, Ed Spencer, Brad Spencer, Marvin Spivey, Kevin Storey, Ron Henry Strait, Derek Stratton, Larry Sunderland, Al Thaggard, Russell Tinsley, Shannon Tompkins, Norm Tremblay, Billy Trimble, Stacy Trimble, Capt. Chuck Uzzle, Wally VanZant, Rod Viator, Stephen Vletas, Mike Verduin, Johnny Walker, John Warren, Ethan Wells, Mitch Whitney, Constance Whiston, Scott Williams, Danno Wise, Bill Waldron, Robert C. Woodruff, Kenneth Zwahr.

My special thanks goes to Mark D. Williams for generously passing on a good idea, and to Darren Brown not only for talking me into the project but supporting it every step of the way.

Introduction

Years ago when I was a boy, my father and his friend, Rudy Real, brought me along on a fishing trip to a ranch in the South Texas brush country not far from the Mexican border. It had taken us the whole morning to drive down from San Antonio and I was excited when we finally pulled up to one of the big stock tanks full of large-mouth. While the grown-ups milled around the car wasting time talking and telling stories, I quickly rigged my rod and headed for the water at a decent pace.

As I neared the shoreline, I saw Rudy Real, rod in hand, go by me at a dead run. He had decided he was going to beat me to the water and make the first cast.

It surprised me because I had never seen a grown-up act that way before.

Decades have gone by since then but I am still amused by the memory of that devilish grin on Rudy Real's face as he ran past me. I have wondered more than once whether he was just having a little fun with me, or, more likely, was as excited as I was about fishing these waters.

Writing this book has been a wonderful adventure that has taken me back to some familiar Texas waters and to many new ones.

Trying to research and write about fly fishing across an area as vast as Texas does not leave a lot of time to do much actual fishing. Most of the time is spent talking to other flyfishers, studying maps, and reviewing logs from previous trips. The experience was not without some exciting moments, however. While walking out on a little peninsula at Choke Canyon State Park a very agitated female alligator came charging out of the water and ran me down the shoreline. That was the first time anything like that has ever happened to me and it changed forever my approach to tranquil pond settings.

My research also took me to resacas in the Rio Grande Valley and to beautiful spring-fed Hill Country streams, where flyfishers can catch Guadalupe bass and Rio Grande perch, two Texas natives. It took me to scenic stretches of the Sabine River on the border with Louisiana, where the primeval bowfin, or grinnel, as they are called by the locals, waits to ambush streamer flies thrown under cypress knees. I learned about the Apache trout in the Guadalupe Mountains of far West Texas.

For the intrepid fly fisher with a sense of adventure, Texas offers an almost endless variety of productive waters and an amazing list of species. In addition to the 191,000 miles of streams and rivers and 212 major lakes and reservoirs, there are resacas, bayous, stock tanks and farm ponds for flyfishers to explore. In some parts of the state, even roadside irrigation ditches hold largemouth and sunfish that will eagerly attack a well placed popping bug.

Thanks to a progressive and forward-looking state parks and wildlife department, and conservation practices supported by the vast majority of anglers, the quality of recreational bass fishing on public lakes and reservoirs, rivers and streams in Texas is excellent, attracting anglers from all over the world. Programs to crossbreed Florida-strain and native-northern largemouth continue to produce bigger bass in Texas lakes. Freshwater flyfishers in Texas now catch largemouth weighing ten pounds or more and a striped bass in the 20 pound class is not out of the question at some lakes and rivers. Texas now offers quality tail water fishing for rainbow and brown trout and there are a number of quality smallmouth waters. Colorful bluegill, redbreast, longear and redear sunfish are abundant targets for flyfishers throughout the state and the white bass that swarm Texas streams and creeks during winter and spring spawning runs are pushovers for small streamers and minnow patterns. In some parts of Texas, flyfishers can also catch yellow bass, walleye, yellow perch and chain pickerel.

Whether the choice is a new or familiar river, lake or stock pond, a largemouth hangout or an open lake with schooling stripers, I hope this guidebook helps flyfishers enjoy many more exciting adventures on Texas waters.

Phil H. Shook
Houston, Texas
January 2001

Texas Facts

Second largest state in the union
Largest state with a largemouth bass population
Second most populated state
267,277 total square miles
5,363 square miles of water
171,057,280 acres
773 miles across
801 miles north to south

Elevations: Sea level to 8,749 feet
Counties: 254
Population: 22.8 million

18	National Wildlife Refuges
5	National Grasslands
4	National Forests
5	State Forests
1	National Seashores
2	National Parks
2	National Recreation Areas
2	National Historical Parks
1	National Monument
1	National Historic Sites
117	State Parks

Primary Industries: Manufacturing, farm products, minerals, financial services, electronics equipment, telecommunications, tourism
Capital: Austin
Bird: Mockingbird
Tree: Pecan
Flower: Bluebonnet
Fish: Guadalupe bass

Sources: Texas Almanac, Texas Parks and Wildlife Department

HUB CITIES

TEXAS
Major Cities, Roads & Rivers

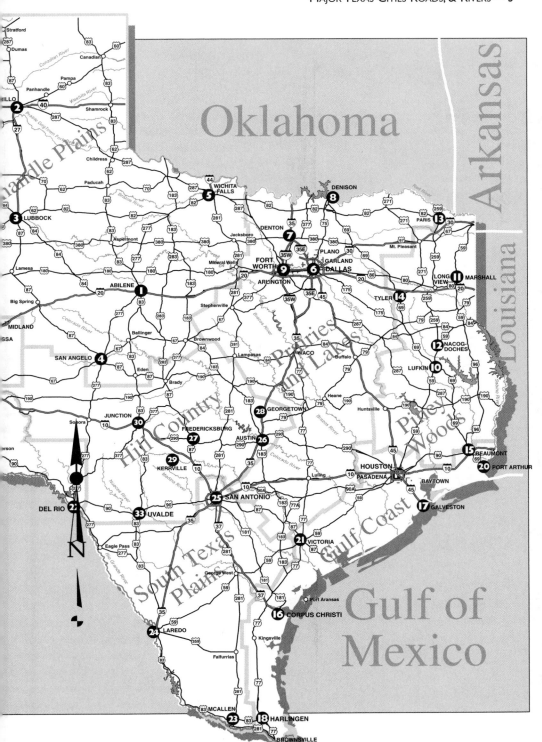

Tips On Using This Book

Within a short drive from every major Texas city is a lake, river or stream where flyfishers have the opportunity to sample some of the most exciting freshwater fishing in the country. The state offers anglers 3,700 named streams, 15 major rivers and 212 major reservoirs. More than 60 state parks offer access to freshwater fishing. To aid the angler in selecting a destination, the state has been divided into seven of its recognized regions: Big Bend Country, Panhandle Plains, Hill Country, South Texas Plains, Prairies and Lakes, Pineywoods, and Gulf Coast. In addition to geographic location, each of the regions has its own distinct natural features, climate, and in many cases, fish species unique to that area.

Within each region are separate listings for rivers, lakes, state park waters, private waters, urban options and border crossings. Before planning a trip, it is advisable to check with the sources listed for the most current conditions of any river, lake or stream.

While more than 90 percent of Texas lands are in private ownership, city, county and state park facilities offer access to a multitude of waterways. The most favorable state park waters for fly fishing are listed in the guide for each region along with information picnic, camping and launch ramp facilities.

A number of scenic, often lightly fished waters ideal for fly fishing lie within the city limits of major cities. These are identified under the heading "Urban Options."

Listed under the heading "Private Waters" are a number of ranches and farms in Texas that offer fishing for a fee on lakes stocked with largemouth, sunfish and other species. In many cases, these private waters are carefully managed to provide high quality fishing in relative solitude for those flyfishers willing to pay for the privilege. Fee-fishing operations can charge in a range of $100 to $275 per day with some providing food and lodging. The fee set by the owners of these fee waters is determined by the level of investment in the management of fish populations, stocking of forage fish, and control of vegetation and water quality. Some of these private waters also have fisheries biologists in residence.

Texas borders four other states, Oklahoma, Arkansa, Louisana, New Mexico, and Mexico. Prime fly fishing waters that lie within close proximity to the Texas border are listed under the heading "Border Crossings."

Profiles on fish species that are more prevalent in a particular section of the state such as Guadalupe bass in the Hill Country Region and bowfin in the Pineywoods Region are included in the appropriate region.

Hub city information in each region provides information on lodging, restaurants, local fly shops and guide services, airport facilities, hospitals and locksmiths.

LODGING PRICE KEY

$	=	$30 - $50 per night
$$	=	$50 - $70 per night
$$$	=	$70 per night and up

RESTAURANT PRICE KEY

$	=	$10 and under per meal
$$	=	$10 - $20 per meal
$$$	=	$20 and up

Fly Fishing Clubs are also listed in the guide by region. In addition to providing monthly programs, fly casting, and fly tying instruction these member clubs of the Federation of Flyfishers provide another way to obtain access to prime fly fishing waters in Texas through their organized outings.

Fishing Regulations

THE FOLLOWING REGULATIONS ARE EFFECTIVE THROUGH 2001

Fishing Licenses

Resident Fishing License $19
All Texas residents who fish in the public waters of the state are required to have this license unless they are under the age of 17, or were born before Sept. 1, 1930.

Temporary (3 day) Resident Fishing $10
Temporary (14-day) Resident Fishing....... $12
Special Resident Fishing.................... $6

This license is required of any Texas resident fishing in the public waters of the state who is at least 65 years of age and was born on Sept. 1, 1930 or , is legally blind.

Non-resident Fishing..................... $30
Required of all non-residents who fish in the public waters of Texas. Not required of any non-resident under 17 years of age, or an Oklahoma resident 64 years of age or older.

Temporary (5-day) Non-resident Fishing.... $20
Valid for 5 consecutive days for non-residents and subject to the same additional requirements stated above under the Non-resident Fishing license.

Fishing Stamp Fees and Tags

Freshwater Trout Stamp Fee $7
This stamp is required in addition to a valid fishing license for those taking or attempting to take any species of freshwater trout.
It is not required for those exempt from holding a fishing license.

Saltwater Fishing Stamp Fee $10
This stamp is required in addition to a valid fishing license in order to fish in the public coastal waters of Texas. It is not required for those who are exempt from holding a fishing license.

License Requirements For Border Waters

Texas-Oklahoma and Texas-Arkansas

To fish in all waters of the Red River along the Texas-Oklahoma or Texas-Arkansas borders, with the exception of that portion which is Texas public waters (consisting of the area from Denison Dam downstream to and including Shawnee Creek), a person must comply with the licensing requirements of Oklahoma or Arkansas, as applicable.

In Lake Texoma, a person may fish in Texas and Oklahoma waters with the appropriate license from each state, or may fish the entire lake with a Lake Texoma fishing license.

Lake Texoma License **$7.50**

The holder of this license, which is in effect through December 31 following the date of issuance, is allowed to fish all Lake Texoma waters without holding any additional Texas or Oklahoma fishing licenses.

Texas-Louisiana

Residents of Texas and Oklahoma who hold valid fishing licenses in their respective states (or are exempt because of age), or persons who hold valid non-resident fishing licenses issued by either state, may fish in any portion of the lakes and rivers of these states that form a common boundary.

Texas-Mexico Fishing License

A fishing license issued by Mexico is required when fishing in Mexican waters.

Statewide Bag and Length Limits

BASS: largemouth, smallmouth, spotted and Guadalupe bass
Daily Bag: 5 (in any combination)
Length in inches (minimum): 14 for largemouth and smallmouth bass; no limited on spotted and Guadalupe bass.

BASS: striped and hybrid striped bass
Daily Bag: 5 (in any combination)
Length in inches (minimum): 18

BASS: white
Daily Bag: 25
Length in inches (minimum): 10

BASS: yellow
Daily Bag: no limit
Length in inches (minimum): no limit*

CATFISH: channel and blue catfish, their hybrids and subspecies
Daily Bag: 25 (in any combination)
Length in inches (minimum): 12

CRAPPIE: white and black crappie, their hybrids and subspecies
Daily Bag: 25 (in any combination)

SUNFISH: various species including bluegill, redear, green, warmouth and longear
Daily bag: no limit
Length in inches (minimum): no limit

TROUT: rainbow and brown trout, their hybrids and subspecies
Daily bag: 5 (in any combination)
Length in inches (minimum): no limit

WALLEYE
Daily bag: 5 (with only two less than 16 inches in length)
Length in inches (minimum): no limit

*There are a number of exceptions to the statewide bag and length limits that apply on specific Texas lakes. Anglers should check these exceptions, which are listed in the Texas Parks and Wildlife Outdoor Annual that is available where fishing licenses are sold. For additional information contact the Texas Parks and Wildlife Department at 1-800-792-1112 or (512) 389-4800.

Texas Parks and Wildlife Inland Fisheries Field Offices
Austin Headquarters/4200 Smith School Road, Austin 78444/800-792-1112

Panhandle Plains/Big Bend Country Region
District 1-A/P.O. Box 835, Canyon 79015/(806) 655-4341
District 1-B/5325 North 3rd, Abilene 79603/(915) 692-0921
District 1-C/4002 North Chadbourne, San Angelo 76903/(915) 655-9413
District 2-E/409 Chester, Wichita Falls 76301/(817) 766-2383

South Texas Plains/Gulf Coast Regions
District 1-D/135 Braniff, San Antonio 78216/(210) 348-6355
District 1-E/P.O. Box 116, Mathis 78368/(512) 547-9712

Prairies and Lakes Region
District 2-A/Route 4, Box 157/Denison 75021/(903) 786-2389
District 2-B/8684 La Village Avenue, Waco 76712/(817) 666-5190
District 2-D/6200 Hatchery Road, Fort Worth 76114/(817) 732-0761

Hill Country Region
District 2-C/Box 947, San Marcos 78667/(512) 353-0072

Pineywoods Region
District 3-A/3802 East End Boulevard, Marshall 75670/(903) 938 1007
District 3-B/2122 Old Henderson Highway, Tyler 75702/(903) 593-5077
District 3-C/11924 FM 848, Tyler 75707/(903) 566-2161
District 3-D/Route 2, Box 535, Jasper 75951/(409) 384-9572
District 3-E/1004 E. 26th Street, Bryan 77803/409 822-5067

Texas State Park Reservation Information
Telephone reservations: (512) 389-8900
FAX Reservations: (512) 389-8959
Internet Reservations: www.tpwd.state.tx.us
E-Mail Reservations: e-mail. reservations@tpwd.state.tx.us
Park Information: (800-) 792-1112
Source: Texas Parks and Wildlife Department

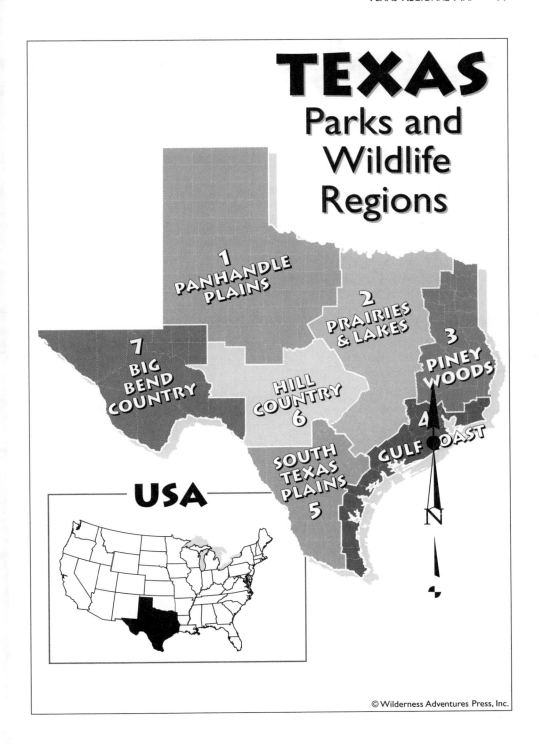

© Wilderness Adventures Press, Inc.

REGION 1

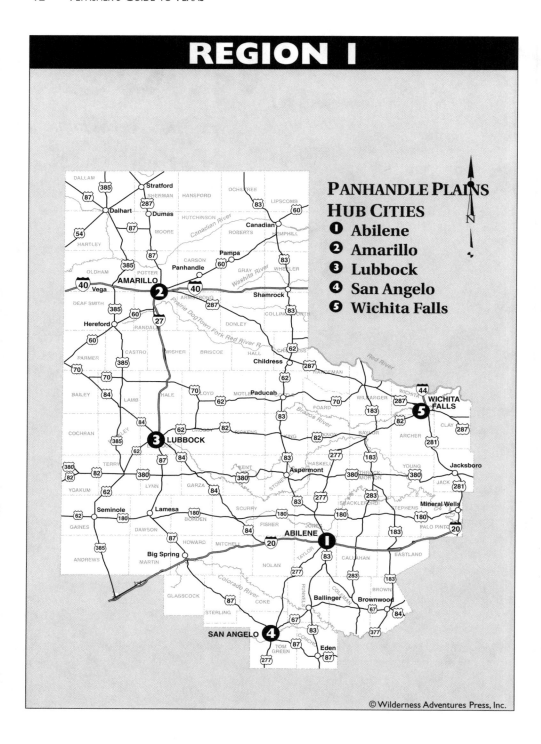

PANHANDLE PLAINS HUB CITIES

❶ **Abilene**
❷ **Amarillo**
❸ **Lubbock**
❹ **San Angelo**
❺ **Wichita Falls**

© Wilderness Adventures Press, Inc.

Panhandle Plains Region

High plains flyfisheries are so diverse you don't have to go to the Great Northwest or the Deep South to catch Kentucky and Alabama spotted bass, yellow perch and walleye.

These fish along with other warm water species can be found in the waters of this vast region called the Panhandle Plains.

The most dramatic feature in this northernmost region of the state is Palo Duro Canyon near Amarillo. Located in one of the state's most popular state parks, this 1,000-foot deep, 120-mile-long canyon surrounded by red cliffs and strips of white caprock suddenly unfolds out of a featureless plain.

On the eastern boundary of the Panhandle Plains, flyfishers can do battle with largemouth on Possum Kingdom Lake or take a float down the clear-flowing stretches of the Brazos River where gangs of white bass often bunch up in the deeper pools eagerly attacking Clousers and other glass minnow fly patterns.

To the south, the flooded timber at Lake O.H. Ivie and the oak-shaded waters of Brady Creek Reservoir provide exciting largemouth and sunfish action.

Dominant features in this region include Palo Duro Canyon, Caprock Canyons, Lubbock Lake Landmark with its archeological exhibits, the frontier forts, including Fort Griffin and Fort Richardson and Lakes Arrowhead, Possum Kingdom, Copper Breaks, Brownwood.

RIVERS

BRAZOS RIVER

The Brazos River System, which begins northwest of Clovis, New Mexico, winds south through an immense area of West Texas, traveling 800 miles to the Gulf of Mexico. Aided by the settling effects of dams on Lakes Possum Kingdom and Whitney, its waters run clear and clean through the limestone cliffs in its midrange, making these stretches of river ideal for floating and fly fishing. The spring and fall months are usually the best times for float trips on this section of the Brazos. Water levels are better at these times and temperatures more moderate. The hot summer months are good only if there is enough water in the river for enjoyable canoeing.

Veteran Brazos River fly fisher Brian Camp says that throughout the length of the Brazos, anglers will find fish congregating where the riffles meet the larger pools. At one of these features the dominant fish may be white bass, and at another it may be Kentucky spotted bass or drum and catfish. The ideal time to fish these features is in the early morning, Camp says, "when every fish in the river seems to move up into these spots."

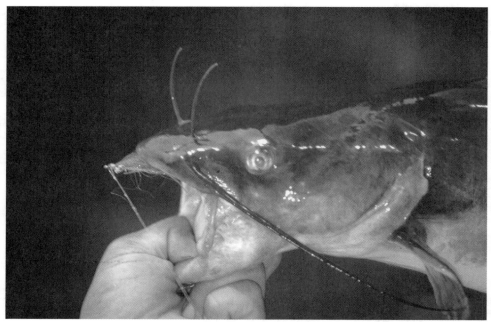

Catfish with fly.

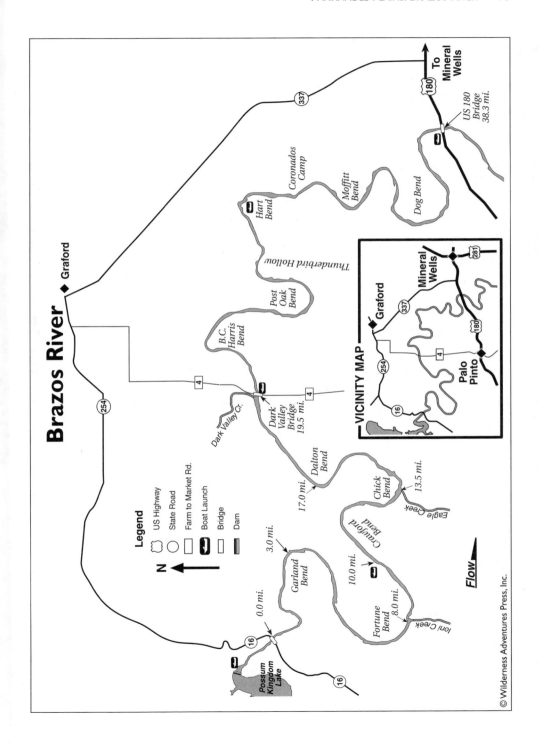

© Wilderness Adventures Press, Inc.

Spotted Bass

The spotted bass (Micropterus punctulatus), *also called the Kentucky spotted bass, is a member of the sunfish family and is often confused with the smallmouth bass and Guadalupe bass in its Texas range.*

Spotted bass have the dark, irregular lateral band of the largemouth bass but a measurably smaller mouth. In addition, the dorsal fin of the spotted bass is not as deeply notched as the largemouth. Spotted bass often live in waters that also hold smallmouth bass but they do not have the vertical barring of the bronzebacks.

A native of the Colorado River drainage system, and other waters to the east, including the upper Brazos, Neches, Sabine and Cypress rivers, the spotted bass is most likely to be found in clear streams with gravel bottoms, riffles and pools or in the deeper waters of reservoirs. Spotted bass are also found in reservoirs in the eastern part of the state including Lake Texoma, Caddo Lake and Sam Rayburn Reservoir.

The diet of the spotted bass is similar to the smallmouth and includes crayfish, small minnows and insects, making it an ideal target for a variety of streamer, nymphs and minnow fly patterns. The growth rate of the spotted bass is not as rapid as the largemouth or smallmouth and the fish will average a half-pound or less after the first year. The average size of mature fish is one to two pounds but specimens weighing in excess of 5 pounds have been taken at Lake O' the Pines.

The Kentucky spotted bass is the main species for flyfishers throughout the Brazos. They are beautiful fish that exhibit a variety of shades sometimes gold and bronze and sometimes green. The average size of these river bass is ten to 12 inches but specimens as big as 4 pounds have been caught on the Brazos.

A primary food source of the spotted bass are mayflies about size 16, Camp says. "They will literally cover you in a hatch, just like in Montana," he says. The same thing applies to caddis-flies, which is a night hatch on the Brazos. Camp says the caddis hatch is found about 16 miles below Possum Kingdom and continues to Lake Granbury.

A variety of dry fly patterns work on the Brazos, including the Adams. Camp says a 4-weight outfit is ideal for the river. "It is a real thrill to dead-drift a true dry fly and catch bass. They fight as hard as a trout, they jump and shake their heads."

Camp notes that other important insects on the Brazos are dragon flies and damsel flies. "You can fish any imitation of these, and the old standby Woolly Bugger in olive does a pretty good job of imitating both of them."

Brazos River tailwaters below Possum Kingdom Dam to Highway 16 Bridge

From December through mid-February, the river just below the dam becomes popular for trout fishing. The Possum Kingdom State Fish Hatchery releases some 3,000 eight- to ten-inch rainbow trout at approximate two-week intervals, to coincide with water releases, beginning in mid-December.

Local fly fishing clubs successfully fought to obtain flow levels from Possum Kingdom Lake to support a trout fishery on tail waters of the Brazos River. Drought conditions have affected Possum Kingdom water levels and resulted in drought contingency management of lake levels in recent years, which also has affected the fishery. Despite this, the put and take fishery in the tail waters below Possum Kingdom Dam continues to do well.

Camp says that in non-drought years when there have been constant flows throughout the summer, the stocked trout will survive through the hotter months. During drought years with flows reduced, it impacts the holdovers but these tail waters still provide quality trout fishing from December through April.

One change in recent years is that the trout stockings are made from the Texas 16 Bridge downstream. So, while there is some trout fishing above the bridge, most is now done downstream from the bridge.

The constant flows on this stretch of the Brazos has had a positive effect on the fishery in that it has improved the insect population, which now includes caddis. "It used to just be midges and that was all," Camp says. "Now there are some caddis, and the little black and white mayflies." So there are now some legitimate hatches on the river, although they are unpredictable.

Caution: When fishing below Possum Kingdom Dam and other tailwater fisheries below large dams, anglers are warned to be on the alert for a horn or siren. Upon hearing such an alarm, move to higher ground immediately. The horn or siren alarm means the authorities are about to open the flood gates to release water.

Fly patterns that have proven to be effective on the Brazos for trout and warm water species include gold-ribbed hare's ear, muskrat, tellico, mosquito emergers, black midges, squirrel nymphs, royal coachman, Woolly Buggers, and elk hair caddis.

The warm water fishery around the tail race has not been affected that much by recent drought conditions, Camp says. "The stripers are still there, the white bass still run up there in the spring, and spotted bass are still there in good numbers."

Float Trip Options

Local canoe outfitters will provide shuttle services for flyfishers to put-ins at the dam for a float down the Brazos to the take-out at the Dark Valley Bridge on Texas 4. They also have a put-in at Crawford Hollow that allows the option of a one-day float to the Dark Valley Bridge.

Camp says the floats offer great opportunities for flyfishers to catch good numbers of bass and big redbreast, or yellow-belly sunfish. The game fish on this stretch of the Brazos are pretty easy to find because they will hold at the head of the deeper pools early and late in the day.

Highway 16 Bridge below Possum Kingdom Dam to Dark Valley Bridge on Texas 4

This 19.5 mile, two day float, with one night spent camping on the river, is considered one of the most remote, scenic, and exciting trips on the Brazos. Noteworthy features on this stretch of river include Flint Bend, Garland Bend, Garland Creek and Fortune Bend.

Canoeists and kayakers will find the first three miles of river into Garland Bend provide changing vistas of bare cliff faces and distant hills. Massive limestone boulders cluster on one shoreline while stately oaks, cottonwoods, and willows surround small, open meadows on the other. In the spring, the brilliant yellow blooms of cactus pear can be seen on the sandy banks overhead.

Ioni Creek

Near Fortune Bend, the Brazos meets Ioni Creek. Here, legend has it, one day in 1873 settlers Jesse Veale and Joe Corbin had gone to set fishing lines, only to tangle with a group of Comanches disgruntled over the loss of their ponies the day before. According to an account related by author John Graves-who wrote an evocative narrative in 1960 of a two-week float down the Brazos-Corbin escaped, but Veale wasn't so lucky. When Corbin came back with help, Veale was found "sitting dead but unscalped against a double elm tree, his pistol gone, Comanche blood on the ground around him."

Anglers on the Brazos have not encountered any Comanches in years and the only attacks today come from packs of white bass, or sandies, as they are called locally, when they gang up to feed on minnows around the gravel bars and fast water.

Veteran Brazos River fly fisher and outfitter Richard Hart of The Brazos Fly fisher, says another popular fly on the river is the *Hexagenia limbata*. He ties the big white Hexagenia wingless on a size 8 or 10 hook with a lot of cream-colored saddle hackle. "It is like a big sofa pillow and looks just like those big spinners on the surface," he says.

These flies are fished most effectively-like others on the Brazos-where the riffles run into the pools. Hart recommends casting into the riffles and letting the fly float down directly into the pool where warmouths, bluegills, redears, pumkinseeds and other sunfish compete with Kentucky spotted bass and largemouth for insects.

A commercial fly tier with a degree in biomedical engineering, Hart offers his clients instruction in stream entomology as well as suggestions on fly selection.

When fishing a lightweight rod for panfish, it is not uncommon to find yourself connected to a hefty largemouth, Hart warns. "A friend of mine sent me a picture of a 21-inch long, 14-inch around, five-pound black bass. He was fishing with a tiny streamer fly, trying for those little Kentucky bass and bingo..."

Hart says he targets the little Kentucky spotted bass along the rocky seams in the fast water. During the day when they are not rising to the surface he recommends casting beadheads or Clousers across the flow and drifting them downstream. "With these impressionistic flies, the faster you strip, the better for the spotted bass," Hart says. "I think the fish see the fly and say, gee, what was that?'"

Fortune Bend

In the sheltered coves around Fortune Bend, carp can be found splashing along weed lines, while alligator gar cruise lazily near the surface. Back in the coves, small but feisty largemouth will take Woolly Buggers tossed up near the bank. The Kentucky spotted bass is one of several prized targets for flyfishers throughout the river. They average 10 to 12 inches, but specimens as large as four pounds have been caught in the river. Fort Worth fly fisher Brian Camp, a veteran of many floats down the Brazos, says some of the best features to fish on this stretch of the river are where the riffles enter the larger pools.

Camp says these bass feed on mayflies and caddisflies, and that most classic dry-fly patterns around size 16 are effective, including the Adams. Brazos River outfitter Richard Hart of The Brazos Fly fisher says another popular fly on the river is the *Hexagenia limbata*. He ties the big white Hexagenia wingless on a size 8 or 10 hook with a lot of cream colored saddle hackle. These flies are fished most effectively, like others on the Brazos, where the riffles run into the pools.

Hart recommends casting into the riffles and letting the fly float down directly into the pool where warmouths, bluegills, redears, pumpkinseeds, and other sunfish compete with Kentucky spotted bass and largemouth for insects.

Crawford Bend

At Crawford Bend, about 10 miles downriver, there is a good stopping point for camping on two day floats. The channels grow deeper, and there are stretches of fast water in narrow shoots. At the foot of the rapids are crystal clear pools with enough depth to conceal the bottom. Throughout the day, these deeper holes are ideal holding areas for white bass.

Eagle Creek

A little past the halfway point of this float around Crawford Bend, there are open gravel bars and split-level banks in stands of huge oaks and cottonwoods that make ideal campsites. Campers can try for the green sunfish and other panfish found in the many small creeks and narrow sandbars of the main river. A bendback streamer fly teased through the nest of sunken branches will draw lots of attention from sunfish.

At daybreak, it is not uncommon to see wild turkeys flying high over the river from their roosts in the stands of tall oaks and pecans along the river banks.

Chick Bend

Even at low water levels, the river starts to deepen in the Chick Bend area 13.5 miles from the Texas 16 Bridge.

On the second day of a two day float from the Texas 16 Bridge below the dam to the Dark Valley Bridge, canoeists and kayakers glide downriver over wide gravel bars, where pods of carp can be seen dashing upstream, nervous at being spotted in the clear, shallow water.

There is the occasional stretch of boulder-filled, relatively mild rapids to break the rhythm of the gentle flow in the deeper stretches of the Brazos. As anglers move downriver into the elbow of Crawford Bend at about the 12-mile point, the channels grow deeper. Midmorning stops at the many gravel bars next to the narrow chutes of fast water can produce nonstop white bass action in the spring and early summer. At the foot of the rapids are clear pools with enough depth to conceal the bottom. A weighted streamer fly dressed with white bucktail and a little flashy material often will draw strikes from the white bass.

Dark Valley Creek

One of the best stretches for casting a Woolly Bugger or one of Richard Hart's Ghost Minnow patterns to largemouth is along the grassy shorelines near the end of the 20-mile float when you can see the Dark Valley (Texas 4) Bridge and the take-out point in the distance.

Rochelle's Canoe Rental, Dark Valley (Texas 4) Bridge, Graford

Rochelle's Canoe Rental in Graford provides canoe rentals and shuttle service for the two-day 19.5-mile float that puts in at the Highway 16 bridge below Possum Kingdom Dam. For information on rental rates and river flows, call Rochelle's at (940) 659 3341. There is overnight camping available at Rochelle's or at motels in nearby Palo Pinto and Mineral Wells. Richard Hart's Brazos Flyfishers in Granbury, (817 279-1169) offers a variety of guided fishing expeditions on the Brazos.

The spring and fall months are usually the best time for float trips on this section of the Brazos. Water levels are better at these times and temperatures more moderate. The hot summer months are good only if there is adequate river flow for enjoyable canoeing.

Dark Valley Bridge (Texas 4) to Hart Bend (Rochelles Shuttle Pick up)
9.5 miles
Rochelle's Canoe Rental located on the east side of the river at the Dark Valley Bridge (Texas 4) can provide access and shuttle service for the 9.5 mile float to Hart Bend, a private access point. This stretch of the Brazos, which holds good numbers of largemouth and spotted bass, can be floated and fished in a half day.

Hart Bend to US 180 Bridge
This 9.3 mile float, which ends at the US 180 Bridge just west of Mineral Wells can be the second leg of a two day float beginning at the Dark Valley Bridge/Rochelle's put-in. There are many primitive camping areas along this stretch of the Brazos. For additional information, contact Rochelle' Canoe Rental at (940) 659-3341.

BOSQUE RIVER

The Bosque River begins near Stephenville in Erath County and runs down toward the communities of Meridian and Clifton. It starts off as a spring-fed river, much like the Paluxy River, and then turns into a runoff dependent river. It is smaller than the nearby Paluxy but there are sections with deeper holes that will hold fish. The species include Kentucky spotted bass, largemouth, catfish, carp and a variety of sunfish. One of the problems with some sections of the Bosque in recent years is the effect of runoff from dairy farms in the area. Erath County is one of the top milk producing counties in north central Texas. In addition to depositing biological pollutants, the runoff creates a nitrogen bloom, which creates algae and can clog up the stream. South of Erath county, the natural ability of the stream to filter itself alleviates the runoff problem making the Bosque a excellent river for flyfishing. "The redbreast sunfish, bluegill and green sunfish are beautiful and it is a great small venue for flyfishers," says Richard Hart, a flyfishing outfitter from Granbury.

The Bosque has deep holes that hold good numbers of bass and sunfish. The headwaters of the Bosque and Paluxy rivers begin in feeder creeks in Erath County near Texas 108 and the community of Huckabay. The Bosque, which is a rain and runoff dependent river, runs south through the community of Hico where it is fed by the Duffau River. The most fishable stretches of the Bosque are along Texas (FM) 6 from the community of Iredell to Meridian and down to Clifton, Hart says. The best way for flyfishers to access this river is to walk in and wadefish short stretches at bridge crossings.

SAN SABA RIVER

"What makes the San Saba River an excellent fly fishing destination (especially for largemouth and sunfish) so much different from Hill Country streams like the Frio and the Llano is that it doesn't have as steep a gradient to it as those rivers do," says Billy Trimble, an Austin fly fisher, who has fished all of these rivers since his boyhood. The San Saba is a small waterway but it is not out of the ordinary for flyfishers to take largemouth there in the 5 pound class, Trimble says.

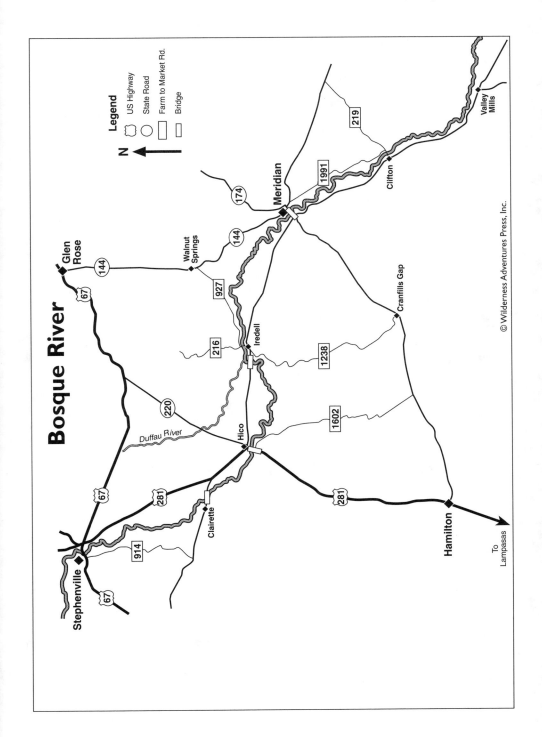

Bosque River

Legend
- US Highway
- State Road
- Farm to Market Rd.
- Bridge

N

© Wilderness Adventures Press, Inc.

San Saba River

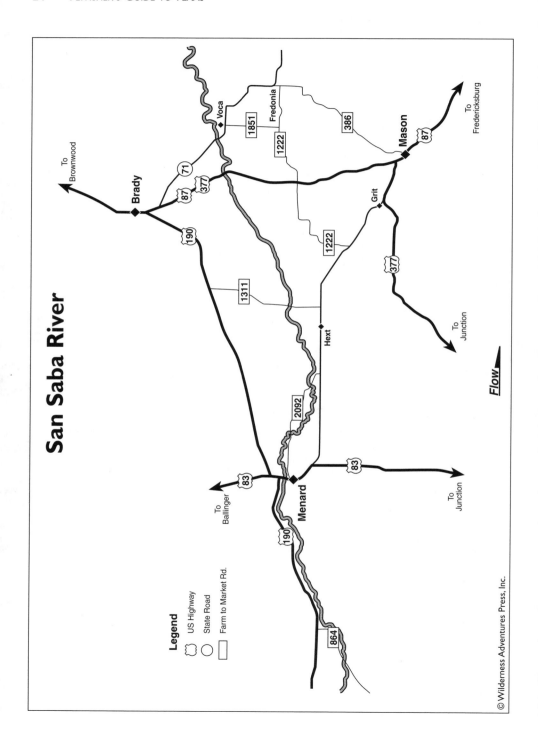

Legend
US Highway
State Road
Farm to Market Rd.

© Wilderness Adventures Press, Inc.

Flow

Anglers are cautioned against taking on too much of the San Saba on floats because a four- or five-mile float on the San Saba can take eight to ten hours and keep an angler on the water from dawn to dark.

The terrain has the feel of the Panhandle Plains region, which is logical since it is in an area that forms a transition from the Hill Country to the south and the Panhandle to the north. A scenic waterway, the San Saba is a slow moving river with deep pools, undercut banks and oaks, pecans, and other thick vegetation growing down to the river's edge. "Once you are on the river, you feel very closed in although you are out in the plains," Trimble says. He notes it is a very small stream, very much like a creek in many places. "It has long slow moving water and deep holes and then it will have a short creek-like channel that will run down to another long, slow-moving hole. And that is what makes it such an excellent largemouth bass fishery," Trimble says.

The San Saba River can be fished year around but Trimble says he leaves it to hunters during the hunting season in the fall and winter.

Public access to the San Saba

The sections of the San Saba that are realistically accessible to the public are all in Menard County, Trimble says. "There are excellent stretches of water in San Saba County but it is bordered there by private ranches and difficult to access," he says. To avoid conflict with landowners over selection of campsites, Trimble recommends day trips on stretches of the San Saba in Menard County. He notes that there are good city park campgrounds in Menard as well as an area to camp at the third crossing downstream from the Texas (FM) 864 crossing northeast of Menard. The river is accessible for floats with canoes, kayaks and johnboats, but boaters should expect to do some walking through some of the riffles. Trimble notes the river is best suited to small watercraft like belly boats. He says he rarely runs into other anglers on the river and that most of the local fishing pressure is on the catfish.

For largemouth, Trimble recommends "working over the banks" with big topwater flies like deer hair muddlers. One of his favorite patterns for the San Saba is the Bob's Baby Doll deer hair bug designed by Texas fly fisher Robert McCurdy.

The San Saba presents "edge type" features with fallen timber and drop-offs for flyfishers to prospect. "Each little hole is a 'lake' and they all have local names," Trimble says.

Toenail Trail Crossing

Beginning near Fort McKavett in Menard County there is a county road crossing and a county park public use area that provides wade fishing access to the river.

Texas (FM) 864 Crossing

Just northeast of Menard there is a crossing on 864 that offers access for wade fishing or approximately a five mile float downriver to the Dixie Allison Road Crossing, which runs behind the Camp Sol Meyer Boy Scout Ranch.

Dixie Allison Road or Dunagan Road Crossing
Located east of Fort McKavett near US 190, this crossing offers a take-out point for floats starting at the Texas (FM) 864 Crossing and a good access point for wade fishing both upstream and downstream.

Byers Road Crossing
A good put-in for a float down to the crossing off County Road 2092 near Menard. Trimble calls this one of the most scenic stretches of the San Saba.

County Road 2092 near Menard
A good put-in for a float into Menard is where the dam backs up to a deep hole.

Menard to Four Mile Crossing on Texas (FM) 2092
This stretch from the bridge crossing in Menard offers slow moving water downstream. Anglers have the opportunity to paddle upstream or downstream to fish a variety of features and shorelines.

Four Mile Crossing at Texas (FM) 2092 to Nine Mile Crossing on 2092
This is another winding, slow-moving stretch of river. The Nine Mile Crossing is also a good put-in for fly fishing upstream and downstream.

Texas (FM) 1311 Crossing
This crossing, which is accessed on Texas (FM) 1311 off Texas 29 in Menard County just west of the Mason County line is another good access point for wade fishing upstream or downstream.

US 87 Crossing, McCulloch County
This crossing provides an access point for wade fishing for largemouth and sunfish. This is also a good put-in for a float downstream past the Texas 71 Crossing to a take-out at one of the two low water crossings north of Voca, one on Texas (FM) 1851 and the other on County Road 212.

Texas (FM) 1851 and County Road 212 Crossings near Voca
These crossings offer good access for upstream and downstream wade fishing for largemouth and sunfish.

As the San Saba runs northward into San Saba County toward the community of San Saba, the river runs through private land that is posted and there is limited fishing access. In addition, in the stretches of river around San Saba, so much water is removed from the river for irrigation purposes that the quality of fishing is adversely affected according to Trimble.

LAKES

LAKE FRYER

Located on Wolf Creek, Lake Fryer is accessible at a county park 12 miles southeast of Perryton off US 83. There is a launch ramp as well as picnic facilities and RV campsites available in the park.

Amarillo angler Rod Brashears says the lake attracts light boat traffic and has excellent features for flyfishers to prospect, including Wolf Creek and the many points around the lake. He says the lake offers many largemouth in the 4 to 5 pound range as well as large sunfish. Small poppers work well on sunfish along the creek banks and Clouser Deep Minnows and streamer patterns like the John Gulley Shad pattern work well on the main lake, Brashears says. This small lake is ideal for fishing from float tubes and small watercraft.

LAKE MARVIN

Located 11 miles east of Canadian off Texas (FM) 2266, this is a small lake in a national grasslands area. The lake is stocked with largemouth, crappie, catfish and sunfish. Picnic grounds, campsites and boat rentals are available.

This lake, which also attracts very light boating activity, is excellent for float tube fishing. Sunfish patterns work well on largemouth in this lake and gold ribbed hare's ears and Woolly Buggers are the choice for the large sunfish population, says Amarillo fly fisher Rod Brashears.

LAKE MEREDITH

Lake Meredith earned a place in fly fishing history in October, 2000 when John Lindsay Jr., a visitor to the lake from Fremont, Calif., cast a small bug with rubber legs into the stilling basin below the lake and hooked and landed a 14.14 pound bass, the largest documented catch of a largemouth on fly tackle. In an effort to keep the fish alive, Lindsay transported the fish from the lake to a marina in a 5-gallon plastic bucket in which he added ice from his drink cooler. With the help of the marina operator and Texas Parks and Wildlife Department game warden Winston Bishop, the fish was revived and placed in the department's Sharelunker Program, where it can be observed and still play a role in the continued development of the state's largemouth fishery. DNA samples from Lindsay's bass showed it to be an "intergrade" largemouth, a fish carrying genes of northern largemouth and Florida largemouth subspecies. It is believed that the genes from the Florida bass, a largemouth subspecies with the genetic predisposition to grow much larger than other largemouth subspecies, combined with those of the native-northern largemouth, a species known for its aggressive feeding characteristics, has lead to these kinds of quality catches on lakes throughout the state.

Lake Fryer

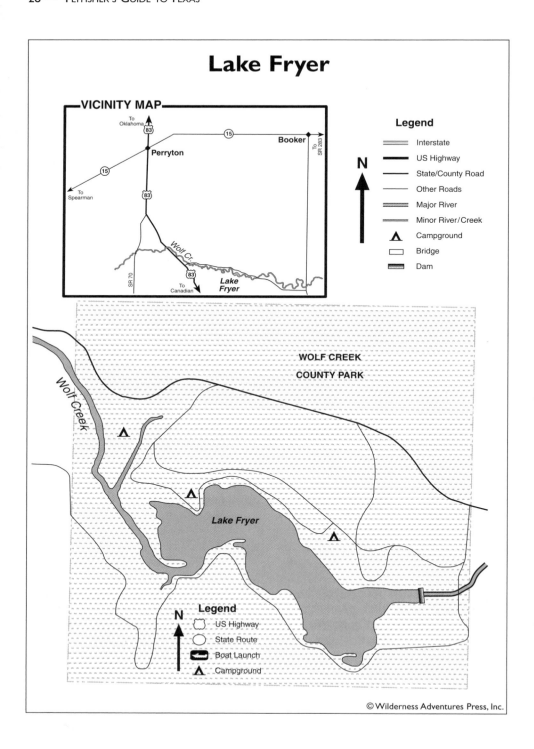

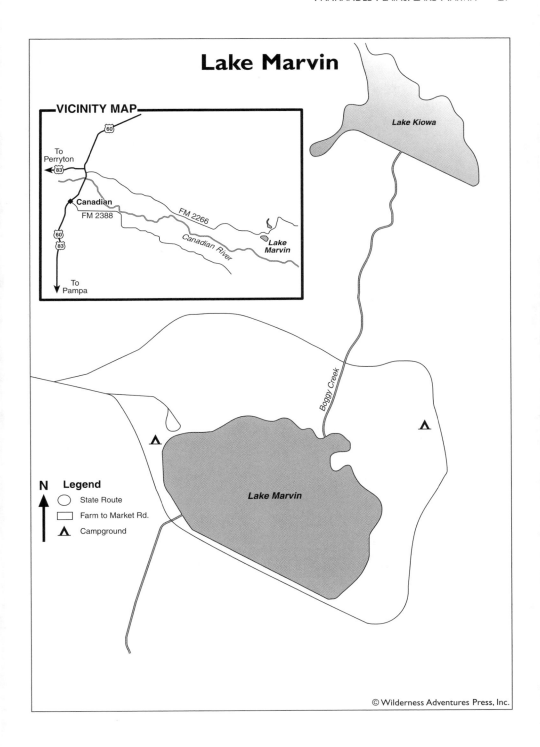

Lake Marvin

Lake Kiowa

VICINITY MAP

60

To Perryton

83

Canadian

FM 2388

FM 2266

Canadian River

Lake Marvin

60

83

To Pampa

Boggy Creek

Lake Marvin

N

Legend

State Route

Farm to Market Rd.

Campground

© Wilderness Adventures Press, Inc.

Lake Meredith

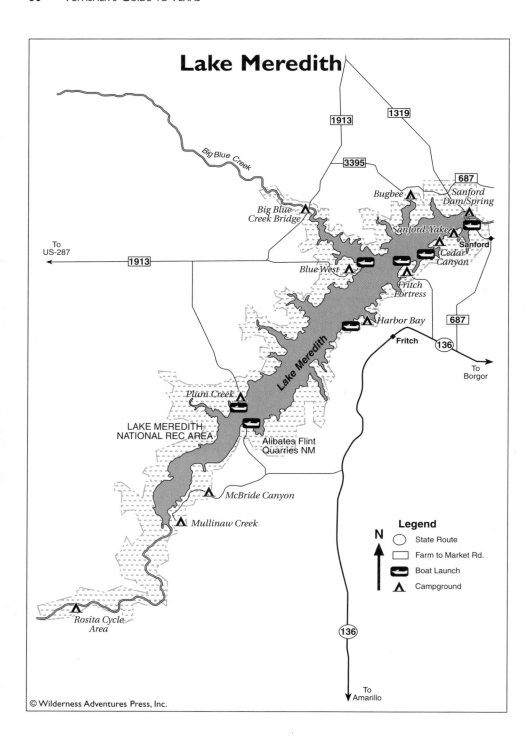

To
US-287

1913

To
Borgor

Fritch

To
Amarillo

Big Blue Creek

1913

1319

3395

687

Bugbee

Sanford
Dam/Spring

Big Blue
Creek Bridge

Sanford-Yake

Sanford

Cedar
Canyon

Blue West

Fritch
Fortress

Harbor Bay

687

136

Lake Meredith

Plum Creek

LAKE MEREDITH
NATIONAL REC AREA

Alibates Flint
Quarries NM

McBride Canyon

Mullinaw Creek

136

Rosita Cycle
Area

Legend

N

◯ State Route

▢ Farm to Market Rd.

▬ Boat Launch

▲ Campground

© Wilderness Adventures Press, Inc.

Joe Kraai, a Texas Parks and Wildlife Department inland fisheries director with 20 years experience on Lake Meredith, noted that the 16-acre, 70 foot deep stilling pool at the base of the spillway is unique in that it has no thermocline and therefore has oxygenated water all the way to the bottom.

Located about 45 miles north of Amarillo, Lake Meredith has been called a rocky canyon filled with water. The lake, which ranges from 9,000 to 16,500 surface acres, holds smallmouth and the strongest self-sustaining population of walleye in the state. Walleyes, mainly residents of the northern US, have thrived in Meredith's rocky habitat since being introduced by the Texas Parks and Wildlife Department in 1965. Other species include white bass, largemouth, catfish and crappie. In 1986, the TPWD stocked 631 Florida-strain largemouth six to eight inches in length. In 1988, about 412,000 Kemp's bass (first generation crosses between northern and Florida largemouth) were stocked, an experiment to see if the Florida fish could survive cold-water temperatures at Meredith. Later collection efforts and laboratory analysis showed that both the Kemp's bass and Florida-strain bass had long-term survival, and spawning had resulted in at least two generations of Florida bass hybrids. Biologist also found that the growth shown by the Kemp's bass of 10 to 12 inches over a two year period was superior to that of the native (northern) bass.

According to Melvin Stovall, Lake Meredith's walleyes move into the shallows to spawn, especially around the riprap of the dam, when the water temperature reaches 44 degrees during March.

Species available on Lake Meredith include largemouth, smallmouth bass, crappie, walleyes, white bass, channel catfish and rainbow trout in the stilling basin below the dam.

LAKE MCCLELLAN

This 325-acre lake, located 28 miles south of Pampa off Texas 70 and Texas (FM) 2477 east, is a popular destination for anglers in the Panhandle. The lake holds a good population of largemouth, crappie and hybrid white/striped bass. Picnic areas, boat ramps and RV hookups are available.

GREENBELT RESERVOIR

This 2,025-acre reservoir on the Salt Fork of the Red River offers flyfishers a crack at walleye, northern pike and yellow perch as well as largemouth, smallmouth, white bass, white crappie and sunfish. It is located in Donley County five miles north of Clarendon off US 287 and Texas 70. Local anglers note that the lake's rich shoreline vegetation offers excellent habitat for largemouth and prime water for topwater bass bug action.

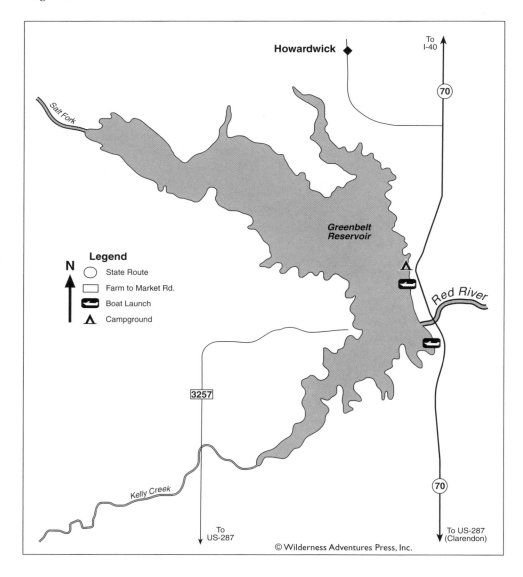

© Wilderness Adventures Press, Inc.

LAKE MACKENZIE

Accessed 12 miles northwest of Silverton off Texas 86 west and Texas and Texas 207 north in the scenic Tule Canyon, deep, clear Lake Mackenzie has large-mouth, walleyes, striped bass, white bass and catfish. The Texas Parks and Wildlife Department also has experimented with rainbow and brown trout in this 900-acre Panhandle lake. Facilities include picnic tables, campsites and RV hookups and boat launches. Palo Duro Canyon State Park is located 25 miles north of the lake.

BAYLOR LAKE

A municipal water supply lake located about 9 miles west of Childress, Baylor Lake has emerged in recent years as one of the favorite big bass destinations in the state. The lake record largemouth scaled almost 15 pounds and each year several dozen bass exceeding 10 pounds are landed at the lake. Catch and release practices are strongly encouraged on this highly productive but relatively small (700 acres) lake.

Flyfishers have the best chance to take a large bass in late February and March when the large females sometimes move up deep channels to feed along brushy shorelines. The lake also has cattails and flooded timber to hold game fish.

For additional information, contact the lake store at (817) 937-2101.

CHILDRESS LAKE

Located 12 miles east of Baylor Lake in Childress County, this 300-acre lake with clear water also holds hefty largemouth up to the eight- and nine-pound class.

A heavy growth of moss in the summer turns off some anglers but it also provides excellent sanctuary and cover for the lake's healthy largemouth population. A boat ramp is available on the west side of the lake for a small fee.

LAKE PAULINE

This 612-acre lake on Wanderers Creek in Hardeman County is stocked with Florida-strain largemouth, crappie and sunfish. It is located about 5 miles east of Quanah off US 287.

DIVERSION LAKE

Located on the Wichita River, a tributary of the Red River, near Wichita Falls, this 3,419-acre reservoir is noted for its hybrid striped bass population. It is susceptible, however, to high winds and turbid water. Boating access to the lake is through privately owned launch ramps for a fee. There are no public campgrounds on the lake. The Lake is located 14 miles west of Holiday off US 277.

Baylor and Childress Lakes

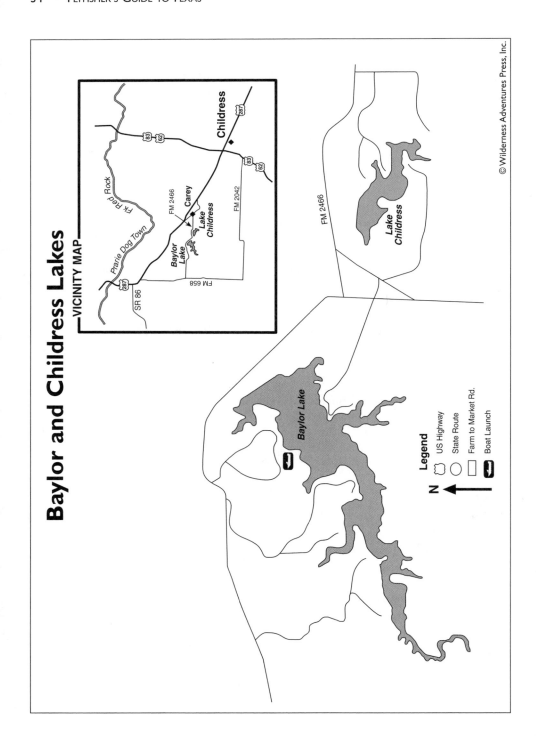

VICINITY MAP

Childress

Carey

Lake Childress

Baylor Lake

Prarie Dog Town

Fk Red Rock

FM 2466

FM 2042

FM 658

SR 86

Lake Childress

FM 2466

Baylor Lake

Legend

US Highway
State Route
Farm to Market Rd.
Boat Launch

N

© Wilderness Adventures Press, Inc.

LAKE WICHITA

This 2,200-acre highly turbid and fertile lake on the southern outskirts of Wichita Falls off Texas 79 holds Florida-strain largemouth and hybrid striped bass. The city provides two public launch ramps and there are two other private marinas that provide boat access to the lake.

LAKE ARROWHEAD

Located on the Little Wichita River about 14 miles southeast of Wichita Falls off US 281 and Texas (FM) 1954, Arrowhead Lake is stocked with Florida-strain largemouth, striped bass, crappie, white bass and sunfish. Shoreline habitat is limited due to fluctuating water levels and turbidity but the lake can offer solid white bass action with schooling fish in open water. Among the fish-holding structures not found in the middle of every bass lake are steel oil derricks reflecting the oil reserves that lie under the waterway. Public access to boat launches and bank fishing is available at Lake Arrowhead State Park. To get to Lake Arrowhead, take US 281 south from Wichita Falls and turn left (east) on Texas (FM) 1954, which leads to the lake

Lake Arrowhead State Park

This 524-acre park located 14 miles south of Wichita Falls provides access to the 13,500-acre Lake Arrowhead.Raccoons, skunks and prairie dogs are among the wildlife that can be viewed at the park. Facilities include campsites, rest rooms with showers, grocery store, fishing pier and boat ramps. For additional information, contact the park at (940) 528-2211.

LAKE KICKAPOO

Located 12 miles northwest of Archer City of Texas (FM) 368, Lake Kickapoo holds a resident population of largemouth, crappie and white bass. Shoreline vegetation is limited due to water level fluctuations and turbidity. There is one boat ramp on the northeast corner of the lake.

LAKE KEMP

A municipal lake for Wichita Falls located 48 miles southwest of the city, Lake Kemp has been stocked with Florida-strain largemouth, striped bass and red drum. The clearest water is found near the dam. Local anglers have had success targeting schooling striped bass in open water on the lake. The city provides several public boat ramps on the lake. The lake is located off US 183 in Baylor County.

ALAN HENRY RESERVOIR

Located south of Post (65 miles southeast of Lubbock) in Garza County, this 3,000-acre water supply lake is situated on the Double Mountain Fork of the Brazos River. In addition to largemouth and smallmouth bass, this is the only lake in the state that also holds the Alabama spotted bass (*Micropterus punctulatus*). Frequently confused with the largemouth, the Alabama spotted bass has a smaller mouth and distinctive rows of tiny blotches extending parallel and below the lateral line. A black spot is located forward of the caudal fin, and, unlike the largemouth, the first and second dorsal fins are clearly connected.

Lake Arrowhead

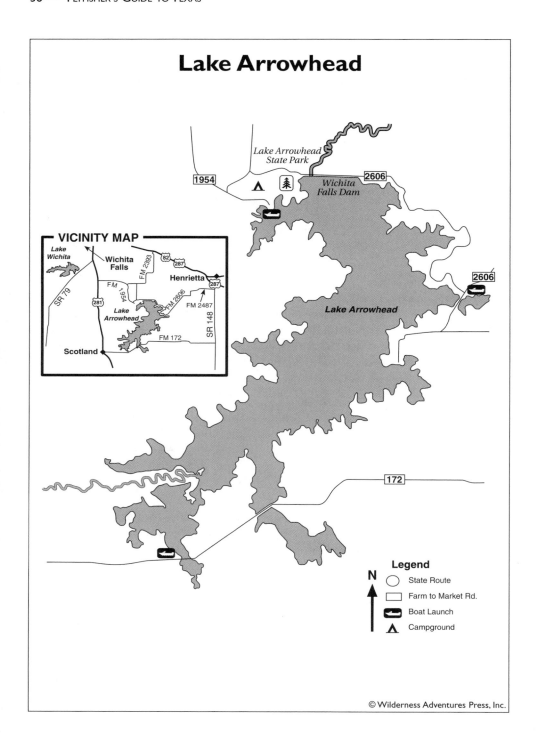

Lake Arrowhead
State Park

1954

Wichita
Falls Dam

2606

2606

VICINITY MAP

Lake
Wichita

Wichita
Falls

FM 2393

82

287

Henrietta

287

FM 1954

SR 79

281

Lake
Arrowhead

FM 2606

FM 2487

SR 148

Scotland

FM 172

Lake Arrowhead

172

Legend

N

◯ State Route

▢ Farm to Market Rd.

🛥 Boat Launch

▲ Campground

© Wilderness Adventures Press, Inc.

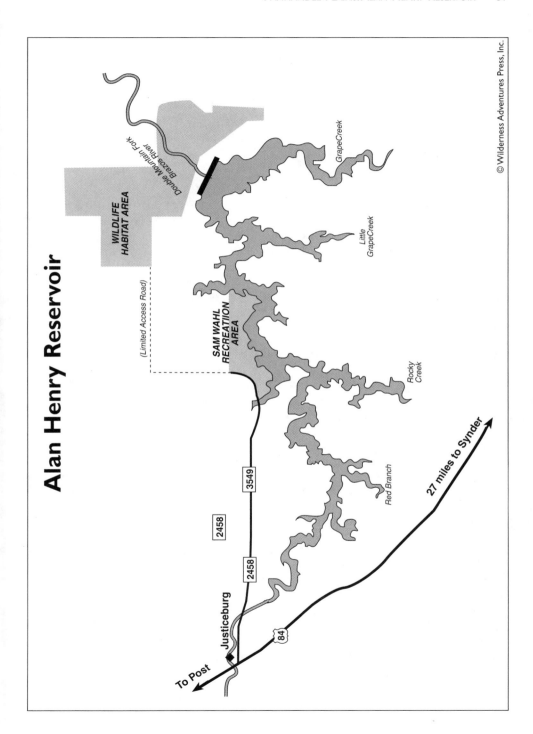

Alan Henry Reservoir

In a cooperative effort with Alabama fisheries officials, Alabama spotted bass have been placed in the lake in the hopes of establishing a population of the species in this lake as well as in other rocky, steep-sided reservoirs of West Texas. Similar restocking efforts with the spotted bass have been successful in California, where a 9 pound 7 ounce Alabama spotted bass holds the IGFA world record.

Alan Henry Reservoir lies next to 4,100 acres that are dedicated to public use and outdoor recreational facilities are currently under construction.

For additional information, contact the Texas Parks and Wildlife Department at (806) 655-4341.

WHITE RIVER LAKE

This 1,808-acre lake is located in the southeast corner of Crosby County, 16 miles southeast of Crosbyton on a tributary of the Salt Fork of the Brazos River. The lake is moderately clear for this part of the state. The aquatic vegetation, flooded brush, gravel bars and riprap at the dam provide excellent fish holding features that are ideal for prospecting with the fly rod. Largemouth weighing in excess of 8 pounds have been taken in the lake and there is also a good population of crappie, small-mouth bass, walleye and hybrid sunfish. Two public boat ramps and campsites are available. To get to the lake, take Texas (FM) 651 south from Crosbyton then turn left (east) on Texas (FM) 2794.

LAKE JACKSBORO

Located off Texas 59 northeast of Jacksboro, is the older twin impoundment to Lost Creek Reservoir. It offers shore fishing on its west end as well as launch sites for canoes, kayaks and johnboats at several park areas along its shorelines. The clear water lake with a rocky bottom is stocked with largemouth and also offers flyfishers action with sunfish and crappie.

LOST CREEK RESERVOIR

Rocky cliffs are among the fish-holding features on this 450-acre lake located two miles downstream from Lake Jacksboro. The lake has a healthy resident population of largemouth, crappie and sunfish. A public boat ramp and dock are located on the southwest side of the Lake just off Texas 59.

LAKE BRYSON

This small lake near the community of   in Jack County has a good numbers of largemouths and is a favorite with flyfishers for its abundant sunfish population. The heavy brush and flooded timber along the shoreline make wade fishing and bank fishing difficult but provide excellent cover and habitat for the gamefish. Float tubes or other small watercraft are ideal on this lake and there is a primitive launch area suitable for a johnboat. Short accurate casts into shaded pockets in thorny brush will tune up casting techniques and catch big sunfish at Bryson. Woolly Buggers, spiders, hopper patterns, hard-bodied bass bugs, Clouser Deep Minnows and bendback streamers are a few of the patterns that work well on the lake's very willing bluegill and redear sunfish and there is always that big, bug-eyed largemouth waiting in the

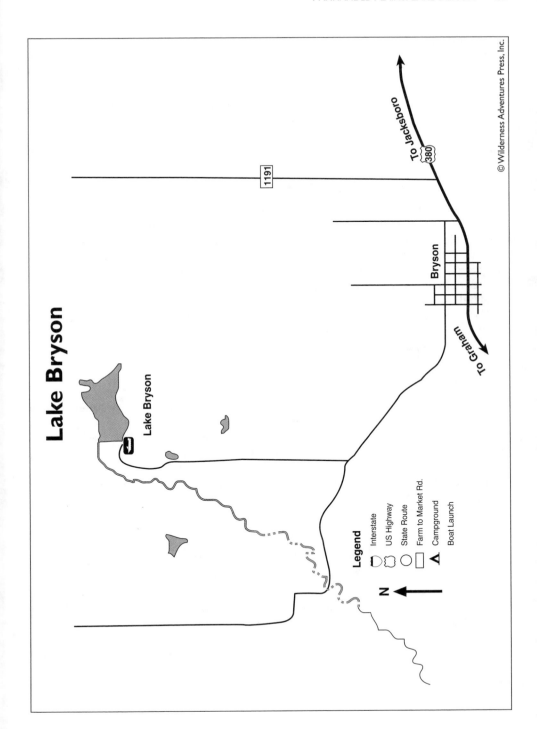

Lake Bryson

To Jacksboro

380

1191

Bryson

To Graham

Lake Bryson

Legend

Interstate
US Highway
State Route
Farm to Market Rd.
Campground
Boat Launch

N

© Wilderness Adventures Press, Inc.

wings to liven up the day. Largemouth in excess of 10 pounds have been taken on the lake. There are no facilities on the lake but there are scenic, shaded areas along the shore for primitive camping. Take a good supply of water and insect repellent. To get to Lake Bryson, travel east from Jacksboro on U.S. 380 to Bryson. In downtown Bryson turn right (north) and travel two blocks through the town then turn left and head west for two miles to an intersection with another road. The road to the right (north) leads to the boat launch area about two miles away. The road continuing west leads to a primitive camping on the west side of the lake about five miles from the intersection.

BLACK CREEK LAKE

One of several small lakes located in the Lyndon B. Johnson National Grassland northwest of Decatur in Wise County, Black Creek Lake is a scenic little jewel that can offer excellent fly fishing for sunfish and small bass. Float tubes and small watercraft are the best way to fish the shorelines and small creeks at this lake. There is a boat ramp and primitive campsites at the lake. Periods of drought can affect water levels on these small lakes in the grasslands so flyfishers should check on current conditions before planning a trip. For information on lakes in the grassland, contact the US Forest Service at (940) 627-5475. To get to Black Creek Lake take Texas (FM) 730 north of Decatur 9.2 miles and turn left (west) on the county road just past the sign for the cemetery and proceed 3.1 miles.

LAKE STAMFORD

Located northeast of Stamford on Paint Creek, a tributary of the Clear Fork of the Brazos, this 4,690-acre impoundment is stocked with Florida-strain largemouth, hybrid striped bass, crappie, and walleye. A fertile lake with turbid water, flyfishers will do best in the spring months. Try casting deer hair and hard-bodied bugs near the reed beds and work streamers and Clouser Deep Minnow patterns around the boat docks for crappie. To get to the lake, travel northeast from Stamford on US 277 and take Texas (FM) 618 east to the lake. A municipal park on the lake offers lodges, cabins and dock facilities.

HUBBARD CREEK LAKE

Located six miles northeast of Breckenridge off US 180 west, Hubbard Creek Lake lies on a tributary of the Clear Fork of the Brazos River and covers 15,250 acres. Stocked with Florida-strain and native-northern largemouth, it offers fairly clear water and a variety of habitat including rocky outcrops and flooded timber along 100 miles of mesquite-lined shores. Flyfishers who launch from Peeler Park can join in the hot winter crappie action by dropping Clouser Deep Minnow patterns dressed in white and chartreuse bucktails along the flooded brush and timber. Seven launch ramps are located around the lake.

LAKE POSSUM KINGDOM

This 65 mile long lake has 310 miles of shoreline. The lake holds a variety of species, including largemouth, striped bass, white bass, crappie, catfish and sunfish. The lake record for largemouth stands at 16.02 pounds caught in 1989.

Flyfishers should be advised that the lake, like other large Texas reservoirs, hosts major bass tournaments with the accompanying boat traffic.

Possum Kingdom is known for exceptional fly fishing for sunfish. On the lower (south) end of the lake near the dam the water is deep with sheer, vertical limestone cliffs from 20 to over 100 feet extending into the clear depths of the lake. Despite the depth, Fort Worth flyfisher Brian Camp says that small surface poppers like the Accardo "Miss Prissy" fished near these cliff faces will draw strikes from large redbreast sunfish that "will materialize out of the depths and slam these poppers." Camp says these sunfish might be used to having bugs blow over the tops of the cliffs and into the water. Casting small popping bugs in the middle of a summer day while drifting this area will get amazing results from sunfish and the occasional bass, he says. "In the clear water, you can see them ten feet down coming up. It is all you can do to avoid striking too soon and pulling it away from them. He says a situation that happens frequently when fly fishing the clear water of the lake is to hook a sunfish and while it is struggling during the fight, attract a hit from a largemouth. Other good areas for sunfish, which include bluegill, longear, warmouth, and redear are at Scenic Point Cove, Cedar Creek adjacent to Possum Kingdom State Park, BRA Cove, and Rainbow Lodge Cove.

Largemouth spawn at Possum Kingdom in March and April and usually move into shallow water during this period seeking out nesting sites and feeding heavily after the winter season. According to Texas Parks and Wildlife fisheries specialists, anglers should target them around flooded timber, brush, standing timber and stumps at Frank Harris Bend, Neeley's Slough, Johnson Bend, Bluff Creek, Hog Bend, Bass Island, Cedar Creek, and Costello Island.

In the fall, many anglers target largemouth around the many creeks flowing into the lake. Casting poppers along the shorelines at night on a full moon can result in explosive strikes on Possum Kingdom.

Possum Kingdom's rocky shorelines provide excellent habitat for Kentucky spotted bass. Among the many areas to target this species are Dam Cove, Caddo Creek Point, Neeley's Slough, Scenic Point Cove, Possum Kingdom State Park, BRA Cove, and Rainbow Lodge Cove.

Smallmouth bass were first stocked in the lake in 1978. Texas Parks and Wildlife fisheries officials say the best areas to target smallmouth on Possum Kingdom are at Scenic Point Cove, Caddo Creek Point, Gaines Bend, and Cedar Creek near Possum Kingdom State Park.

For more information on lake conditions, contact the Texas Parks and Wildlife Department at (817) 549-1803.

Lake Possum Kingdom

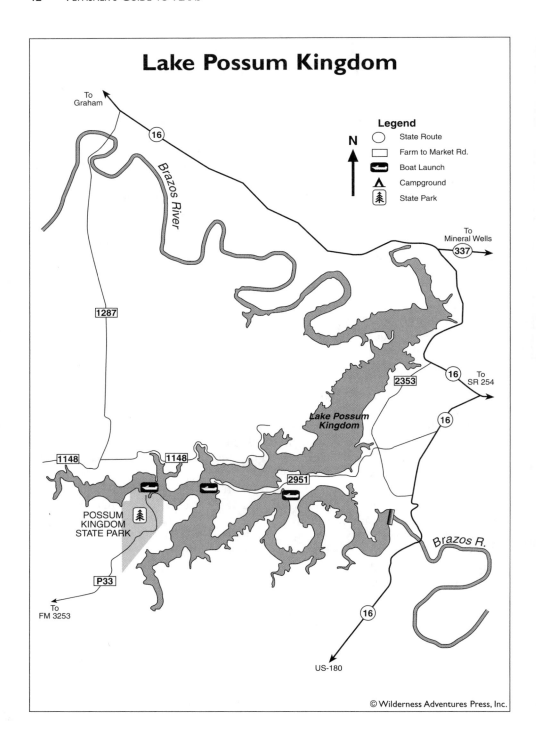

To
Graham

16

Brazos River

Legend

N

State Route
Farm to Market Rd.
Boat Launch
Campground
State Park

To
Mineral Wells

337

1287

16
To
SR 254

2353

16

Lake Possum
Kingdom

1148

1148

2951

POSSUM
KINGDOM
STATE PARK

Brazos R.

P33

To
FM 3253

16

US-180

© Wilderness Adventures Press, Inc.

Possum Kingdom State Park

Located in the Brazos River canyon country of the Palo Pinto Mountains, 17 miles north of Caddo at US180, between Palo Pinto and Breckenridge, this 1,724-acre park is situated at the southwest corner of Possum Kingdom Lake. From the park entrance, the road leads through wooded limestone bluffs to a broad peninsula at the Spanish Oaks camping area. Here, the road branches off to other campgrounds, all of which are near the water. The park, which is situated on the west side of the 20,000-acre Possum Kingdom Lake, is an excellent access point for fishing its nearby shorelines, lined in juniper, oak, and mesquite. To get to the park, travel west of Mineral Wells on US 180 past the community of Palo Pinto to the Caddo community. At Caddo, take Park Road 33 north to the park. For more information about park facilities, contact Possum Kingdom State Park at (817) 549-1803.

LAKE PALO PINTO

Located on Palo Pinto Creek, a tributary of the Brazos River, this 2,660-acre power plant lake is located 25 miles south of Palo Pinto. A fishery with fairly turbid water, the best opportunity for flyfishers comes in the winter when power plant discharges warm the water and white bass and crappie fishing turns on. Palo Pinto Creek is also a good spring destination for crappie. The lake is also stocked with largemouth. Much of the lake is surrounded by private homes, which limit access, but there are several public boat ramps and private marinas where anglers can launch boats. To get to the dam at Palo Pinto Lake travel 20 mile south from Palo Pinto on Texas (FM) 4.

LAKE FORT PHANTOM HILL

Located north of Abilene on the Clear Fork of the Brazos, this 4,245-acre lake is stocked with Florida-strain and native-northern largemouth, hybrid striped bass, walleye, white bass, crappie, and redear sunfish. Walleye exceeding 7 pounds have been taken from this lake. Surrounded by featureless farm land and exposed to the wind, this lake is often in a turbid state. There are two public parks and three public launch ramps that provide boat and bank access to the lake. To get to the lake, head 10 miles north of Abilene on Texas (FM) 600.

LAKE SWEETWATER

Located 8 miles southeast of Sweetwater on two creek tributaries of the Clear Fork of the Brazos River, this fairly turbid 630-acre lake has been known to produce large redear sunfish and is also home to good numbers of largemouth, crappie and walleye. Another advantage for flyfishers is that it attracts less fishing pressure than some of the other more popular area lakes. Surrounding the lake and open to the public for a nominal fee is a city-operated municipal park which has camping and picnicking areas and a paved launch ramp. To get to the lake, take Interstate 20 east from Sweetwater, turn right (south) on Texas (FM) 1856 and follow it to the lake.

TRAMMAL LAKE

Located about 10 miles south of Sweetwater, this small lake is used for fishing only and has a good population of largemouth and sunfish. Take Texas 70 south from Sweetwater and turn right (west) on Texas (FM) 1809 and follow it to the lake.

OAK CREEK RESERVOIR

Located 30 miles southeast of Sweetwater, this 2,375-acre power plant reservoir is the largest of the city's three area lakes. The water is surprisingly clear for this region of red clay and sandstone. Game fish species present include Florida-strain and native-northern largemouth, smallmouth and sunfish. An abundant forage fish population that includes golden shiners and threadfin shad make this a good lake for white and olive streamer fly patterns topped off with silver flash material. To get to Oak Creek Reservoir, take Texas 70 south from Sweetwater through the community of Blackwell and then turn left (east) on Texas (FM) 3399.

LEON RESERVOIR

Located six miles southeast of Eastland, this 1,590-acre lake on the Leon River attracts anglers, water sports enthusiasts and campers. Turbid conditions and the lack of significant shoreline structure for game fish habitat make this a problematical choice for flyfishers. Shoreline weed beds and docks offer the best bet for flyfishers casting streamers and bass bugs to the lake's considerable largemouth population. Hybrid striped bass and tiger muskie were stocked in the lake in the mid 1970s. To get to the lake, travel south from Ranger on Texas (FM) 2461 to the lake or travel east from Eastland on Texas (FM) 570 and turn right (south) on Texas (FM) 2214 and follow it to the lake.

LAKE COLORADO CITY

Located about 7 miles southwest of Colorado City in Mitchell County, this 1,612-acre power plant lake on the Colorado River supports a population of game fish that includes Florida-strain and native-northern largemouth, hybrid striped bass, red drum and walleye. Fishing on this lake is best during the coldest days of the winter when hybrid striped bass and other game fish are more concentrated around the warm water discharges. Fishing with intermediate sink and full sink fly lines and dropping weighted streamers including Clouser Deep Minnow patterns is a good way to connect with the hybrid striped bass. While the lake's turbidity increases with stiff southerly winds, the lower end of the lake is known to hold clear water fairly consistently. In the summer months redfish will school on the surface and are good targets at this time for streamers dressed in white bucktail with some flash material. Camping, picnicking and boat launch facilities are available at city and state parks (See Lake Colorado City State Park in State Park Waters, page 46). To get to the lake, take Interstate 20 west from Colorado City and turn left (south) on Texas (FM) 2836 to the lake. The state park is located on the southwest corner of the lake.

Lake Colorado City

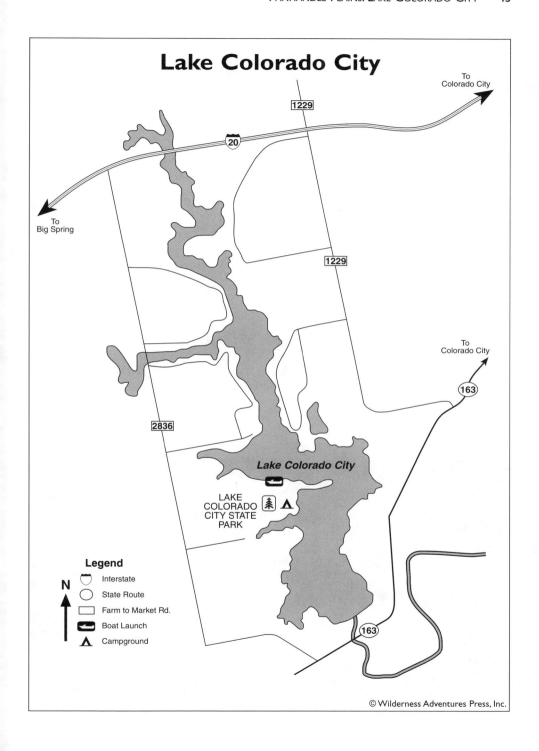

To
Colorado City

1229

20

To
Big Spring

1229

To
Colorado City

163

2836

Lake Colorado City

LAKE
COLORADO
CITY STATE
PARK

Legend

N

Interstate
State Route
Farm to Market Rd.
Boat Launch
Campground

163

163

© Wilderness Adventures Press, Inc.

Lake Colorado City State Park

Located on the southwest shore of Lake Colorado City, this park provides developed campsites, fishing piers, boat and bank fishing access to the 1,600-acre power plant lake. The lake is a popular destination during the coldest winter days because the warm water outflows from the power plant can make the resident population of largemouth, hybrid striped bass and red drum particularly active. For additional information, contact the park at (915) 728-3931.

E.V. SPENCE RESERVOIR

This 14,950-acre lake located west of Robert Lee in Coke County is a pioneer Texas fishery for transplanted striped bass and is still considered one of the best in the state for these hard-fighting game fish. The lake record for striped bass exceeds 35 pounds. This lake is known for its dramatic sandstone and red clay bluffs and clear water. Other game fish present include Florida-strain largemouth, hybrid striped bass, white bass, hybrid sunfish and smallmouths. There are four parks that provide access to the lake. To get to E.V. Spence, travel west from Robert Lee on Texas 158 or on Texas (FM) 1904.

LAKE COLEMAN

This 2,000-acre lake on Pecan Bayou, a tributary of the Colorado River, is located 17 miles north of Coleman. Generally clear water with excellent game fish habitat in the form of flooded timber, gravel bars, and creek mouths make this lake an excellent fly fishing destination. Florida-strain and native-northern largemouth, hybrid striped bass and sunfish are the prime targets. To get to Lake Coleman, take US 283 north from Coleman, turn left (west) on Texas (FM) 1274, which leads to the lake.

Striped bass with Texas state flower, the bluebonnet.

E.V. Spence Reservoir

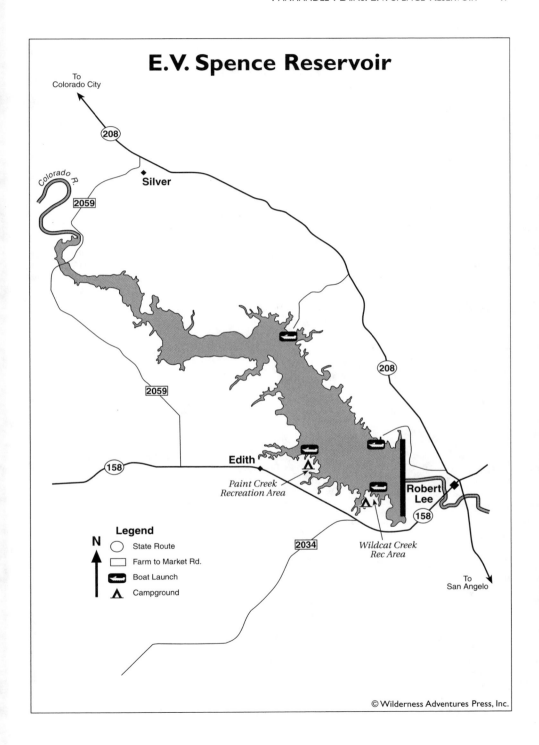

To
Colorado City

208

Colorado R.

Silver

2059

2059

158

208

Edith

Paint Creek
Recreation Area

Robert
Lee

158

2034

Wildcat Creek
Rec Area

To
San Angelo

Legend

N

○ State Route

▭ Farm to Market Rd.

🛥 Boat Launch

⛺ Campground

© Wilderness Adventures Press, Inc.

White Crappie

White crappie (Pomoxis annuaris) *are found statewide, but most often in the relatively hard waters of the Trinity River drainage.*

Black Crappie

Black crappie (Pomoxis nigromaculatus) *are far more numerous in the clear, acidic to slightly alkaline waters of east Texas.*

Although frequently misidentified during the spawning season when male white crappie and black crappie both develop dark markings over most of their body, the two species can be easily distinguished. The white crappie has five or six spines in the dorsal fin and vertical black bars on the sides. the black crappie has seven or eight spines in the dorsal fin and the black coloration on the sides appears as random markings or spots rather than vertical bars.

Crappie have voracious appetites, feeding on threadfin and gizzard shad and insect larvae, especially mayflies. They also will eat minnows, small sunfish, carp, catfish, black bass, striped bass, freshwater drum, and other crappie.

Crappie can be caught year round, but the ideal time for flyfishers to target them is during the spring spawning season when they move into shallow water and congregate in large schools. From mid-February to mid-June, crappie are generally found in less than 15 feet of water in coves, along submerged creek channels, around submerged islands and around flooded timber and subsurface vegetation.

HORDS CREEK LAKE

Located about eight miles west of Coleman off Texas 153, Hords Creek Lake is a 510-acre US Corps of Engineers reservoir on Hords Creek, a tributary of Pecan Bayou. It was designed for flood control and recreational fishing. There are three park areas and eight launch ramps at the lake.

The lake has a good population of largemouth, black and white crappie, sunfish, and channel catfish. Flyfishers should target largemouth in the March to May spawning period around the many coves that have partially flooded or submerged brush. During the summer months, early morning, late evening, and night fishing can provide exciting topwater action with deer hair and hard-bodied bass bugs. During the fall, largemouth move into shallow water along the shorelines.

Crappie fishing is best on Hords Creek during spring and fall when the fish have moved up into shallow water. Like the largemouth this time of year, crappie also will be found in the coves around flooded timber and over gravel bottoms. In the summer crappie are most active at sunset and at night. Use full-sink lines with Clouser Deep Minnow patterns to prospect for them on the ledges below Flatrock Park and at the fishing piers at the dam and at Lakeside Park.

Bluegill and redbreast are the most common sunfish at Hords Creek. They are aggressive feeders and provide great sport for flyfishers during their nesting period from April to July. For additional information, contact Texas Parks and Wildlife Department (915) 692-0921 or US Corps of Engineers (915) 625-2322.

LAKE BROWNWOOD

One of Texas' oldest reservoirs, the 7,300-acre Lake Brownwood has more than 93 miles of scenic shoreline.

The lake, which has a maximum depth of 55 feet, attracts a lot of angler activity. Primary species are white bass, or sand bass, and hybrid striped bass or "wipers," a hatchery produced fish resulting from crossing white bass and stripers. The white bass average one to 1½ pounds while the hybrids grow much larger, with 10 pound fish caught frequently.

The hybrids were first stocked in Lake Brownwood in 1980 and have been restocked on a regular basis since then.

Night fishing around lighted boat docks in the early spring can be productive for flyfishers.

Hybrid fishing can be good around the Jim Ned Arm from Mountain View to the dam and in Pecan Bayou from Sunken Island to the dam. Florida-strain largemouth were first stocked in Lake Brownwood in 1975.

Veteran Lake Brownwood anglers recommend "beating the banks" and fishing around the docks on this relatively shallow water lake. The 538-acre Lake Brownwood State Park provides bank and pier fishing access and boat launches.

To get to Lake Brownwood, take Texas (FM) 2125 or Texas (FM) 2623 to the south shore or Texas 279, which leads to the north shore and Lake Brownwood State Park.

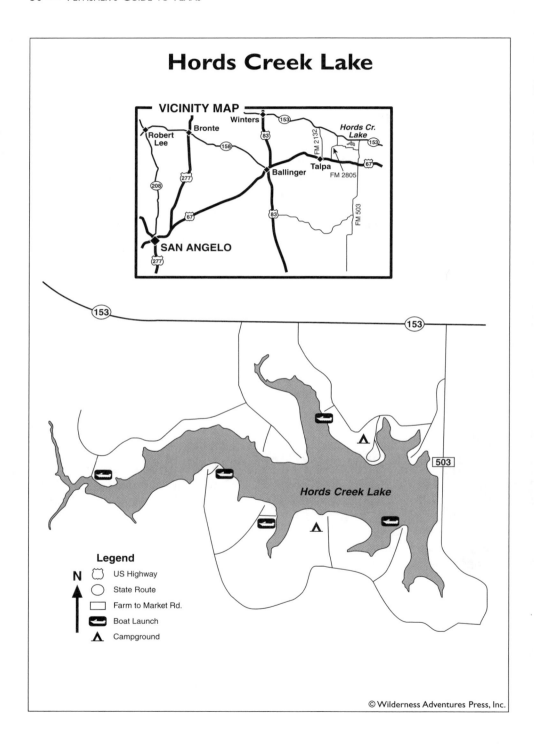

Hords Creek Lake

VICINITY MAP

Winters · 153
Bronte · 83
Robert Lee
158
FM 2132
Hords Cr. Lake · 153
277
Ballinger
Talpa · 67
FM 2805
208
67
83
FM 503
SAN ANGELO
277

153

153

503

Hords Creek Lake

Legend

N

US Highway
State Route
Farm to Market Rd.
Boat Launch
Campground

© Wilderness Adventures Press, Inc.

Lake Brownwood

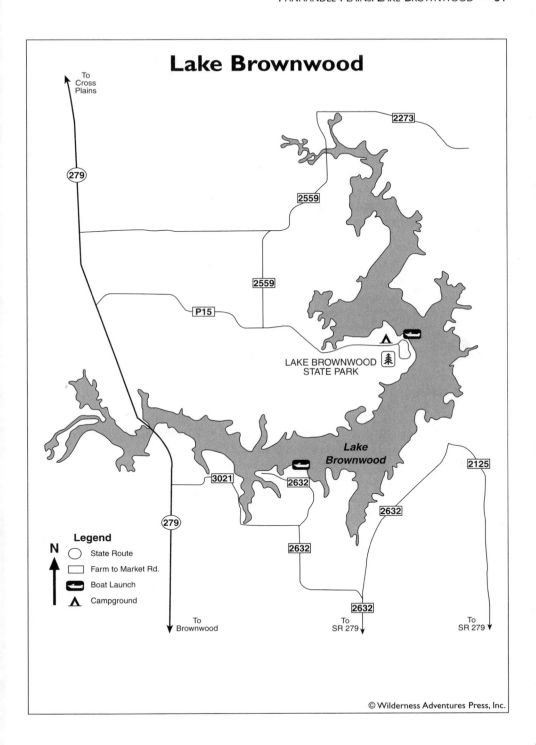

To Cross Plains

279

2273

2559

2559

P15

LAKE BROWNWOOD
STATE PARK

Lake
Brownwood

2125

3021

2632

2632

2632

279

Legend

N

◯ State Route

☐ Farm to Market Rd.

⬭ Boat Launch

⛺ Campground

2632

To
Brownwood

To
SR 279

To
SR 279

© Wilderness Adventures Press, Inc.

Lake Brownwood State Park

Located on the southern shoreline of Lake Brownwood, the 538-acre park offers 90 campsites and 17 log cabins built in the 1930s. About 250,000 people visit the park annually. There are three launch ramps, a number of boat stalls and a lighted fishing pier on the park property. To get to the park from US 67/377 take Texas 279 northwest to Park Road 15 and proceed five miles down the park road to the entrance. For more information on Lake Brownwood State Park, call (915) 784-5223 between 8 a.m. and 5 p.m. seven days a week. The central reservation number for all Texas state parks is (512) 389-8900.

LAKE PROCTOR

This 4,610-acre US Corps of Engineers conservation, flood control and recreational waterway is located eight miles south of DeLeon in Comanche County. Surrounded by sandy loam farm lands, this lake is generally turbid and fertile but a healthy forage fish population can kick off surface feeding hybrid striped bass. Other species include Florida-strain and native-northern largemouth, crappie, and sunfish. The US Corps of Engineers has provided excellent park facilities along the lakefront including concrete boat ramps, picnic tables and campsites. To get to Lake Proctor, take Texas 16 south from DeLeon to the Downing community and from there look for Texas (FM) 2318 and Texas (FM) 2861, which lead to the lake.

TWIN BUTTES RESERVOIR

This 9,080-acre reservoir is comprised of two separate pools behind one of the longest earth fill dams ever built by the US Bureau of Reclamation. Largemouth up to 13 pounds, smallmouth exceeding 5 pounds and walleye exceeding 8 pounds have been taken on this lake. The lake, which holds clear water, also produces good numbers of white bass, striped bass and hybrid striped bass. Flyfishers should target largemouth around flooded salt cedar and mesquite brush in the flats and flyfishers should also be alert for top water action from schooling white bass and striped bass early and late in the day.

Veteran San Angelo angler Russell Smith says flyfishers should look for largemouth and crappie action in both pools, around riprap near the dam, and on the mouths of the rivers that feed into the lake. There is access to bank fishing around the creeks and rivers that feed into the west side of the reservoir.

Periods of drought can adversely affect the quality of fishing and access to launch ramps on Twin Buttes Reservoir. Under normal conditions, boat launch access is available for a nominal fee at private facilities on the north side of the lake.

Access to the lake is available for a small fee at the Twin Buttes Marina launch ramp located off US 67 on the north side (North Pool) of the lake. The site also offers RV campgrounds and covered picnic tables.

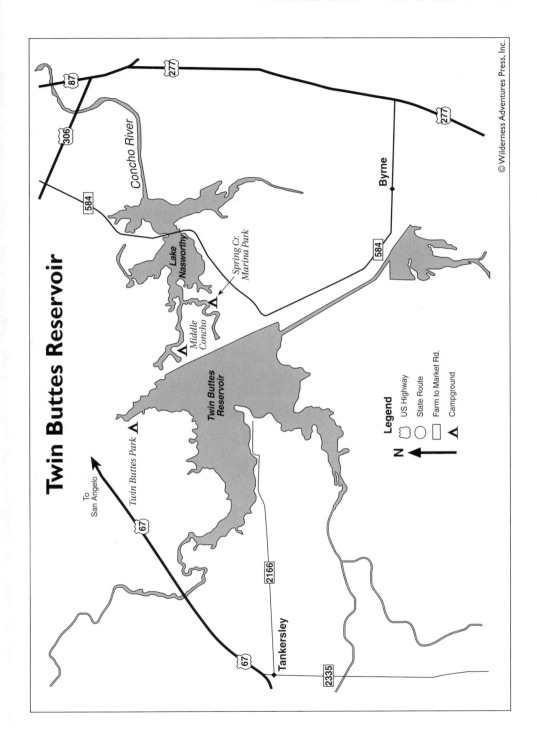

Twin Buttes Reservoir

Concho River

Lake Nasworthy

Spring Cr.
Marina Park

Middle Concho

Twin Buttes Reservoir

Twin Buttes Park

To San Angelo

Tankersley

Byrne

Legend

N

- US Highway
- State Route
- Farm to Market Rd.
- Campground

© Wilderness Adventures Press, Inc.

O.C. FISHER LAKE

Located three miles northwest of San Angelo in Tom Green County, the 5,440-acre O.C. Fisher Lake, also called North Concho Lake and Lake San Angelo, has been heavily stocked over the years with a variety of game fish including Florida-strain and native-northern largemouth, white crappie, walleye and sunfish. Seasonal fluctuations in water levels can affect the quality of fishing and shoreline features and game fish habitat along its 26 miles of shoreline are somewhat limited. Nonetheless, walleye exceeding 7 pounds and largemouth exceeding 12 pounds have been taken from this lake. Flyfishers should look for the large schools of white bass that blow up on the surface during the summer months, says veteran San Angelo angler and outdoor writer Russell Smith. He says O.C. Fisher's spillway, riprap and rocky banks are accessible for bank fishing.

Shoreline parks on the west side of the lake offer boat ramps and picnic areas. For information on current lake conditions, contact the Texas Parks and Wildlife fisheries office in San Angelo at (915) 655-9413. O.C. Fisher Lake is located on the northwest side of San Angelo. To get to the lakeside parks from San Angelo, take Texas (FM) 2288, which runs along the west side of the lake.

San Angelo State Park

Located on the shores of the 5,440-acre O.C. Fisher Reservoir, just west of the city of San Angelo, this park offers camping facilities and boat access to the the lake. For additional information, contact the park at (915) 949-4757.

LAKE NASWORTHY

Located in the Middle Concho River drainage six miles southwest of San Angelo just below Twin Buttes Reservoir, Lake Nasworthy is a fertile, turbid power plant lake with an average depth of about 4 feet. Shoreline features and game fish habitat are limited but it is stocked with Florida-strain and native-northern largemouth, striped bass, hybrid striped bass and red drum. Texas Parks and Wildlife Department surveys have indicated a higher than average population of sunfish. The lake produces double digit largemouth and red drum and striped bass exceeding 15 pounds. In addition to red drum, Texas Parks and Wildlife fisheries specialists have experimented on Lake Nasworthy with stockings of orangemouth corvina from California's Salton Sea. Flyfishers can have good white bass action and avoid daytime water skiing activity by fishing around lighted docks at night.

Excellent public access to lakeside facilities including picnic grounds, camping areas, a lighted fishing pier and paved launch ramps are provided by the city for a nominal fee. To get to the lake from the southwest side of San Angelo, take Texas (FM) 584.

O.H. IVIE RESERVOIR

At various times the Texas Parks and Wildlife Department has stocked more than 500,000 Florida largemouth bass and 300,000 smallmouth bass fry and fingerlings in the lake, along with quantities of channel, blue and flathead catfish, plus crappie and striped bass.

The lake has an 18 inch minimum length and three fish per day bag limit on black bass (largemouth, smallmouth and spotted).

To get to Lake O.H. Ivie from San Angelo, take Texas (FM) 380 for 28 miles to Paint Rock, turn north on US 83 for about three miles. Turn east again on Texas (FM) 1929 for about 10 miles until the road ends at Texas (FM) 2134. Then turn northeast for about three miles. The Concho site is a left turn onto a caliche road at the sign.

The three public recreation areas at the lake are Concho, on the south side; Padgitt on the north side, and the Kennedy Area near the north end of the dam. To get to the Padgitt site from Ballinger, take US 67 east to Valera and turn south on FM 503 for 10 miles to Voss. One mile south of Voss, turn west on FM 2134 and follow the signs to the site.

BRADY CREEK RESERVOIR

Located 3 miles west of Brady, the 1,020-acre Brady Creek Reservoir is a scenic fishery reflecting its setting among live oaks on the northern boundary of the Texas Hill Country region. Its attractive location, abundance of wildlife, clear water and good numbers of largemouth, crappie, sunfish and the occasional smallmouth make this a favorite with flyfishers and other light tackle anglers. Flyfishers should prospect around the flooded timber and brush piles at the creek mouth. Private marinas provide camping areas, fishing piers and boat access to the lake. To get to the lake, travel west from Brady on Texas (FM)2028.

STATE PARK WATERS

FORT GRIFFIN STATE HISTORICAL PARK

Located in Shackelford County, this 506-acre park offers campsites, showers and picnic tables and access to fishing on the Clear Fork of the Brazos River. Fort Griffin was the primary supply point for units attempting to force the Comanches onto Oklahoma reservations. The fort was abandoned in 1881. Today, besides sampling the fishing on the Brazos river, visitors can view the park's herd of Longhorn cattle. For additional information, contact the park at (915) 762-3592. The park is located off US 283 between Albany and Throckmorton.

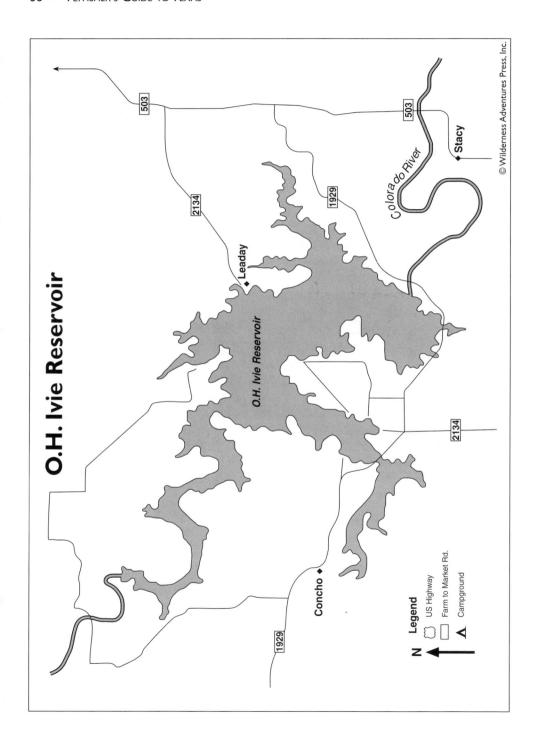

O.H. Ivie Reservoir

Brady Creek Reservoir

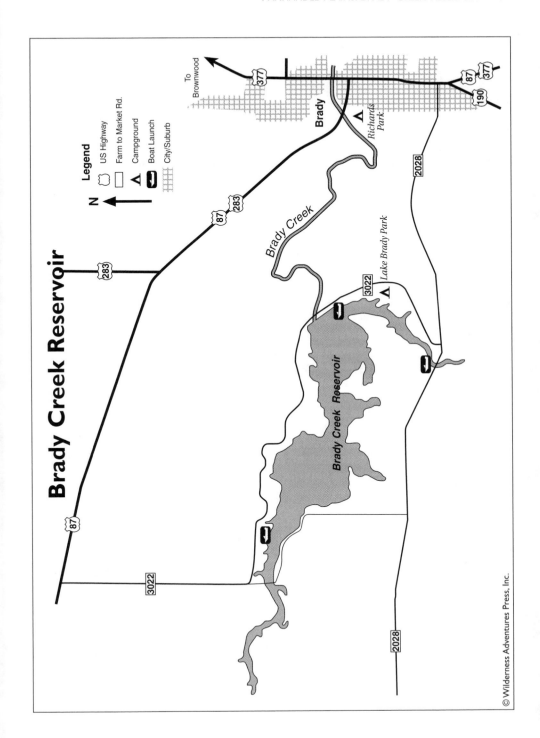

CAPROCK CANYONS STATE PARK

Located among rugged canyons on the eastern side of the High Plains in Briscoe County, 13,906-acre Caprock Canyons State Park offers a dramatic setting for fly fishing on a small lake stocked with largemouth and sunfish. The 100-acre Lake Theo can be fished from float tubes, small watercraft or johnboats and a no-wake rule for power boats is enforced. Lake levels can vary widely, especially during drought years. For information on lake conditions, contact park officials at (806) 455-1492. Wildlife present in the area include mule deer, bobcats, coyotes, porcupine, and jackrabbits. Aoudads, or Barbary sheep, exotic transplants from North Africa, have also taken hold in this rugged and beautiful country since they were introduced in the late 1950s. For the adventurous, the park offers one of the most unique features in the state - an abandoned railroad line that has been converted into a combination hiking, biking, and equestrian trail. The 64-mile trail traverses rugged Quitaque Canyon, and crosses many elevated trestles as it climbs the caprock into the High Plains. Shuttles are provided to take visitors to the west end of the trail, allowing a downhill descent through some of the most scenic sections of the trail. To get to Caprock Canyons State Park, take Interstate 27 south from Amarillo to the community of Tulia. At Tulia, proceed east on Texas 86 the park, which is located near the community of Quitaque.

COPPER BREAKS STATE PARK

Located 12 miles south of Quanah off Texas 6 in Hardeman County, Copper Breaks State Park, formerly a working ranch, is a scenic park in a stark, dramatic setting with grass and mesquite mesas and juniper breaks. Near the present park area, Cynthia Ann Parker was recaptured from a band of Comanche Indians and subsequently reunited with her relatives. She had been captured as a small child by a raiding party near Mexia and grew up among the Indians. Her son, Quanah Parker, was to become the last great war chief of the Comanche nation.

The park offers many opportunities for viewing wildlife, which includes mule deer, bobcats, porcupines, raccoons and coyotes. The park is also home for the official state herd of Texas Longhorn cattle. Located in the 1,800-acre park is Lake Copper Breaks, Big Pond and a smaller pond, which are stocked with largemouth, crappie, sunfish and rainbow trout in the winter. The lakes are ideal for float tubes and small watercraft. Bass boats are allowed on the lakes but a 5-mile-per-hour speed limit is enforced. The lake is set among red-rock escarpments and there is access to bank and pier fishing. For further information, contact the park at (512) 389-8900.

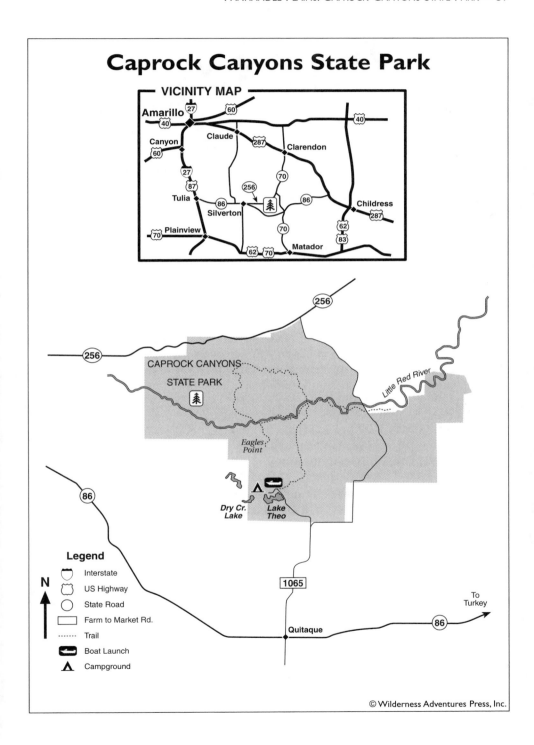

Caprock Canyons State Park

PRIVATE WATERS

HAGGARD LAKE

Located north of Stephenville off US 281 and Texas (FM) 1188 in Erath County, this 8 acre lake built in the 1970s offers solid largemouth action for fish in the 2- to 5-pound range. Fish-holding structure includes flooded timber, lay-downs and floating vegetation.

Flyfishers can cast from the bank or use small watercraft or boats with electric trolling motors.

Access to catch and release fly fishing on Haggard Lake is offered through membership in The Great Texas Bass Club. In addition to the annual membership fee, which allows access to lakes throughout the state, the day use fee at Haggard Lake is $35, half day $20, with children under 12 free.

For additional information, contact The Great Texas Bass Club at (214) 954-1818.

CENTENNIAL TANKS

Located south of Desdemona off Texas 16, Centennial Tanks is composed of two irrigation conservation lakes. The 17- and 22-acre lakes are within walking distance of each other and available for fishing. Each has a variety of fish-holding structure and is stocked with largemouth and sunfish. Largemouth up to 9 pounds have been taken from these waters. Fishing pressure is controlled on these lakes to enhance the quality of the fishing and day use is limited to two anglers per lake.

Small RVs are allowed but there are no hookups. There is a tent camping area near a picnic table at the smaller lake. There is a fee for overnight camping.

Access to catch and release fly fishing on Centennial Tanks is offered through membership in The Great Texas Bass Club. In addition to the annual membership fee, which allows access to lakes throughout the state, the day use fee at Centennial Tanks is $35, half day $20, with children under 12 free.

PARK TANK

Located south of Eastland off Texas 6, this 8-acre lake is situated in a wooded area that gives it a park-lie feel. Tree limbs and brush provide excellent cover for the lake's ample population of largemouth. Bass in excess of 7 pounds have been caught in the lake.

Access to catch and release fly fishing on Park Tank is offered through membership in The Great Texas Bass Club. In addition to the annual membership fee, which allows access to lakes throughout the state, the day use fee at Park Tank is $35, half day $20, with children under 12 free. Overnight tent and RV campsites are available for a fee.

BORDER CROSSINGS

LAKE CARL ETLING

Located near Boise City, Oklahoma, this lake is about a 3 hour drive for Texas flyfishers from Amarillo. The spring-fed lake located about 30 miles from the Texas border. It is stocked with rainbow trout from November through April. The lake also holds largemouth, smallmouth, Kentucky spotted bass and walleye.

WICHITA MOUNTAINS WILDLIFE REFUGE

Located in south-central Oklahoma, 20 miles northwest of Lawton, the Wichita Mountains Wildlife Refuge offers 12 lakes, a couple of streams and a variety of fishing opportunities.

The waters hold largemouth and smallmouth bass, sunfish and chain pickerel. Three weight to six weight fly rod outfits are ideal for these waters. Weight forward, floating lines and long leaders are recommended in the clear water. A variety of flies will produce on these waters including small poppers, sliders, and large nymphs.

The park has camping facilities and water. To get to the Wichita Mountains Wildlife Refuge, travel north from Wichita Falls on I-44 to Lawton, cross town and exit at SH 49. Then travel west for 20 miles to the park entrance.

For additional information, contact the park at (405) 429-3221.

Sunfish (pumpkinseed).

Panhandle Plains Hub Cities
Amarillo

Population - 174,541	**Elevation - 3,676'**
Area Code - 806	**County - Potter/Randall**

ACCOMMODATIONS
Holiday Inn - I-40, 1911 I-40 East/372-8741/248 rooms/$$$
Best Western - Amarillo Inn, 1610 Coulter Drive / 358-7861 / 103 rooms / $$
Hampton Inn, 1700 IH-40 East / 379-8807 / 116 rooms / $$
Quality Inn and Suites - Airport, 1803 Lakeside / 102 rooms / $$$

BED AND BREAKFASTS
Auntie's House Bed and Breakfast, 410 E. Corsicana Street / four rooms / $$$

CAMPGROUNDS
Amarillo KOA, 1100 Folsom Rd. Amarillo 1-800-562-3431 806-335-1792
Information www.koa.com

RESTAURANTS
Macaroni Joe's Pasta House, Wellington Square, I-40 and Georgia Street / 358-8990 / $
Chili's Bar and Grill, 3810 Interstate 40 West / 379-6118 / $
The Black-Eyed Pea, 3820 Interstate 40 West / 355-9816 / $
Big Texan Steak Ranch, 7701 Interstate 40 East / 372-6000 / $

FLY SHOPS AND GUIDE SERVICES
RiverFields, 2465 I-40 West / 351-0980
Top Notch Outfitters, 2617 Wolflin Village / 353-9468

SPORTING GOODS STORES
Academy Sports, LP 335 & 45th Ave / 468-6314
Anchor Marine, 4217 Canyon Drive / 353-9511

AIRPORTS
Amarillo International Airport / 335-1671 / American Airlines-American Eagle:
800-433-7300 / Atlantic Southeast Airlines (Delta):800-282-3424 / Continental
Express:800-525-0280 / Southwest Airlines 800-435-9792

FOR MORE INFORMATION
Amarillo Convention and Visitors Bureau
1101 North First Street
Amarillo, TX 79105
374-1497

Wichita Falls

Population - 99,440　　**Elevation - 946'**
Area Code - 940　　**County - Wichita**

ACCOMMODATIONS
Best Western - Towne Crest Inn, 1601 Eighth Street / 322-1182 / 42 rooms / $
Holiday Inn Hotel and Suites, 401 Broad Street / 766-6000 / 241 rooms / $$
La Quinta Inn - Wichita Falls, 1128 Central Freeway North / 139 rooms / $$

RESTAURANTS
Hacienda Hernandez, 1105 Broadway / 767-5932 / open Monday through Saturday for lunch and dinner / $
Branding Iron, 1041 Scott / 723-0338 / $
McBride Land and Cattle Co., 501 Scott / Open weekdays for lunch and dinner, weekends for dinner only / $

AIRPORTS
Wichita Falls Municipal Airport / 855-3621 / American Airlines-American Eagle: 800-433-7300 / Atlantic Southeast Airlines (Delta): 800-282-3424

SPORTING GOOD STORES
Big 5, 3808 Kemp Blvd / 691-3628

FOR MORE INFORMATION
Wichita Falls Convention and Visitors Bureau
P.O. Box 630
Wichita Falls, TX 76307
716-5500

LODGING PRICE KEY

$	=	$30 - $50 per night
$$	=	$50 - $70 per night
$$$	=	$70 per night and up

RESTAURANT PRICE KEY

$	=	$10 and under per meal
$$	=	$10 - $20 per meal
$$$	=	$20 and up

Lubbock

Population - 194,799   **Elevation - 3,241'**
Area Code - 806   **County - Lubbock**

ACCOMMODATIONS

Lubbock Inn, 3901 19th Street / 792-1319 / 117 rooms / $$
Howard Johnson Express Inn, 4801 Avenue Q, Highway 84 / 800-747-3668 / 56 rooms / $
La Quinta Inn - Civic Center, 601 Avenue Q / 800-531-5900 / 137 rooms / $$
Residence Inn by Marriott, 2551 S. Loop 289 / 745-1963 / 80 rooms / $$

BED AND BREAKFASTS

Country Place Bed and Breakfast, 16004 Country Road 1600 / 863-2030 / 5 rooms / $$

CAMPGROUNDS

Lubbock RV Park, Tent Sites Available4811 N I-27 Lubbock 806-747-2366 lubbockrv@gocampingamerica.com www.gocampingamerica.com
Lubbock KOA, 5502 County Rd. 6300 Lubbock 1-800-562-8643 Free Reservations 806-762-8653 Information

RESTAURANTS

Josie's Restaurant, 212 University Avenue / 747-8546 / $
Tommy's Famous Burgers, 117 University Avenue / 763-5424 / $
Orlando's, 2402 Avenue Q / 747-5998 / open Monday through Saturday for lunch and dinner, dinner only on Sunday / $$
Don Pablo's, 4625 50th Street / open for lunch and dinner / $
Lone Star Oyster Bar, 5116-C 58th / open daily for lunch and dinner / 797-3773 / $

SPORTING GOODS STORES

Outdoorsman, Inc., 6602 Slide Road / 794-6666
Mountain Hideaway, 4816 50th Street / 762-8416
Fishermans Headquarters, 2388 509th St. / 793-5822
Oshman's, 7020 Quaker Avenue, F / 792-1964

AIRPORTS

Lubbock International Airport / 775-2046 / American Airlines-American Eagle:800-433-7300 / Continental Airlines: 800-525-0280 / Southwest Airlines: 800-435-9792

FOR MORE INFORMATION

Lubbock Visitors and Conventions Bureau
1301 Broadway, No. 200
Lubbock, TX 79401
763-4666

Abilene

Population - 117,074　　　**Elevation - 1,738'**
Area Code - 915　　　**County - Taylor**

ACCOMMODATIONS

Best Western - Mall South, 3950 Ridgemont Drive / 800-346-1574 / 61 rooms / $$
Embassy Suites Hotel, 4250 Ridgemont Drive / 698-1234 / 176 rooms / $$$
La Quinta, 3501 West Lake Road / 800-531-5900 / 105 rooms / $$

BED AND BREAKFASTS

BJ's Bed and Breakfast, 508 Mulberry Street / 800-673-5855 / four rooms / $$

CAMPGROUNDS

Abilene KOA, 4851 W. Stamford St., Abilene - 1-800-562-3651 Reservations 915-672-3681 information www.koa.com

RESTAURANTS

John Zentner's Daughter Steak House, 4358 Sayles Boulevard / 695-4290 / Open daily for lunch and dinner / $
Joe Allen's Pit Bar-B-Que, 1233 South Treadway / 672-6082 / Open Monday through Saturday for lunch and dinner / $
Dos Amigos / 3650 North 6th Street / 672-2992 / Open Monday through Saturday for lunch and dinner / $

HOSPITALS

Hendrick Health System, 1242 N. 19th Street / 670-2000

AIRPORTS

Abilene Regional Airport / 676-6367 / American Airlines-American Eagle:800-433-7300

SPORTING GOODS STORES

Academy Sports, 3950 Knox Dr. / 698-5490
Dry Creek Anglers, 3301 South 14th St / 698-7801

FOR MORE INFORMATION

Abilene Convention and Visitors Bureau
1101 North First
Abilene, Texas 79601
676-2556

San Angelo

Population - 90,187	Elevation - 184'
Area Code - 915	County - Tom Green

ACCOMMODATIONS

Best Western - San Angelo Inn West, 415 West Beauregard / 800-582-9668 /
75 rooms / $

Hampton Inn, 2959 Loop 306 / 942-9622 / 64 rooms / $

La Quinta Inn Conference Center, 2307 Loop 306 / 168 rooms / $$

CAMPGROUNDS

San Angelo KOA, 6699 Kinickerbocker Rd. San Angelo / 1-800-562-7519 /
Reservations / 915-949-3242 Information

Spring Creek Marina & RV Park, Tent sites and cabin rentals available as well as
RV lots. / 45 Fishermans Rd. San Angelo / 1-800-500-7801 Toll Free / 915-944-
3850 Local / www.springcreekmarina@gocampingamerica.com

RESTAURANTS

Las Dos Hermanas, 1406 South Chadbourne / 655-6057 / Open Sunday through
Thursday 7 a.m. to 10 p.m., Friday and Saturday 7 a.m. to 11 p.m.

Spaghetti Western Italian Grill, 26 East Concho Avenue / 653-1300 / $

Zentner's Daughter Steak House, 1901 Knickerbocker / 949-2821 / $

AIRPORTS

Mathis Field Airport / 659-6409 / American Airlines:800-433-7300

SPORTING GOODS STORES

Field and Stream Sporting Goods, 3812 Houston Harte / 944-7094

FOR MORE INFORMATION

San Angelo Convention and Visitors Bureau
500 Rio Concho Drive
San Angelo, TX 76903
653-1206

FLY FISHING CLUBS:

Golden Spread Flyfishers, Amarillo. For information on membership, programs,
and outings, contact Rod Brashears at 353-8379.

A hefty largemouth bass taken on a fly.

REGION 2

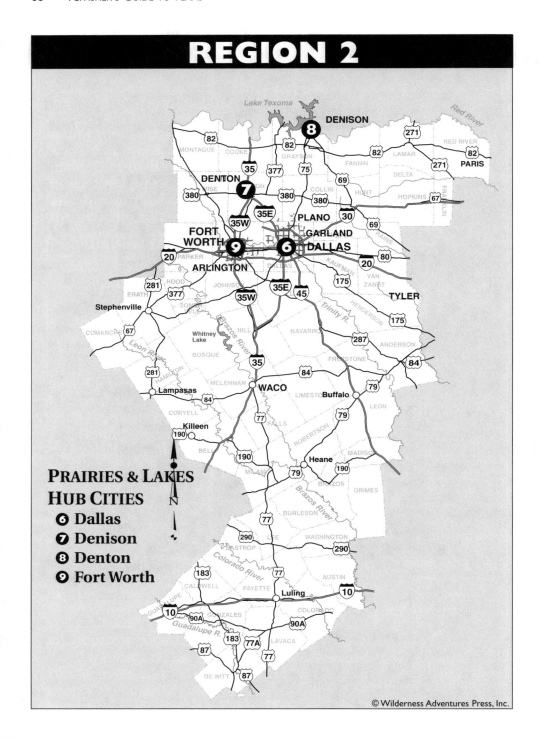

PRAIRIES & LAKES
HUB CITIES

6 Dallas
7 Denison
8 Denton
9 Fort Worth

© Wilderness Adventures Press, Inc.

Prairies and Lakes

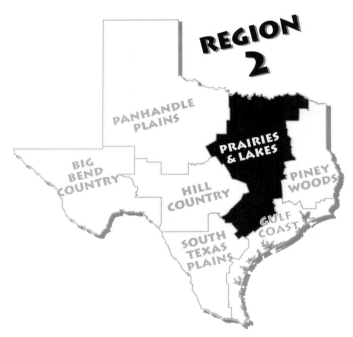

This region, which extends from the Red River on the Oklahoma border almost to the Gulf of Mexico, could also be described simply as "Bass Country" because of the multitude of waters that are home to large-mouth.

Even President George W. Bush has his own bass lake in this region.

From small state park lakes like Purtis Creek to massive reservoirs like Whitney and Richland-Chambers, this is the region where bucketmouth Florida-strain largemouth thrive. The region's waters also offer many other intriguing options for flyfishers with good populations of sunfish, striped bass, smallmouth bass, white bass, and hybrid striped bass.

Located in north-central and central Texas, this region of blackland prairies and oak "Cross Timbers" is a transition zone between the pineywoods of East Texas and the western plains.

The Cross Timbers terrain included in this region is a narrow band of heavily wooded land dominated by post oaks, blackjack oaks, black hickories and winged elms. These trees rooted in sandstone form a thick canopy called the Cross Timbers forest.

This is where dinosaurs roamed millions of years ago and only a century ago, Kiowa and Comanche warriors fought with pioneer farmers and ranchers. Cities in the region include Dallas and Fort Worth, Waco, Gainesville, Denison and Sherman.

RIVERS

RED RIVER

Fly rodders have successfully prospected the prolific striper fishery below Denison Dam for a number of years, casting Deceiver patterns and Clouser Deep Minnow flies from rocky banks at sunset or throwing big poppers at dawn when the stripers are chasing bait on the surface.

Experienced fly casters swim flies along the rock-strewn shoreline near the dam when water is being released, or wade the flats downstream near the river channel during low water periods.

*Flyfisher on airboat with a striper on the Red
River below Denison Dam (Lake Texoma).*

Weight-forward floating lines handle well on the river in most conditions although a clear, intermediate line like the Scientific Anglers Striper Line offers more flexibility when there is moving water. A uniform density line with a sink rate of three to five inches per second is also a good option when the conditions require the angler to counter the heavy currents and get flies down to reach stripers holding at deeper depths. With floating lines, use a six- to nine-foot leader with a 10- or 12-pound tippet. The same leader system that works well on Gulf Coast redfish and seatrout does the job for stripers. With the uniform density lines, use a short, two- to three- foot section of 12- or 15-pound monofilament. The short leader is important with the sinking line to keep the fly at the same depth as the line and to allow the angler maximum contact with the fly.

While Lefty's Deceivers dressed in white bucktail are proven killers on the river, a variety of other fly patterns and colors work as well. The stripers will inhale Clouser Deep Minnow patterns tied on #1 hooks as well as six-inch long sailfish streamers on 3/0 hooks. A simple but effective pattern that works well on these stripers is a Seaducer tied with gray hackle with a few strands of Flashabou. Fort Worth angler and fly tier Brian Camp also has had a lot of success with this pattern on stripers on the Brazos River below the dam at Possum Kingdom Lake. The fly has a tantalizing swimming action in the fast water and can be dead-drifted around the deep holes down the river.

Saltwater poppers and skipping bugs on 2/0 hooks also take Red River stripers in the early morning and late evening when the fish are chasing bait and feeding aggressively on the surface.

During the heavy spring runs, the striper that takes the fly may be a feisty 15-inch schoolie or a 20-pound bruiser that will put a deep bow in an eight-weight rod.

Red River airboats have the choice of fishing near the dam during periods of heavy flow or traveling downstream to fish around the rocky shoals and deep holes.

The airboat guides, who can measure in tons the stripers that have been taken by their clients on conventional tackle, seem to enjoy the fly fishing trips as much as the fly fishers. Often when they spot flyfishers along the shore, they will throw live shad in the area to attract stripers so they can watch the results.

While the action can be fast and furious near the dam when water is being released, guide Harold Speed, who operates a fleet of four airboats on the river, says the best fly fishing is downstream during low water periods when the fish are concentrated in deeper holes.

Speed uses a number of tricks to put flyfishers on stripers during low water periods. When the power generation is in the cycle of being halted around midnight and then starting back up around 11 a.m., Speed starts out the morning fishing the shallow pools around the dam. When the water comes on it is time to haul it down- river five or six miles to try another hole. After about an hour and a half, the downstream flow will catch up with the boat and it is time to move downriver until everyone has put a day in fishing the choice spots where the fish are concentrated.

When conditions are right downriver, fly rodders also have the option of getting out of the airboat and fishing the holes from float tubes.

The spring trips offer some of the hottest fishing with big numbers of fish in the river as well as a chance to hook one of the heavy spawners. Speed's airboat clients took more than 90 stripers of 30 pounds or more in one three-year period, with most of the bigger fish taken in the spring.

Fall fishing on the Red River offers eagle watching as a bonus. The mottled brown and black juveniles as well as the unmistakable white-headed adults can be easily spotted flying overhead or nesting in the dead trees along the river bank just downstream from the dam.

Speed's airboats are ideal for the river because, in addition to their stability in the fast water, they allow him to navigate the rocky shoals and deep holes downriver. Frequent fluctuations in river flows, shifting sandbars and floating debris make conventional outboards a risky proposition on the river.

Speed designed his 23-foot airboats with high gunwales and 8½-foot beams. They can carry a lot of people and gear and there is ample room for two or three fly casters to have loops in the air at the same time. The airboats come equipped with 85-pound anchors made from flat chunks of railroad steel, the only thing that will hold on the flat, mossy river bottom.

With Lake Texoma as its mother lode, the quality striper fishing on this stretch of the Red River is not likely to decline anytime soon. First stocked in the mid-1960s, stripers adapted well to the lake's high salinity and favorable habitat and began reproducing on a wide scale in 1974.

According to Texas Parks and Wildlife Department data, as many as 970,000 striped bass are caught by anglers on the lake annually.

There is a five-fish bag limit for stripers on the river with no maximum length restriction. Speed says he has verified a 41-pound striper taken from the river.

To fish from a boat in the river, or from the bank on the north (Oklahoma) side of the river requires an Oklahoma fishing license. Information on fishing licenses is available on the river at Damsite Bait Shop, (903) 465- 0165 or at the Tackle Box in nearby Pottsboro, (903) 786-9010.

For information on fly fishing from airboats on the Red River, contact Harold Speed at Silver Dollar Striper Guide Service 800-462-9711, (580) 838-2578 or 838-2297. For information on river flows, contact the US Army Corps of Engineers at (903) 465-1491.

Below Denison Dam on the Red River, Texas residents holding a Texas fishing license may fish from the bank on the south (Texas) side of the river between the dam and Shawnee Creek, a distance of a half mile or less. However, to fish from a boat in the river, or from the bank on the north side, an Oklahoma fishing license is required. The special Lake Texoma fishing license is not valid in the Red River below the dam.

TRINITY RIVER

Feeder creeks to the Trinity include Johnson Creek at Six Flags Over Texas at Arlington, Denton Creek at Lake Grapevine, White Rock Creek, Duck Creek and Spring Creek.

The Clear Fork and the West Fork of the Trinity join in Fort Worth. A slower, smaller branch of the Trinity, the Clear Fork begins south of the West Fork and flows into Lake Weatherford and Benbrook Lake. The East Fork and Elm Fork of the Trinity have their headwaters north of Dallas.

The West Fork begins 145 miles west of Fort Worth in Archer County and flows into Lake Bridgeport, Eagle Mountain Lake and Lake Worth. It joins the Clear Fork of the Trinity in Fort Worth.

The different forks of the Trinity river join south of Dallas then the river flows almost due south into Freestone County, where it forms Fairfield Lake and into Leon and Houston Counties, where it forms Houston County Lake.

In the Dallas-Fort Worth Metroplex area, the main branches of the Trinity River are susceptible to urban runoff and wide variations in flow that can adversely affect the quality of the fishing. Flyfishers in the area, nonetheless, say it can produce excellent carp action at times.

Crestland Cutoff

A good stretch of the Trinity River that is well worth exploring by flyfishers is an oxbow section near the community of Trinidad, which is located west of Athens on Texas 34 west of Texas 274 in Henderson County. This part of the river is called Crestland Cutoff and has the look of an old bayou with Spanish moss hanging from trees along the bank. There is a launch ramp for putting in a small boat, kayak or canoe. In addition to largemouth and sunfish, there is a resident population of alligator gar and spotted gar that can provide a lot of action for fly rodders.

NAVASOTA RIVER

The Navasota begins in Limestone County and flows into Lake Mexia and Lake Limestone before forming the boundary for Robertson and Madison counties and eventually joining the Brazos River at Washington on the Brazos in Washington County.

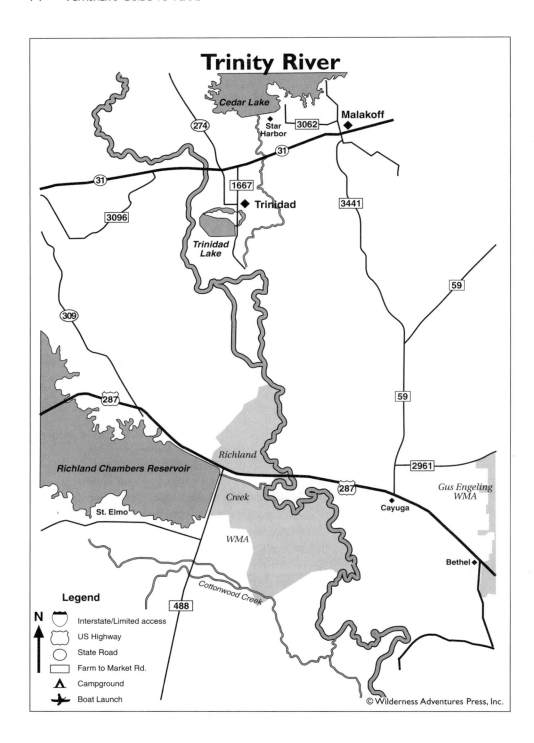

ALLIGATOR GAR (Lepisosteus spatula)

Texas rivers and lakes hold several species of gar. Alligator gar (Lepisosteus spatula), *the largest, prefer big, slow moving rivers and reservoirs. They are also found in the mouths of rivers along the coast and in brackish water environments. Alligator gar under 25 pounds is considered small and specimens weighing in at more than 100 pounds are common. There are three other smaller species of gar in Texas waters, the shortnose gar* (Lepisosteus platostomus), *longnose gar* (Lepisosteus osseus) *and spotted gar,* (Lepisosteus oculatus). *The longnose gar, or needle-nosed gar, has one row of teeth while the alligator gar has a double row. The shortnose gar has no spots and the spotted gar has large spots on its head.*

Alligator gar.

BRAZOS RIVER

The Brazos River System, which begins northwest of Clovis, New Mexico, winds south through an immense area of West Texas, traveling 800 miles to the Gulf of Mexico. Aided by the settling effects of dams on Lake Possum Kingdom and Lake Whitney, its waters run clear and clean through the limestone cliffs in its midrange, making these stretches of river ideal for floating and fly fishing. The spring and fall months are usually the best times for float trips on this section of the Brazos. Water levels are better at these times and temperatures more moderate. The hot summer months are good only if there is enough flow for enjoyable canoeing.

On the Brazos, the well-equipped fly fisher will bring a floating line and a uniform density full-sinking line. Stripers and white bass hold in depressions where shallow water drops off into deeper holes. Lake Whitney fly fishing guide Charlie Cypert says that on the days when these fish are aggressively feeding, they can be caught on floating lines and sink tips or shooting heads. But he says that after he started using uniform density sinking lines, he caught three to four times as many fish as he caught with floating lines on a daily average. On some days, the sinking line made the difference between catching no fish and having a good day, especially with white bass and stripers. The reason is that if these fish are not feeding aggressively, they will hold down in the bottom of the holes, and you often need to bring a fly right in front of them to take the fish. Cypert often uses a 6 weight sinking line on a 5 weight rod.

Cypert recommends sinking lines for fishing deeper holes in the river. He says he uses sinking lines in the river 60 percent of the time. Cypert says he always carries one fly line rigged with floating line and one rigged with sinking lines for his clients. "Some days a floating line will work because the fish are moving up to take baitfish," he says. "But most of the time they are in the deeper holes and you have to go down for them especially with stripers and white bass."

Cypert says he uses sinking line in the river during white bass season 90 percent of the time. Being on the bottom makes a big difference.

In the hot part of the summer, Cypert says the water in the tailrace area of Brazos "goes dead" after receiving flows from oxygen depleted water at the bottom of Lake Whitney. When water is being generated off the bottom of the lake, there is such low oxygen that the fish will turn off from feeding. He says it takes about 24 hours for the fish to begin aggressively feeding again.

Interstate 20 to Lake Granbury

During the spring white bass runs, which typically take place from mid-February through mid-March, Brian Camp says he likes to target a stretch of the Brazos downstream from Interstate 20 to Lake Granbury. The white bass, or "sandies" will be moving upriver from Lake Granbury. A good technique, Camp says, is to put-in at one of the public fishing camps with a johnboat and trolling motor and look for some of the deeper holes where the fish are concentrating, or in the shallow riffles, where they are spawning. A good approach is to use sink tip or full sink, uniform density lines with small white or chartreuse streamers, white Woolly Buggers or Cypert Mylar

Minnows. "The sand bass will be on the bottom and you need to get your fly down to them," Camp says.

Interstate 20 / US 80 Crossing to Dennis
Put-in and take-out points for fishing this stretch of the Brazos include the Interstate 20 / US 80 crossing in Parker County. Contact Brazos River Resort (817) 596-2994 for information on camping, river access, flow levels and canoe rentals) or the Texas (FM) 1189 Crossing 12.6 miles downriver at the Dennis Community.

Lake Granbury Dam to Upper Lake Whitney
Fort Worth fly fisher Brian Camp says this stretch of the Brazos has been extremely productive for fly fishing in recent years with stripers in the tailrace area near the dam. The area downstream from the dam, from the crossing on Texas (FM) 67 down-river, has developed into a decent smallmouth stream. The reason is that the smallmouth that have been in Lake Whitney for years have gotten established and moved up the river. "You can now catch smallmouth all the way up the Lake Granbury tailrace, but from 67 downstream it is almost expected that you will catch smallmouth," Camp says. He recommends using black or olive Woolly Buggers for these bronzebacks.

Several fishing camps located on Texas (FM) 199 and Texas (FM) 200 along the Brazos River between Granbury and Lake Whitney offer information on flow levels as well as campsites, access to the river and shuttle service for a fee. These include Oakdale's Camp 'N' Fish (254) 897-2321, Rhodes Canoe Rental (254) 897-4214, and Low Water Bridge Canoe Rental (254) 897-3666.

Mitchell Ford Crossing to Texas (FM) 200 Crossing
Located west of Texas (FM) 2174, the Mitchell Ford Crossing offers access to 15.5 miles of river downstream to the Texas (FM) 200 Crossing. This is a scenic, winding stretch of river through rolling hills lined with cedar and live oak.

Texas (FM) 200 Crossing south of Rainbow Community to Braden's Camp
The Texas 200 Bridge Crossing allows good public access for take-out, as well as a put-in for the 13 mile float to Braden's Camp on the south bank just below the bridge crossing on County Road 1118 / 1175 east of the Brazos Point community. An interesting feature for fly fishers to target on this float is the intersection of the Paluxy River just below the put-in.

Lake Whitney to Waco (Cameron Park)
This stretch of the Brazos, where the river flows through Hood, Somervell and Johnson counties, is one of the most attractive and productive stretches to fly fish. Charlie Cypert notes that there is one deep hole after another beginning on the downstream section of the Brazos just below the Lake Whitney Dam. Smallmouth in the 6.5 to 7 pound class have been caught in deep holes in this stretch of the Brazos.

Brazos River

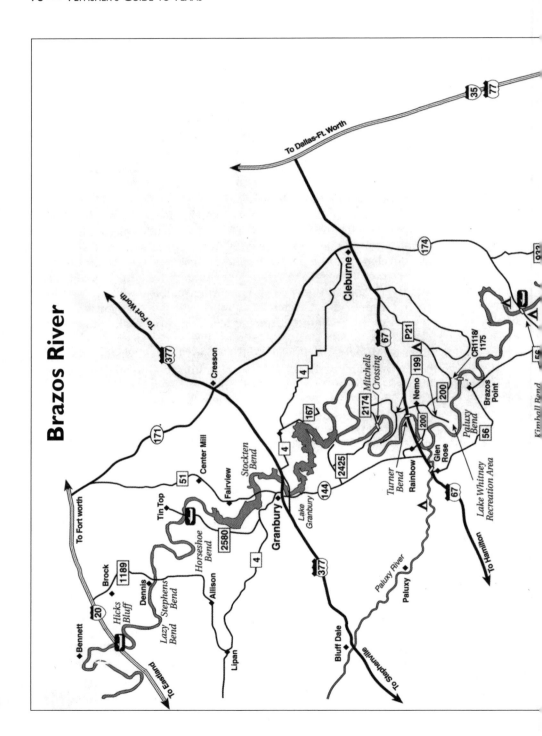

To Dallas-Ft. Worth

35
77

174

923

To Fort Worth

377

Cresson

Cleburne

67

P21

174

Mitchells
Crossing

2174

Nemo

199

CR118/
1175

4

167

200

200

Brazos
Point

56

Kimball Bend

To Fort worth

171

Center Mill

Fairview

Stockten
Bend

4

51

2425

144

Turner
Bend

Rainbow

360

Glen
Rose

Paluxy
Bend

56

Lake Whitney
Recreation Area

67

Tin Top

2580

Lake
Granbury

Granbury

To Hamilton

Horseshoe
Bend

Allison

4

377

Paluxy River

20

Brock

1189

Dennis

Hicks
Bluff

Stephens
Bend

Lazy
Bend

Lipan

Bluff Dale

Paluxy

Bennett

To Eastland

To Stephanville

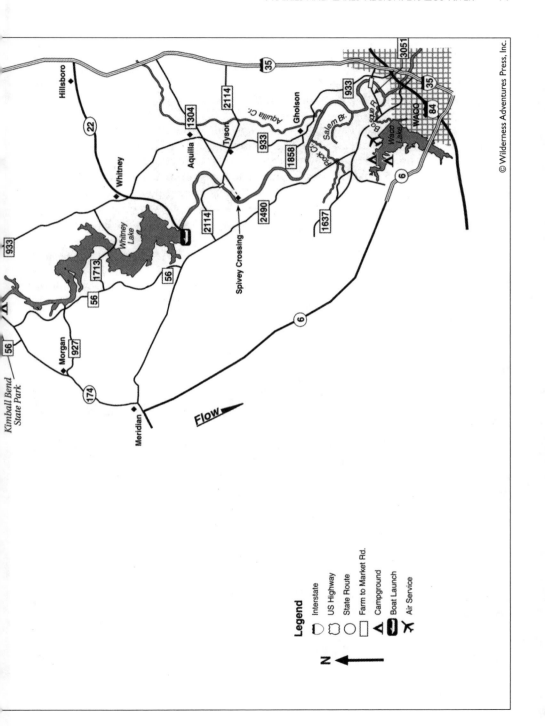

© Wilderness Adventures Press, Inc.

Anglers should look for fallen trees around the holes to find the bass and crappie. The smallmouth will hold out along the rocks and gravel near the faster water.

Heavy flows and high water, while good for navigation, can present problems for fishing. "When water is being generated, the water comes up four or five feet. But the only place where the fishing is good during those periods is just below the dam in the tail water," Cypert notes.

The Brazos River runs extremely clear, especially when there hasn't been recent heavy rains. This clear water feature of the river makes it a challenge sometimes to present a fly to game fish because they can see the offering so clearly.

An excellent fish-holding area is just below the dam where two runs come together, Cypert says. The best areas downstream during generation periods are where fast water is running over a shoal into a deeper hole and eddies are created. These are good areas to fish but technically difficult. "Unless the fly fisher can drift with the current it is hard to get even a sinking line down deep," he says.

Flyfishers go down the river in flat bottom johnboats, but Cypert says kayaks and canoes are much easier because of the shallow sections in the river. On an 8-mile float from the dam to the bridge on Texas 2114, anglers might have to drag a johnboat a mile and a half over rocks and gravel and it can be a tough trip.

During floats on this stretch of the Brazos, flyfishers can wade shallow areas and cast into deeper holes. Also, many people put-in behind the dam and walk

*Flyfisher with canoe on Brazos River float on a stretch below
Possum Kingdom Dam.*

downriver to wade. On floats downstream from the dam when the generators are cut off, flyfishers on float trips can follow the falling water downstream and catch fish, Cypert says. Stripers will also work their way downriver to deeper holes and anglers can follow them.

Flyfishers can also walk about a quarter mile downriver from the dam and find excellent stretches for wade fishing. Cypert says he has caught striped bass up to 22.5 pounds and smallmouth to 5 pounds on this stretch below the dam. He says some of the best fishing is about 2½ miles below Whitney Dam.

Lake Whitney Dam to Texas (FM) 2114 Crossing (The Outpost - Dick's Place)

Just below Whitney dam on the east bank is an easy put-in for downstream floats. There is usually clear water flowing over sand and gravel bottom in this stretch with many clear flowing springs. Spring and autumn offer optimum conditions for float trips on this section of river. The put-in is immediately below Lake Whitney Dam. The access can be found on the the road to the river off Texas 22 on the west side of the dam.

This 8.33 mile stretch holds largemouth, smallmouth, Kentucky spotted bass, white bass and striped bass. The fly fishing can be excellent on this float from April through June and again beginning in September until the first frost. It is a scenic trip through limestone bluffs and over rocky, gravel bottoms. There are several very shallow stretches to cross and during periods of low flow, anglers may have to get out and drag boats to the next stretch of deep water. Canoes, kayaks or lightweight johnboats are recommended for this section that offers opportunities to fish a variety of fish-holding features.

The Outpost - Dick's Place (254-622-8364), is located at the (FM) 2114 Crossing. The owners offer shuttle services and put-in and take-out access downstream from their property or for floats starting at the dam for their own rental canoes.

For a two-day trip, flyfishers can continue downriver another 13.2 miles to Reddell's Camp at the Gholson community. Another 13-mile stretch downriver that ends in Waco at the Waco Drive Bridge can make the float into a three-day trip.

Texas (FM) 2114 Crossing to Brazos River RV Park and Reddell's Camp

This 13.2 mile stretch of the Brazos maintains adequate flows for floats throughout the year and offers many deep holes, sand and gravel bars, limestone bluffs and springs for fly-fishers to prospect for largemouth, Kentucky spotted bass, smallmouth, white bass and striped bass.

For a fee, Reddell's offers camping areas, R.V. hookups, restrooms, a pavilion, and fire grates.

Reddell's Camp to Waco (Cameron Park) and Texas (FM) 3051 Crossing

This 14.4-mile stretch to Waco will take boaters past several feeder creek mouths and springs and the option at the end of the float just below the Texas (FM) 3051 Crossing to take a 4 mile side trip down the Bosque River toward Lake Waco.

PALUXY RIVER

Located in an ecological transition zone of north-central Texas called the Cross Timbers, this clear, spring creek-fed river begins near Bluff Dale in Erath County and winds for about 35 miles through Hood and Somervell counties until it joins the Brazos River below Glen Rose.

The river is too small to float but there are a number of access points for wade fishing. Fly fishing guide and outfitter Richard Hart of Glen Rose calls the Paluxy River one of the state's hidden fly fishing jewels. "This river is spring-fed, small and clean," Hart says. "Access is limited but the locals you run into are friendly and usually offer advice."

Hart explains that several spring creeks-the North Fork, the South Fork and Berry's Creek converge near the community of Bluff Dale to form the headwaters of the Paluxy. The upper stretch of the Paluxy has a sandy bottom and vegetation that supports a variety of aquatic insects, minnows and amphibians. "The limestone streambed provides a slight alkalinity to the water that encourages most aquatic insect growth," according to Hart.

The lower Paluxy, which runs through Dinosaur Valley State Park near Glen Rose, is faster moving because of its hard, smooth limestone bottom. Re-regulation dams were built in the 1930s on the Paluxy to supply water for the town of Glen Rose and these small rock dams have created deep pools that hold bass and sunfish. Downstream from Glen Rose, the river widens and moves more slowly as it approaches "Tres Rios," where it meets the Brazos River and Squaw Creek. Hart says the sandy flats that have formed along this section of the river provide flyfishers an opportunity to cast to carp, especially during the summer. "The carp move out of the main river channel and feed over these flats in the early evening," Hart says. "The water is shallow and they tail and even enter water that allows their backs to be exposed while they are mudding around on the bottom trying to scare out the stray nymph."

For carp action, Hart recommends casting a nymph ahead of the fish and waiting for them to move up to "find" the fly. "A slight movement will either get their full attention or scare them away," Hart says. "These guys can tax all your fly fishing skills."

Hart points out that the Paluxy is a clear running river and the fish are extremely wary. Proper fly fishing technique and thoughtful fly selection is important. Hart says smaller, lighter rods are the best choice for the headwater streams and upper sections of the Paluxy and its feeder creeks. He says some of the pools are deep and wide, and these are fished just as you would any pond or small lake-wading down the middle and casting to the edges of the grass-covered banks.

Hart also recommends flyfishers target the fallen timber and large tree roots that hold the larger spotted bass and largemouth. During the middle of the day when the sun is high, Hart will cast a small hopper or cricket pattern up into the grass along the shoreline and let it fall down off the bank-a trick that almost always draws a strike. Hart says the sunfish are pushovers for nymphs and small poppers cast up to the edge of the shore vegetation and then worked back to the middle of the pool.

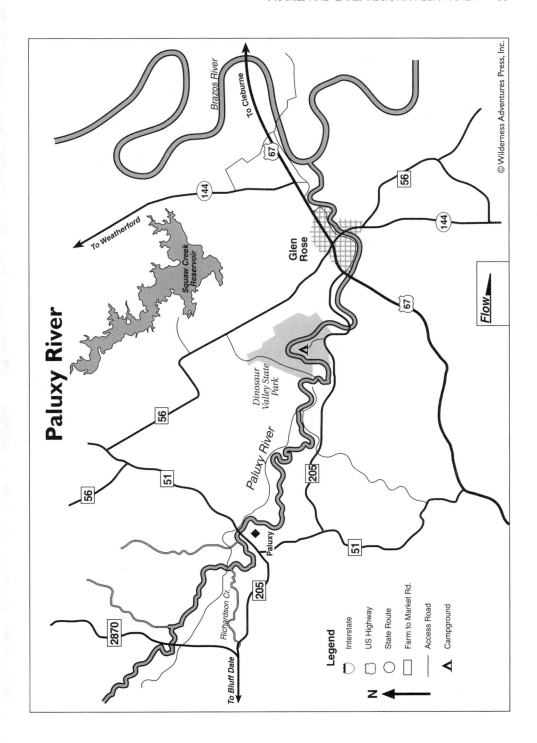

Paluxy River

© Wilderness Adventures Press, Inc.

Legend

- Interstate
- US Highway
- State Route
- Farm to Market Rd.
- Access Road
- Campground

N

For the riffles that feed the pools, Hart recommends the "high stick" nymphing technique of letting the fly float down on a dead-drift to the head of the pool where the fish are stacked up. "Keep a fairly tight line so you can feel when the take occurs," Hart says. "The floating portion of your line will just stop, giving the indication that you have stuck on the bottom or you have a bite." Another productive technique is to cast a small crawfish pattern to the middle of these pools and make a trail with it on the sandy bottom as it is retrieved. When a fish takes in these pools, the first run can be sudden and dazzling. Hart says that the most prevalent aquatic insects on the Paluxy are of the genus *Odonata* — damselflies and dragonflies. The most common damsels are the Ruby Spot, (*Hetaerina Americana*) and the Blue Damsel (*Argia moesta*). Hart notes that both of these have a tan or olive colored larvae that is ¼ to 1 inch long. The most common dragonflies are the Green Darter (*Aeshnidae anax junius*) and the River Cruiser (*Macromiidae illinoiensis*).

The Green Darter has a torpedo shaped nymph that is an aggressive feeder while the River Cruiser is a large flat or round body nymph that doesn't swim around as actively as the River Cruiser nymph. Hart recommends tying these nymphs in olive to get action from bass and sunfish. He says a floating adult dragon or damsel will draw a strike from largemouth and spotted bass.

Dinosaur Valley State Park

Located northwest of Glen Rose in Somervell County, Dinosaur Valley State Park offers flyfishers the opportunity to fish along the Paluxy River while wading in the footsteps of the three-toed Acrocanthosaurus, a cousin of Tyrannosaurus rex, and other animals who roamed the area in the early Cretaceous period. Besides the dinosaur footprints preserved in the river bottom, visitors to the 1,274-acre park often can observe a variety of present-era wildlife, including wild turkey, raccoons, armadillos, and coyotes.

The park has a small campground with partial hookups, showers and picnic tables for day use. For additional information, contact the park at (817) 897-4588.

Flyfisher casting on Colorado River below Austin.

COLORADO RIVER

Austin to the Gulf of Mexico

Once the Colorado River, which begins in Dawson County 900 miles from the Gulf of Mexico, passes Longhorn Dam below Town Lake in Austin, it slows down as it flows across fertile, gently rolling grasslands and blackland prairies. This 290-mile segment of river, whose banks are shaded by post oak, hickory, hackberry and elm trees, is lightly traveled and offers excellent fly fishing on float trips. This scenic waterway holds a healthy population of Guadalupe bass, spotted bass, largemouth, sunfish, yellow cats and other species.

The stretch from Austin to LaGrange offers float trips of varying lengths, from one day outings between access points on the upper part of this section to overnight trips on the 38-mile stretch from Smithville to LaGrange. Veteran anglers on the lower Colorado say one of the best times to fish the river is in the fall when the Lower Colorado River Authority (LCRA) reduces the river flow and the water level drops and clears. Canoes and kayaks work well on the river but a flat bottom johnboat is more comfortable and advisable for longer floats.

On this lightly traveled, scenic stretch of the Colorado, anglers get to sample a taste of the Wild West and the Deep South with action from Guadalupes and Kentucky spotted bass in the fast water and yellow cats and spotted gar in the deeper holes. As the sun get lower, largemouth join in, waiting in ambush along banks.

The large variety of warm water species in the Colorado, which also includes white crappie, Rio Grande perch, smallmouth, drum and the occasional striped bass,

Colorado River
Austin to the Gulf of Mexico

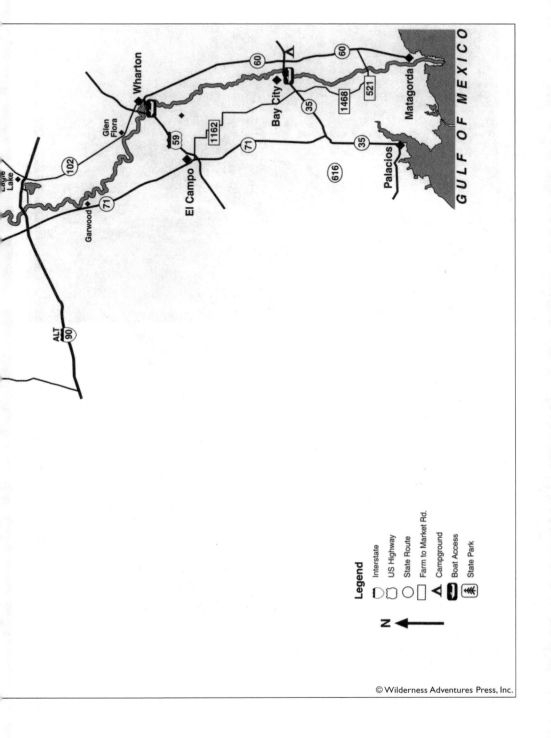

Legend

Interstate
US Highway
State Route
Farm to Market Rd.
Campground
Boat Access
State Park

N

© Wilderness Adventures Press, Inc.

*Flyfishers on Colorado River below Austin casting
shoreline structure from western style driftboat.*

provides flyfishers with a wide range of choices in fishing strategies, fly selection, tackle and watercraft.

A native Texas bass, the Guadalupes are the dominant species in this section of the river. Although they are small, mostly under a pound, it is exciting to see a Guadalupe come charging out from under a log or a shaded bank in the clear green water to pounce on a popper or muddler minnow fly. Rods in the 3 weight to 6 weight range provide great sport in the faster water.

On the other hand, largemouth in the four to five pound range are not uncommon on the river and may require heavier tackle. And when blind casting across deeper sections of the river, a big bow in a 6- or seven-weight rod can mean a yellow cat has added Woolly Buggers to its diet.

Muddler Minnow patterns fished in the fast water around the tails of pools and along seams and channels are top producers on the Colorado. Small hard-bodied poppers worked into the current around the gravel bars or dropped into the shaded pockets along the banks also produce well.

Matching the hatch on the Lower Colorado means using a streamer or glass minnow pattern that imitates or simulates the black tail shiner - a silvery minnow that grows to about 4 inches and has a black spot on its tail - or the red shiner, also a silvery minnow but with a deeper, shad-like body.

Mayfly, damsel and caddisflies also are prevalent on the river and a good choice to match for dry fly sunfish action. A reason to take along a selection of Woolly Bugger and Flashabugger patterns in black and olive is the large local population of hellgrammites, the larval stage of a dobson fly, a favorite natural bait of local anglers.

A float down the Colorado will result in many sightings and the occasional slashing surface strike from the spotted gars that are abundant in the river. The larger alligator gars also are in the river in lesser numbers.

Beginning in West Texas almost 900 river miles from the Gulf of Mexico, the Colorado River has a much higher profile with recreational users to the north where it forms large reservoirs, including Lake Buchanan, Inks Lake, Lake LBJ, Lake Marble Falls, Lake Austin and Town Lake.

Below Austin, the Lower Colorado, as it is called in its final run to the Gulf, offers solitude as well as excellent fly fishing action in big or small doses.

Bryan Cook, environmental coordinator for the Lower Colorado River Authority, the government agency that oversees the waterway, says the stretch of water from Longhorn Dam in Austin to Smithville. This 70-mile stretch is ideal for fly fishing because of its clear water, wadable flats, pools and riffles. Below Smithville, the look of the waterway changes and it becomes more turbid, like most Texas rivers flowing downstream off the Edwards Plateau onto the blackland prairies.

Besides a geographical transition point, this link of the Colorado River also offers a blend of warm water species that is not found many other places in the state. Guadalupe bass, whose range is centered more in the Hill Country to the northwest coexist here with Kentucky spotted bass, whose range is primarily in East Texas, Cook says. This stretch of the Lower Colorado is also the northernmost range of the Rio Grande perch, a feisty Texas cichlid related to the peacock bass that will aggressively take a fly.

Also present are a variety of sunfish species including the ubiquitous bluegill, redbreast, longear and green sunfish, or warmouth. Cook says the white crappie congregate around flooded gravel pits off the main river channel on the stretch of river above the Little Webberville Park.

In addition to yellow or flathead catfish who feed primarily on minnows in open water, Cook says there also is a strong population of bottom feeding channel cats in this stretch of river.

Flyfishers on this stretch of the Colorado have used johnboats, canoes and kayaks as well as western style drift boats to prospect the variety of features over the five-mile section of river between Little Webberville Park and Big Webberville Park.

Launch ramps at public parks in the community of Webberville, less than an hours drive from Austin's crowded freeways, offer easy access to the river.

Veteran Colorado River hands say that fishing can be good during high flow or low flow conditions but the river's personality changes significantly with changes in river flows.

From roughly March to October, water is released at an average rate of 1500 cubic feet per second (cfs) which translates to a river flow of about 2 miles per hour.

Colorado River scene.

With a little paddling, the average canoeist will travel about 3-4 mph, depending on skill level and paddling rate, according to officials with the Lower Colorado River Authority. On the Lower Colorado, the average canoeist is doing well to cover 10 river miles in one day.

From October to March, release rates are cut back to about 300-350 cfs, which make for a very slow moving river. During these months the river flows at a rate of less than 1 mph, which means nearly all forward progress depends on paddling. The low flow periods also mean more obstacles must be navigated. During this time of year, old river hands recommend planning for floating no more than 5 miles of river per day.

Almost all of the land outside of the riverbed is privately owned. The LCRA advises that boaters encountering hazards like log jams, low-water dams, or other obstructions may get out on the bank and scout for a safe route or portage but any intrusion on private land should be kept to a minimum.

The LCRA recommends camping on float trips at public parks but it is permissible to camp on an island or gravel bar in the riverbed.

Longer float trips and overnight camping are also possible on the Colorado.

Ronnie Ray and his wife, Sherri, outfitters and fly fishing guides on this stretch of the Colorado below Austin, offer half day and full day float trips aboard their western style, 14-foot Hyde drift boat. In addition to trailering the drift boat to public ramps along the river, the Rays are landowners with access to the river between the towns of Smithville and La Grange.

One of the reasons for the level of solitude that can be enjoyed on this stretch of the Colorado, so close to a major Texas city, is the limited number of access points which are located primarily at relatively isolated local parks, bridge and road cross-ings. And like many Texas rivers, most of the land that borders the waterway is private property. As a "navigable" waterway, boaters and anglers have the right to wade or float the river and in some cases, camp on its islands, but the surrounding countryside, with the exceptions of the public parks and right of ways is off limits. In addition, it is prudent to contact the LCRA or an experienced river guide for informa-tion on river flows.

Access Points for Float Trips on the Colorado River

Colorado River Below Longhorn Dam

Texas Parks and Wildlife biologist Steve Magnelia says there is excellent habi-tat for and large bass in the stretch of river starting below Longhorn Dam to Little Webberville Park. Canoeists and kayakers also have the option of launching at Little Webberville Park and paddling upstream to fish this favorable stretch of water.

There is an access point below Longhorn Dam at the undeveloped Austin city park, called Colorado River Park, in Travis County just west of US 183 (Bastrop Highway). It is located in Austin south of the Texas State School for the Deaf, East Campus. There is also a put-in-point below the US. 183 Bridge where it crosses the Colorado, but this is not a very easy access. A put-in at these access points would allow for a manageable one day float of about 10 miles to Little Webberville Park, Magnelia says.

There also is access to the Colorado at the Del Valle Bridge that is limited to a roadway right of way.

Little Webberville Park to Big Webberville Park

Little Webberville Park, a county operated facility, is located off Texas (FM) 969 just north of the Bastrop-Travis County line on the east bank of the Colorado. The park has paved roadways, a boat ramp, picnic sites, and a chemical toilet. Flyfishers floating the 5 mile stretch downriver to Big Webberville Park can start the float by paddling upstream a half mile or so to sample the excellent fishing opportunities for spotted bass, largemouth and sunfish along the creek mouths, shoals and fishing piers.

On this float, anglers are often treated to the sight of solitary blue herons, flights of egrets and black-bellied tree ducks. Usually there are only a few other boaters encountered on this river, mostly recreational canoeists and locals in johnboats run-ning trotlines. The river bottom provides excellent habitat for red tailed hawks and horned owls and bald eagles are a common sight in the winter and spring months

The five mile float can be tackled in a half day or full day depending on the num-ber of stops made to sample the many inviting riffles, runs, gravel bars, deep pools and shorelines that hold a variety of game fish.

If the fishing slows for a period, it usually is only a matter of finding the right gravel bar or shoreline where the packs of Guadalupes are hanging out to get the action started again. Sometimes the hottest action can come at midday. The take-out for this float at Big Webberville Park is an improved boat ramp. The park is located on Park Lane off Webberville Drive west of Texas (FM) 969.

Utley to Fisherman's Park in Bastrop

Local fisheries biologists report good habitat in this section of river but samplings indicate lower fish populations than sections above and below. While easily floated in a canoe and kayak, this section can be hazardous to boating with an outboard motor because there are many large submerged boulders near the surface.

Flyfisher casting from float tube on the Colorado River.

SAN MARCOS RIVER

This stretch of the San Marcos in the Prairies and Lakes Region is not as crystal clear as the upper part of the river beginning in the community of San Marcos, which sometimes is an advantage in approaching the population of largemouth, Guadalupe bass, spotted bass and sunfish that hold along the banks and around overhanging trees and submerged stumps.

Access points for floats on the San Marcos River:

Texas (FM) 1979 Crossing

Located in Caldwell County, west of the Martindale Community, this bridge crossing offers public access to the river along the road. Shady Grove Campground (512-499-8432) is located nearby and offers launch facilities, canoe rentals and shuttle service. San Marcos River flyfishing guides Marcus Rodriguez and Johnny Quiroz say this is an excellent put-in point for the 5 mile float to the Staples Community. Excellent fly fishing opportunities are available on this stretch for largemouth, smallmouth, and spotted bass as well as Rio Grande perch, the guides say. Anglers in kayaks and canoes will experience a steady flow for the first three miles with the river slowing down significantly over the last two miles because of the back up of water caused by the Staples Dam. Rodriguez and Quiroz say the largest bass and sunfish hold very close to shoreline and other midstream structure on this stretch. Other ideal fish-holding habitat on this stretch includes runs, riffles, seams between fast moving and slower moving water, undercut banks, and the heads of pools.

Texas (FM) 1977 near Staples Community

Located east of the Staples Community, this access provides a put-in and take-out point for floats as well as access to bank fishing.

This is a good area to fish that gets light angling pressure. There are many cutbanks that hold fish but approach should be from the bank because of tricky rapids caused by logjams. The Staples Dam below the crossing requires portaging either on the right side of the dam or on the left side along the dam buttress.

Texas (FM) 20

Crossing located west of Fentress community in Caldwell County. Access for wade fishing and bank fishing along the road.

Texas (CR) 247

Crossing located off Texas (CR) 249 in Caldwell County west of Prairie Lea community.

Texas (CR) 116

Crossing located west of Texas (SH) 80. that provides access to wade fishing along the road.

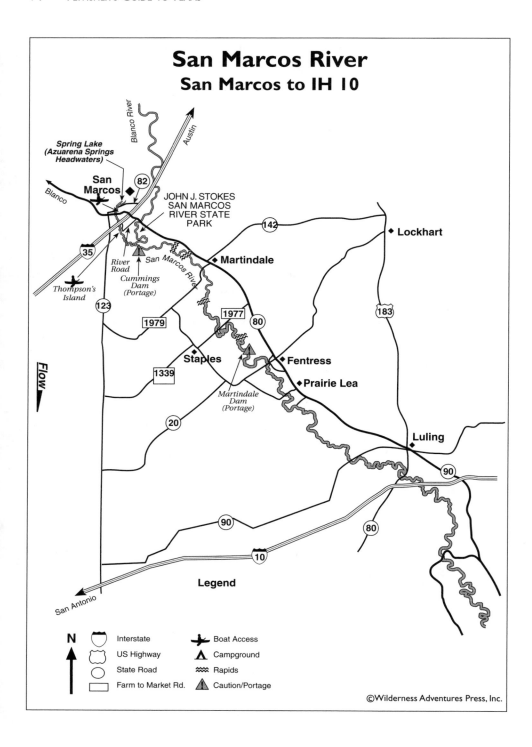

San Marcos River
San Marcos to IH 10

Blanco River

Austin

Spring Lake
(Azuarena Springs
Headwaters)

San
Marcos

Blanco

82

JOHN J. STOKES
SAN MARCOS
RIVER STATE
PARK

142

Lockhart

35

River
Road

San Marcos River

Martindale

Cummings
Dam
(Portage)

Thompson's
Island

123

1979

1977

80

183

Flow

Staples

1339

Martindale
Dam
(Portage)

Fentress

Prairie Lea

20

Luling

90

90

80

10

San Antonio

Legend

N

⬡ Interstate	✈ Boat Access
⬠ US Highway	▲ Campground
◯ State Road	〰 Rapids
▭ Farm to Market Rd.	⚠ Caution/Portage

©Wilderness Adventures Press, Inc.

Texas (CR) 119
Bridge crossing located west of Stairtown community in Caldwell County, access to the San Marcos River is available on the southwest end of the bridge.

US 90
Crossing west of Luling, offers roadside access to river about a mile from the bridge.

Luling City Park
Located off US 80 south of Luling in Caldwell County, offers public access to river.

SAN GABRIEL RIVER

The North and South Forks of the San Gabriel River flow eastward through Williamson County until they join in Georgetown to form the main one river. The deep pools on this small, gently flowing river hold largemouth, smallmouth, sunfish and catfish and offer solitude as well as sight casting opportunities to the stealthy fly fisher.

This is a river that can reward the fly fisher willing to learn its unique features with surprisingly consistent catches. Wally Van Zandt, a veteran of the San Gabriel, says he is attracted to the river because it offers a wild and remote setting in relatively close proximity to his home in Austin. A small waterway, he says the San Gabriel is better suited for wade fishing and scouting along its banks than for floating. Traveling through limestone canyons and blackland prairie, it requires an understanding of its mixed terrain. "A fly fisher can be walking a nice limestone bottom and then suddenly be in mud up to the knees," he says.

Van Zandt says he likes to walk above the river to pick out game fish along its pools and banks. "They will stage in the deeper pools. You can spot them and then look for the best place to go and cast to them."

The successful fly fisher on the San Gabriel will wear drab clothes and remain out of full view from the water. Anglers on many stretches of the San Gabriel will spend more time walking the banks than wading, making comfortable hiking shoes more useful than felt-soled wading boots, Van Zandt says. He has been successful using some of the same tactics on the San Gabriel that he has used to stalk wild trout on Colorado streams. "All of the good fishing locations take a little work to get to," he says. Van Zandt prefers shorter length fly rods-from six foot long 4-weights to seven foot long 6-weights-when stalking fish on the San Gabriel. "Skill casting" is not required on this river, Van Zandt says, and a stiff rod can make the short casts that are most effective.

Flies that are effective on other Texas rivers including Woolly Buggers in black and olive, Muddler Minnow patterns, and popping bugs also work well on the San Gabriel according to Van Zandt says. One pattern that has proved to be particularly effective on the San Gabriel is a Muddler Minnow tied with a very tight head. "When I fish for bass, I like to weight the line in front of the fly, because on these little rivers I run the streamer across the stream instead of doing a dead-drift." An effective technique is to cast downstream and then strip the fly very slowly back into the current. "I have found a lot of times that my strikes come when I have stripped it and rested and counted 12 to 15 seconds before the fish strikes," Van Zandt says. He says he puts a "good size" split shot about 12 or 14 inches in front of the Muddler. "The current on the San Gabriel is normally not fast enough to pull it down and the muddler will actually float. That is why I tie the Muddlers with really tight heads. I even tie a foam body underneath to give them more floatation."

Other patterns that work well on the San Gabriel include the Clouser Crayfish, Damsel nymph, Mickey Finn, Clouser Minnow, and black and red ant patterns.

The San Gabriel, like other Hill Country streams with stretches of limestone bottoms, offers the opportunity to fish dry flies on occasion. Van Zandt says he always carries a supply of Adams and Humpys. "When the mayflies are coming off here, they are absolutely enormous, up to two inches long and the dry fly fishing becomes spectacular," he says. Van Zandt says he reverts to a dead-drift when dry fly fishing on the San Gabriel. "But you can also cast downstream and strip it back into the current. You can go at these fish with about every tactic there is."

A bonus on the San Gabriel is the occasional hookup of a monster largemouth, probably refugees from flooded farm ponds. "That is why I get excited about fishing the San Gabriel after a big flood," Van Zandt says.

A catch and release philosophy is especially important on the San Gabriel, a river that doesn't receive any stocked fish. "If you catch a large fish, it is probably part of the breeding population so it is a good idea to leave it in the river," Van Zandt says.

Access can be a problem for flyfishers on the San Gabriel. With large game ranches along some stretches of the river, conflict with landowners is a fact of life on the San Gabriel. Streamside properties are heavily patrolled to prevent trespassing and game poaching, and this often results in confrontations between property owners and anglers who have gained legal public access and are fishing within the stream banks. Arguing with landowners over access rights to stream fishing is unwise. However, anglers, as well as property owners, have the right to report any unreasonable conduct to the local sheriff.

Van Zandt lists the following walk-in access points as among the most user-friendly on the San Gabriel.

San Gabriel, North Fork

US 183 Crossing

Good parking and walk-in access to the river here. Van Zandt says the farther upriver that flyfishers hike from this access, the better the fishing.

County Road 256 Crossing

Take Texas (FM) 3405 east off US 183 to this crossing. Good wade fishing is available upstream and downstream.

County Road 258 Crossing

This access is reached by traveling north from Leander on US 183. Turn west off 183 onto County Road 258 and follow it to the crossing. This is the location of Tejas Camp, a popular white bass fishing destination in the early spring. Van Zandt advises flyfishers to walk upstream to find the best action. Tail waters below Lake Georgetown - Flyfishers should prospect a good distance downstream.

San Gabriel, South Fork

Texas (FM) 1174 Crossing

Located south of the community of Bertram in Burnet County, there is a deep pool on the upstream side of the crossing that produces solid sunfish action.

US 183 Crossing

This bridge crossing located north of Leander offers largemouth action for a good half mile in both directions. Fish early and late or hike a distance from the bridge to avoid swimmers in summer months.

County Road 270 Crossing

Best fishing at that low water bridge crossing begins about a half mile downstream.

County Road 268 Crossing

Located off Texas 29 west of Georgetown, this crossing offers easy parking access and good numbers of sunfish up and down the river.

Interstate 35 Crossing at Georgetown

This spot is popular with locals. Good for sunfish as well as the occasional largemouth and bronzeback.

LAKES

MOSS LAKE

Located about 12 miles northwest of Gainesville in Cooke County, this scenic and very fishable lake gets its name not from a form of aquatic vegetation but from Hubert H. Moss. The 1,125-acre lake is stocked with Florida-strain and native-northern largemouth, Kentucky spotted bass, smallmouth bass, walleye, white bass, crappie and sunfish.

Excellent white bass action is available for flyfishers on Lake Moss in April and May as the fish move into North and South Fish Creeks. Look for schools of these "sandies" around the mouths of the creeks a few weeks before they begin their spawning runs. During the rest of the year, look for surface activity on the open lake.

Texas Parks and Wildlife fisheries specialists at Lake Moss say anglers will have the most success targeting largemouth around the aquatic vegetation near the south boat ramp, along the dam, and the upper end of the South Fish Creek Arm, Timber Cove, and Turtle Cove. Some of the largest bass taken at the lake have come out of Timber and Turtle Coves.

During the summer months it is best to target largemouth in the early morning, beginning just prior to dawn.

Kentucky spotted bass and smallmouth are best targeted along the lakes rocky shorelines, with crawfish patterns topping the list of effective flies. Full sink lines and minnow patterns fished deep along the same habitat might draw the attention of one of the lakes more elusive walleye.

Flyfishers can best target the lake's abundant crappie population in the late fall and winter when the fish tend to school in large numbers around boat houses, submerged trees, creek channels and brush piles. In the spring months, crappie can be found in the shallows where they are moving to build spawning nests. Dropping Clousers dressed in white and olive bucktail down among submerged timber and tree limbs in the backs of the coves is an effective fly fishing tactic during this time of year.

Sunfish, including warmouth, bluegill, green sunfish, longear, and redear are also best targeted near boat Houses, piers, stumps, brush and aquatic vegetation.

Managed by the city of Gainesville, facilities at the lake include two public boat ramps, the north boat ramp is located on the north side of the lake near the North Fish Creek Arm of the lake and the south boat ramp is located south of the dam. Boaters are required to obtain a lake permit to operate on the waterway.

For additional information, contact the city of Gainesville at (817) 665-8871 or Texas Parks and Wildlife Department at (903) 786-2389.

LAKE TEXOMA

Lake Texoma, located on the Texas-Oklahoma border, has 89,000 acres of water surface and a winding 580-mile shoreline. The 40-mile-long lake meanders through the eastern belt of the Cross Timbers region of the state, a gently rolling, north-south band of brush and stunted trees including blackjack oak, cedar elm, post oak, hackberry and hickory. Most of the game fish at Texoma were introduced after the lake was impounded on the Red River. Native fish included flathead, blue and channel catfish and alligator gar. The lake created a much larger, deeper and cooler body of water that allowed other fish species to survive.

Striped bass, introduced in the late 1960s, are now the most sought after species on the lake. Water flowing into Lake Texoma from the Red and Washita Rivers is relatively salty, allowing striped bass, a saltwater native, to reproduce. The lake record striper, caught in 1984, weighed 35 pounds, two ounces. Smallmouth were introduced in the lake in 1981 and can be found along the lake's limestone bluffs. Creel surveys over the last decade have shown a 100 percent increase in the per hour catch rate of smallmouth bass.

Some of the best areas to fish for smallmouth on Lake Texoma include the bluffs from Navigation Point, along Eisenhower State Park to the dam and north along the dam. The Willow Springs area has produced some of the biggest smallmouths for biologists during routine electro shocking surveys and has a record of producing some of the biggest for anglers as well.

Guide's sign on Lake Texoma.

Striped bass with flyrod and popper.

In general, smallmouth can be found from Willow springs in the Washita River Arm to the west end of the islands near Mill Creek in the Red River Arm of the lake. Smallmouth prefer rocky or gravel shorelines and sandy points or beaches with submerged structure, such as large rocks, stumps, brush or logs. During most of the year this type of structure is visible in depths to five or six feet.

Dallas fly fisher Norm Goheen has experienced some of the exciting topwater striper action on the lake. Topwater action with streamers or bass bugs is one of the most exciting ways to fish the lake in the spring and fall, says veteran Texoma guide Polly Polishuk.

Beginning in September and continuing through fall, the swarming presence of seagulls and other birds is an easy tip-off to stripers attacking baitfish on the surface. This is the time of year when topwater flies bring explosive strikes. "All you have to do is find some birds flying and it's automatic fish," says Polishuk. "I tell my clients that if you can't catch fish around the birds, I'll pay you." Anglers planning to sample Lake Texoma's considerable fishing opportunities should be aware that fishing regulations and license requirements are a bit more complicated on the Texas-Oklahoma border reservoir than on reservoirs entirely within Texas.

Texas Parks and Wildlife Department officials point out that Texas residents with resident fishing or combination hunting / fishing licenses can legally fish only waters on the Texas side of the reservoir. However, a special $7.50 Lake Texoma Fishing License enables the holder to fish anywhere on the lake proper. Unlike other Texas fishing licenses, the Texoma license expires on December 31 each year instead of August 31.

On the lake proper, bag and length limits for sport fish species vary between the two states, except for black (largemouth, smallmouth and spotted) basses and striped

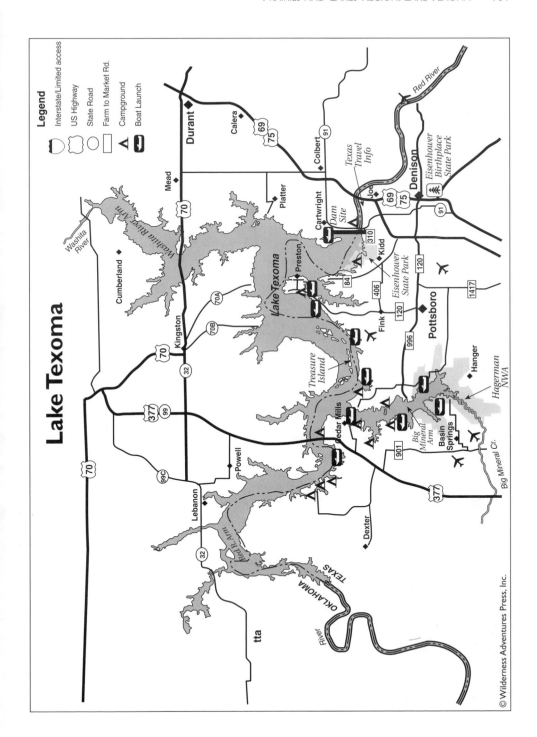

Lake Texoma

Legend

Interstate/Limited access
US Highway
State Road
Farm to Market Rd.
Campground
Boat Launch

© Wilderness Adventures Press, Inc.

bass. The daily limit for black bass throughout the lake is five in the aggregate, with a 14-inch minimum length limit. The striped bass limit is 15 per day with no minimum length limit, except that no more than one striper 20 inches or more may be retained each day. Below Denison Dam, there are variations between the two states' bag and length limits on virtually all species of fish. Prospective Texoma anglers are advised to write, call or visit the Texas Parks and Wildlife Department's Lake Texoma Fisheries Station, Route 4, Box 157, Denison, Texas 75020, (903) 786-2389. Station personnel have a variety of literature, including complete Texas and Oklahoma fishing regulations and fishing advice for visitors.

Other species caught in the lake include largemouth, spotted bass, white bass and white and black crappie.

Dallas fly fisher Charlie Ducote says he fishes for stripers below the dam on the Red River and does well with the Cypert Mylar Minnow, a Clouser Deep Minnow in white with a little red in the wing. He says the key is to fish the Red River during periods when water is coming through the dam and the generators are on, which draws the stripers to waters near the dam.

Red River guide holding large striped bass.

Eisenhower State Park to the Dam

Eisenhower State Park provides access to shorelines with giant boulders, which over the centuries have broken off from the Oklahoma side and fallen into the water. Largemouth, smallmouth up to 3½ pounds, and catfish up to the 10-pound class are taken here on fly tackle.

There are two launch ramps on the lake near the north side of Lake Texoma Dam. This allows fly casters to fish the waters near the dam, rocky points and big boulders in the water all the way to Little Mineral, an arm-like feature on the lake near the dam.

This is good shoreline fishing because it doesn't get a lot of interest from other boaters and anglers. Most anglers fish in the Big Mineral area, the big, open parts of the lake and the deep humps, Ducote says. "Most of the time I have the whole Eisenhower State Park shoreline to myself," he says. This area gives the fly fisher six or seven different species to target, including buffalo, he says. "I have a buffalo still heading up the river with half of my leader," he says. In Eisenhower State Park Ducote says he likes to begin fishing on the shoreline near the Eisenhower Yacht Club and marina in Eisenhower State Park and fish it eastward to the Elm Point camping area. There are large boulders extending out of the water along this shoreline that are excellent holding areas for stripers and other game fish. Sometimes the stripers prefer smaller flies like damselfly nymphs on this stretch, he says.

Ducote says there are stripers on the north part of the lake near the Oklahoma shoreline but that he rarely fishes that area. He points out that Texas anglers must purchase either a Texoma Lake license or an Oklahoma license because the state boundaries are not always clear on the lake. The Texoma Lake license allows anglers to fish either side of the lake.

School stripers in the two-pound class turn up along these shorelines and Ducote says he uses minnow patterns (similar to the Cypert Mylar Minnow) tied on size 8 to 10 hooks to take these fish. Another good pattern is the damsel fly nymph, with an olive body, rubber legs with black tail and red flash material and silver bead chain eye. Ducote says he allows it to get down in the big boulders in eight to 12 feet of water and works it slow.

Eisenhower State Park

Located along rocky bluffs on the shores of Lake Texoma, Eisenhower State Park provides access to prime shoreline habitat for largemouth, striped bass and white bass.

Veteran flyfishers say that some of the best areas to fish for smallmouth on Lake Texoma include the bluffs from Navigation Point, along Eisenhower State Park to the dam and north along the dam. Park facilities include large campgrounds, full RV hookups, screened shelters, picnic areas and a marina.

The 457-acre state park is located one mile west of the south end of Denison Dam on Lake Texoma. For additional information call (903) 465 1956.

WATERLOO LAKE

A 50-acre water supply lake for Denison, Waterloo Lake offers flyfishers a chance at prolific numbers of sunfish. The lake is located next to a park and is open to canoes and kayaks but no gasoline powered boats.

Proceeding north from Dallas on US 75, take the Loy Lake Exit in Denison and turn right(east) off the access road and proceed to a stop sign. Turn right (east) at the stop sign and follow the road 1 mile. After passing under an overpass make a hard left (northwest) and follow the road to the next intersection. Turn left and proceed through the park area to the lake. For additional information contact the park at (903) 463-5116.

LAKE BONHAM

Lake Bonham, located off Texas 121 in Fannin County, is a relatively shallow lake of slightly more than 1,000 acres. The lake holds a population of largemouth bass, hybrid striped bass, crappie and sunfish. A park near the dam includes picnic sites, restrooms and two public boat ramps. For additional information, contact the park at (903) 583-5022

COOPER LAKE

An 18,000-acre impoundment on the Sulphur River, Cooper Lake was opened to recreational fishing in 1993 after being stocked with Florida-strain bass prior to flooding. It has proven itself to be a top producer under mild wind conditions. Top fish taken here have already exceeded 15 pounds and catch rates are high. A three-bass, 18-inch minimum length limit should keep fishing quality high on this lake.

East Texas fly fishing guide Robert Woodruff says Cooper is one of the rising stars among quality fisheries in the northeast part of the state but that it is a relatively open lake that can be "white capped" under a 10 mph wind. In addition to quality largemouth fishing, the lake offers fly fishers excellent surface action for white bass throughout the summer.

Prime fishing on Cooper will be similar to other top East Texas lakes with February through November the best months. "It warms a little quicker than Lake Fork because it is muddy and shallow, and you cannot get on it on many days because it is so rough," he says.

The lake is expected to emerge as an excellent hybrid striper destination in the coming years, after stockings of 45,000 fish two years ago. The lake also has received stockings of Florida-strain largemouth, crappie, and sunfish, and fisheries officials expect this to be one of the top fishing lake in the region as it matures.

Located on the South Sulphur River in Delta and Hopkins counties, the lake is configured in two units, the Doctor's Creek unit on the north side of the dam and the South Sulphur Unit on the south side of the lake. Cooper Lake State Park is located on the lake and camping facilities, boat ramps, and picnic facilities are available at both units. The lake is located between Commerce and Cooper off Texas 24 and Texas (FM) 1528 out of Klondike and Texas (FM) 1529 out of Cooper.

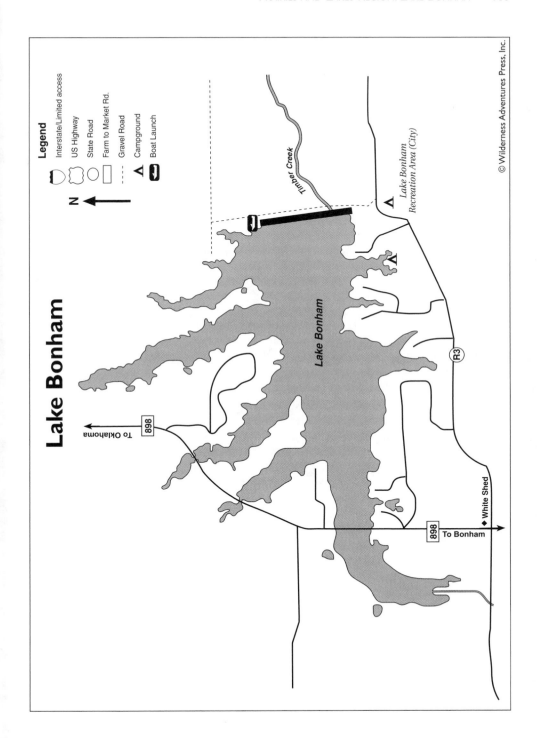

Lake Bonham

Legend

Interstate/Limited access
US Highway
State Road
Farm to Market Rd.
Gravel Road
Campground
Boat Launch

N

Timber Creek

Lake Bonham

Lake Bonham
Recreation Area (City)

To Oklahoma

898

898   To Bonham

◆ White Shed

R3

© Wilderness Adventures Press, Inc.

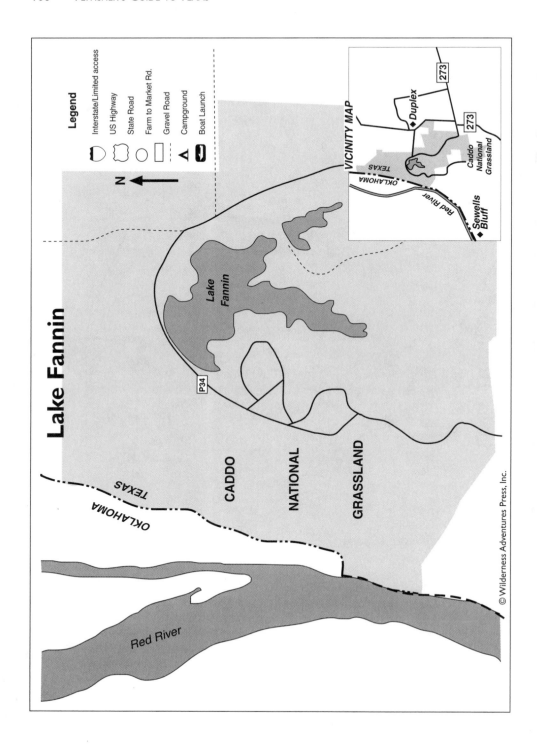

Lake Fannin

Legend

Interstate/Limited access

US Highway

State Road

Farm to Market Rd.

Gravel Road

Campground

Boat Launch

N

P34

CADDO

NATIONAL

GRASSLAND

OKLAHOMA

TEXAS

Red River

Lake Fannin

VICINITY MAP

273

Duplex

273

Caddo National Grassland

OKLAHOMA

TEXAS

Red River

Sewells Bluff

© Wilderness Adventures Press, Inc.

Cooper Lake State Park

Composed of two units, Doctors Creek and South Sulphur, Cooper Lake State Park offers bank and boat access to the 19,280-acre Cooper Lake on the South Sulphur River in Cooper and Hopkins counties. Both units of the park offer camping with partial hookups, picnic areas, fishing piers, and boat ramps. Doctors Creek has screened shelters, and South Sulphur has cabins. Two boat ramps separate from the main park units also provide access to the lake. In addition to providing camping, picnicking and access to angling on the lake, the park offers a unique opportunity for viewing wildlife. White-tailed deer, opossums, armadillos, rabbits, raccoons, wild turkeys, falcons, and bald eagles have been sighted in the park and along the lake shorelines. For additional information, contact the park at (903) 395-3100.

LAKE FANNIN

Located north of Bonham, Lake Fannin offers excellent fly fishing for sunfish and also holds some largemouth. This small scenic lake is best fished in the spring and early summer because the heavy vegetation growth makes it difficult to maneuver even a kickboat later in the year.

LEWISVILLE LAKE

Formerly known as Lake Dallas, this 23,280-acre lake is located on the Elm Fork of the Trinity River just north of Dallas off Interstate 35.

Dallas fly fisher Charles Ducote calls Lewisville an excellent fly fishing lake for largemouth, striped bass, hefty sunfish and buffalo. A large lake (200 miles of shoreline), it has a number of sloughs off the main body of water where, Ducote says, buffalo can be spotted pushing wakes up in the sloughs along the shorelines when they are spawning. He has had success taking them there on small crawfish patterns. Lake Lewisville is also considered an excellent destination for open water white bass action during the warmer months. White bass and white crappie in excess of 3 pounds have been caught in this lake. The city of Lewisville manages two parks on the lake, Hidden Cove Park on the east shore and Lake Park on the south shore. Facilities at the parks include picnic areas, RV and tent campsites, marinas, boat rental facilities and launch ramps. For additional information, contact the City of Lewisville Parks and Leisure Services (972) 219-3550.

AMON G. CARTER RESERVOIR

Located northwest of Fort Worth, this 1,848-acre waterway on Big Sandy Creek in Montague County offers fly fishers a shot at Florida-strain and native-northern largemouth, crappie and sunfish. Picnic, camping facilities, and a launch ramp are available at a 35-acre public park on the lake. For additional information, contact Texas Parks and Wildlife Department at (903) 786-2389. To get to the lake, take Texas (FM) 1125 south from Bowie.

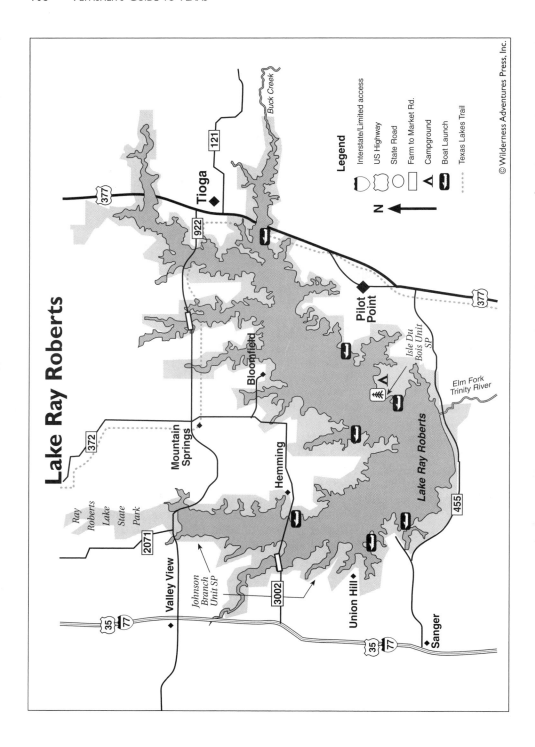

Lake Ray Roberts

Buck Creek

Tioga

Pilot Point

Isle Du Bois Unit SP

Elm Fork Trinity River

Lake Ray Roberts

Bloomfield

Mountain Springs

Hemming

Ray Roberts Lake State Park

Johnson Branch Unit SP

Valley View

Union Hill

Sanger

Legend

N

Interstate/Limited access
US Highway
State Road
Farm to Market Rd.
Campground
Boat Launch
Texas Lakes Trail

© Wilderness Adventures Press, Inc.

LAKE RAY ROBERTS

This large reservoir offers fly fishers a shot at a variety of species, including heavyweight largemouth and white bass. Fort Worth fly fisher Brian Camp calls Lake Ray Roberts, a 29,000 acre lake located north of Denton on the Elm Fork of the Trinity River, an excellent fly fishing destination. Configured similar to Lake Fork in that it has twin forks on a large reservoir, Lake Ray Roberts provides better than average water clarity, protected shorelines, narrow fingers and coves with flooded timber that is ideal for fly fishing under varied wind conditions. Access to productive shorelines near bridge crossings is available along Texas (FM) 3002 and Texas (FM) 922 on the western fork of the lake. Camp notes that there are also shorelines on the north end of the lake along Texas FM 922, where flyfishers can fish from float tubes, kickboats and kayaks.

The Isle Du Bois Unit and Johnson Branch Unit state parks as well as Jordan Park and Culp Branch Park also offer great access to the lake.

A good access point for fly fishers at Ray Roberts is Buck Creek. It is located north of Pilot Point. Take Texas 377 to the launch ramp on the eastern fork of the lake below the Tioga community. This ramp offers access to the southern shoreline, which is attractive to flyfishers since the prevailing wind is out of the south. There is also a launch ramp at the state park nearby.

This is an open lake that can become very rough on short notice. Anglers should be extremely cautious about weather conditions when boating on this lake.

There is also access to excellent fly fishing on the Elm Fork of the Trinity River below the lake, which can be accessed through a trail system. This is also a good place to put in a canoe or kayak for a downstream float with take-out areas at a number of bridge crossings.

The lake holds solid numbers of largemouth and sunfish, and the white bass fishing can be excellent for flyfishers during the summer months when the fish school up on the surface on the main lake. Boaters should look for surface activity and then throw any white streamer pattern into the melee. Camp says he has had success with chartreuse and olive Dahlberg Divers for topwater largemouth action.

Lake Ray Roberts State Park

Made up of the 1,687-acre Isle Du Bois Unit set in wooded hills near the Lake Ray Roberts Dam on the south side of he lake and the 1,514-acre Johnson Branch Unit on the north side of the lake, Ray Roberts State Park offers bank and boat access to Lake Ray Roberts as well as a large number of campsites and day use facilities. In addition to boat ramps within the parks, there are several other ramps with restrooms around the lake.

The parks are located off Interstate 35 near the Sanger community. For additional information, contact the park at (817) 686-2148.

LAKE BRIDGEPORT

This 13,000-acre impoundment on the West Fork of the Trinity River west of Bridgeport in Wise County holds clear water and is stocked with Florida-strain and native-northern largemouth, hybrid striped bass, crappie, and coppernose bluegill.

Public boat launch areas are located around the lake and a campground is available at Wise County Park.

For additional information, contact the Texas Parks and Wildlife Department at (817) 335-2491. To get to the lake, take Texas (FM) 1658 or US 380 west from Bridgeport.

LOY LAKE

Located along Texas 75, Loy Lake is a city lake on the western edge of Denison. Very lightly fished, it has a large population of sunfish. There is a park adjacent to the lake and a launch ramp. Gasoline powered outboards are not allowed on the lake but it is ideal for kickboats, canoes and kayaks.

LAKE GRAPEVINE

Located in Tarrant County north of Dallas-Fort Worth Regional Airport off Texas 114, Lake Grapevine offers 60 miles of shoreline with a variety of habitat from steep cliff faces to shallow flats with heavy vegetation. In addition to a large population of Florida-strain and native-northern largemouth, the lake also is a good producer of hybrid striped bass, crappie and white bass.

Flyfisher releasing largemouth.

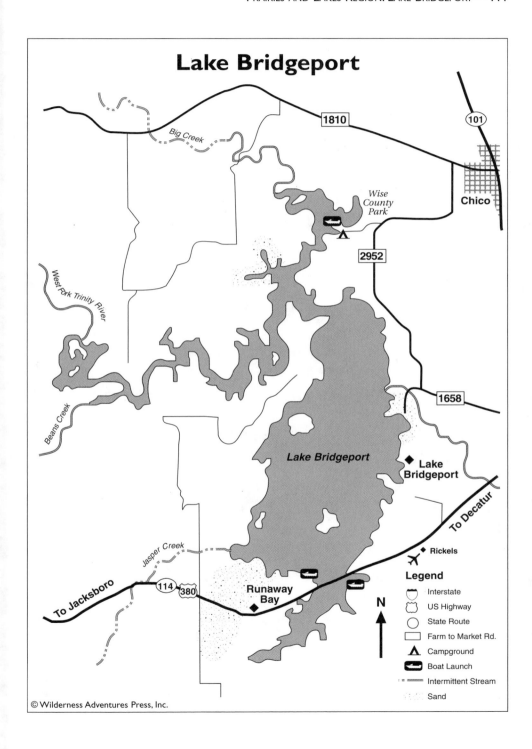

Lake Bridgeport

Big Creek

1810

101

Wise
County
Park

Chico

2952

West Fork Trinity River

Beans Creek

1658

Lake Bridgeport

◆ Lake
Bridgeport

To Decatur

Jasper Creek

Rickels

Legend

To Jacksboro

114 380

Runaway
Bay
◆

N

Interstate

US Highway

State Route

Farm to Market Rd.

▲ Campground

Boat Launch

Intermittent Stream

Sand

© Wilderness Adventures Press, Inc.

Eagle Mountain Lake

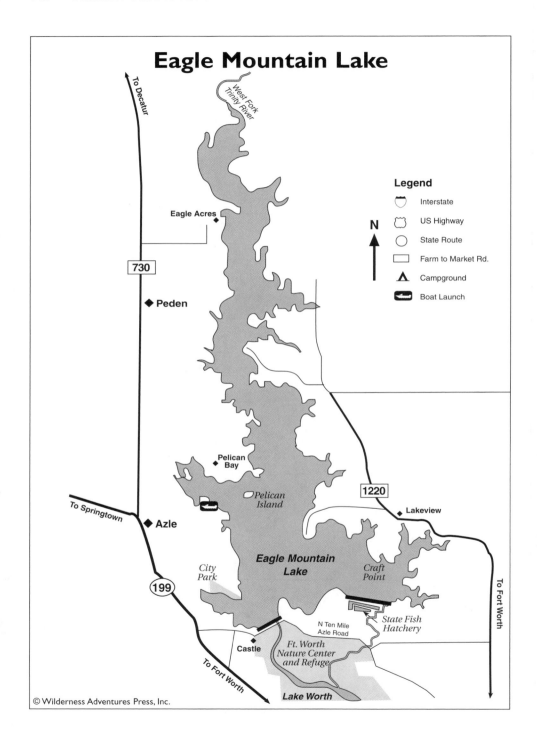

West Fork
Trinty River

To Decatur

Eagle Acres

Legend

Interstate

US Highway

N

State Route

Farm to Market Rd.

Campground

Boat Launch

730

◆ **Peden**

Pelican
Bay

*Pelican
Island*

1220

To Springtown

◆ **Azle**

Lakeview

*City
Park*

**Eagle Mountain
Lake**

*Craft
Point*

199

*State Fish
Hatchery*

To Fort Worth

N Ten Mile
Azle Road

*Ft. Worth
Nature Center
and Refuge*

Castle

To Fort Worth

Lake Worth

EAGLE MOUNTAIN LAKE

Eagle Mountain Lake is located in Tarrant County on the West Fork of the Trinity River on the northwest side of Fort Worth. Like conventional tackle anglers, flyfishers target largemouth in the spring around boat docks and several islands on this 9,200-acre lake. Hybrid stripers and white bass can sometimes be spotted schooling and crashing bait on the surface.

LAKE WEATHERFORD

Located on the Clear Fork of the Trinity River just off Interstate 20 east of the town of Weatherford, Lake Weatherford is a 1,144-acre lake stocked with native-northern and Florida-strain largemouth. Texas Parks and Wildlife officials note that the lake was stocked in the late 1970s with a yellow-striped bass hybrid nicknamed the "sunshine bass." The lake also has received significant stockings of walleye over the years but the species has not taken hold in the somewhat turbid lake environment.

LAKE RAY HUBBARD

Approachable on US 30 east of Dallas, Lake Ray Hubbard is a 22,745-acre reservoir on the Trinity River that is considered an excellent hybrid striper lake, especially during the spring months. The lake is also stocked with largemouth, striped bass, white bass and crappie.

Flyrod with sunfish.

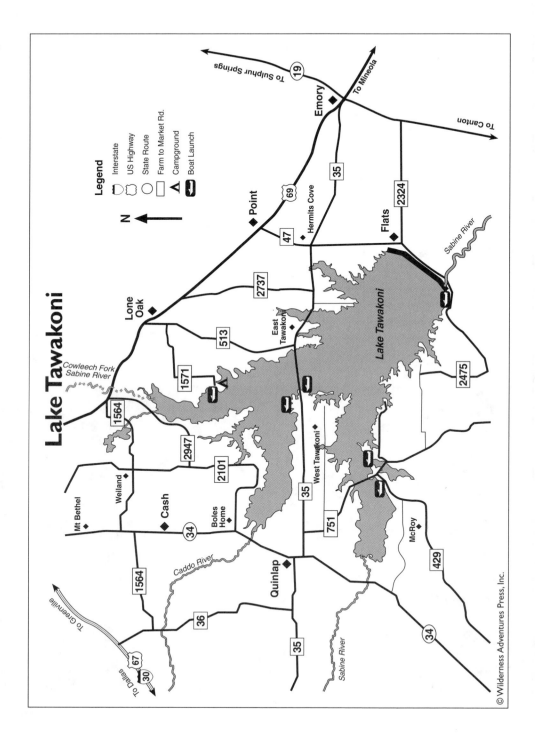

Lake Tawakoni

Legend

Interstate
US Highway
State Route
Farm to Market Rd.
Campground
Boat Launch

N

To Sulphur Springs

To Mineola

To Canton

Emory

19

35

Point

69

Hermits Cove

47

2324

Flats

Sabine River

2737

Lone Oak

East Tawakoni

513

Lake Tawakoni

1571

Cowleech Fork Sabine River

1564

2947

2101

West Tawakoni

2475

Mt Bethel

Welland

Cash

35

Boles Home

34

751

McRoy

Caddo River

Quinlap

36

429

1564

To Greenville

67

30

35

To Dallas

34

Sabine River

© Wilderness Adventures Press, Inc.

LAKE TAWAKONI

A large reservoir that lies on the Sabine River in Hunt, Rains and Van Zandt counties, Lake Tawakoni averages 12 feet deep. Most of the native flooded timber has rotted away but the lake has remained productive for Florida-strain largemouth, striped bass, crappie, hybrid striped bass, white bass and sunfish.

This is another excellent lake for hybrid striped bass and most of the action for them is surface action in the deep water by the dam. That is where the fly rodder will have the best opportunity for action, says central Texas fly fishing guide Charlie Cypert. "Normally, there is more surface action on Tawakoni than on Lake Whitney," he says.

Lake Tawakoni State Park

Located in Hunt County south of Greenville, Lake Tawakoni State Park is expected to open in 2001. It will offer shore and boat access to 36,700-acre Lake Tawakoni. The 376-acre park is situated along 5.2 miles of Lake Tawakoni shoreline and will include campsites, picnic sites, a boat ramp and a breakwater levee suitable for fishing from the shore.

For additional information, contact the park at (903) 560- 1795.

MEACHAM FIELD LAKE

Located on the north end of Meacham Field between the end of the field and US 820 Loop on the west side of Fort Worth is a small lake operated by the Tarrant County Regional Water District. Parking and walk-in fishing is available and the lake holds good numbers of sunfish and small bass.

BENBROOK LAKE

Benbrook Lake is located on the Trinity River ten miles southwest of Fort Worth off US 377. Flyfishers can prospect for bass along the flooded timber on the east side and upper end of the lake. A number of feeder creeks provide prime habitat for largemouth, crappie and white bass especially during the spring.

White bass and hybrid stripers also congregate around the dam within casting distance of shore anglers.

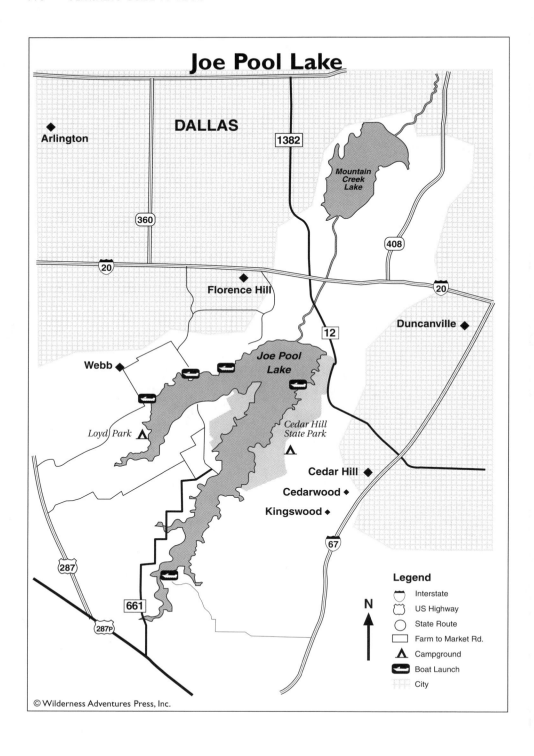

Joe Pool Lake

DALLAS

Arlington

1382

Mountain
Creek
Lake

360

408

20

Florence Hill

Duncanville

12

20

Webb

Joe Pool
Lake

Loyd Park

Cedar Hill
State Park

Cedar Hill

Cedarwood

Kingswood

67

287

661

287P

Legend

N

⬡ Interstate
⬭ US Highway
○ State Route
▭ Farm to Market Rd.
▲ Campground
⬛ Boat Launch
▦ City

© Wilderness Adventures Press, Inc.

JOE POOL LAKE

Located between Dallas and Fort Worth, 7,470-acre Joe Pool Lake is a relatively new reservoir opened to recreational fishing in 1989. Heavy stockings of Florida-strain largemouth and coppernose bluegill predated the opening by as much as seven years.

Cedar Hill State Park

Located on the southeast side of Joe Pool Reservoir in Dallas County, the 1,811-acre Cedar Hill State Park provides bank and boat ramp access to the 7,500-acre lake. The park offers a large number of campsites, picnic tables, a park store and grill.

For additional information, contact the park at (214) 291-3900. To get to the park, take Texas (FM) 1382 off Interstate 20 south of Grand Prairie.

Small Watercraft for Texas Streams and Lakes

PONTOON BOATS
Advantage: These boats are more than float tubes, like sitting in a lawn chair. Flyfishers can remove the oar systems and replace them with swim fins worn over rigid boots. They can be helpful when fishing tail races.

FLOAT TUBES
Advantages: Extremely portable and stealthy for fishing small bodies of water, stock tanks and farm ponds. Disadvantages: Slow, with limited maneuverability. Three feet of body rests in water, not practical or safe for tailraces.

KICKBOATS
Advantages: Lightweight, durable, give comfortable ride, easy to fish out of. Disadvantages: Blown styrofoam materials can be released into environment.

INFLATABLES
Advantages: Compact, quiet on the water. Disadvantages: Limited range.

KAYAKS
Advantages: Highly maneuverable, seaworthy, allow user significant range. Disadvantages: Not the most comfortable to fish out of along shorelines.

CANOES
Advantages: Maneuverable and versatile, comfortable fishing and range. Disadvantages: Less Stability, particularly in swift water

Lake Granbury

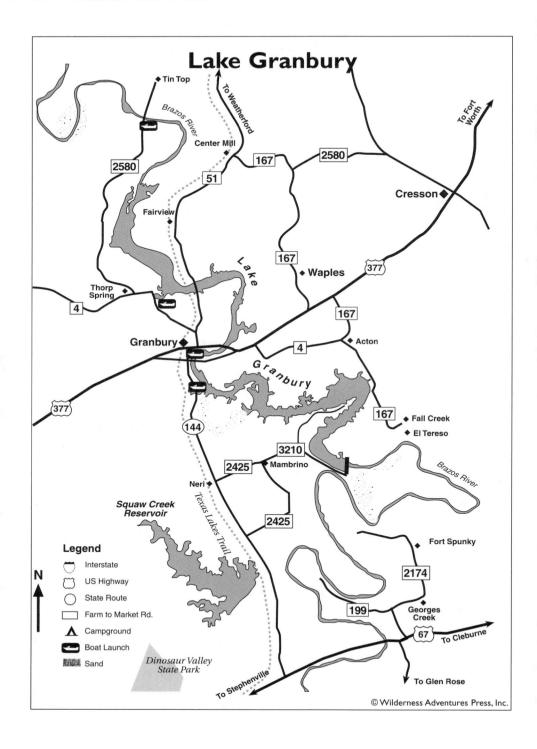

Tin Top

To Weatherford

Brazos River

Center Mill

2580

167

2580

51

To Fort Worth

Cresson

Fairview

Lake

167

Waples

377

Thorp Spring

4

167

Granbury

4

Acton

Granbury

167

Fall Creek

El Tereso

377

144

3210

Brazos River

2425

Mambrino

Neri

2425

Squaw Creek Reservoir

Texas Lakes Trail

Fort Spunky

2174

Georges Creek

199

67

To Cleburne

Legend

N

🡑

⬭ Interstate
⬭ US Highway
◯ State Route
▭ Farm to Market Rd.
▲ Campground
⬍ Boat Launch
▦ Sand

Dinosaur Valley State Park

To Stephenville

To Glen Rose

© Wilderness Adventures Press, Inc.

LAKE GRANBURY

Located on the Brazos River 33 miles southwest of Fort Worth in Hood and Parker counties, this 8,700-acre lake offers flyfishers a chance at Florida-strain largemouth, striped bass and white bass.

Lake Granbury has ample public access and is long and narrow with many coves and features attractive to fly fishing. A good technique is to work the shorelines with the standard bass bugs, streamers and sunfish flies, says Fort Worth flyfisher Brian Camp, who frequently fishes the lake.

Flyfishers also have the option of fishing the tailrace area below the dam. Veteran fly fishing guide Charlie Cypert says the tailrace below Lake Granbury offers some of the best fishing in this area of the state in the spring when striped bass and white bass are moving upstream. The action is especially frantic after the spring floods when fish stack up below the dam. Cypert says the best way to fish the tailrace area is with a small watercraft such as a canoe, kayak or kickboat when water is being released from one gate on the west side of the dam. He says anglers should look for flow conditions in which there is slow water in the middle of the pool allowing boaters to anchor safely. Under heavy flow situations, anglers must cast from the shoreline. "Under the right conditions, I have caught more than 100 white bass and stripers in a half day and had large stripers break me off several times on the boulders," Cypert says.

SQUAW CREEK RESERVOIR

A 3,272-acre reservoir fed by tributaries of the Brazos, Squaw Creek is located four miles north of Glen Rose. It is attractive to flyfishers for its clear water and variety of fish species including smallmouth and walleye pike. Squaw creek is a power plant lake serving Texas Utilities' Comanche Peak Nuclear Power Plant. Due to warm water runoff, this a good lake to fish in the winter. Docks and piers that are largely ignored by anglers in bass boats are good structures for flyfishers to prospect. A 90-acre park provides access to the lake. Entry is limited to daylight hours and there is a fee.

Below the Squaw Creek Dam off Texas 144 south of Granbury, there is a road crossing on Texas (FM) 302 that provides access to wade fishing on the tail waters of Squaw Creek.

MILL CREEK LAKE

A 364-acre lake that lies just south of Canton, off Texas 19 or Texas (FM) 1654 in Van Zandt County, Mill Creek has a history of producing quality largemouth bass fishing. Known locally as the new Canton City Lake, it produced at 16.77 pounds largemouth in 1990. When its catch rate for trophy bass dipped, it became the focus of recent stocking programs by the Texas Parks and Wildlife Department. The stocking was designed to alter the genetic make-up and rejuvenate the lake's bass population. Toward that end, TPWD released 36,000 Florida-strain bass fingerlings in the lake in 1998. "History has shown this lake has the potential to produce big bass and we want to put the trophy bass fishery back on track," says TPWD biologist Steve Poarch.

LAKE PAT CLEBURNE

Located on the Nolan River southwest of Cleburne off US 67 in Johnson County, Lake Pat Cleburne is stocked with largemouth and crappie. Overshadowed by the many opportunities at nearby Lake Whitney and Lake Granbury, Lake Pat Cleburne's off color water is a challenge to flyfishers but not to crappie fishermen using live minnows.

LAKE CLARK

Located next to US 287 in Ellis County at Ennis, Lake Clark is an old city water supply lake and is an excellent destination for fly fishing out of a float tube, kayak or canoe. The 150-acre lake has lush shoreline vegetation that provides prime habitat for large sunfish and largemouth. This lightly fished lake, which is more than a hundred years old, has a diverse native plant community including white and yellow water lilies as well as submerged plants that provide habitat for fish and make the lake a unique fishing environment.

LAKE WAXAHACHIE

A small lake with a good population of largemouth, 645-acre Lake Waxahachie holds relatively clear water despite a caliche bottom. Located on the south side of Waxahachie in Ellis County, the lake holds both largemouth and sunfish.

To get to the lake, travel south on Texas (FM) 877 (Howard Lane) off Interstate 35 on the south side of Waxahachie.

CEDAR CREEK RESERVOIR

Cedar Creek Reservoir, a big, wide-open lake located west of Athens in Henderson and Van Zandt counties, offers flyfishers an excellent opportunity to catch hybrid stripers, especially when they are working shad on the surface in the spring. A boat with an adequate outboard motor to cover the water is required. The trick is to watch for the birds and catch the fish on the surface, which doesn't last long, says Richard Ott, a biologist with the Texas Parks and Wildlife Department.

Early morning is best and one of the most productive sites is at the face of the dam. Another advantage of fishing this area is that the dam structure is large enough to delay the morning light as the sun comes up, prolonging the bite, Ott says. "The hybrids will come and push those shad up against the dam."

Other species present in the 34,300-acre lake include Florida-strain and native-northern largemouth, crappie, white bass and sunfish. Other prime fish-holding features on Cedar Creek are boat docks, coves, and aquatic vegetation.

To get to Cedar Creek Reservoir, take US 175 south from Dallas and take either Texas 274 south of Kemp or Texas 198 at Mabank to Gun Barrel City to reach private marinas and launch ramps on either side of the lake.

Texas Freshwater Fisheries Center

Besides celebrating the Texas freshwater angling experience and show-casing the state's freshwater species in their natural habitat, the Texas Freshwater Fisheries Center in Athens is the center of a serious research effort designed to produce the next world record largemouth bass. For visitors of all ages and interests, the center provides a journey of learning about Texas freshwater fisheries that has the look and feel of an adventure in the wild.

The trip begins at the entrance to the center where visitors cross over a replica of a Hill Country stream. The stream gallery is patterned after Onion Creek at McKinney Falls State Park in Austin. Other major inland aquatic habitats depicted include rocky, spring-fed western streams such as the Devils' River and tannin-stained waters like Caddo Lake, whose fish species and wildlife can be viewed on the shore and below the surface.

The pond gallery exhibit represents the many farm ponds built throughout the state for watering livestock, irrigation and flood control. These ponds frequently support healthy sport fish populations. A sunfish spawning area provides a close-up look at spawning behavior of the popular species.

The 178,000-gallon reservoir habitat, the largest exhibit at the center, has three large viewing walls, including a concave bubble wall designed to give visitors the sensation of actually standing on the bottom of a lake surrounded by largemouth bass, blue and flathead catfish, freshwater drum, and other species.

The 1.2-acre casting pond, stocked with thousands of rainbow trout and channel catfish, provides parents with a unique opportunity to intro-duce youngsters to fishing. The adjacent Angler's Pavilion has soft drinks and fishing equipment for visitors.

Indoors at the center's 150-seat theater and aquarium, wide-eyed visitors can watch a subsurface show whose stars include crappie, sun-fish, catfish, and largemouth including wide-bodied females weighing 14 pounds or more.

One of the most famous residents of the center's aquarium was Texas Star, a 14-year-old largemouth that weighed almost 19 pounds when she died in 2000. Two more recent arrivals, an 18-pounder, and a 14-pounder caught by a fly fisher in the Canadian River below Lake Meredith have assumed headliner roles at the aquarium.

In addition to films describing the evolution of the state's diverse waters and ambitious fisheries projects, the programs at the theater and aquarium include question and answer sessions with a diver in the 26,000-gallon tank.

Galleries display collections of antique lures, rods and reels and honor the state's angling legends. In the Fisheries Management Gallery, there is information on the techniques that Texas Parks and Wildlife Department biologists use to improve fishing, including stocking programs, harvest management and regulations, habitat control and research. From a open display window, visitors get a good look at the research side of the facility, which includes a 24,000-square-foot building that Houses raceways and vats holding forage fish, rainbow trout and bass that are part of the Texas Parks and Wildlife Department's ShareLunker program. At the Research Center, hatchery technicians and fisheries biologists work on projects designed to maintain and enhance the quality of the state's freshwater fishing experience. Among the efforts under way are work in DNA genetic analysis to determine if certain largemouth from Texas waters possess the high growth Florida-strain genes. Inside the laboratory, biologists conduct research on genetics, diagnose diseases, analyze water quality, and monitor plankton. This well equipped laboratory is the headquarters for the state's ShareLunker program and its breeding operations. Production of Florida-strain largemouth bass from the hatchery and adjacent rearing ponds exceeds 6 million fingerlings per year.

The hatchery facility is the headquarters for the state's successful ShareLunker Program, which encourages Texas anglers to donate, live, any largemouth weighing 13 pounds or more for use as brood fish. In return, the angler is given a fiberglass replica of the catch. The ShareLunker hotline number for anglers lucky enough to have caught a 13-pound plus largemouth is (888) 784-0600. Row after row of half acre hatchery ponds bearing game fish in various stages of their life cycle are carefully regulated and monitored to produce quality fish for research and stocking in the state's waters. Water from Lake Athens stored in a 6-acre pond feeds the hatchery ponds. At the manager's residence, a 24-hour security system monitors the hatchery operations. Among many special events held at the center is the annual Fly Fish Texas show, which draws thousands of visitors each year.

The Texas Freshwater Fisheries Center is located just east of Athens near the north shore of Lake Athens. The center is open daily from 10 a.m. to 5 p.m. There is a fee for admission to the center and tours of the laboratory and rearing pond operations are also available by reservation for groups and professionals from the scientific community.

LAKE ATHENS

This is a great lake for flyfishers because of an exceptional population of sunfish. Richard Ott, the TPWD biologist who manages this lake, says flyfishers using canoes or kayaks should target the area from the bridge up toward the upper end of the lake. He says another hot spot is the island near the dam. "In the summer when it starts to get too warm for bass, you can start to work on those sunfish," Ott says. "The redear will come on the beds the earliest-March through April-while the bluegills stay on the beds year around."

In addition to its noted sunfish population, the 1,500-acre lake is stocked with Florida-strain and native-northern largemouth, crappie and catfish.

Boat ramps, a commercial marina, picnic sites, and camping areas with RV hook-ups are located near the Texas (FM) 2495 Bridge. For additional information, contact the marina at (903) 677-7490, or Texas Parks and Wildlife Department at (903) 566-2161. To get to the lake, take Texas (FM) 2495 about 3 miles east from Athens.

RICHLAND-CHAMBERS RESERVOIR

Located southeast of Corsicana, 44,752-acre Richland Chambers is the third largest reservoir situated totally within the state's boundaries. It includes the flooded watersheds of Richland and Chambers creeks, giving the reservoir a wishbone shape. The hardwoods along those creeks have provided excellent habitat for largemouth bass. Experienced conventional anglers frequently take bass in the double-digit class here.

There are five improved public boat ramps, two fee ramps and many old road beds, which provide adequate launching facilities. There are large areas of standing and submerged timber in both arms of the reservoir and brushy areas are found along most of the shoreline. Excellent habitat exists in the form of abundant creek channels, old levees, old stock tank dams and roadbeds. Fall can be an excellent time for top water bass bugging around shorelines.

The reservoir provides fly fishing opportunities for largemouth, black and white crappie, white bass and the occasional hybrid striped bass, escapees from Navarro Mills Reservoir. The Texas Parks and Wildlife Department stocked Florida-strain largemouth bass in the lake in the late 1980s and early 1990s.

White crappie have adapted well to the more turbid alkaline waters in this central Texas region. In the spring, crappie can be found spawning in shallow brushy areas and near the bridges at Highway 31 and IH 45. Clouser Deep Minnows in white or chartreuse on No. 2 or No. 1 hooks are effective for the crappie. In the summer, crappie can be found around the brush piles and treetops and heavier timber.

In early spring, white bass, or sand bass as they are called locally, move upstream into streams and feeder creeks to spawn. In March, they usually can be found far up these creeks near the bridges at Highway 31 and IH 45. Later in the spring, white bass travel in large schools on the main body of the reservoir. Diving gulls often will give away schools of white bass feeding on the surface.

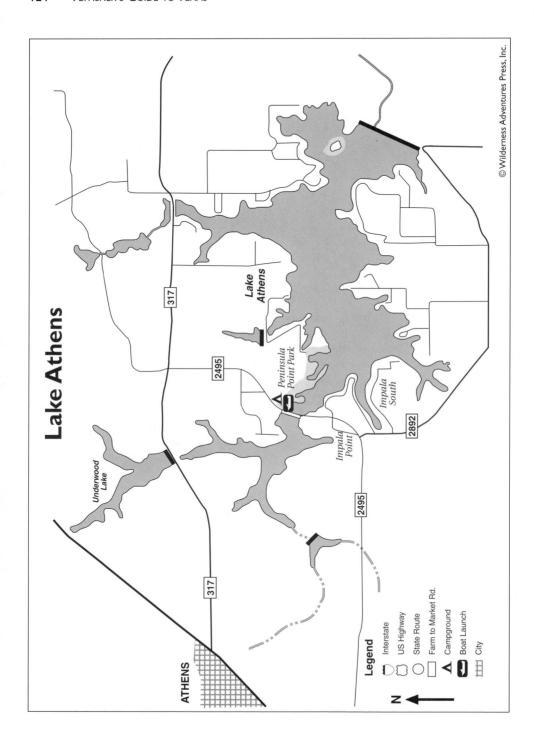

Lake Athens

ATHENS

Lake Athens

Peninsula Point Park

Impala Point

Impala South

Underwood Lake

317

2495

2495

2892

Legend

Interstate
US Highway
State Route
Farm to Market Rd.
Campground
Boat Launch
City

N

© Wilderness Adventures Press, Inc.

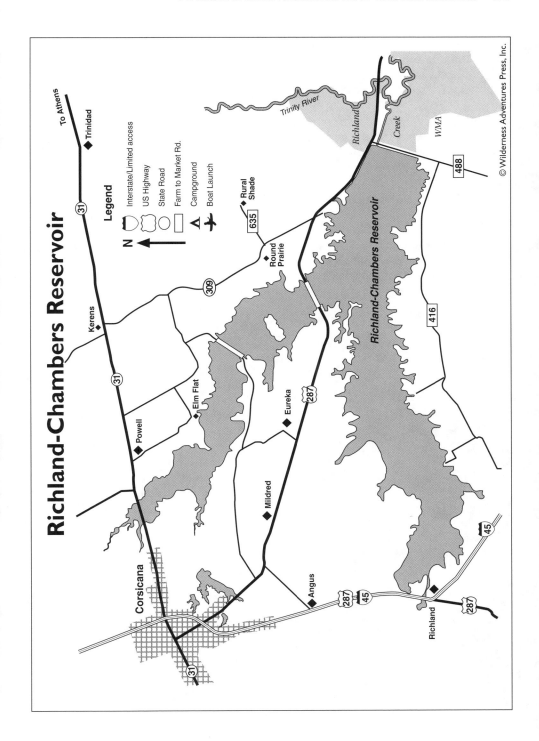

Richland-Chambers Reservoir

Legend

Interstate/Limited access
US Highway
State Road
Farm to Market Rd.
Campground
Boat Launch

N

To Athens
Trinidad
Kerens
Elm Flat
Powell
Corsicana
Mildred
Eureka
Round Prairie
Rural Shade
Angus
Richland
Richland-Chambers Reservoir
Trinity River
Richland
Creek
WMA

© Wilderness Adventures Press, Inc.

Boaters should keep themselves informed on the weather when out on this lake, just as they should when out on any large reservoir in the state, because conditions can become very rough very quickly on Richland-Chambers. At the first sign of a thunderstorm or high winds, anglers should seek shelter or return to a boat ramp to get off the water.

Richland-Chambers is an excellent white bass lake all year long, says fly fishing guide Charlie Cypert. In the spring, fly fishermen will find white bass typically moving up Richland and Chambers creeks if there is water flowing in those creeks. The tailrace area east of the dam also provides access to good white bass fishing during the spring.

White bass also will school on the surface with hybrid striped bass, and mixed in with these feeding frenzies fly rodders often will find largemouth in the three- to four-pound class. One of the best areas is on lower, southeast end of the lake within four miles of the dam, says Cypert. "I have seen times when there are schools of white bass as far as you can see- tens of thousands." Cypert says the best time to target the action is from daylight to mid-morning, and picking up again the last two hours of daylight. On rainy days, he notes, the action may extend throughout the entire day.

The topwater action on Richland-Chambers usually begins in the late spring after the spawn and continues into the fall. For surface action, Cypert says he uses his 1/0 and 2/0 poppers, which work well on stripers, black bass and smallmouths.

There are two marina launch points on the lower end of the lake on the west side. For more information on Richland-Chambers Reservoir, contact the Texas Parks and Wildlife Department in Tyler at (903) 566-2161 or the Tarrant County Water Control and Improvement District office, (903) 389-3928.

Flyfisher with heavyweight largemouth.

Striped Bass and Hybrid Striped Bass in Texas

Striped bass (Morone Saxatilis) *and hybrid stripers thrive in many Texas lakes and reservoirs. South Carolina biologists discovered in 1954 that striped bass that had become landlocked in Santee-Cooper Reservoir were capable of completing their entire life cycle in fresh water. Stocking programs were launched after they also found that the species not only demonstrated excellent sport fishing qualities in fresh water but also fed aggressively on gizzard shad, an often overabundant prey species in many reservoirs.*

In 1965, South Carolina biologists also were successful in crossbreeding striped bass and white bass. Additional research revealed the resulting hybrid had a faster growth than the striped bass in the first years of life, a better survival record and higher catch rates. While displaying the desirable traits of the parent species, the white bass / striped bass hybrid showed very limited reproductive capability. The hybrid striped bass is therefore utilized in put-grow-and-take fisheries and periodic stockings are required to maintain lake populations. The Texas Parks and Wildlife Department's striped bass / hybrid program has continued to expand since the first stockings in 1967. The state now has one of the largest freshwater striped bass and hybrid stocking programs in the nation. While many freshwater game species in Texas prefer inshore areas and require shallow water habitat for spawning and nursery areas, striped bass and hybrid striped bass prefer open water and therefore coexist well with the inshore species.

While striped bass and hybrids have many similar characteristics, their differences dictate their management by fisheries officials and often their location. Striped bass grow larger, prefer cooler water, and are better suited to large, deep reservoirs, fisheries officials say. Hybrids are smaller, tolerate warmer water, and are therefore better suited to smaller, shallow reservoirs.

LAKE WHITNEY

A long river-like reservoir, Lake Whitney lies on the Brazos and Nolan Rivers on Texas 22 about 30 miles north of Waco. The lake winds 40 miles through blackland prairie habitat and limestone bluffs. Much of the native timber is still present, providing, along with gravel shoals and rocky points, excellent habitat for game fish. In addition to resident populations of largemouth and striped bass, Lake Whitney is considered one of the top smallmouth destinations in the state.

Whitney offers flyfishers an excellent striped bass fishery, with the average fish in the lake running three to six pounds. The lake record is 39 pounds. Veteran Lake Whitney fly fishing guide Charlie Cypert says most fish caught by flyfishers are hooked while blind casting, and that 95 percent of the fishing he does on the lake is blind casting. "There will be some surface action occasionally," Cypert says. "You mark fish on fish finder equipment or find birds-gulls and terns- feeding on crippled shad on the surface. On those occasions, there may be a swirl on the surface where a striper has followed a fish up to get it." In the winter, when the stripers are feeding on very small redfin shad, they can be taken most easily on a fly, Cypert says. He says his Scissortail Clouser pattern is the best pattern he has found to take stripers. "We have tried a variety of flies, but it is the most productive. You can work it slow under the birds where the fish are feeding, especially if you can get them in one of the shallower creeks in water 4 to 10 feet deep, where you can get your fly down on the bottom." Cypert points out that the smaller stripers will cripple a lot more fish than they will eat and the bigger fish just follow them around and pick up the leavings. To target the larger stripers, Cypert says he fishes a large streamer-with short strips and pauses-like it is a dying shad. "When a big striper takes it, your line will just tighten up. The fish will just move off because he is not hitting the shad hard, just sucking them in."

Cypert recommends a hard hook set, two or three times when the take comes. "I have caught stripers in the 8 or 9 pound range with a 9-weight rod and hit them three or four times-what I thought was hard-with the rod tip lowered, but when you get them in the net, the hook falls out." Cypert says he noticed that most often when he used bigger, heavier saltwater hooks. Now, he has switched to the Tiemco 8089 Bass Bug Hook, a number 6 with the wide gap is about equivalent to 3/0 or 4/0 in a standard hook. "It has a real fine diameter wire and a real small barb, and everybody sticks them with that," Cypert says. Before he switched to the bass bug hook, 90 percent of his clients lost their bigger smallmouth, blacks and stripers because they were not setting the hook hard enough. "With these small diameter wire hooks, even when they don't set it hard, they usually get good penetration," Cypert says.

Cypert, who has guided and fished on a number of central Texas lakes, says Lake Whitney is the best all-around lake for having a chance at a combination of species.

The white bass season on Whitney begins in late winter-January and February-when fish begin congregating for the spawning run and it extends until mid-April. Cypert recommends fishing the "backwaters" of the lake and the riverbed as the fish gradually move up into those areas. By March, they are up the river spawning.

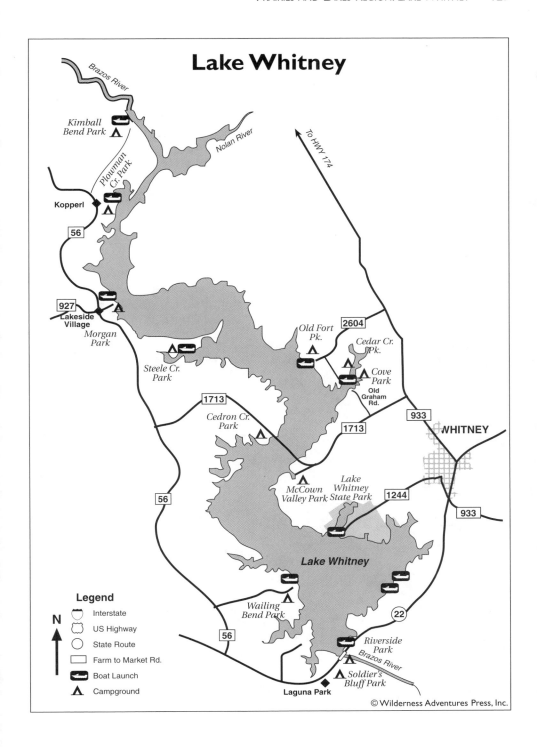

Lake Whitney

Brazos River

Nolan River

To HWY 174

Kimball
Bend Park

Plowman
Cr. Park

Kopperl

56

927

**Lakeside
Village**

*Morgan
Park*

*Steele Cr.
Park*

Old Fort
Pk.

2604

*Cedar Cr.
Pk.*

*Cove
Park*

**Old
Graham
Rd.**

933

WHITNEY

1713

*Cedron Cr.
Park*

1713

*McCown
Valley Park*

*Lake
Whitney
State Park*

1244

933

56

Lake Whitney

Legend

N

⌒ Interstate

⌒ US Highway

◯ State Route

▭ Farm to Market Rd.

▬ Boat Launch

▲ Campground

*Wailing
Bend Park*

22

56

*Riverside
Park*

Brazos River

▲ *Soldier's
Bluff Park*

Laguna Park

© Wilderness Adventures Press, Inc.

In late spring and summer, the surface action from white bass and stripers will kick off on Lake Whitney. And while the surface action might not be as good as it gets on Richland-Chambers, Cypert says Whitney's strength is always the variety of game fish offered to flyfishers, including stripers, smallmouth, hybrid striped bass and white bass. Since shad and minnows make up the primary food source for fish in Whitney, flies that match them do well. You can catch everything in the lake on one or two minnow patterns, Cypert says. "Just match the fly to the size of the bait-fish that the game fish are feeding on."

The Maribou Minnow, a maribou chenille fly created by Cypert, works well on white bass, black bass and smallmouth. He has taken stripers up to 9 pounds on it and smallmouth to 6.5 pounds.

The maribou pattern is extremely effective on white bass from the last part of December through March, Cypert says, when the fish are moving upstream to spawn. "When the water is super cold, the Maribou Minnow is the fly to use. It will out fish the Clouser and Mylar Minnow (another Cypert pattern) ten to one when you work it very slow right along the bottom with short hops. Once the water begins to warm up around the end of February, then the Clouser Minnow and Mylar Minnow patterns become the best choices." Cypert says.

In clear water, Cypert recommends the white Mylar Minnow pattern or a clear sparkle pattern. The Mylar Minnow is tied on a size 10 to size 4 hook. Any hook above a size 4 hasn't worked well, Cypert notes. He says he has seen stripers up to nine pounds taken on size 6 Mylar Minnow flies. Cypert coats these flies with a material that hardens and sparkles in a clear and chartreuse finish.

Cypert's Scissortail Clouser, a Clouser Deep Minnow variation, is tied sparsely for clear water fishing. "These patterns will catch a much higher percentage of fish than flies tied with bulkier materials," Cypert says. "If

Cowboy flyfisherman.

you see a fish follow a fly but not take it even after you put action on it to make it look like a crippled baitfish, that is when it is necessary to use a more sparsely tied fly."

Cypert also has success with his hair bug pattern on Lake Whitney. "The way to fish it is to strip it in continuously so it makes a wake on the top of the water. A crippled shad will stick its nose out of the water with its tail hanging down, and they will move across the surface making a small wake, and often a striper will come up and take it." Cypert says he ties his Hair bugs in light colors for Whitney stripers.

Another effective pattern on Whitney is a diver pattern. It is stripped so it will dive and wiggle down and then float back to the surface. It can be used with a sinking line to keep it down. A 5- or 6- weight fly rod will do the job at Whitney in most circumstances but an 8 weight is needed in windy conditions. Cypert recommends flyfishers bring a full sink or sink tip fly line in addition to a floating line because of the variety of situations that can be encountered in a fishing day on Lake Whitney. Situations may call for casting in deepwater to smallmouth along a rock strewn shoreline, casting along a shallow shoreline for largemouth or throwing poppers to schooling white bass and stripers in open water. Cypert recommends a 2½ to 3 foot leader with sinking lines and never more than 4 feet. "If the leader is too long, it is difficult to feel the fish because it has to pull the leader so far before it tightens up. The fish will spit the fly out and most people won't know it had the fly."

Bank fishing and boat access to Lake Whitney is available at Lake Whitney State Park. The 955-acre park offers campsites, RV hookups, showers, screened shelters and a paved airstrip.

Lake Whitney State Park

Located on a peninsula on the shore of 23,560-acre Lake Whitney among scattered groves of live oak, Lake Whitney State Park offers boat and bank access to the lake's abundant population of striped bass, white bass, hybrid striped bass, largemouth and smallmouth. The 955-acre park offers campsites, RV hookups, showers, screened shelters and a paved airstrip.

To get to the park, take Texas 22 west from Hillsboro to the Whitney community. From Whitney, take Texas (FM) 1244 to the park entrance. For additional information, contact the park at (817) 694-3793.

NAVARRO MILLS LAKE

Navarro Mills Lake offers limited opportunities for flyfishers unless channel catfish are the target. Clear-cutting and other agriculture and land use practices around the lake have created heavy siltation and have had an adverse effect on game fish habitat on a good part of the lake.

FAIRFIELD LAKE

Texas Parks and Wildlife biologist Richard Ott says Fairfield Lake holds more big bass than most of the lakes in the region. He says that in the spring when they are up in the shallows spawning and the water levels are up, the fish will get up along the shoreline in the grass and cattails. Flycasters can do extremely well working this structure. "Watch the reeds move and cast toward the movement," Ott says. Sometimes the activity is made by carp, so the angler has a mixed bag to choose from on Fairfield's shorelines in the spring.

One of the best shorelines to fish is around Fairfield State Park opposite the shoreline that is the site of the Texas Utilities Company power plant. There are two public boat ramps on the side of the lake where the park is located.

This is a large open lake that requires a boat, and anglers are advised to fish Fairfield early in the year-late winter to early spring-because of the heavy growth of hydrilla which builds up during the warmer months, much earlier than at other area lakes. Being a power plant lake with a warm water discharge, Fairfields largemouth bite kicks off in the wintertime.

Fairfield Lake State Park

Located on rolling hills and woodlands called the post oak savannah, Fairfield Lake State Park shares shorelines with 2,400-acre Fairfield. Texas Parks and Wildlife fisheries biologists who do shocking surveys to measure and manage game fish populations have expressed amazement at the numbers of quality largemouth along many of the lake's shorelines. As a cooling water supplier to an electric power generating plant, the lake is recharged with warm water, providing a year-round fishery.

In addition to the largemouth, hybrid striped bass and crappie population, experiments with stockings of red drum and African perch, or tilapia, have been successful in the lake. Largemouth up to 13 pounds and redfish in excess of 20 pounds have been landed at Fairfield Lake. The park also is an excellent site for viewing and photographing wildlife.

Facilities at the 1,460-acre park include campgrounds with showers and picnic areas. For additional information, contact the park at (903) 389-4514.

To get to the park, take Texas (FM) east from Fairfield Texas (FM) 2570, and then turn right (east) on Texas (FM) 3285 to the park.

LAKE WACO

Located on the Bosque River within the city limits of Waco in McLennan County, Lake Waco offers anglers 60 miles of shoreline in a blackland prairie setting. This 7,270-acre lake is stocked with Florida-strain largemouth, crappie and sunfish.

Tributaries to the lake, including the north, south, and middle Forks of the Bosque River provide excellent white bass fishing in the spring.

There are six parks that provide access at paved launch ramps. For additional information, contact the US Army Corps of Engineers (254) 694-3189 or the Texas Parks and Wildlife Department (254) 666-5190.

TRADING HOUSE CREEK RESERVOIR

Located five miles east of Waco in McLennan County, Trading House Creek Reservoir is a power plant lake that holds a good population of Florida-strain and native-northern largemouth, striped bass, and crappie. Texas Parks and Wildlife has experimented with other "exotic" species in this lake, including peacock bass, but results to date have not made this another Lake Guri. On the other hand, red drum, another Trading House Creek transplant with a black spot on its tail, have fared well in this year-round warmwater environment.

There are two boat ramps on the south side of the lake. For additional information, contact Texas Parks and Wildlife Department at (817) 799-5190.

HOUSTON COUNTY LAKE

Houston County Lake on Little Elkhart Creek is located northwest of Crockett, off Texas (FM) 229 in Houston County. The lake is stocked with native-northern and Florida-strain largemouth, black crappie, striped bass, redear sunfish and hybrid striped bass.

A scenic lake surrounded by East Texas hardwoods and stately pines, this clear water lake offers flyfishers an excellent shot at hefty largemouth around a variety of cover, from flooded timber to hydrilla. The spring is a prime time for all species including very large redear sunfish.

LAKE LIMESTONE

Located in Leon, Robertson and Limestone counties, Lake Limestone can be reached on Texas (FM) 3371 south of Groesbeck. A variety of shoreline structure such as flooded timber and aquatic plants provide good habitat for largemouth, hybrid striped bass, crappie and sunfish. Water conditions range from moderately clear to off color.

LAKE BELTON

Located five miles northwest of Belton off Texas (FM) 317 or Texas (FM) 36, Lake Belton offers flyfishers a variety of shoreline structure for bass bugging as well as opportunities for schooling hybrid striped bass in open water.

GIBBONS CREEK RESERVOIR

A power plant reservoir, Gibbons Creek is located east of Bryan-College Station, off Texas 30 near Carlos in Grimes County. The lake is catch and release only for its Florida-strain largemouth. A good population of redear sunfish and coppernose bluegill are also found in the lake.

There is a $2 entry fee per car and $1.50 per person for anyone 13 years or older. Lake access is offered to the public during daylight hours.

LAKE SOMMERVILLE

Located on Middle Yequa Creek ten miles northwest of Brenham off Texas 36, Lake Somerville is an 11,460-acre lake that is stocked with Florida-strain and native-northern largemouth, hybrid striped bass, crappie and sunfish.

The lake offers 85 miles of shoreline and the tailrace below the dam is considered one of the best in the region for shore casting to white bass.

Lake Sommerville State Park

Comprised of two units, Nails Creek and the Birch Creek, the expansive Lake Sommerville State Park covers almost 6,000 acres surrounding Lake Sommerville. Park facilities include campgrounds, boat ramps, picnic areas and nature trails. Commonly sighted in the park are white-tailed deer, raccoons, coyotes and rabbits, as well as a wide variety of bird life.

The park units provide bank and boat access to 11,460-acre Lake Sommerville that holds good numbers of largemouth, white bass and crappie.

For additional information, contact the Birch Creek Unit at (409) 535-7763 or the Nails Creek unit at (409) 289-2392.

LAKE BASTROP

Located three miles northeast of Bastrop off Texas (FM) 1441, this small (906-acre) lake holds Florida-strain largemouth, hybrid striped bass, crappie and sunfish. Although the results did not meet expectations, this lake was chosen for stockings in the late 1970s of South American peacock bass.

A warmwater, cooling lake for a power generation plant, Lake Bastrop is an excellent destination for largemouth action on the worst winter days.

LAKE FAYETTE

Located 15 miles northeast of La Grange off Texas 159, Lake Fayette (formerly called Fayette County Lake) is another power plant reservoir that offers excellent winter largemouth action. Access is provided at two launch ramps for a nominal fee. Flyfishers have the opportunity to launch canoes, kayaks, float tubes or kickboats from two parks to fish nearby coves and shorelines that offer prime largemouth habitat including flooded timber and hydrilla beds - the most problematic aquatic plant in the U.S..

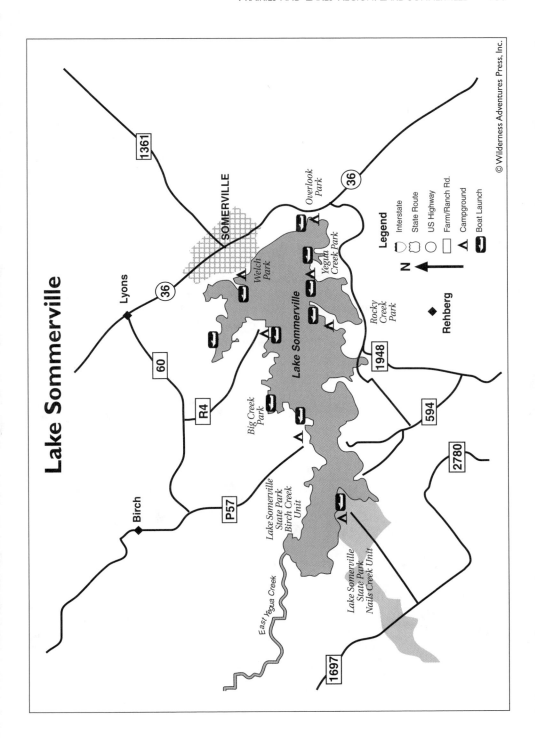

Lake Sommerville

STATE PARK WATERS

BONHAM STATE PARK

Located just south of Bonham off Texas 78 and Texas (FM) 271, Bonham State Park's 65-acre lake offers lots of walk-in fishing for largemouth, sunfish and large-mouth.

Operators of boats with outboards are required to observe a 5 mph speed limit on the lake, encouraging an environment that is ideal for flyfishers and game fish alike.

Among the facilities offered at the 261-acre park are campsites with partial RV hookups, showers, picnic tables and canoe rentals during the summer.

For additional information, contact the park at (903) 583-5022.

LAKE MINERAL WELLS STATE PARK

This 3,010-acre state park located in the Cross Timbers region of the state, where rolling hills are covered in post oak, blackjack oak, juniper and mesquite, offers bank and boat access to 646-acre Lake Mineral Wells. Park facilities include a large camp-ground with RV hookups, several fishing piers and boat ramps.

For additional information, contact the park at (817) 328-1171.

Catch and release notice on Purtis Creek State Park lake.

PURTIS CREEK STATE PARK

Purtis Creek State Park is a 1,533-acre state recreational area with a 355-acre lake that is considered one of the top fly fishing destinations in the region. It is located 70 miles south of Dallas via US 175 near the town of Eustace. The lake, which is restricted to catch and release only angling for its abundant largemouth bass population, offers flyfishers realistic opportunities to do battle with bucketmouth bass in the eight to 10 pounds range. Managed for large sunfish, it has produced a 1.88 pound bluegill, the state record.

A small impoundment by Texas standards, the lake at Purtis Creek Park has a number of regulations that make it attractive for anglers and flyfishers.

Instead of the thunderous sound of bass boats taking off at dawn and the silhouettes of waterskiers bouncing across wakes, there's an all-too-rare sense of tranquility at Purtis creek. The peace is broken only by the whirring of trolling motors and the "plop-plop" of Dahlberg Divers chugging through the lily pads.

Filled with flooded timber and ringed by red oaks, dogwoods and black walnuts, Purtis Creek is an angler's lake by design. Relatively manageable in size, its heavy cover, flooded levees, numerous flats and coves make it particularly attractive to flyfishers. A Woolly Bugger teased along the bank in the spring can produce a 6-inch bream on one cast and a 6-pound bass on the next.

In the decade since it was opened, Purtis Creek has earned a reputation for producing black bass in quality and quantity. Bass in excess of 13 pounds have been weighed on hand-held scales and at least one 11-pound fish reportedly has been taken there on a fly rod.

Wade fishing is unrestricted and boats of all sizes, including float tubes, are allowed but require a daily use permit. There is a nominal fee for entering the park. A "no wake" restriction is enforced for power boats and no more than 50 boats are permitted on the lake during the daylight fishing hours.

A variety of streamers, hard-bodied and deer hair bugs in sizes 10 to 4 are used by flyfishers at Purtis Creek. Woolly Buggers and Flashabuggers in black, brown and olive produce well on the lake.

In addition to Florida-strain largemouth, the lake is also stocked with coppernose bluegills, redear sunfish, channel catfish and crappie, all of which anglers may keep, subject to state-wide bag limits. Ponds below the dam are stocked with trout in the winter months.

Park visitors are also allowed to fish the four small ponds that surround the lake. The heavy fishing traffic that Purtis Creek received in its early years has dropped off, making it even more attractive for flyfishers. Late winter, early spring, and fall are prime times for action on Purtis Creek.

High quality bass fishing so close to a large urban center didn't happen by chance at Purtis Creek. Stocked with pure Florida-strain largemouth in 1984, Purtis Creek opened four years later as the only lake of its size in the state where catch-and-release was used to develop a superior fishery. State fisheries officials say quality fishing didn't occur at Purtis Creek only because of a catch-and-release edict.

Purtis Creek State Park

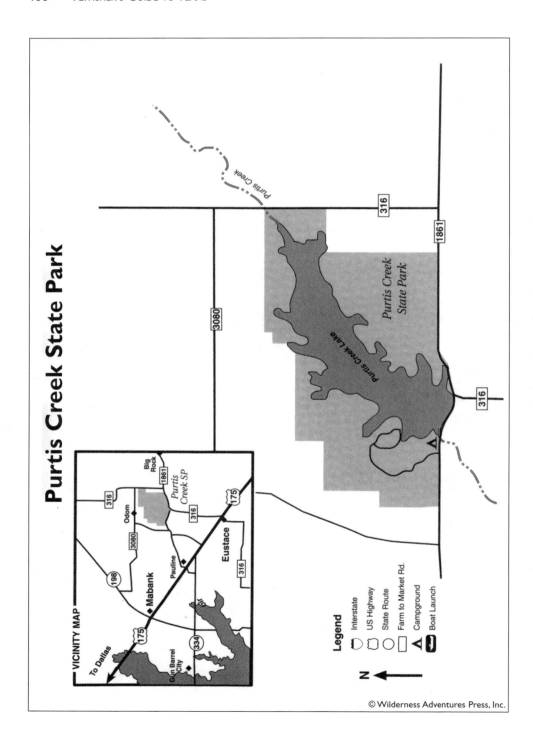

© Wilderness Adventures Press, Inc.

The immensely popular fishery has been carefully managed and has proven to be remarkably resilient through a stressful period just after startup in 1988.

Dallas fly fisher Charles Ducote's favorite fly pattern for Purtis Creek is an orange bead head Maribou Leech on a No. 8 hook. He also uses a Scates Shrimp pattern tied like a crawfish on freshwater hook with a reddish body and a lighter tan and white tail.

Casting a fly around the lighted piers in the early morning after most of the live bait anglers have left can be extremely productive for flyfishers. Look for smaller bass attacking minnows attracted to the lights and use glass minnow patterns, Deceivers and Clousers in brown and black. Cast the fly around the edges of the lights or "walk it" along the edge of the pier pilings. Largemouth of eight pounds and more have been caught and released off these piers at night.

Ideal for float tubes, canoes, and kayaks, the park lake can also be waded or fished from the bank in many places along scenic trails.

Park facilities include campgrounds with partial hookups and showers, primitive backpacking campsites, fishing piers and launch ramps. For additional information, contact the park at (903) 425-2332.

To get to the park, take US 175 south from Dallas and at the community of Eustace take Texas (FM) 316 north for 4.8 miles to the park entrance.

Flyfisher fighting bass out of a float tube in Purtis Creek State Park.

Flyfisher in float tube with a nice largemouth in Purtis Creek State Park.

CLEBURNE STATE PARK

A 116-acre spring-fed lake designed specifically for fishing offers an ideal fly fishing setting at this scenic 529-acre park between Glen Rose and Cleburne in Johnson County. The lake is ideal for targeting the resident population of bass and sunfish from a float tube, kayak or canoe and a 5 mph speed limit is enforced for outboards.

There are campsites with RV hookups, screened shelters and showers available at the park. For additional information, contact the park at (817) 645-4215.

MERIDIAN STATE PARK

Upstaged by nearby Lake Whitney, Meridian State Park's 72-acre, spring-fed lake also offers largemouth and smallmouth in a much smaller setting. Rainbow trout are released in the lake during the winter months. The park is located two miles west of Meridian off Texas 22.

CONFEDERATE REUNION CAMPGROUNDS STATE HISTORICAL PARK

This 77-acre park near the confluence of the Navasota River and Jack's Creek served as the reunion site for Confederate Civil War veterans for more than 50 years. The park offers picnic facilities and access for flyfishers to launch canoes or kayaks for fishing on the Navasota River. To get to the park, take Texas(FM) 27 west from the Wortham community. For additional information, contact nearby Fort Parker State Park at (817) 562-5751.

FORT PARKER STATE PARK

Located eight miles south of Mexia in Limestone County, Fort Parker State Park has a lake and access to the Navasota River. Another nearby option for flyfishers is the three-acre Lake Springfield next to the park. A long leader and a stealthy approach can translate into a surprisingly large bass on this clear, spring-fed lake. Fort Parker State Park is located in rolling oak woodlands between Interstate 35 and Interstate 45, six miles southwest of Mexia by way of Texas 14 or 50 miles east of Waco via US 84. The 1,485 acre park includes the 750-acre Lake Fort Parker, a shallow lake not suitable for large boats or water skiing but ideal for flyfishers using small boats, canoes and kayaks. The lake holds largemouth, crappie, sunfish and catfish. Rainbow trout are stocked each winter in Springfield Lake, located on the southeast end of the park. A boat launch is available at the park store and fishing piers are located at the campground and at the group area. Camping facilities include a 25-site campground, 10 screened shelters, a day use group activity center and overnight barracks-type group lodging with a separate kitchen / dining recreation hall. For additional information, contact the park office at (817) 562-5751.

MOTHER NEFF STATE PARK

Located above Lake Belton off US 35 north of Temple, the park waters offer flyfishers excellent white bass fishing in the spring as the fish make their spawning run upstream from Lake Belton. There is access for launching johnboats or other small watercraft from the bank. Park waters are usually stocked with rainbows during the winter months. Camping facilities are available in a scenic hardwood bottomland. For additional information, contact the park at (817) 853-2389.

BASTROP STATE PARK

No motorized boats are allowed on the small (10-acre) lake at Bastrop State Park, making makes it ideal for flyfishers stalking bedding sunfish or launching canoes, kayaks or kickboats to cast deer hair bugs along the banks for the local largemouth. There are camping facilities, RV hookups, showers and cabins at the park. This lake should not be confused with Lake Bastrop, a 900-acre power plant reservoir just across Texas 21 from the park. The park is located on the east side of Bastrop at the intersection of Loop 150 and Texas 21. For more information, contact the park at (512) 321-2101.

BUESCHER STATE PARK

Bastrop State Park and Buescher State Park are located in close proximity and offer flyfishers two small scenic waters ideal for fly fishing. The dam at Buescher Lake was washed out by record rainfall in the winter of 1991, but Texas Parks and Wildlife fisheries biologists say the largemouth bass population, which had to sustain low water conditions, bounced back strongly after the dam was repaired. The 30-acre lake offers bank fishing as well as float tube, canoe and kayak options for flyfishers targeting a good population largemouth and sunfish. Rainbow trout are stocked in the lake during the winter months.

LOCKHART STATE PARK

Located along Clear Fork Creek, Lockhart State Park is situated in the Blackland Prairie region of the state. The park, which includes a 9-hole golf course and swimming pool, offers flyfishers the opportunity to cast to largemouth and sunfish on the creek.

The 264-acre park has campsites and picnic facilities. For additional information, contact the park at (512) 398-3479. To get to the park, take Texas (FM) 20 2.8 miles west from Lockhart and turn left on Park Road 10.

PALMETTO STATE PARK

At Palmetto State Park, flyfishers can sample lake and river fishing in a scenic swamp setting. Sunfish are the prime target in the four-acre pond, while largemouth, Guadalupe bass and Rio Grande perch are part of the mixed bag on the river.

The park offers flyfishers an excellent put-in or take-out point for a five or six mile float on the San Marcos River. Floaters can use the county road 232 crossing as a take-out, or put-in at Luling and take- out at the park.

The park is located off US 183 between Luling and Gonzales.

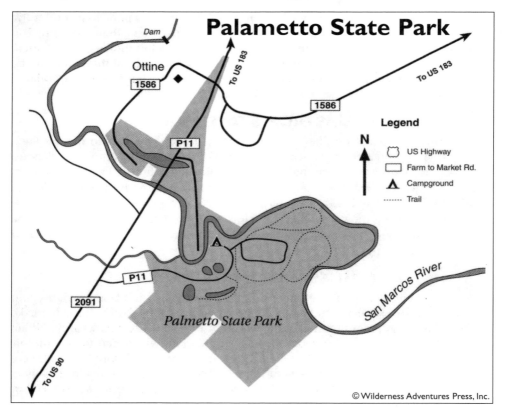

URBAN OPTIONS

There are a number of community lakes and creeks in the Dallas-Fort Worth area that offer flyfishers everything from a scenic venue and proper surface tension for fly casting practice to surprisingly good fishing for largemouth, white bass, crappie and sunfish.

WHITE ROCK LAKE

Located within a city park about five miles from downtown Dallas, this 1,120-acre lake offers excellent largemouth bass, sunfish and crappie fishing.

There is ample bank fishing access and a public launch ramp on the west side of the lake. A 10 horsepower limit is enforced on power boats on the lake.

For additional information, contact the Dallas Parks and Recreation Department at (214) 670-4100.

BACHMAN LAKE

Located off US 75 and Northwest Highway in Dallas, this attractive 132-acre lake holds largemouth, white bass and sunfish. There is bank fishing access and picnic areas.

For additional information, contact the Dallas Parks and Recreation Department at (214) 670-1923.

LAKE ARLINGTON

This 2,275-acre power plant lake in Arlington holds largemouth, hybrid striped bass and crappie. Two parks with public boat launches border it. Flyfishers should schedule visits early and late during weekdays, if possible, since the lake is popular with recreational boaters on weekends.

The lake is located off Interstate 30 west. Turn south off Interstate 30 on East Chase Parkway and continue as East Chase becomes Green Oaks. Turn west on Arkansas Lake and continue to the lake.

TRINITY RIVER (FORT WORTH)

There are a number of access points to the Trinity River along park property in Fort Worth, including a stretch just north of Interstate 30 on University Drive across from the Botanic Gardens.

Species range from largemouth, sunfish and catfish to carp and gar.

PRIVATE WATERS

PETTIGREW RANCH

Flyfishers travel from across the country to fish on the 2,600-acre Pettigrew Ranch near Ennis in Navarro County, where they have a shot at Florida-strain largemouth that can push the double digit class. Barry Austin and other family members personally guide every angler, and insist that all bass caught be carefully released to maintain the quality of the fishery. Novices shouldn't expect explosive action with every poorly thrown loop. Flyfishers should know how to make an accurate cast, as Pettigrew's banks are steep and provide the structure that most of the bigger fish prefer. This ranch is located near Chatfield, about 52 miles south of Dallas, and its Florida-strain bass thrive in a winding waterway that was once a gravel quarry. A half-day of fishing for two people costs $165. For information, contact owner Barry Austin at (903) 345-7331.

BED ROCK RANCH

Located west of Denton off Texas (FM) 455 in Wise County, this cattle ranch offers catch and release bank fishing access to a 4-acre stock tank that holds largemouth up to 7 pounds. Access to fishing on Red Rock Ranch is offered through membership in The Great Texas Bass Club. In addition to the annual membership fee, which allows access to lakes throughout the state, the day use fee at the ranch is $35, half day $20, children under 12 are free. For additional information, contact The Great Texas Bass Club at 888-303-4822 or (214) 954-1818.

BORDER CROSSINGS

BLUE RIVER

Located about 110 miles north of Dallas near Tishomingo, Oklahoma, is the Blue River, a scenic tail water fishery with largemouth, smallmouth and Kentucky spotted bass. A section of the river spanning limestone ledges and falls is also stocked with rainbow trout during the winter months. The trout fishing season on the Blue River runs from the last Saturday in October through the end of March the following year. The trout fishing area is located four miles east of Tishomingo on Oklahoma 78 in the Blue River Campground and the Carl R. And Ruth Walker Landrum Wilderness Area.

Dallas fly fisher Jeff Hines notes that the limestone bottom is irregular and sharp edged and says felt soled and studded wading shoes are essential for wading the trout waters on the Blue River. Hines says wet flies dead-drifted behind strike indicators are the best bet for taking rainbows in this tail water fishery. Among the effective patterns are weighted Woolly Buggers, Prince nymphs, and soft hackle, casual dress, in size 12 and smaller.

For additional information, contact the Oklahoma Department of Wildlife Conservation, 1801 North Lincoln, Oklahoma City, OK 73105.

Prairies and Lakes Hub Cities
Dallas

Population - 1,086,248   **Elevation - 512'**
Area Code - 214   **County - Dallas**

ACCOMMODATIONS

Courtyard by Marriott, Richardson / 800-321-2211 / 149 rooms / $59 - 135
Comfort Suites, 2287 W. Northwest Hwy. / 350-4011 / 103 rooms / $59 - $139
Crown Plaza, 7050 Stemmons Freeway / 630-8500 / 354 rooms / $79 -$169
Best Western - Market Center, 2023 Market Center Blvd. / 800-275-7419 /
    98 rooms / $69 - $109

BED AND BREAKFAST

Country Rose Bed and Breakfast, 616 East Beltline Road, Lancaster / 218-5017 /
    3 rooms / $

CAMPGROUNDS

Dallas East/Rowlett KOA, 108 Marina Circle Rowlett, TX / 1-972-475-3824
    Information / Call ahead. www.koa.com / $ to $$$

RESTAURANTS

Chuy's, 4544 McKinney Avenue / 559-2489 / $
Good Eats Cafe, 3888 Oak Lawn / 522-3287 / $
Lombardi's, 311 North Market Street / 747-0322 / $ to $$
Sonny Bryan's Smokehouse, 302 North Market Street / 744-1610 / $

FLY SHOPS AND GUIDES

Backwoods, 1453 West Campbell Road, Richardson / (972) 671-0372
Barlow's Tackle Shop, 451 North Central Expressway, Richardson
Orvis, 10720 Preston Road / 265-1600 / outfitting, casting instruction, guide
    services
Pocket Sports Company, 7235 Syracuse Drive / 553-0347
Westbank Angler, Inwood Village on Lovers Lane / 350-4665 / outfitting,
    travel services, guided fishing, casting instruction

SPORTING GOODS

Oshman's, 501 South Plano Road, Richardson / 972-783-1598
Fishn' World, 4609 W. Lover Lane / 214-358-4941
Gun and Tackle Store, 6041 Forest Lane / 214-239-8181
Rays Hardware and Sporting Goods, 730 Singleton / 214-747-7916
Oshman's, 9100 N. Central Expressway, #123 / 214-363-8441
Oshman's, 15490 Dallas Pkwy / 972-991-3533

HOSPITALS
Methodist Hospitals of Dallas, 1441 North Beckley at Colorado
Trinity Medical Center, 4343 North Josey Lane, Carrollton / 972-492-1010

AIRPORTS
Dallas Love Field, 670-6073 / American Airlines:(800-) 242-4444 / Continental
Airlines: (800-) 525-0289 / Southwest Airlines: 800-435-9792
Dallas / Fort Worth / DFW International Airport / 972-574-8888 /
Aeromexico:800-237-6639 / America West: 800-235-9292 / American Airlines
/ American Eagle: 800-433-7300 / Atlantic Southeast Airlines (Delta):800-282-
3424 / British Airways:800-247-9297 / Continental Airlines: 800-525-0280 /
Delta:800-221-1212 / Japan Air:800-525-3663 / KLM Royal Dutch Airlines: 800-
374-7747 / Korean Air:800-438-5000 / Lufthansa:800-645-3880 / Northwest
Airlines: 800-225-2525 / Swiss Air: 800-221-4750 / TACA International
Airlines:800-535-8780 / United Airlines: 800-241-6522 / US Air:800-428-4322

FOR MORE INFORMATION
Dallas Convention and Visitors Bureau
1201 Elm, Suite 2000
Dallas, TX 75270
571 1000

Flyfisher casting on Colorado River below Austin

Population - 495,418   Elevation - 670'
Area Code - 817   County - Tarrant

ACCOMMODATIONS

Fairfield Inn by Marriott, 3701 NE Loop 820 / 232 5700 / 106 Rooms / $49 - $99

Hampton Inn, 2700 Cherry Lane / 125 Rooms / 426 7866 / $49 to $69

Holiday Inn - Fort Worth / North, 2540 Meacham Blvd. / 247 rooms / 625 9911

Holiday Inn South and Conference Center, 100 Alta Mesa Blvd. / 247 rooms / 293 3088 / $59 - $79

Canada Inn Midtown, 1401 University Dr. / 336 9311 / $72

BED AND BREAKFASTS

Azalea Plantation Bed and Breakfast Inn, 1400 Robinwood Dr. / 838 5882 / 4 rooms / $110 - $159

Texas White House, 1417 Eighth Avenue / 800-279 6491, TexaswhiteHouse.com / three rooms / $105-$125

RESTAURANTS

Spaghetti Warehouse, 600 East Exchange / 625 4171

Angelo's Barbecue, 2533 White Settlement Road / 332 0357 / hickory-smoked brisket, pork ribs and chicken.

Booger Red's Restaurant and Saloon, Stockyards Hotel, Stockyards District / 625 6427 / open 6:30 am to 11 p.m.

FLY SHOPS

Main Street Outfitters, 501 Main Street, 332 4144

Backwoods, 3212 Camp Bowie / 332-2423

SPORTING GOODS STORES

Oshman's, 8555 Airport Freeway, North Richland Hills / 428-5512

Academy Sports, 6101 I-20 A Bryant Irvin Road / 817-346-6622

Oshman's, 4830 S.W. Loop 820 / 817-377-1515

Oshman's, 1250 Green Oaks Road / 817-731-8578

Texas Outdoors, 3821 SW Blvd / 817-731-3402

HOSPITALS

Baylor Health Care Systems Medical Center, 1999 Forest Ridge Road, Sherwood Gardens, Bedford / 283-3322

AIRPORTS

Dallas / Fort Worth / DFW International Airport, 972-574-8888 / Aeromexico:800-237-6639 / America West: 800-235-9292 / American Airlines / American Eagle: 800-433-7300 / Atlantic Southeast Airlines (Delta):800-282-3424 / British Airways:800-247-9297 / Continental Airlines: 800-525-0280 / Delta:800-221-1212 / Japan Air:800-525-3663 / KLM Royal Dutch Airlines: 800-374-7747 / Korean Air:800-438-5000 / Lufthansa:800-645-3880 / Northwest Airlines: 800-225-2525 / Swiss Air: 800-221-4750 / TACA International Airlines:800-535-8780 / United Airlines: 800-241-6522 / US Air:800-428-4322

FOR MORE INFORMATION

Fort Worth Convention and Visitors Bureau
415 Throckmorton
Fort Worth, Texas

DENISON

Population - 27,667	**Elevation - 767'**
Area Code - 903	**County - Grayson**

ACCOMMODATIONS

Ramada Inn, 1600 South Austin Avenue / 465-6800 / $45 to $70
Fink Motel, Pottsboro

CAMPING

Eisenhower State Park (see State Park Waters)

RESTAURANTS

Sonic Drive-In, 2405 South Austin Street / 465 2562 and 3325 Texas (FM) 120 West 465 5720

FLY SHOPS AND SPORTING GOODS

Daves Ski and Tackle, 3714 N Hwy 91 / 963-465-6160
Wal-Mart, 401 N US Hwy 75 / 963-465-0684

FOR MORE INFORMATION

Denison Area Chamber of Commerce
P.O. Box 325
Denison, TX 75021
465-1551

Denton

Population - 86,341   **Elevation - 620'**
Area Code - 940   **County - Denton**

ACCOMMODATIONS

La Quinta Inn, 700 Fort Worth Dr. / 800-531 5900 / $67 to $78
Motel 6, 4125 IH-35 North / 591 0981 / $40
Royal Hotel Suites, 1210 N. IH-35 E. at McCormick St. Exit / 383 2007

CAMPING

KOA Campground, 7100 South Stemmons Freeway / 497 3353 / $19 for a tent site, $26 for an RV site, $28 for a camping cabin
Dallas Destiny RV Resort, Tent and RV Sites Available / 7100 South I-35 Corinth, TX / 940-497-3353 Information / dallasrv@gocampingamerica.com

RESTAURANTS

Sweetwater Grill and Tavern, 115 South Elm Street / 484 2888
Good Eats Grill, 5812 Interstate 35 North / 387 3500
The Black-Eyed Pea, 2420 Interstate 35 East / 320 4140

SPORTING GOODS

Oshman's, 2201 South I-35, Space P-7 / 940-566-3902

FOR MORE INFORMATION

Denton Convention and Visitors Bureau
P.O. Drawer P
Denton, TX 76202
382-7895

FLYFISHING CLUBS

Dallas Flyfishers, P.O. Box 8553, Carrollton, TX 75011. Meets monthly at Addison Conference Center, Airport Drive, Addison. For additional information, contact Jere Anderson (972) 618-6714

LODGING PRICE KEY

$	=	$30 - $50 per night
$$	=	$50 - $70 per night
$$$	=	$70 per night and up

RESTAURANT PRICE KEY

$	=	$10 and under per meal
$$	=	$10 - $20 per meal
$$$	=	$20 and up

REGION 3

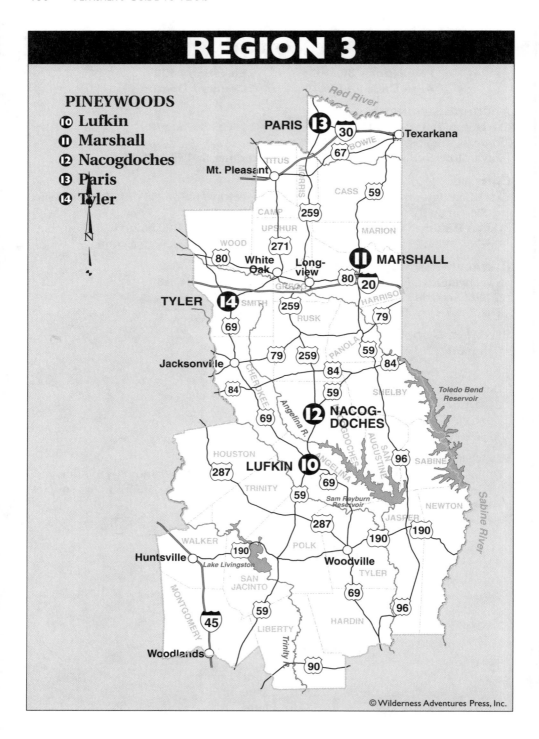

PINEYWOODS
- ⑩ **Lufkin**
- ⑪ **Marshall**
- ⑫ **Nacogdoches**
- ⑬ **Paris**
- ⑭ **Tyler**

N

PARIS ⑬ 30 Texarkana
67
Mt. Pleasant TITUS BOWIE CASS 59
MORRIS
259 CAMP
UPSHUR MARION
WOOD 271
80 White Oak Long-view ⑪ MARSHALL
GREGG 80 20
TYLER ⑭ SMITH HARRISON
259 RUSK 79
69
Jacksonville 79 259 PANOLA 59
84 84
84 SHELBY Toledo Bend Reservoir
59
69 Angelina R. ⑫ NACOG-DOCHES
SAN AUGUSTINE
HOUSTON 96 SABINE
287 LUFKIN ⑩
TRINITY 69
59 Sam Rayburn Reservoir NEWTON
JASPER
287 190 190
Huntsville 190 POLK
Lake Livingston Woodville
SAN JACINTO TYLER
MONTGOMERY 69
45 59 HARDIN 96
Woodlands LIBERTY
Trinity R. 90

Sabine River

© Wilderness Adventures Press, Inc.

Pineywoods

REGION 3

PANHANDLE PLAINS

BIG BEND COUNTRY

PRAIRIES & LAKES

HILL COUNTRY

PINEY WOODS

GULF COAST

SOUTH TEXAS PLAINS

Blossoming dog-woods and red-buds welcome the spring. Slow moving rivers drift under stands of stately, moss draped cypresses and the calls of birds can be heard through the woodlands and scattered swamps.

This easternmost region of Texas is also characterized by loblolly and short leaf pines. Houston writer Shannon Tompkins, an east Texas native, describes lakes and streams in the Pineywoods Region as much more laid back and isolated than in other regions of the state. "It's farther between bridges and access points. The water flows slowly, sometimes almost imperceptibly on these rivers. They are deeper, with their water often a thin, reddish brown from the tannin leeched from tree detritus."

And instead of the rocks that line the bottoms and form winding pathways for the clear running waters of Hill Country rivers, east Texas waterways have sand bottoms that pile up into broad bars, offering excellent locations for camping or wade fishing.

And unlike the property around Hill Country rivers, which is virtually all privately owned and off limits to boaters, much of the land along east Texas waterways is held in public trust, or at least protected by private conservation groups. For example, the big Thicket National Preserve lines the entire length of the Neches River from Steinhagen Lake to Beaumont, a distance of almost 70 river miles.

Information on river conditions in the region can be obtained from the Big Thicket National Preserve information office, (409) 246 2337, or on the Web at www.nps.gov / bith. Information on the area is also available through the US Geological Survey's Texas website at http://txwww.cr.usgs.gov

RIVERS

BIG CYPRESS BAYOU

Big Cypress Bayou is a scenic east Texas waterway that winds along cypress and oak shaded banks and flooded timber from Lake O' the Pines to Caddo Lake. Once a navigable waterway for steamboats transporting pineywoods lumber from the bustling port of Jefferson to New Orleans, the river now offers anglers a step back in history and some excellent fly fishing for bass and sunfish.

Lake O' the Pines to Jefferson Park in the town of Jefferson

Canoes, kayaks and small flat-bottomed boats are able to navigate this scenic 20-mile stretch of river for most of the year but river trips can be affected by log jams and low water during the summer months when discharges from the lake are less than 500 cubic feet per second (cfs), says the Texas Parks and Wildlife Department. The occasional hefty largemouth is always possible amid the more frequent action with smallish spotted bass and sunfish in this wild and scenic setting.

The tailrace below Lake O' The Pines also offers walk-in access to bank fishing and a chance at largemouth, spotted bass, crappie, white bass, yellow bass, hybrid striped bass and sunfish.

Late winter and spring are the most productive times for white bass. Float trips are not recommended on this reach of Big Cypress if Bayou discharge rates from Lake O' The Pines exceed 1,500 cfs.

Jefferson to Caddo Lake State Park

This lower segment of Big Cypress Bayou also offers flyfishers a 20-mile float in a scenic East Texas setting. Flyfishers can cast to a variety of fish species and enjoy viewing wild game and bird life along its shorelines.

Put-ins include Texas (FM) 134 in Jefferson, Thompson Camp off Texas 49 north of Jefferson, the Texas 43 bridge crossing, and at Caddo Lake State Park near Karnack. The Black Cypress and Little Cypress Rivers flow into Big Cypress Bayou at Thompson Camp as well as three miles below it, prime holding areas for a variety of species.

This reach of the Big Cypress Bayou is much wider, deeper and easier to navigate than the section from Lake O' The Pines to Jefferson Park but anglers on float trips should be watchful for submerged stumps and fallen trees on all parts of the river, according to the Texas Parks and Wildlife Department.

SABINE RIVER

The stretch of Sabine River that runs along the east Texas border with Louisiana near Orange offers exciting backcountry fly fishing on a swampy, tannin-stained waterway. Largemouth and sunfish share creek banks and shorelines lined with cypress and gum trees with the primordial looking bowfin.

The stretch of the river from near Deweyville downstream to Orange also offers excellent Kentucky spotted bass fishing. There is a boat launch at Niblett's Bluff Park on the Louisiana side of the river. Flyfishers should target largemouth around lily pad shorelines and spotted bass holding in rocky shoal areas. Those who launch from the Louisiana side are required to have a Louisiana fishing license.

In addition to the largemouth and sunfish, the Sabine and other east Texas waterways are home to a healthy population of bowfins, or grinnel, as they are affectionately known locally. And while the grinnel's reputation for fooling anglers into thinking they have hooked a giant largemouth and their tendency to savage expensive bass lures have not endeared them to the local levelwind set, they have attracted a strong following among flyfishers.

The bowfin (*Amia Calva*)

Commonly called the grinnel in Texas, it is the last survivor of Amiidae, an ancient, primitive family of fishes. In Texas, found in the far eastern portion of the state, the fish has a large mouth filled with sharp teeth. The dorsal fin runs more than half the length of the body. The fish is olive or dark green in coloration on the back and lighter green on the sides with a light cream-colored belly. The males have a large, black spot on the tail, which is bordered in orange. The average size is 4 to 8 pounds although fish exceeding 17 pounds have been caught in Texas waters.

Sabine River

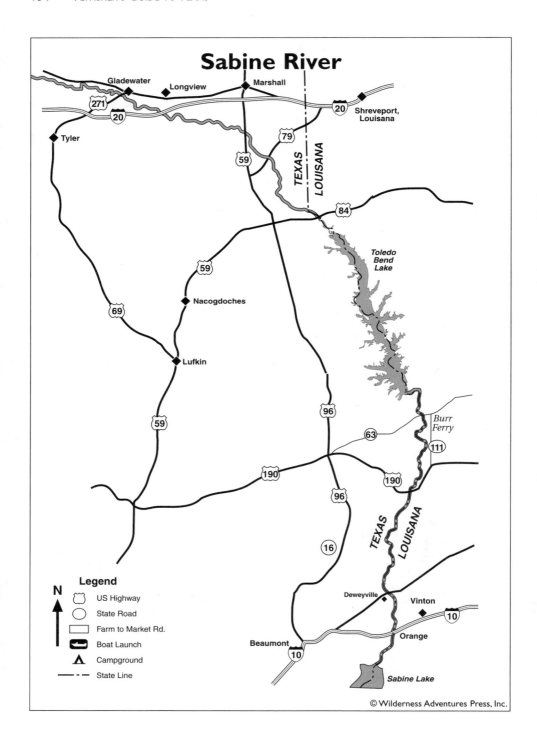

The word is out that there are some bowfin in the Sabine and nearby Neches rivers big enough to dwarf some of the existing IGFA fly rod line-class records. This ancient and primitive fish with a mouthful of small, sharp teeth strikes flies hard and puts up a strong fight. "They will back up against the bank, and they work off strictly ambush tactics," says Ronnie Robison, a veteran Sabine River fly fisher.

Fly fishing guide Robert Woodruff says he fishes for bowfin in sloughs off the Sabine River. He presents light colored, slow sinking flies to the fish finning on the surface. For bowfin, Woodruff says he uses all of his Lake Fork bass flies that "have gotten ratty" because bowfin have a mouth full of teeth and are notoriously hard on flies. He says another proven pattern for bowfin is the Simple Shiner pattern by John Likikas.

Bowfin have a long undulating dorsal fin that gives them a snakelike appearance. The males also have a large, black spot bordered in orange near the tail.

There is an opportunity to sight cast to these fish but most are taken blind casting. "You are looking for a stationary fish, his fin will be moving," says Robison. Bowfin will hit streamer flies and poppers with bright colors with white and chartreuse the most effective.

Flyfishers casting Sabine River shoreline.

Sabine River Access Points
The stretch of river that runs from Gladewater to Longview offers good float trip possibilities, according to Woodruff.

Orange, Texas Area
Boat access to the Sabine River is available at several launch ramps, marinas, and parks in Orange and nearby Vinton, Louisiana. A public launch ramp in Orange next to Bluebird Fish Camp, just off Interstate 10 on Simmons Drive, provides access to Square Lake and to the Sabine River via the Gulf States Canal.

Niblett's Bluff Park, Louisiana
Camping and launch facilities are also available on the Louisiana side of the Sabine near Vinton at Niblett's Bluff Park, a onetime supply center for Confederate troops. The park can be reached by traveling east on Interstate 10, exiting at the Toomey Starks exit and then proceeding north on Louisiana 109 to the park entrance. For information, contact park officials at (409) 886-5222.

NECHES RIVER
The Neches River begins east of Colfax in eastern Van Zandt County and flows southeast for more than 400 miles to its mouth on Sabine Lake at Port Arthur. Lake Palestine and Lake B.A. Steinhagen are located on the Neches. Major tributaries include the Angelina River and Village Creek. Selected stretches of the Neches pro-

Largemouth caught on the Sabine River.

Flyfisher casting at Cypress Trunk, Sabine River.

vide excellent habitat in scenic settings for largemouth and sunfish action. Because the river runs through a forested region in its upper reaches, there are also stretches that suffer from natural pollution in the form of decaying vegetation. Discharges from oil refineries and chemical plants on the lower reaches of the river around the Beaumont / Port Arthur-Orange area have also had an adverse effect on the water quality of the river.

A good stretch to float on the Neches River is from Lake Palestine south. There is a crossing at Texas 175 that offers a good put-in access to the next bridge take-out. Shuttles between bridges have to be worked out in advance because there are no commercial canoe outfitters in the area. Good water clarity and scenic Pineywoods river bottom habitat makes this an ideal fly fishing option for bass and sunfish, says Richard Ott, Texas Parks and Wildlife biologist for the region

TEN MILE BAYOU

Located east of Beaumont about four miles above the Interstate 10 Bridge crossing on the Neches River, Ten Mile Bayou can be reached from Beard's Boat Launch on Interstate 10. One of the most scenic and unique waterways in East Texas, it has feeder creeks and huge stumps at the water's edge from what is left of virgin cypress trees. Bowfin will often wait in ambush around these dramatic features. The area also holds river largemouth and is protected from the wind.

VILLAGE CREEK

Located between Kountze and Silsbee, Village Creek has an irregular flow through the Big Thicket of east Texas. Floats of ten miles or less can be made between bridges on Village Creek.

Quiet, isolated and wild, Village Creek offers excellent fly fishing for spotted bass, bluegill and longear sunfish along sandbars and ridges lined with beech and magnolias. Look for largemouth in the deep pools where current moves at a lazy pace. Look for spotted bass around structure in the faster water, where they wait to attack a moveable feast of baitfish. While most of the action will come from the typical small river largemouth, spotted bass and sunfish, the occasional bucketmouth bass awaits the fly fisher with the skills to patiently prospect the deeper holes.

This stream is rich in wildlife and underutilized by anglers. Stable water levels and pleasant weather make the fall months (September through November) an ideal time to fish the Village Creek area.

A captivating float trip that offers a real taste of this scenic waterway and its prolific fishery can begin at the Texas 418 Bridge and end at the Texas 327 crossing, a nine mile stretch that runs through the Roy Larsen Sandyland Sanctuary, a 5,600 acre tract owned by The Nature Conservancy.

Outfitters for float trips on Village Creek include James and Nelda Overstreet, Timber Ridge Tours, Kountze (409) 246-3107 and Perry and Robin Humphrey, Easttex Canoes, Silsbee, (409) 385-4700 or (800) 814-7390.

Flyfishing for smallmouth.

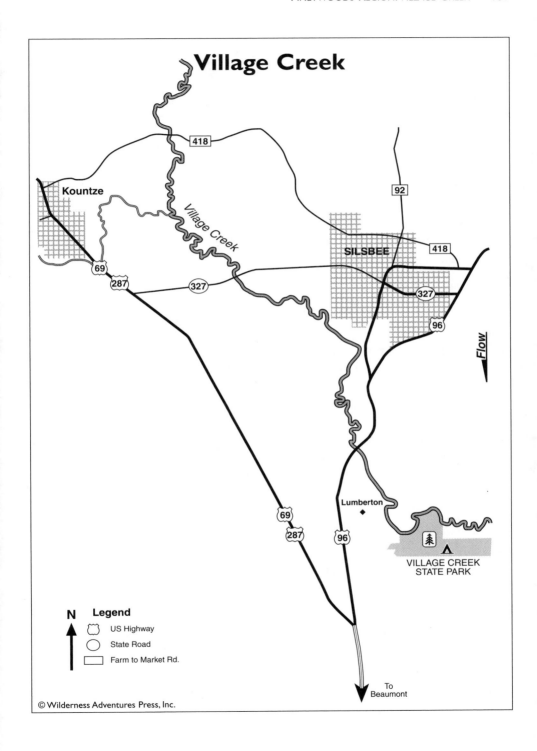

Village Creek

Village Creek

418

Kountze

92

69

287

327

418

SILSBEE

327

96

Flow

Lumberton

69

287

96

VILLAGE CREEK
STATE PARK

To
Beaumont

N

Legend

US Highway

State Road

Farm to Market Rd.

© Wilderness Adventures Press, Inc.

LAKES

PAT MAYSE LAKE

This 5,993-acre Corps of Engineers impoundment is located 13 miles north of Paris in Lamar County on Sanders Creek, a tributary of the Red River. It offers 62 miles of shoreline and is stocked with Florida-strain and native-northern large-mouth, hybrid striped bass, crappie and sunfish. Surrounded by blackland prairie, this lake is considered one of the top lakes in the state for hybrid striped bass. Shoreline parks offer picnic areas, boat ramps and campgrounds. To get to park facilities on the north side of the lake, take US north from Paris and turn west on Texas (FM) 906 at Midcity.

LAKE CROOK

Located 3 miles northwest of Paris in a scenic setting, this 920-acre lake is stocked with largemouth, hybrid striped bass, crappie and sunfish.

WRIGHT PATMAN LAKE

Located on the Sulphur River in Bowie and Cass counties just southeast of Texarkana, Lake Wright Patman, originally known as Lake Texarkana, covers 20,300 acres and has an average depth of 7.6 feet. The lake has 170 miles of shoreline that provides prime habitat for game fish that include largemouth bass, white bass and sunfish.

The lake has been stocked with Florida-strain largemouth and Texas Parks and Wildlife officials say catch rates for bass are good throughout the year on Wright Patman. Peak spawning time occurs when the water temperature exceeds 62.5 degrees in March and April. Prime habitat for bass includes shorelines with sub-merged brush and aquatic vegetation, flooded timber, ridges and creek channels.

Parks and Wildlife officials report high growth rates for white bass on the lake, with fish in the 15-inch class abundant. The months of January through April provide the best fishing as the white bass begin their upstream migration to spawn in the Sulphur River and its tributaries. Within the reservoir, major points, creek channels, and open water areas adjacent to the dam provide action from May through August. Flyfishers should look for seagulls or schools of shad on the surface to indicate feeding white bass.

White and black crappie are also present in the lake with the former being the most prevalent. Peak fishing for crappie occurs from winter through spring as fish begin to congregate prior to spawning. The river channel in the lower end of the reservoir attracts many anglers during this time of year. In the spring as water temperatures begin to warm, crappie are targeted in shallower water, five feet or less, near islands and flooded brush. Bluegill and redear sunfish are also abundant on the lake and provide additional action for flyfishers on Wright Patman.

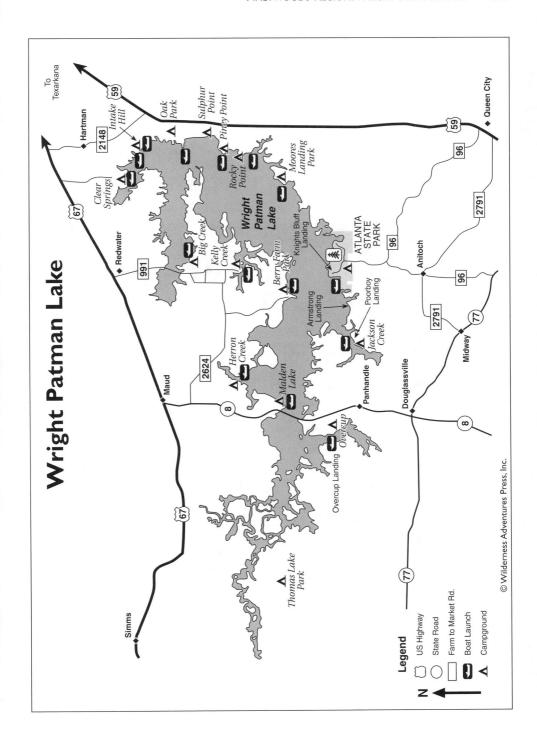

Wright Patman Lake

Legend

US Highway
State Road
Farm to Market Rd.
Boat Launch
Campground

© Wilderness Adventures Press, Inc.

Atlanta State Park

Located on the shoreline of Wright Patman Lake in Cass County, Atlanta State Park is situated in scenic wooded hills covered in thick stands of oaks, pines and sweet gums. In addition to bank fishing access, the 1,475-acre park is an excellent put-in for flyfishers to prospect nearby shorelines of Wright Patman Lake from float tubes, canoes and kayaks. Park facilities including campgrounds with full and partial RV hookups and boat ramps.

To get to the park, take Texas (FM) 96 northwest from Atlanta and turn right (north) on Texas (FM) 1154, which leads to the park. For additional information, contact Texas Parks and Wildlife Department at (903) 796-6476.

Open mouth of a largemouth bass.

LAKE WELSH

A 1,365-acre impoundment located off Texas (FM) 1735, six miles southeast of Mount Pleasant in Titus County, Lake Welsh offers flyfishers a shot at chain pickerel as well as Florida-strain largemouth, sunfish and crappie. Launch facilities are limited to one public ramp and one private marina.

LAKE MONTICELLO

A small, power plant lake located in Titus County just west of Mount Pleasant, Monticello provides lots of winter season action. Features along the 2,000-acre lake include cattails, heavy moss beds and some standing timber on one end.

The primary species at Monticello is largemouth but it also holds coppernose bluegill which grow to large size in the warm water environment.

Robert Woodruff, who guides on the lake from January through May and then from mid-November through December, says he will begin to fish the lake as soon as the photo period (daylight hours) begins to lengthen and water temperatures climb to 80 degree levels and the bass think it is spring. A cooling pond for a coal fired plant, lake temperatures stay warm in the winter and the bass begin to spawn around January 15. The best fishing runs from January through May and then it tapers off because the water gets too hot, with surface temperatures as high as 100 degrees. Woodruff says April is a good month for topwater action at Monticello. Eighty degree water temperature and 30 degree air temperatures during the winter can create steamy conditions and difficult visibility.

There are no marina facilities on Lake Monticello but there is a single two-lane ramp and the lake can be fished from a canoe or kayak.

LAKE BOB SANDLIN

Located south of Mount Pleasant on the Big Cypress River off Texas (FM) 127 in Titus and Camp counties, 9,460-acre Lake Bob Sandlin is an excellent lake for largemouth and white bass.

Fly fishing guide Robert Woodruff notes that the lake is one of the few in the state that runs east and west and is therefore fishable during winter cold fronts, "northers", and in heavy wind conditions that "roll up" most other lakes. Camping facilities at the lake consist of 75 multi-use campsites and 20 shelters. The shelters are completely enclosed with glass windows that can be opened and shut. Most of the shelters have a view of the lake, and several back up to it. For more information on current lake conditions, write Lake Bob Sandlin State Park, Route 5, Box 224, Pittsburg, TX 75686, (903) 572-5531.

Lake Bob Sandlin State Park

Located on the north shore of Lake Bob Sandlin this park provides fly fishing access to prime largemouth habitat along the lake's many coves and bays as well as a jumping off point for fishing adjacent Lakes Cypress Springs and Monticello.

The park also offers access to bank fishing, a lighted pier for night fishing, a boat ramp, camping and picnic facilities.

For additional information, contact the park at (903) 572-5531.

LAKE CYPRESS SPRINGS

Located on Big Cypress Creek, 11 miles southeast of Mount Vernon on Texas (FM) 3007 in Franklin County, Lake Cypress Springs is another lake with an east-west configuration that is fishable during heavy north winds.

The 3,000-acre lake is adjacent to Lake Bob Sandlin. It receives considerable fishing pressure but is a good producer of Florida-strain and native-northern large-mouth, crappie, and redear sunfish.

Set in scenic pineywoods, Cypress Springs has five parks along its shores that offer camping facilities, picnic tables, commercial marinas, RV hookups, boat ramps and beaches. To get to lakeside facilities at Cypress Springs, proceed on Texas 37 south from Mount Vernon and turn east on Texas (FM) 21 and south on Texas (FM) 2723 to the lake.

LAKE WINNSBORO

Lake Winnsboro is located in northern Wood County southwest of Winnsboro off Texas 37 and is an excellent lake for largemouth as well as one of the best lakes for redear sunfish in the region. A redear specimen that exceeded 3 pounds., Florida-strain largemouth in excess of 10 pounds and black crappie in excess of 3 pounds have also been taken in this 1,100-acre lake. Flooded weed beds and standing timber provide habitat and prime fishing targets on this scenic, clear-water lake. Facilities provided by Wood County include free boat ramps, picnic grounds and campsites.

To get to Lake Winnesboro, take Texas 37 south from the Winnesboro community and access one of the county roads that run west to the lake.

LAKE QUITMAN

Lake Quitman is an 814-acre lake located just off Texas (FM) 69 about 10 miles southwest of Winnsboro. Quitman is among several Wood County lakes including Hawkins and Winnesboro that have received bass from Lake Fork. This small lake situated in the pineywoods holds clear water and is stocked with Florida-strain largemouth, striped bass, crappie and hybrid sunfish. Flyfishers should target these species around shoreline vegetation.

There are unimproved campsites and four launch ramps along the lake shore. For information on current lake conditions, contact Texas Parks and Wildlife Department at (903) 593-5077.

To get to Lake Quitman, take Texas 37 north from Quitman and then take Texas (FM) 69 north to the lake.

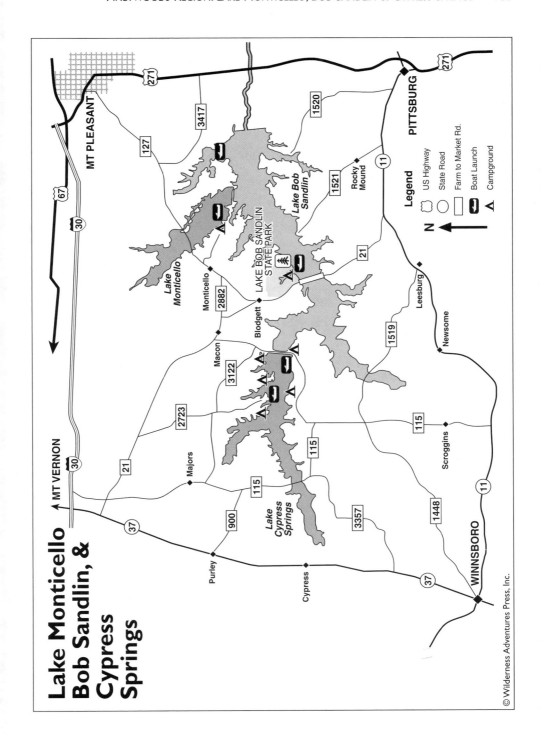

Lake Monticello
Bob Sandlin, &
Cypress
Springs

MT VERNON

MT PLEASANT

PITTSBURG

WINNSBORO

Lake Monticello

Lake Bob Sandlin

LAKE BOB SANDLIN STATE PARK

Lake Cypress Springs

Monticello

Blodgett

Macon

Majors

Purley

Cypress

Rocky Mound

Leesburg

Newsome

Scroggins

271

67

30

127

3417

1520

1521

11

21

2882

3122

2723

21

900

115

115

115

1519

115

3357

1448

37

37

11

30

Legend

N

US Highway

State Road

Farm to Market Rd.

Boat Launch

Campground

© Wilderness Adventures Press, Inc.

Lake Winnsboro

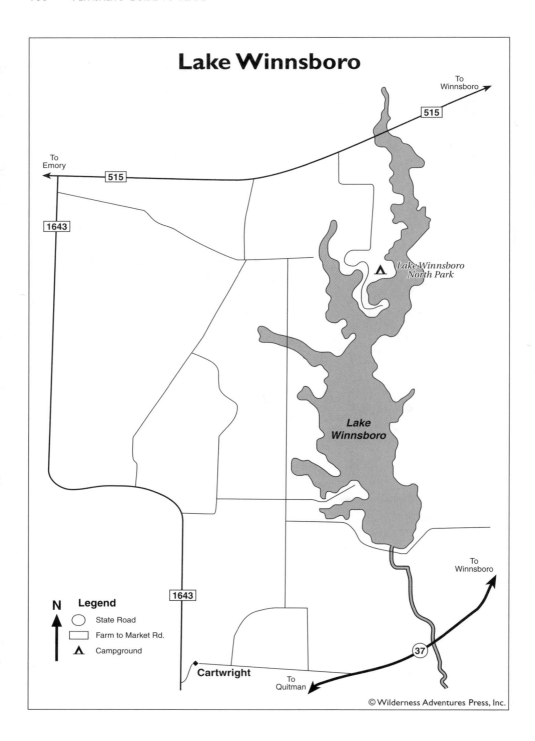

To Winnsboro

515

To Emory

515

1643

Lake Winnsboro North Park

Lake Winnsboro

To Winnsboro

N

Legend

State Road

Farm to Market Rd.

Campground

1643

37

Cartwright

To Quitman

© Wilderness Adventures Press, Inc.

Largemouth Bass in Texas

Bass native to Florida and other southeastern states are called Florida-strain largemouth (Micropterus salmoides floridanus). *They enjoy long growing seasons in the warm climates of their native states, and it is not uncommon for them to grow into the double digits. They have relatively long lives, often living into their teenage years. While known to be aggressive feeders and strikers of artificial lures and flies, some bass anglers say the Florida subspecies has a tendency to contract lockjaw on occasion.*

Bass native to the eastern half of the United States excluding Florida and New England, are called native-northern largemouth (Micropterus salmoides salmoides). *Scientists tell us that they don't as a rule grow as big nor live as long as the Florida-strain fish but their reputation for aggressiveness when it comes to an artificial lure is unblemished. Both are subspecies of largemouth bass* (Micropterus salmoides salmoides) *and both are common to Texas waters.*

Biologists have found that crossbreeding the subspecies combines the best traits of both fish. The term "F1" is used to describe the first generation of largemouth that result from the cross between Florida-strain and native-northern fish.

Since it was introduced in Texas waters in the mid-1970s, the Florida bass has been the primary ingredient in Texas Parks and Wildlife Department's efforts to create trophy largemouth bass in Texas. By crossing pure Florida bass with the native-northern subspecies and stocking those hybrid fish in Texas lakes, fisheries scientists have begun to see the potential for creating trophy class bass with optimum genetic traits for Texas.

Parks and Wildlife officials note that the 14.14 pound largemouth caught by a fly fisher in 2000 in the Panhandle Plains Region below Lake Meredith was a native-northern / Florida-strain hybrid. The specimen also illustrates how the crosses may be more tolerant of colder climates than the pure Florida-strain largemouth.

Lake Fork and Lake Quitman

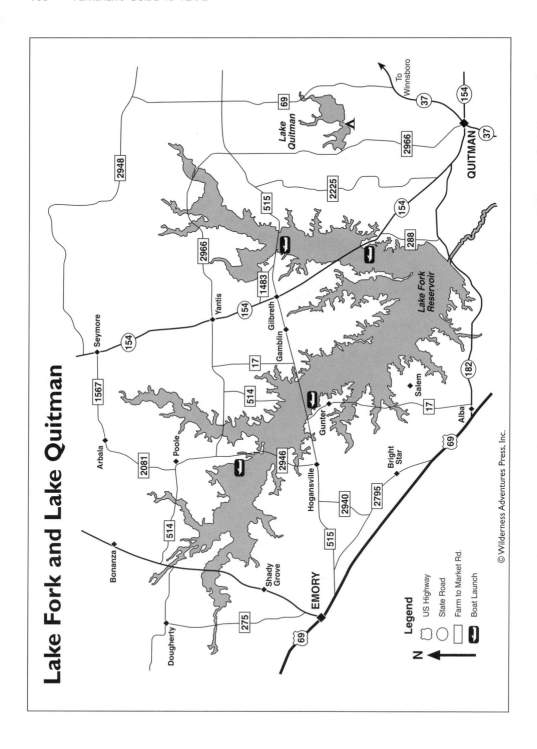

Legend

US Highway
State Road
Farm to Market Rd.
Boat Launch

© Wilderness Adventures Press, Inc.

LAKE FORK

A 28,000-acre impoundment located about 90 miles from Dallas, Lake Fork has produced more big bass than any Texas lake, and it has sustained that record for 15 years. As of May 1996, 36 of the state's top 50 largemouth were caught at Fork. The state-record largemouth, an 18.18-pound fish, was caught in Lake Fork in 1992. Thanks for the most part to the rapid growth rate of the lake's Florida-strain largemouth, anglers now have to catch a bass weighing more than 15 pounds to make the Texas Top 50.

Scientists believe that the nutrient runoff from dairy farms located around the lake has contributed to the large size and rapid growth of the bass. In addition, bottom contours such as the sharp drop-offs near shore keep shallow-water vegetation from taking over. A large amount of timber was left in place when the lake was designed, providing prime habitat for the game fish.

Flyfisher fighting bass at Lake Fork.

Lake Fork was one of the first lakes in Texas with more restrictive bag and size limits. The lake opened with a five bass daily limit, instead of the 10-fish limit then in effect on other Texas lakes. The limit was later reduced to three fish, with a slot limit between 14 and 21 inches to protect brood bass. The bag limit at Fork is now back at five fish a day, and only one fish can be bigger than 21 inches.

Despite the increased bag limit, a strong catch-and-release ethic has been cultivated among guides and anglers on Lake Fork. Creel surveys show a near universal practice of catch and release on the lake. "You don't dare try to clean a bass near Lake Fork," says Steve Poarch, who is in charge of managing Lake Fork for the Texas Parks and Wildlife Department. "You will get looks and you will hear some dirty words."

Robert C. Woodruff is a Lake Fork fly fishing guide whose clients have taken largemouth up to 10 pounds along Lake Fork's weed lines and flooded timber.

Woodruff says a 7- or 8-weight rod will work on the lake but he says the ideal outfit is a 9-weight rod matched to a bass-taper floating line, and a 7-foot leader of 17-pound-test monofilament for Lake Fork bass fishing. He recommends fly-fishers carry along an extra fly line because he has seen lines destroyed by large bass sawing them over logs and brush.

It is important to bring a quality pair of polarized sunglasses designed for angling, preferably with brown lenses, and a hat with a brim. This helps flyfishers catch more fish because they can see the fish hit. "What I have seen through the years is that you won't hang up as much because you see that stump, you don't set the hook on it, you let the fly work over it. You also don't fall down as much because you see the rocks and see the bottom."

Selection of bass flies for Lake Fork.

Woodruff recommends bringing a sink tip or full sinking line to get the fly below the surface. "You can fish fairly deep with a floating line but a sinking line is also needed and is often left out."

Good heavy tippet material is also a must on Lake Fork, Woodruff says. "I don't use tippet or leader anymore but prefer a straight 7½ ft. to 8 ft. length of monofilament. Once he works it down to about 6 feet, he starts over with a fresh, full-length leader. "I don't splice a leader together because every knot will catch moss."

Lake Fork Fly Selection

Woodruff says flyfishers often restrict themselves to poppers and divers at Lake Fork but they also need patterns that will get down in the water column. A variety of flies are needed because when even a mild cold front comes through, it will drop the bass off the topwater bite. He recommends Clousers and streamers. Most of the flies he ties are underwater patterns because he says there are so many good poppers on the market.

Popping bugs are good for a couple of months out of the year and early and late into the fall but for the day in day out, all day long fishing, flyfishers need to be able to vary the fly fishing presentation.

The marinas at Fork don't have a lot of information for fly fishing but there is no substitute for local knowledge about what is working. Woodruff says he has learned through the years at Fork that it pays to pay attention to what is happening with the soft plastic lures because he suspects the color preference is a function of water clarity and quality at a given time at Fork.

"If black / blue lizards are working, I will pull out that Lake Fork Leech with the blue tail if what I am using is not working," Woodruff says. He says he ties a lot of flies that will fill in niches that are filled by conventional lures.

A productive method at Fork in February and early March is to work a Rattletrap over the grass flats and let it kick the top of the grass. To fill that niche, Woodruff says he designed the Swamp Rabbit fly. It has a rattle in it, and he can swim it over the top of the grass. "It is a real effective pattern in an area I wasn't capitalizing on in fly fishing."

A bass boat is a good platform for fly fishing if there is a deck and all the fittings are recessed. Float tubes, kayaks and pontoon boats also work well at Fork, but tubers should be careful to avoid stickups which might have exposed hooks from the thousands of misdirected artificial lures that end up on submerged structures.

The biggest advantage in using kayaks and small watercraft is that they are low to the water and extremely stealthy, but that is also their biggest drawback because it is difficult to see the fish.

A big advantage of having a small watercraft on Fork and on other east Texas lakes is that there are many access points for launching them off county roads. Often the road bed is a good fish holding feature because it is a hump running out into a clear area.

Rules of the "road" for Lake Fork.

Everybody has big bass in mind when they go to Lake Fork and there is no shortage of shoreline structure to fish. But Woodruff says it is impossible to cover the water with fly rods as thoroughly as someone can do it with conventional tackle. He recommends flyfishers be selective in their casts. "Fork has 28,000 acres and all of it looks bassy", Woodruff says. "It is covered with timber and there are moss beds and other structure."

Lake Fork Strategies

A general rule is that in late February and March anglers should go as far north and west as possible on any East Texas reservoir because the water will warm faster on those shores. The northwest side is exposed to the sun during the day and will warm up relatively quickly. The second thing to look for, Woodruff says, is slightly stained water, which will warm faster because the particles will absorb the solar radiation. A third feature in addition to a feature on the northwest side in slightly stained water would be a hill or swale on the bank that protects the stretch of water from a cold front. Under these conditions, the warmer water will draw the baitfish and if the bass are thinking about spawning, they will be pulled toward those shorelines.

In the spring, Woodruff says he tries to find 53 degree water, and it is remarkable how much the water temperature can vary on the lake. It might be 53 degrees on one part of the lake and 60 degrees on the northwest side the same day.

Another tip-off to warmer water are coves that have a lot of turtle activity, Woodruff says. They are cold blooded and are dormant at temperatures below 50 degrees but get out and move around more in warmer coves. The coves that have more activity will be warming faster, he says.

An ideal feature in March would be a point off a fence row near a spawning creek. This provides cover and protection to the bass along with a variation in depth that they can move up and down with changes in water temperature and barometric pressure. Any cover like cattails is also a plus, Woodruff says.

Water gap fence extensions are a good place to fly fish, Woodruff says. "Anywhere there is a water gap, you can bet that before the lake was built, there was a fence line extending out into the lake. You can find the line of trees and line up with them and make long parallel casts," he says. This feature will provide good cover for bass and it allows the fly fisher to work a fly from six inches deep to 10 feet deep in one cast. The bass will be moving up and down that feature in the early spring based on the barometric pressure until they find a comfort zone.

Lake Fork fly fisher Charles Ducote says he likes to avoid the open water on the north side of the lake, which can take the brunt of the wind and turn rough. But he says he can launch on the side of the lake near the intersection of Texas 514 and Texas 2946 and find protected shorelines. He finds protection from the prevailing south wind on Fork by fishing in the Mustang Creek area.

Fly Patterns Effective on Lake Fork

Fly patterns effective on Lake Fork mimic the threadfin, gizzard shad and sunfish that make up the main forage for largemouth and other predator species in the lake. Woodruff says effective subsurface shad imitations include mylar Minnows, Clouser Minnows, and streamers in combinations of gray, white, silver, and chartreuse.

Selection of bass flies for Lake Fork.

"There is no such thing as too much Flashabou or Krystal Flash in a Lake Fork fly," Woodruff notes. "So add plenty to any pattern you tie."

Woodruff says one of his most effective subsurface fly patterns on Lake Fork is his '57 Chevy Bugger, a Woolly Bugger tied on a size 4 or 6 hook with a tail of gray marabou and pearl Krystal Flash, a silver-tinsel chenille body, and light-blue dun hackle. He says the fly looks flashy in the water and is quick and easy to tie, an important quality in flies used on a lake with so many fly-snagging features.

For topwater action on Fork, Woodruff recommends shad-imitating Dahlberg Divers, poppers (both in deer hair and foam), and sliders-all tied in the same colors-(gray, white, silver, and chartreuse) as the wet flies. The Cypert foil-covered balsa poppers also are effective on Lake Fork bass when they are attacking shad on the surface, Woodruff says.

The Nix Woolhead, Whitlock's Sheep, Zonkers and a sunfish-pattern Dahlberg Diver are among Woodruff's favorite subsurface sunfish imitations.

If flies in the more natural colors are not working on a given day, Woodruff switches to bright colors. "On days when the shad and bream patterns are not doing the trick, I go to a red-and-orange version of Dan Blanton's Punch Fly or my own Swamp Rabbit for subsurface presentations, or a red Ric McNulty Twitch Fly for fishing on top."

Woodruff ties his Swamp Rabbit pattern on a size 2/0 Mustad 3366 or 3366B hook. He uses half of a Stanley Jigs Pro Trailer with rattle unit or a large Wapsi Fly Tail for the tail of the fly. Red rabbit fur strips make up the body and 1/36-ounce lead dumbbell eyes are tied in at the hook eye.

The I.C. Fly, another effective Lake Fork streamer fly designed by Woodruff is tied on a size 2/0 Mustad 3366. For eyes, Woodruff uses 1/36 ounce dumbbells with silver 1/8 inch stick-on eyes. One half of a spinner bait replacement skirt or 40 strands of Wapsi Sili legs is used for the tail. For the body, Woodruff matches colors of a chenille underbody with a large Ice Chenille or Estaz over wrap.

Seasonal Options at Lake Fork

Woodruff believes the fall months of October, November and the first few weeks of December are usually the best times to fly fish on Lake Fork. "While the fall may not offer as many double-digit bass, it more than makes up for it with the best topwater action of the year and less crowded conditions," Woodruff says. It is this time of year, as the water begins to cool, that bass begin moving into open coves, flats, and the backs of creeks, chasing the dense schools of shad that congregate in these areas. Bass begin to prowl the edges of weed beds, keying on the sunfish that are holding there. "These behavioral patterns are the keys for the fall fly fisherman (on Fork)," Woodruff says.

A good fall strategy for flyfishers, is to begin the day probing the edges of weed beds with a topwater fly such as a deer-hair popper. As the sun gets higher, he recommends switching to a diver type fly, or moving onto an adjacent flat to prospect for suspended fish. If suspended bass are located on a fish finder, a Clouser Minnow pattern fished at the appropriate depth will draw strikes. All the while, Woodruff says, anglers should keep an eye out for the activity that erupts when schools of bass drive shad to the surface. When fish are breaking the surface, s he uses a trolling motor to ease into casting range with shad-colored surface flies.

Schooling largemouth on Lake Fork are not always the typical 1- to 2-pound school fish found on other large lakes. "They could just as easily be 4- to 5-pounders, with a few larger fish thrown in," he says. "These larger bass often hang underneath the schools, vacuuming up crippled shad fluttering down from the melee on the surface." Woodruff says an effective means of targeting the largest bass in a school is to try to drop a weighted fly through the surface-feeding fish to the bigger fish lurking below.

Lake Fork also has a yellow bass run. They are a forage fish for bass and also a predator fish because they eat shad. They tend to concentrate in deeper water so flyfishers don't always encounter them when fishing shoreline structure.

Deepwater Fly Fishing at Lake Fork

Woodruff says he also targets bass in deep water with uniform density sinking lines. During some times of the year the strategy is to fish poppers early and late in the day and go to the deep water in between.

Boaters Take Caution

Woodruff cautions flyfishers and other anglers that Lake Fork can become extremely rough on windy days and during storms. And like on other large lakes and reservoirs in Texas, almost every year Lake Fork claims the lives of boaters who did not heed the warnings and stayed out in hazardous conditions.

Anglers on Lake Fork should also learn the waters they are fishing and always keep boats at manageable and prudent speeds. "Shops that repair fiberglass and motors do a brisk business patching up boats that have encountered the standing and floating timber in the lake," Woodruff says. "When you're going 60 miles an hour, a collision with an oak tree the size of a bus may do more than damage the lower unit."

Beef Up Tackle for Lake Fork Largemouth

Woodruff has taken largemouth up to 11 pounds 8 oz. on fly tackle on Lake fork but he says fish in the 5.5 to 6.5 pounds range are a better fight on fly rods because they can still get out of the water. He says he has caught a 9 pounds 4 oz. this year and fish in this class are strong but they kind of wallow around.

Woodruff recommends scaling up the fly tackle when hunting Lake Fork bass in heavy cover. He says he had a client hook "an honest 10 pounds fish" on a recent Lake Fork outing and the loop connector came off the fly line. "We are in that heavy cover and heavy hydrilla and so it is not delicate work," Woodruff says. "I throw 9 weight rods and use a seven and a half foot, 20 pounds straight piece of Stren Super Tough as a leader." He says he prefers knotless leaders because every blood knot in a leader can collect moss.

Largemouth caught on large crawfish fly pattern, Lake Fork.

Woodruff says sunfish are a bonus for flyfishers at Lake Fork especially in the fall. "Flyfishers can catch redear sunfish all day long and very few other anglers even know they are there," he says, adding that he is learning how to catch the big ones consistently.

Seasonal Patterns at Lake Fork

After a cold front comes through, bass that were holing on the points the day before when the temperature was 72 do not disappear, they stay in the area, Woodruff says. When the temperature drops, he recommends looking for a nearby creek channel or depression. "They will be sluggish and you will have to knock them on the head to get a bite, but if you know where they are and you keep putting the fly in there, they will come around."

In late March and April, largemouth at Lake Fork will start moving back into the main creeks where they spawn. They will spawn on the west side of the lake because that is where they find warmer water temperatures. Woodruff says this is a good time to fish because the big females tend to hang out in the creek channels. "They are still eating and they are aggressive," Woodruff says. "You have the males doing their 'race tracking,' staking out the territory where they are going to nest, swimming over an elliptical path. They are particularly territorial. At that time bream and lizard patterns really pull the trigger on them. They don't like those in that area." To exploit this behavior, Woodruff says flyfishers should throw fly patterns like Lefty's Deceivers with a weed guard added. He adds olive grizzly feather on top and an orange belly to create a sunfish imitation. "The male bass will unload on it," Woodruff says.

Woodruff says the big female bass will prefer something that is more like a lizard. The Lake Fork Leech tied by Woodruff in black to imitate a water dog is a very effective pattern under these conditions.

Later in the year as the water begins to warm, Woodruff suggests anglers look for any kind of depression off the main lake. These will begin to hold bass and the fish will begin to bed when the water hits 58 to 60 degrees.

Ethical Considerations During The Spawn

It is at this time when flyfishers have to deal with ethical considerations. Bedded bass are easy to catch. Woodruff admits that if can be fun to sight fish for these, wide-bodied targets but the problem at Lake Fork is that if one angler does it, another 14 anglers might catch that fish during the same day and stress out a big female. "A big fish is a proven producer and has proven genetics to get big, so the effect would be to cull off the top of the big bass crop by stressing these fish," Woodruff says. "It is a vulnerable time, it is a time when the practice could hurt the bass population five years down the road." Woodruff also points out that every time a bedded fish is pulled off a nest, every sunfish and crawfish in the neighborhood has an all-you-can-eat buffet while that bass is not guarding the bed.

Woodruff says he does not condone nor does he fish for bedded fish at the time that they are on the beds. He says that on Lake Fork and other big reservoirs in Texas, the spawn proceeds from the north to the south and if anglers know the water, they will never have to target bedded fish.

Targeting Pre-Spawn Bass on Lake Fork

The pre-spawn fish are aggressive and an angler is not hurting them by catching them, Woodruff says. And if anglers stay south of the spawn, they can stay on fish all the way down to the dam in May at Lake Fork. The same applies in April when anglers can "jump back over the band of spawning fish" and get to the post-spawn fish that are hungry and have recuperated.

So anglers don't have to catch the spawning fish, Woodruff says. He points out that casting to bedded fish is not really angling. "If you dropped a white rock or marble in the nest, the female or the male guarding the nest will pick it up and move it," Woodruff. "You are not fishing, the bass are just cleaning their House."

The Post-spawn Period

During the post-spawn period, the bass will move out into the middle of the creeks and to humps in the middle of the lake. Woodruff says this is the time of the year to use an electronic fish finder to locate suspended fish. "Around the full moon in May, you can find fish suspended in about 9 feet of water." The strategy is to count down a baitfish pattern and keep working it in that depth zone. "They will not come up and hit a popper at that time, and they probably will not dive down and hit something on the bottom, but if you put the fly right in their zone, they will eat it eventually." Woodruff says the bass are in a recovery period at this time. "They have done their spawning for the year, but it is a good time to catch a big fish."

Late Spring Conditions

In early spring, flyfishers look for the warmest water on the lake. Later in the spring, mid-May into June, the strategy is to find the coolest water. That is when overhead cover becomes important. This can be a boat house. Woodruff notes that Lake Fork is not a lake where anglers can "make a living" throwing flies at every boat house. He says it is important to find a boat house that has some other feature associated with it such as a small creek nearby or some type of bottom contour to attract fish. The same applies to docks. Look for docks near areas with other attractive features.

Woodruff says that with a little practice fly fishers can develop a skip cast-a firm chopping motion at a 45 degree angle -and skip a fly seven or eight feet back up under the dock and put it where no one else has put a lure.

Maps of Lake Fork can be obtained from Fishing Hot Spots, (800) ALL-MAPS; A.I.D. Associates, (800) AID-MAPS, and Kingfisher Maps, (800) 326-0257.

Flyfisher with Lake Fork bass.

Boat docks hold large-mouths and provide targets for flyfishers on Lake Fork and other East Texas Lakes.

Flyfisher with Lake Fork bass.

ELLISON CREEK RESERVOIR (LONE STAR LAKE)

Located eight miles south of Daingerfield in Morris County, this 1,516-acre lake was created as a water supply for a private industrial user. The lake has been stocked with Florida-strain largemouth and hybrid striped bass, but flyfishers might wish to target the healthy population of bluegill and redear sunfish that build beds along its sandy shorelines in the spring.

The lake gets light fishing pressure and there is boat access for a fee at private fishing camps.

LAKE O' THE PINES

A northeast Texas reservoir, Lake O' the Pines covers 18,700 acres, has an average depth of 14 feet and is surrounded by 138 miles of shoreline. Named after the tall pine-hardwood forests that border the reservoir, the lake is a prime destination for largemouth bass and also holds spotted bass, white bass, yellow bass, white and black crappie, chain pickerel and sunfish. Florida-strain bass were introduced into the lake in the early 1980s.

In the spring, the lily pad field surrounding the lake can be very productive for flyfishers. Effective fly patterns around the lilypads include black Dahlberg Divers, deer hair frogs and chartreuse poppers.

Flyfishers should also target weed beds next to creek channels. An ideal scenario is to fish a black or chartreuse diver over the tops of weed beds that are one to two feet beneath the surface. An alternative tactic is to use a bottom bouncing rabbit strip fly fished down the deep edge of the weed line. Whitlock's Eelworm streamer is an effective pattern for this approach.

The upper end of the lake has a variety of channels that meander around dozens of small islands, providing a variety of fish holding features. Flyfishers using large nymph patterns and Woolly Buggers will take redear sunfish holding near the intersections of the channels.

Chain pickerel provide exciting fly fishing action on Lake O' the Pines. A white Deceiver fished on the edge of a weed bed will often entice a savage strike from this smaller cousin of the northern pike.

Lake facilities include four modern campgrounds with a total of 245 RV and 125 tent sites. There are nine commercial boat ramps as well as several commercial operations that provide camping facilities.

Willow Point Marina on the upper part of the lake offers cabins, campsites and rental boats. The Willow Point area provides launch access for canoes, kayaks and other small watercraft to fish a prime area of the lake. For information on Willow Point Marina, contact Jack Hudson at (214) 775-2912.

For more information on Lake O' The Pines, contact the Texas Parks and Wildlife Department Inland Fisheries Field Office, 3802 East End Blvd., Marshall, Texas 75670. (903) 938-1007 or contact the Lake O' the Pines Chamber of Commerce, P.O. Box 648, Jefferson, TX 75657. (903) 665-3229.

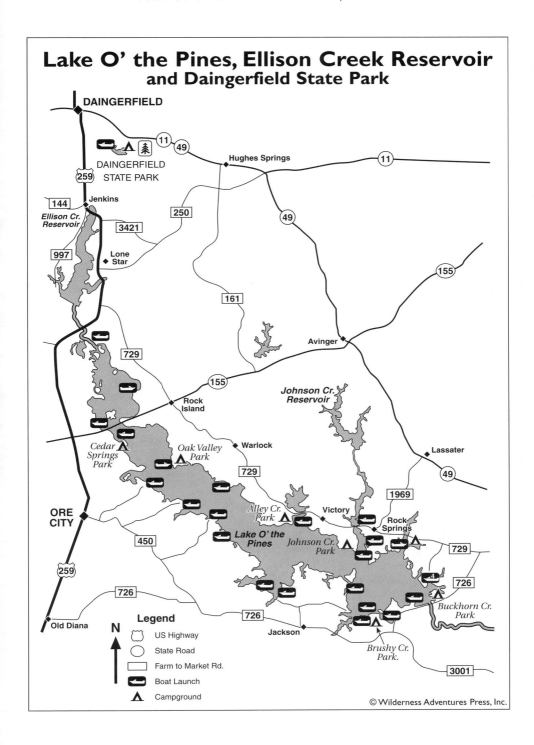

Lake O' the Pines, Ellison Creek Reservoir
and Daingerfield State Park

DAINGERFIELD

11
49

Hughes Springs

11

DAINGERFIELD
STATE PARK

259

Jenkins

144

Ellison Cr.
Reservoir

250

49

3421

Lone
Star

997

155

161

Avinger

729

155

Johnson Cr.
Reservoir

Rock
Island

Cedar
Springs
Park

Oak Valley
Park

Warlock

Lassater

49

729

1969

ORE
CITY

Alley Cr.
Park

Victory

Rock
Springs

Lake O' the
Pines

Johnson Cr.
Park

729

450

4

726

259

726

Buckhorn Cr.
Park

Old Diana

726

Jackson

Brushy Cr.
Park.

3001

Legend

N

US Highway

State Road

Farm to Market Rd.

Boat Launch

Campground

© Wilderness Adventures Press, Inc.

CADDO LAKE

The largest natural lake in Texas, Caddo Lake is located in the Lower Cypress Bayou Basin on the northeast Texas-Louisiana border. It offers flyfishers a chance at a diverse number of game fish including largemouth, spotted bass, crappie, white and yellow bass, sunfish, chain pickerel and catfish in a beautiful setting amid thick stands of moss-draped bald cypress. Seventy species of fish have been documented in the Lower Cypress Bayou Basin.

Caddo is a cypress swamp with relatively shallow water, which makes it especially attractive for fly fishing. The cypress trees form islands that provide areas protected from the wind that are excellent for fly fishing. If the wind is blowing out of the south, the prevailing wind on Caddo, anglers can fish the north side. And if the wind is blowing hard on the main lake, the back side of the lake offers protection.

Much of the lake's 30,000 acres are made up of twisting bayous and sloughs that wander through inundated, moss-draped cypress swamps and bottom land hardwoods. On Caddo, a drab looking bayou in winter turns into a lush green display of aquatic and terrestrial vegetation in the spring. White and yellow water lilies cover the lake in the summer and the lake explodes in brilliant colors in the East Texas fall.

Fishing around the flooded bald cypress trees and aquatic vegetation can be productive for largemouth during fall, winter and spring.

Big Cypress Bayou offers opportunities for bass fishing during the summer months when aquatic vegetation reduces fishing access on the main lake.

Florida-strain largemouth bass were successfully introduced in the lake in 1981 and 1982, and double digit fish have been caught by anglers since the late 1980s.

Kentucky spotted bass, the smaller but hard fighting cousin of the largemouth, are present in good numbers in Big Cypress Bayou above Caddo Lake. They are differentiated from largemouth bass by the rows of spots below the lateral band. In addition, the tongue of the spotted bass has the texture of sandpaper compared to the smooth tongue of the largemouth bass.

Texas Parks and Wildlife Department says the spotted bass generally spawn earlier than largemouth bass, with peak activity occurring in late February and early March. They also tend to prefer deeper water than largemouth. Spotted bass weighing in excess of 5 pounds have been caught from the Big Cypress system.

Caddo holds large numbers of bluegill, redear sunfish and warmouth (goggle-eye). Texas Parks and Wildlife biologists say the best time to fish for sunfish is from late spring through early summer. Look for action around inundated cypress breaks, duck blinds and boat docks as well as around submerged vegetation.

White bass, called sand bass locally, and yellow bass, called bar fish, are also present in good numbers in Caddo Lake. Peak fishing for these species occurs from January through April as they begin their migration upstream in conjunction with spawning. Flyfishers can find white bass and yellow bass in Big Cypress Bayou (Upper and Lower Government Ditches and the mouth of Black Cypress Bayou) and in the main lake (Devil's elbow, Alligator Bayou, and Britt's Gap). White bass are also frequently found schooling on the surface of the main lake during the summer and the fall.

White crappie and black crappie are part of the mixed bag of freshwater species in Caddo Lake. Quality fish in the ten-inch range are abundant, say Parks and Wildlife officials. Peak fishing for crappie occurs from winter through spring in conjunction with spawning. The fish begin to congregate in deeper water, 15 feet or more, in December and January in Big Cypress Bayou above the lake and Alligator Bayou within Caddo Lake. During this time, they will feed actively in preparation for spawning. As water temperatures begin to warm in the late winter and early spring, the crappie will migrate into shallower water and begin to spawn. During the spring, flyfishers should target them with lead-eyed Clouser Deep Minnow patterns in white, yellow and chartreuse around isolated stands of cypress trees in the main lake.

Chain pickerel are also common in the lower Cypress River drainage and Caddo Lake, according to Parks and Wildlife officials. A smaller but aggressive cousin of the northern pike, this fish is most active in winter and early spring with the onset of spawning. Their preferred habitat at Caddo includes aquatic vegetation, and they will typically lay motionless along the edge of these weed beds to ambush baitfish. Anglers fishing Caddo Lake have taken chain pickerel weighing in excess of four pounds.

Boating access to Caddo Lake is available at the Caddo Lake State Park and many fishing camps bordering the lake. Several of these privately owned camps are located in the community of Uncertain. Lodging also is available in the communities of Jefferson and Marshall approximately 20 miles away.

Caddo Lake State Park and Wildlife Management Area located on Big Cypress Bayou upstream from the lake, provides camping, canoe rental, picnicking, hiking and nature trails, and bank fishing. A variety of campsites, including screened shelters and cabins, are available but advance reservations are required. For information contact the park superintendent, Caddo Lake State Park, Route 2, Box 15, Karnak, TX 75661. (903) 679-3351. For information about lodging in the area, contact the Marshall Chamber of Commerce, 213 W. Austin St., Marshall, Texas 75670, (903) 935-7868 or the Jefferson Chamber of Commerce, 116 W. Austin St., Jefferson, TX. 75657, (903) 665-2672.

Dallas fly fisher Charles Ducote, who has fished this lake frequently, says fishing around cypress trees on Lake Caddo is totally different than fishing the trees at Toledo Bend, for example. He says this is because different parts of a tree form different parts of structure. "With (Caddo) and the cypresses, you have the doughnut and the cypress knees and then grass and then lily pads creating four or five different types of structure. So it gets difficult to fish, but an angler can spend all day fishing a very small area."

Caddo is a big lake but it is well protected against the wind. In 1982, Florida bass were stocked in the lake and now it holds some monsters in the 10-12 pound class.

At Caddo Lake flyfishers can not only catch bass, sunfish and crappie but also the pickerel, called pike or jackfish in East Texas and Louisiana. "They are not only

Caddo Lake
and Caddo Lake State Park

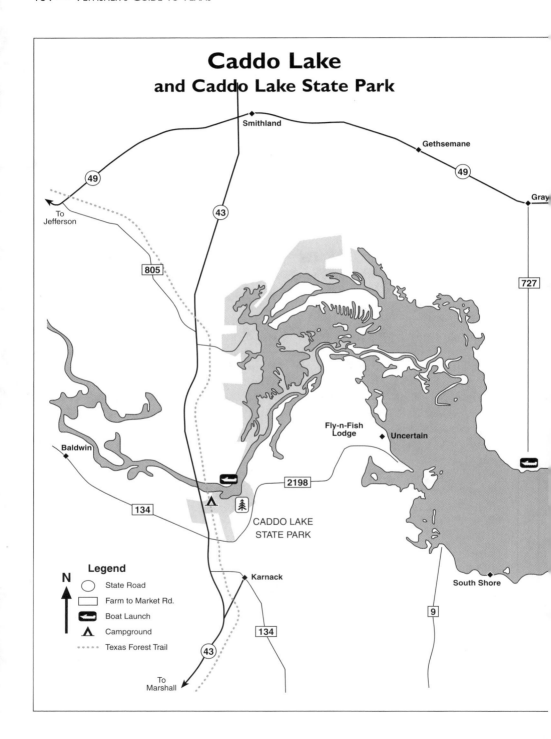

Smithland

Gethsemane

49

49

Gray

To
Jefferson

43

805

727

Baldwin

Fly-n-Fish
Lodge

Uncertain

2198

134

CADDO LAKE
STATE PARK

South Shore

Legend

N

State Road
Farm to Market Rd.
Boat Launch
Campground
Texas Forest Trail

Karnack

9

134

43

To
Marshall

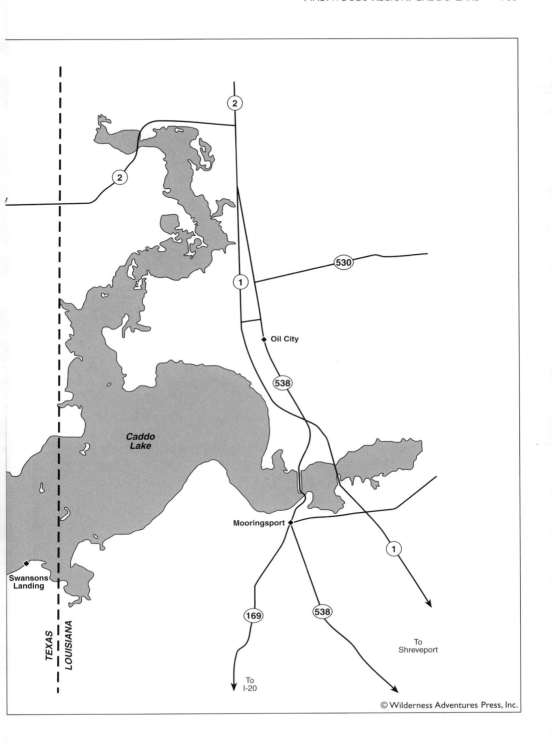

© Wilderness Adventures Press, Inc.

a lot of fun but will drive you crazy when you find them in the deep grass," Ducote says.

Ducote notes that the easiest access points to Caddo Lake are north of Shreveport via US 71. The part of the lake on the Texas side, which has a state park, is very heavy with grass, Ducote says. "After June or July it can be tough to navigate a boat through the grass in some areas," he says, adding that there are areas on the Louisiana side that are more open, have less grass, and are more accessible. Anglers can fish either side of the lake with either a Texas or Louisiana fishing license.

The area called James Bayou (on the North Fork, which is primarily in Louisiana) is full of oil rigs and cypress trees and is excellent fishing for bass and pike.

A good map is necessary for visitors to Lake Caddo, Ducote says, because the boatways are clearly marked but if the angler gets off track, there is the risk of encountering submerged cypress trees that might be a half million years old that can take the bottom out of a boat. So despite the hazards, there are safe access points, including those at the boat ramp by the dam, near the community of Mooringsport, Louisiana which is accessed north of I-20 on Louisiana 169.

On the Texas side of the lake, there is also an access point on the west side of the lake in Harrison County off of Texas (FM) 9 north of Waskom.

Bass boats, johnboats, kayaks and canoes all work well on Caddo Lake. Because the prevailing wind on Caddo is out of the south, Ducote says the entire southern shoreline normally is protected from the wind and can be fished effectively from small watercraft. The James Bayou area on the east side of the North Fork is protected from the wind and offers a number of launch ramps.

Largemouth are the primary target on Caddo but there are many varieties of sunfish as well as "jackfish." These chain pickerel, average about 2.5 to 3 pounds but can get up to around 5 pounds and are ferocious and acrobatic fighters that are fun to take on topwater flies.

In the fall months, when the water begins to cool, the bass and the pike get competitive for food. The optimum time to target pike is during these fall months when the water temperature drops down into the low 60s; the pike are active and the bass are feeding for the winter. During this time, Dahlberg Divers and other hair bugs tied with inverted hooks make it easier for flyfishers to work around the lily pads and grass on the lake.

Spring is also a good time to fish Caddo, Ducote says, but the weather is not quite as stable as it is in the fall.

Flyfishers have a chance at landing a double digit bass on Caddo Lake in the heavy cover as well as finding good numbers of schooling bass in the 2.5 to 3.5 pound class. "If you go to Lake Caddo and put on a little yellow sponge spider, you are going to catch 20 to 30 fish in an afternoon," Ducote says.

Caddo Lake State Park

Located on the west side of Caddo Lake, Caddo Lake State Park sits in a lush setting of magnolia, oak, and loblolly pine. The 7,090-acre park offers anglers excellent access to the upper end of the 32,700-care lake and its maze of bayous, sloughs and ponds. The park provides cabins, campgrounds, picnic areas, canoe rentals, a fishing pier and boat ramp. For additional information, contact the park at (903) 679-3351. To get to the park, take Texas 43 east from Marshall and turn right (east) on Texas (FM) 2198 north of Karnack.

LAKE HOLBROOK

Located on Keyes Creek two miles northwest of Mineola off Texas (FM) 1799 in Wood County, Lake Holbrook attracts only modest boat traffic and offers flyfishers opportunities for action with Florida-strain largemouth, crappie and sunfish. This 1,050 acre lake has a variety of fishable habitat including shoreline vegetation, flooded timber and riprap around the dam.

LAKE GLADEWATER

Situated on two small creeks, Lake Gladewater can be reached north of Interstate 20 in Gregg and Upshur counties. The lake offers clear water and excellent habitat for bass bugging along shoreline vegetation. Stockings in the lake over the last 30 years include Florida-strain and native-northern largemouth, yellow-striped bass hybrids and redbreast sunfish. Shoreline access is limited by private homes but there is a boat ramp and fishing pier where johnboats, canoes and kayaks can be launched to fish this 700-acre lake.

BRANDY BRANCH RESERVOIR

This 1,242-acre power plant cooling reservoir located in Harrison County between Marshall and Longview has been stocked with Florida-strain largemouth, black and white crappie, coppernose and readear sunfish. Flyfishers will find this an excellent lake for sunfish action, especially in the spring. There are no camping facilities on the lake but there is a public boat ramp on the southeast side of the lake.

For current information about lake conditions, contact the Texas Parks and Wildlife Department at (903) 938-1007. To get to Brandy Branch Reservoir, take US west of Marshall, turn south on Loop 390 and then turn left (south) on Texas (FM) 3251, which leads to the lake.

LAKE STRIKER

This 2,400-acre lake, formerly known as Striker Creek Reservoir, is located 18 miles southwest of Henderson in Cherokee and Rusk counties. It is known to hold a high percentage of Florida-strain largemouth due to stockings dating back to 1976. Other species present include hybrid striped bass, crappie and sunfish. Fish-holding features include flooded timber in the middle and upper end of the lake. This lake doesn't seem to get the higher angler traffic of the better know area lakes like Lake Palestine and Sam Rayburn.

There is a marina and launch ramp on the property and picnic grounds for day use. To get to Lake Striker, take US 79 east from Jacksonville or southwest from Henderson. For updated information on fishing conditions and lake levels, contact the Texas Parks and Wildlife office in Tyler at (903) 566-2161.

Lake Hawkins

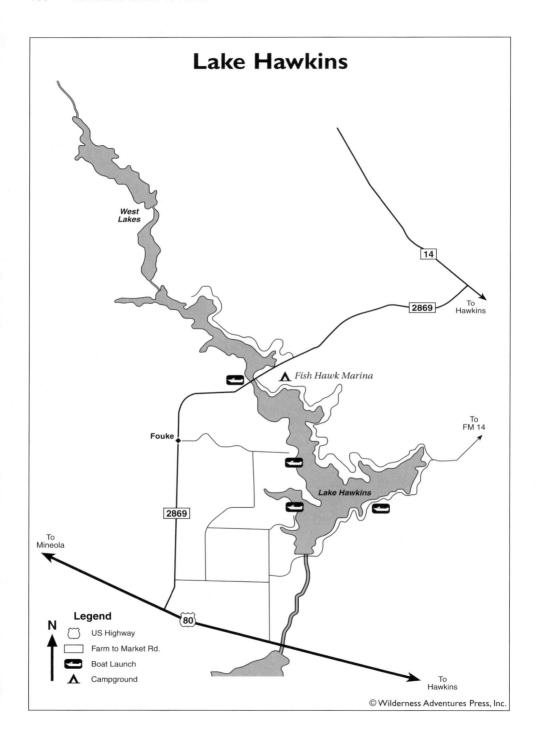

West
Lakes

14

2869   To
Hawkins

Fish Hawk Marina

To
FM 14

Fouke

Lake Hawkins

2869

To
Mineola

80

Legend

N

US Highway

Farm to Market Rd.

Boat Launch

Campground

To
Hawkins

© Wilderness Adventures Press, Inc.

LAKE HAWKINS

Located 100 miles east of Dallas between the towns of Hawkins and Mineola, just north of Texas 80, 776-acre Lake Hawkins offers flyfishers a shot at largemouth, spotted bass, crappie, sunfish and chain pickerel. Hawkins is not thought of as a "trophy" bass lake like nearby Lake Fork but anglers routinely catch largemouth in the five-pound range, and the lake record is in double figures. The lake is attractive to flyfishers because it is virtually ignored by the fleets of bass boats and pleasure craft found on most of the larger East Texas reservoirs. "Unless you are there on a big weekend in the summer when you have skiers and pleasure boaters, there is not much activity," says Steve Poarch, a Texas Parks and Wildlife official. "There are just a few that fish it regularly."

Campsites are available at the Wood County RV Park located 13 miles east of Mineola on US 80. For information call (903) 769-4545.

VAN CITY LAKE

Located at the community of Van on the border between Smith and Van Zant counties off Texas 110, this small lake offers excellent fly fishing for largemouth and sunfish from a small boat, kayak or float tube.

Heavily flooded timber, typical of many Piney Woods lakes.

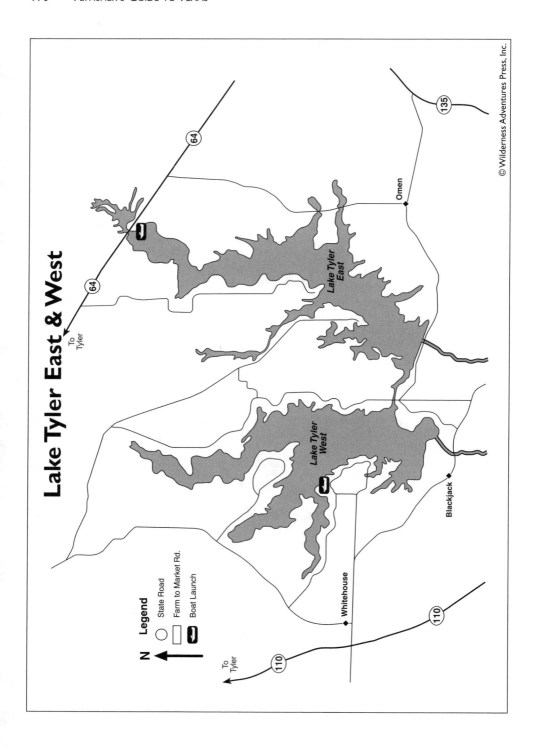

Lake Tyler East & West

© Wilderness Adventures Press, Inc.

LAKE TYLER EAST AND WEST

These twin lakes are located in Smith County about eight miles east of Tyler off Texas (FM) 346. The two lakes are connected. Lake Tyler East is 2,530 acres and was impounded in 1968 and Lake Tyler West at 2,450 acres, was impounded in 1951.

There are a number of city parks at Lake Tyler West that provide access to the water. Lake Tyler East offers three launch ramps. There are excellent features on both lakes for prospecting by flyfishers, says Richard Ott, TPWD biologist. He says the East Lake in particular has a lot of vegetation that holds fish. In addition to largemouth, the East Lake has an excellent population of redear sunfish, with Olman Cove a hot spot.

These lakes can be fished from float tubes but there are times when the jet ski activity makes it impractical near open water. Recent TPWD samplings have found chain pickerel in these lakes, which provide another target for flyfishers.

LAKE BELLWOOD

Located about five miles west of Tyler off Texas 64, this 170-acre lake, which formerly supplied water for Tyler, has an excellent bass and sunfish population. Very lightly fished, it is a perfect lake for float tubes.

MARTIN CREEK LAKE

Located between Carthage and Henderson on a tributary of the Sabine River, Martin Creek Lake can be reached off Texas (FM) 2658 in Rusk and Panola counties. Double digit largemouth have been caught out of this lake around flooded timber and shoreline vegetation. Other species available to fly rodders are hybrid striped bass, redbreast sunfish and walleye pike. A nearby state park has day use facilities for launching boats and picnicking.

Martin Creek Lake State Park

The community of Mt. Pleasant, located 12 miles northeast of Martin Creek Lake State Park, refers to itself the bass capital of Texas. There is a $2 entrance fee at the park, $4 for primitive backpack camping and $9 for a campsite with water / electricity hookup. Shelters are $12 with a maximum of eight people. For information, write to Lake Bob Sandlin State Park, Route 5, Box 224, Pittsburg, Texas, 75686, (903) 572-5531

LAKE PALESTINE

Located on the Neches River, southeast of Tyler, Lake Palestine is a long, narrow waterway bisected by Texas 155. In addition to largemouth action, the lake offers flyfishers opportunities for double-digit hybrid striped bass.

East Texas fly fishing guide Robert Woodruff says he targets hybrid striped bass with uniform density sinking lines with baitfish patterns when they can be located. In the winter months, he looks for birds to indicate hybrids on the surface, and he then works poppers on the surface or streamers just under the surface. He advises flyfishers to approach these schools cautiously and not motor up to them. "Use a trolling motor and approach from above the school and don't cast right in the middle of the school because it will put them down," he says.

Richard Ott, the Texas Parks and Wildlife Department biologist who oversees the fisheries management at Lake Palestine, says most of the hybrid striper action takes place from the Villages Marina to the south, and the biggest concentrations are due south of the Texas 155 Bridge, adjacent to the mouth of Saline Bay. Another good area that attracts fish is at the mouth of Chimney Creek, which is down near the dam. Vegetation has been limited in recent years, which means anglers hunting largemouth must look for them in the back ends of coves. The Highsaw Ledbetter coves, north of the Texas 155 Bridge are good areas for largemouth.

LAKE MURVAUL

Located on Murvaul Creek 7 miles southeast of Carthage off Texas 1970 in Panola County, this 3,800-acre lake is stocked with Florida-strain and native-northern large-mouth, crappie and sunfish. There is a county park with a picnic area and overnight campground.

LAKE JACKSONVILLE

Fed by Gum Creek in the Neches River drainage, Lake Jacksonville is located on Texas (FM) 747 southwest of Jacksonville in Cherokee County. The 1,352-acre lake provides a clear water habitat for a variety of game fish including Florida-strain and native-northern largemouth, hybrid striped bass and crappie. It can be more difficult for fly fishers than most East Texas lakes for because most of its prime habitat is in deep water, but it can also be excellent for shoreline topwater bass bug action in the fall.

LAKE NACOGDOCHES

This 2,200-acre lake is located on a tributary of the Angelina River west of Nacogdoches on Texas (FM) 225. Fishing the edges of flooded weed beds with deer hair and hard-bodied poppers can attract the attention of the local largemouth population.

Lake Palestine

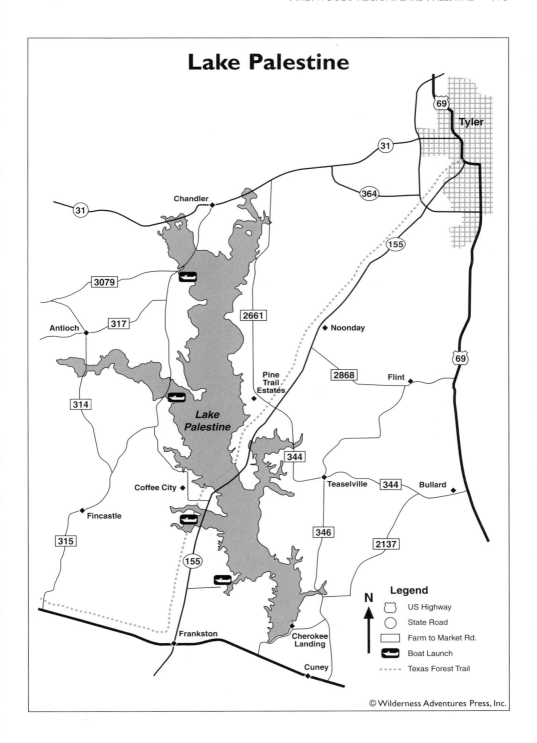

Tyler

Chandler

Antioch

Noonday

Pine Trail Estates

Flint

Lake Palestine

Coffee City

Teaselville

Bullard

Fincastle

Frankston

Cherokee Landing

Cuney

Legend

N

US Highway
State Road
Farm to Market Rd.
Boat Launch
Texas Forest Trail

© Wilderness Adventures Press, Inc.

TOLEDO BEND

A 185,000-acre lake, which lies on the Sabine River at the Louisiana border just northeast of Jasper, Toledo Bend offers flyfishers clear water, flooded timber and aquatic grasses along 1,200 miles of shoreline.

One of the most famous destinations in the country for largemouth bass fishing, Toledo Bend also is a haven for large sunfish and crappie. It is considered by many to be the best lake in the state for "bull" bluegill.

Both the Texas Parks and Wildlife Department and the Louisiana Department of Wildlife and Fisheries have stocked Florida-strain largemouth in the lake over the years. Prespawn action begins in February as the largemouth stage along creek channels or move into shallow coves or the edges of weed beds. During the summer months, throwing deer hair or hard-bodied bugs into weed pockets can produce explosive fly fishing action.

East Texas flyfishers Chuck Uzzle and Ronnie Robison say they have found excellent opportunities for fly fishing on the southernmost end of Toledo Bend Reservoir from the Hemphill community south, at launch ramps off Texas 87.

Robison says favorite access points are at 944 Park, Sandy Creek, and Housen Bend- lightly traveled areas of the lake that offer a number of coves to prospect. "No matter what the weather is, you can find a place to fly fish," Robison says. "I have taken six- and seven-pound bass out of those coves."

Indian Creek on the extreme south end of the lake off of Texas 255 is pockmarked with coves and is another good destination for fly fishing, Uzzle says. He says there are a number of "neighborhood launch ramps" in the area that provide easy access to these shorelines.

When it comes to waters in the southern part of the Pineywoods Region, Robison says that the 944 Park at Toledo Bend would be his first choice for a large bass on a fly rod. Uzzle says he would also choose Toledo Bend if the target is large bass.

Robison recommends flyfishers throw patterns that imitate or simulate leeches. A Zonker or black Woolly Bugger on a size 2 hook is an ideal choice for fishing the variety of structure on Toledo Bend, he says.

Both Louisiana and Texas have conducted stocking programs in the lake and Florida-strain bass were added to the mix in the mid- 1980s.

Lake maps of Toledo Bend can be obtained from Fishing Hot Spots, (800) ALL-MAPS; A.I.D. Associates, (800) AID-MAPS, and Kingfisher Maps, (800) 326-0257.

SAM RAYBURN RESERVOIR

Located between Lufkin and Hemphill just northeast of US 69, Sam Rayburn's 114,500 acres of water on the Angelina River represent the largest reservoir located within the state. It has 560 miles of shoreline that extent into five counties. Flooded or fallen timber in uncleared areas provides prime fish habitat but a good part of the lake is open water that attracts heavy, high speed boating activity.

Sam Rayburn has a reputation for producing some of the largest bass in the state year after year, and for this reason it attracts heavy angling and tournament activity. "Fishing Sam Rayburn would be like fishing downtown Houston," says Ronnie Robison, a veteran East Texas fly fisher. "It heats up to a faster pace than Toledo Bend but it keeps producing great fishing."

Ten-pound bass have been common at Sam Rayburn over the years. Five new lake records have been set at the lake since 1993, with the top fish weighing in near 17 pounds.

At Sam Rayburn, anglers can target prespawn largemouth staging along ditches that the fish use as routes to spawning areas. The postspawn period also can provide hot action with streamer patterns and topwater bugs in pockets and around grass lines in the main lake.

A popular launch site on the southern end of the lake is at Twin Dykes Marina and Campground. A trip down Texas 255 toward the dam with stops at Powell Park on Sam Rayburn can offer anglers famous cheeseburgers as well as access to nearby coves that offer excellent fly fishing, including Powell Creek.

Continue up Texas 6996 to Mill Creek where anglers can put-in and access shorelines that have a variety of fish-holding features including buck brush, exposed grass, button willows, grass flats and feeder creeks.

Another good tour is along Texas 63 toward Texas 187 to launch and fish around the Black Forest and the 147 Bridge.

Piney Woods largemouth.

Toledo Bend

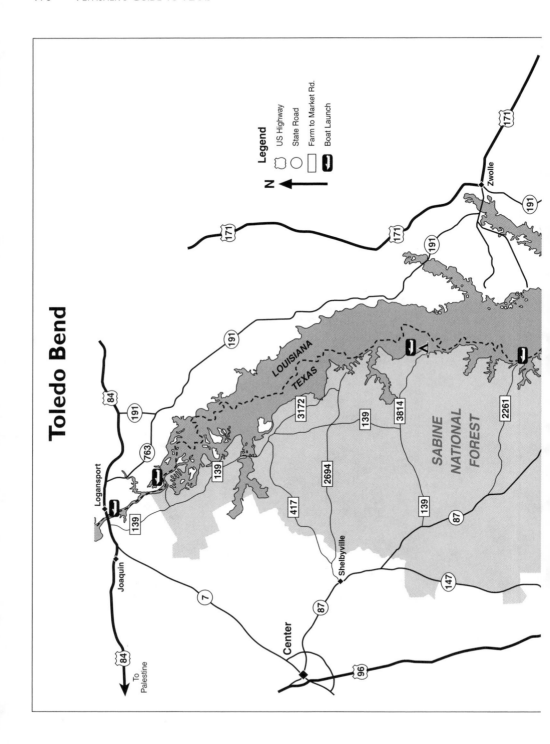

Legend

US Highway
State Road
Farm to Market Rd.
Boat Launch

N

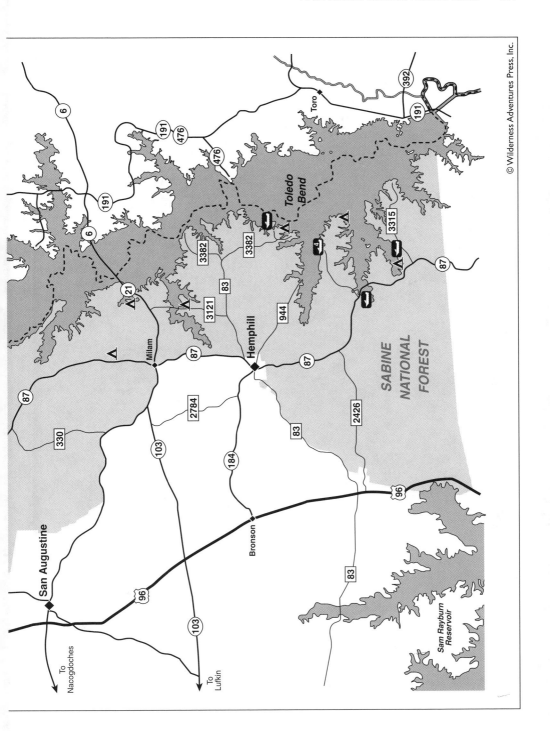

Sam Rayburn Reservoir

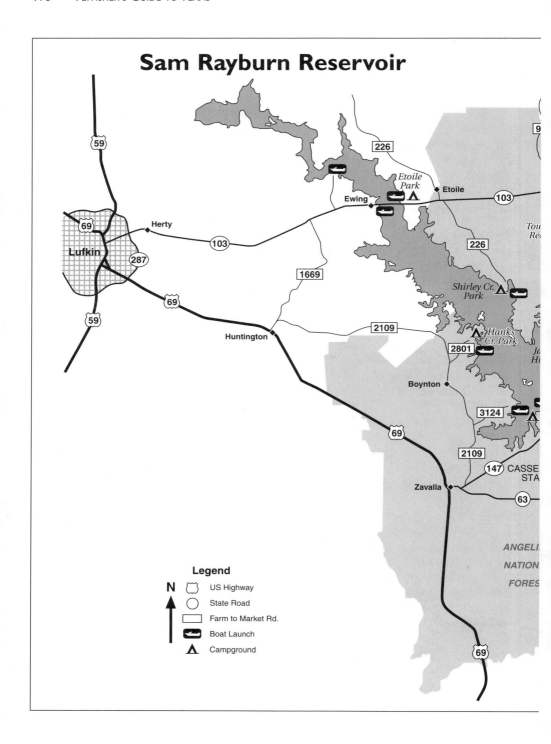

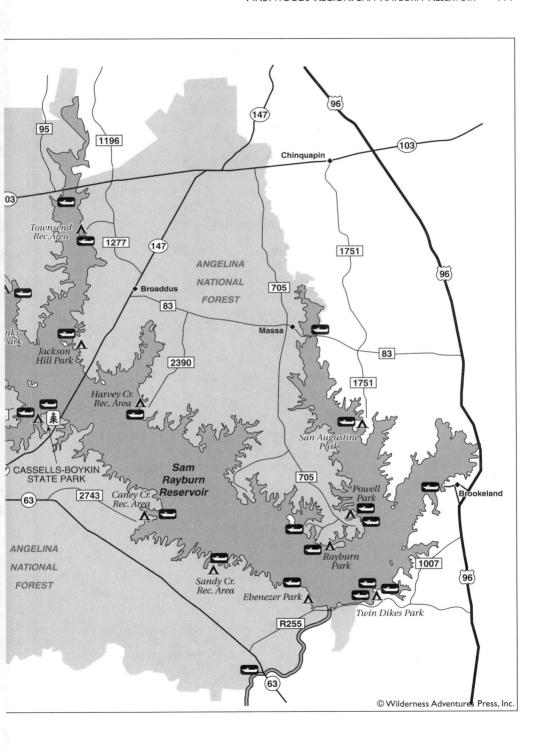

© Wilderness Adventures Press, Inc.

B.A. Steinhagen Lake
and Martin Dies, Jr. State Park

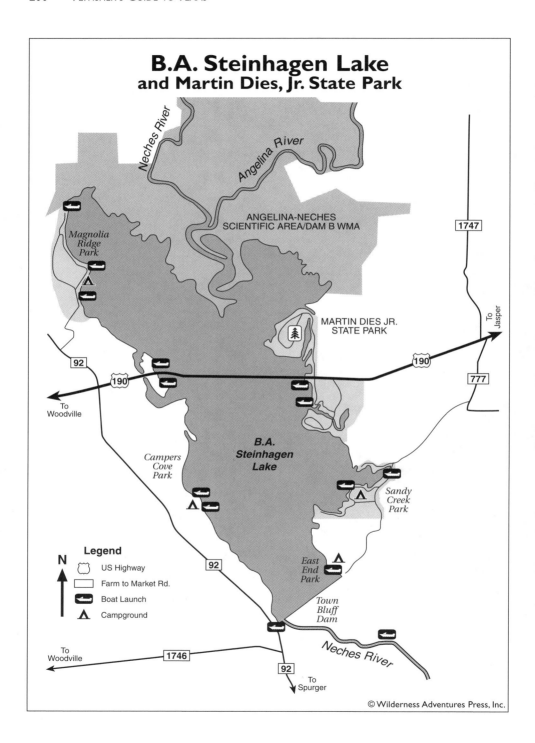

Neches River

Angelina River

ANGELINA-NECHES
SCIENTIFIC AREA/DAM B WMA

1747

Magnolia
Ridge
Park

MARTIN DIES JR.
STATE PARK

To
Jasper

92

190

190

777

To
Woodville

B.A.
Steinhagen
Lake

Campers
Cove
Park

Sandy
Creek
Park

Legend

N

US Highway

Farm to Market Rd.

Boat Launch

Campground

92

East
End
Park

To
Woodville

1746

92

Town
Bluff
Dam

Neches River

To
Spurger

© Wilderness Adventures Press, Inc.

B.A. STEINHAGEN LAKE

A 13,500-acre reservoir on the Neches River west of Jasper off US 190, Steinhagen Lake, also known as Dam B or B.A. Steinhagen, is a shallow open reservoir marked with mud flats. It holds good numbers of largemouth and sunfish and is accessible to small craft including johnboats, canoes and kayaks. Resembling a flood plain, Steinhagen is a wide open lake and fishing conditions are subject to frequent changes in wind direction and velocity. A plus is that it does not receive the heavy angler and boating traffic that is present on Sam Rayburn. Flyfishers will find the best features along protected coves.

Martin Dies Jr. State Park

To get to Martin Dies Jr. State Park, located in Tyler and Jasper Counties, travel 12 miles west of Jasper on US 190 to Park Road 48, or 15 miles east of Woodville on US 190 to Park Road 48. B.A. Steinhagen Lake, located in the park, offers flyfishers a shot at largemouth bass and crappie. The park staff offers a five hour, guided float down the Angelina River on the third Saturday of each month for a $25 fee, which includes the canoe rental. The fee for those that bring their own canoe is $20. Reservations are required and can be obtained by contacting the park staff at (409) 384-5231.

LAKE LIVINGSTON

Located about 70 miles north of Houston off US 190, Lake Livingston lies on the Trinity River and encompasses 90,000 acres. Its shorelines are ringed with pine and hardwoods. In addition to largemouth and sunfish, Livingston is known for its hybrid striped bass, white bass and striper population.

Lake Livingston State Park

Located in Polk County, 1 mile south of Livingston on US 59, Lake Livingston State Park is situated among tall loblolly pines and water oaks. It offers 2½ miles of shoreline access to Lake Livingston as well as fishing piers and boat ramps. The park also offers campsites and screened shelters with water and electricity as well as a day use area with tables and grills. For additional information, write Lake Livingston State Park, Route 9, Box 1300, Livingston, TX 77351, (409) 365 2201.

LAKE CONROE

A 21,000-acre lake north of Houston on Interstate 45, Lake Conroe is fed by the West Fork of the San Jacinto River. A popular lake with recreational boaters from Houston, in recent years Conroe has begun to produce some of the largest black bass in the state. The lake attracts a lot of party barges and jetski traffic on weekends during the summer months but also offers protected water and coves ideal for fly fishing. The large number of boat docks are excellent structure to target for bass action during the day or at night under the lights. There are a number of launch ramps on the southernmost end of the lake off Texas 105.

SQUARE LAKE

A small lake located in a city park accessible from Interstate 10 at Orange, Square Lake offers flyfishers the opportunity to launch canoes or kayaks and fish scenic shorelines marked with towering cypress and tupelo gum trees.

STATE PARK WATERS

Daingerfield State Park

Located on Texas 11, west of Daingerfield, this park (see map on page 181) offers flyfishers a shot at chain pickerel on a 47-acre, spring-fed lake. Anglers can access the lake with float tubes, kayaks or pontoon boats. A bonus for flyfishers on the lake is the fact that it is situated in a depression which reduces the wind on the water and makes it a good alternate destination when wind and cold weather conditions make it difficult to fish other lakes. Clouser Deep Minnows or Zonker patterns in white or chartreuse with flash or sparkle material work well on the lake.

A peak time to try for chain pickerel is in February, says Robert Woodruff, who has caught them up to 3.5 pounds on this lake. Largemouth and sunfish can also be caught in the clear waters of the lake.

Tyler State Park

Tyler State Park is located in Smith County, 8 miles north of Tyler on Texas (FM) 14 and 2 miles north of US 20. Located in densely wooded hills, the park has a 64-acre lake that is ideal for canoes, kayaks and other small watercraft. The lake offers exceptional fly fishing for redbreast sunfish and is stocked with rainbows during the winter months.

For additional information write to Tyler State Park, 789 Park Road 16, Tyler, TX 75706-9141, (903) 597- 5338.

Texas Railroad State Historical Park and
Rusk and Palestine State Parks

Located in a scenic setting among loblolly pines, oaks, sweet gums and elms on either end of the Texas State Railroad line, these are the only state parks where flyfishers have a chance to catch a big sunfish while hearing a steam whistle from a passing train, notes Richard Ott, a Texas Parks and Wildlife Department biologist.

Texas State Railroad Unit

The Texas Railroad Unit is located on 499 acres. Visitors can board the steam trains at both the Palestine and the Palestine depots at either end of the line that connects the two units of Palestine / Palestine State Park. The trains operate year-round on weekends and reservations are recommended. Trains depart from both stations at 11 a.m. and return at 3 p.m. Ice chests and food may be taken on the trains and food service is available at each depot. For additional information and reservations for the train rides, contact the park at (903) 683-2561 or (800-) 442-8951.

Rusk Unit

The Rusk Unit is located 3 miles west of Rusk, adjacent to the Texas State Railroad Rusk Depot off US Highway 84. There is an old depot building; tennis courts; a 15-acre lake; and a .25-mile nature trail.

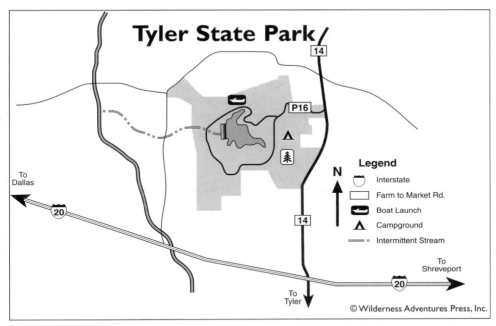

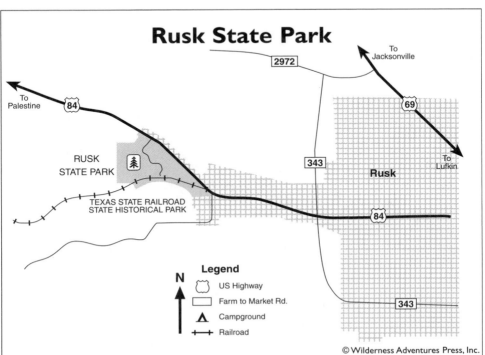

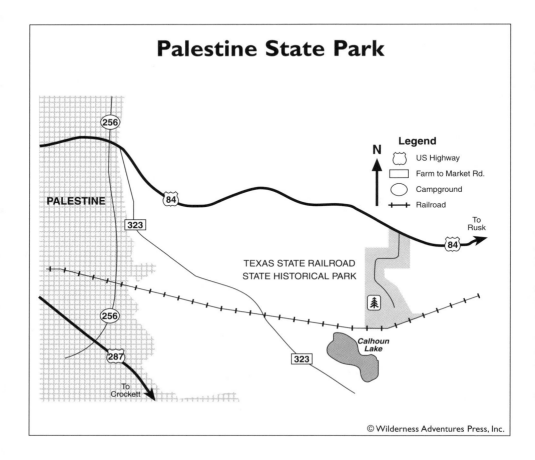

Palestine Unit

It is located 3 miles east of Palestine on US Highway 84, adjacent to the Texas State Railroad State Historical Park Palestine depot.

Palestine is open 7 days a week except for annual closure December 1 through February 28 to correspond with the closure of the Texas State Railroad for maintenance purposes. Busy Seasons are spring and fall.

Nearby attractions include Jim Hogg and Mission Tejas State Historical Parks and Lake Livingston and Fairfield Lake State Parks. Other attractions within a 1½-hour's drive of Rusk are Toledo Bend Reservoir, which is located on the Texas/Louisiana state line, and Lake Livingston, which is south on US Highway 59. For reservations, call 512/389-8900. Current weather conditions, including fire bans and water levels, can vary from day to day. For more details, call the park or Park Information at 1-800-792-1112.

Mission Tejas State Historical Park

Located south of Alto in Cherokee County near the Neches River, the 363-acre Mission Tejas State Historical Park, the site of a mission established by Spanish colonizers in the 1690s, offers a campground, picnic facilities and a small pond that offers bank fishing for bass and sunfish in a scenic woodland setting. For additional information, contact the park at (936) 687-2394.

Huntsville State Park

Scenic Lake Raven in Huntsville State Park offers excellent shore features and coves with good fish-holding habitat including floating vegetation and flooded timber. This small lake with clear water can be fished effectively from a kayak, canoe or kickboat. This lake is known for producing monster redear sunfish.

Surrounded by loblolly and shortleaf pines with a scattering of willow, water oak, and black gum, the 2,083-acre park offers the chance to view white-tailed deer, fox squirrels, raccoons, opossums and alligators as well as a variety of bird life.

Facilities include a large campground, screened shelters, a fishing pier and boat ramp. For more information, contact the park at (409) 295-5644.

Village Creek State Park

Located in Hardin County 10 miles north of Beaumont, Village Creek State Park offers bank fishing and access by canoes and kayaks. The park offers flyfishers more than a mile of shoreline on Village Creek, a clean, sand-bottomed, free-flowing tributary of the Neches River. Floats can also be launched upstream from the park at road intersections including US 296, Texas 327 or Texas (FM) 418. There is also a floatable four mile stretch downstream to the juncture of Village Creek and the Neches River. At that point, boaters can paddle upstream on the Neches a short distance and take-out in the Big Thicket Preserve on the Orange County side of the river. The river holds a variety of freshwater species including largemouth, sunfish, crappie and channel catfish. For more information contact the park at (409) 756-7322.

PRIVATE WATERS

FLAG LAKES

Located east of Jefferson off Texas (FM) 248 in Marion County, Flag Lakes offers four fishable waters ranging in size from ½ acre to 4 acres. The lakes are stocked with Florida-strain largemouth. Small watercraft are allowed on the larger lakes and bank fishing access is available on the half an acre lake. Open year-round, a cabin as well as RV and tent campsites are available on the property for a fee.

Access to Flag Lakes is offered through membership in The Great Texas Bass Club. In addition to the annual membership fee, which allows access to lakes throughout the state, the day use fee at Flag Lakes is $35, half day $20, children under 12 are free.

For additional information, contact The Great Texas Bass Club at (214) 954-1818.

ROBIN LAKE

Located west of Jefferson off Texas 49 in Marion County, this 20-acre lake is ideal for canoes, kayaks and small watercraft with trolling motors. This clear-water lake in a wooded setting has produced largemouth up to 12 pounds.

Access to catch and release fly fishing on Robin Lake is offered through membership in The Great Texas Bass Club. In addition to the annual membership fee, which allows access to lakes throughout the state, the day use fee at Robin Lake is $35, half day $20, children under 12 are free.

For additional information, contact The Great Texas Bass Club at (214) 954-1818.

HIDDEN LAKE

Located north of Tyler off Texas (FM) 2015 in Smith County, Hidden Lake is situated among East Texas pines. The 45-acre lake holds good numbers of largemouth in the 1.5- to 6-pound range and there are a variety of fish-holding features including flooded timber, floating vegetation and brush piles.

There is no bank fishing allowed so flyfishers should come equipped with a float tube, canoe, kayak or other small watercraft.

Access to catch and release fly fishing on Hidden Lake is offered through membership in The Great Texas Bass Club. In addition to the annual membership fee, which allows access to lakes throughout the state, the day use fee at Hidden Lake is $35, half day $20, children under 12 are free.

For additional information, contact The Great Texas Bass Club at (214) 954-1818.

NEW FRONTIER LAKE

Located south of Brownsboro off Texas (FM) 317 in Henderson County, this 35-acre lake is stocked with Florida-strain largemouth and coppernose bluegill. The lake has a variety of fish-holding structure and can be fished from a bass boat with a trolling motor. Canoes, kayaks, or other small watercraft are also permitted. Largemouth in the 8- to 10-pound range have been caught in the lake.

Facilities include a concrete patio, picnic tables, charcoal grill and a fishing pier. RV and tent campsites are available on the property for a fee.

Access to catch-and-release fly fishing on New Frontier Lake is offered through membership in The Great Texas Bass Club. In addition to the annual membership fee, which allows access to lakes throughout the state, the day use fee at New Frontier Lake is $35, half day $20, children under 12 are free.

BORDER CROSSINGS

Mountain Fork River, Oklahoma

Species available in this river and a nearby lake in Beavers Bend State Park in southeastern Oklahoma include rainbow and brown trout as well as walleye below the dam. In the cold water river section above the lake, and in the lake, there are smallmouth, spotted bass and largemouth. Trout can be caught year around with smallmouth caught from mid-April through November. Wading fisherman in the river should use felt-soled or studded shoes because of slick shale bottoms.

Fly fishing guide Robert Woodruff recommends 5- or 6-weight outfits for fishing both the river and lake. A variety of classic nymphs such as gold ribbed hare's ears and pheasant tails as well as Woolly Buggers and other large streamers work well for trout. There is some dry fly fishing during black caddis hatches. Flyfishers can practice a variety of trout fishing techniques on small stream (Spillway Creek) and big river environments.

To the north of the reservoir, there are also a variety of creek and river small-mouth fisheries, including the Upper Mountain Fork and Glover River.

To reach the Mountain Fork River, proceed east from Mount Pleasant for 18 miles and turn north on US 259. Proceed north on US 259 for approximately 30 miles into Oklahoma and through the communities of Idabel and Broken Bow. Approximately 7 miles north of Broken Bow, turn east on US 259A and proceed four miles to the park entrance.

The Mountain Fork River below Mountain Fork Lake and Beavers Bend State Park in Oklahoma offers fly fishing for rainbow and brown trout. The most produc-tive areas are nearest the dams but there is wade fishing access to 12 miles of the river.

The area below the park dam is a popular stretch for fly fishing. Regulations include catch and release only on brown trout and "artificial and fly lure only" from the Park Re-Regulation Dam for 3.7 miles downstream to the Corps of Engineers Re-Regulation Dam.

The area near the Corps of Engineers Re-Regulation Dam located off US 70 has campsites and offers access to productive stretches of river starting near the dam. Fish the river during periods when there is no power generation.

Presbyterian Falls is an area that offers public access to the river over half a mile downstream from the Beavers Bend State Park Re-Regulation Dam.

Effective fly patterns on the Mountain Fork include Elk Hair Caddis, Adams, and Renegades for dry fly fishing and Woolly Worms, Woolly Buggers, gold ribbed hairs ears and soft hackle patterns for nymphing. Select hook sizes from 16 to 10. An Oklahoma license and trout stamp available at two stores within the park are required for fishing the Mountain Fork.

Beavers Bend offers flyfishers 13½ miles of rainbow and brown trout on a small stream and big river. For an annual fee of $25, it also offers access to 930,000 acres of Weyerhaeuser timberland and National Forest lands with smallmouth and sunfish waters that are very lightly fished. The river also offers flyfishers a shot at walleye during spawning runs in February north of the lake. In March, there is a spawning run of large white bass. Smallmouth action heats up in mid-April after the water warms up.

LAKE VERNON AND ANACOCO LAKE, LOUISANA

Considered one of the top largemouth lakes in Louisiana, Lake Vernon is located in Vernon Parish near the south end of Toledo Bend Reservoir, about 40 miles east of Jasper, Texas. Veteran Louisiana flyfisher and flytyer Tom Nixon recommends launching a skiff or bass boat at the dam on the south end of the lake and prospecting the lake's west shoreline with popping bugs and streamers. Creek channels and flats are also accessible from launch points around the dam. Rip-rap around the dam and flooded timber in other parts of the lake offer prime fish-holding structure for flyfishers. The lake also holds a thriving population of sunfish, Nixon says.

Also recommended in the area is Anacoco Lake, which lies just to the south of Lake Vernon. Nixon says the lake has been drained, re-flooded and restocked and now holds good numbers of small to medium largemouths.

For additional information, contact the Vernon Parish Tourist Commission at (318) 238-0783. To get to Lake Vernon, travel west from Leesville on Route 8 for about 7 miles. Look for the sign on the right for the dam. Take the road to the right and proceed to the dam.

Pineywoods Hub Cities
Paris

Population - 26,471
Area Code - 903

Elevation - 592'
County - Lamar

ACCOMMODATIONS
Best Western Inn, 3755 N.E. Loop 286 / 785-5566 / 80 rooms / $$
Comfort Inn, 3505 N.E. Loop 286 / 784-7481 / 62 rooms / $$

BED AND BREAKFAST
Fisher Farm Bed and Breakfast, Country Club Road off Texas 450 / 660-2978 / $$$

RESTAURANTS
Johnny Cace's Seafood and Steak House, 1501 East Marshall (US 80 East) / 753-7691 / Lunch and dinner served
Tuesday through Saturday, dinner only on Sunday and Monday / $ to $$
Lupe's / 809 Pine Tree / 297-6916 / $

SPORTING GOODS STORES
Wal-Mart, 3855 Lamar Ave / 903-785-7168

FOR MORE INFORMATION
Longview Convention and Visitors Bureau
P.O. Box 472
Longview, TX 75606
753-3281

LODGING PRICE KEY
$	=	$30 - $50 per night
$$	=	$50 - $70 per night
$$$	=	$70 per night and up

RESTAURANT PRICE KEY
$	=	$10 and under per meal
$$	=	$10 - $20 per meal
$$$	=	$20 and up

Marshall

Population - 24,684	Elevation - 375'
Area Code - 903	County - Harrison

ACCOMMODATIONS

Best Western Inn of Marshall, 5555 East End Boulevard, South / 935-1941 / 100 rooms / $$

Hampton Inn - Marshall, 5100 S. East End Boulevard / 68 rooms / $$$

Super 8 Motel, 6002 East End Boulevard / 800-800-8000 / 40 rooms / $$

BED AND BREAKFAST

Maison Bayou Waterfront Bed and Breakfast, 300 Bayou Street, Jefferson / 11 rooms / $$ to $$$

Steamboat Inn, 114 North Marshall, Jefferson / 665-8946 / $$ to $$$

CAMPGROUNDS

Country Pines RV Park, Tent and RV Sites Available. / 5935 Highway 59 North Marshall, TX / 800-848-7087 Information

RESTAURANTS

Bodacious Bar-B-Q, 2018 Victory Drive / 938-4880 / $

Porky's Smokehouse and Grill, 504 East Carolanne at Hwy. 59 South / 927-2144 / $

Homero's Mexican Restaurant, 111 East Houston / 938 2803 / $

SPORTING GOODS

Shooter's Sporting Goods, 909 E. End Blvd. / 938-0738

HOSPITALS

Marshall Regional Medical Center, 811 South Washington / 927-6000

FOR MORE INFORMATION

Marshall Chamber of Commerce
P.O. Box 520
Marshall, TX 75671
935-7868

Tyler

Population - 83,678   **Elevation - 558'**
Area Code - 903   **County - Smith**

ACCOMMODATIONS
Best Western - Tyler Inn and Suites, 2828 West Northwest Loop 323 / (800-) BWTYLER / 90 rooms / $$
Fairfield Inn, 1945 West Southwest Loop 323 / 561-2535 / 64 rooms / $$
Ramada, 2631 West NW Loop 323 / 593-7391 / 78 rooms / $$

BED AND BREAKFAST
Seasons Bed and Breakfast Inn, 313 East Charnwood / 533-0803 / 4 rooms / $$ to $$$
Woldert-Spence Manor, 611 West Woldert Street / (800-) WOLDERT / 7 rooms / $$ to $$$

CAMPGROUNDS
Lake Palestine Campground and Lodge: Tent and RV sites as well as 10 cabins available / Hwy 15, South at Echo Hills Rd. Frankston, TX / 876-2253 / Ltolner@aol.com www.lakepalestine.net
Whispering Pines RV Resort, Tent and RV sites available. / 5583 FR 16 East Tyler, TX / 858-2405 Local / 800-559-3817 Reservations / whisperingpinestx@ gocampingamerica.com

RESTAURANTS
Cace's Seafood, 7011 South Broadway, 581-0744 / $
The Black-Eyed Pea, 322 E. Southeast Loop 323 / 581-0242 / $
The Potpourri House, 2301 S. Broadway / 592-4171 / Open Monday through Saturday, 11 a.m. to 3 p.m. / $

FLY SHOPS AND GUIDES
Jones Creek, 2301 South Broadway #A7 / 526-3474

SPORTING GOODS STORES
Oshman's, 4023 South Broadway / 581-7888
Sporster, 4542 S. Broadway / 903-561-5505
Backcountry, 3320 Troup hwy #125 / 593-4602

FOR MORE INFORMATION
Tyler Area Chamber of Commerce
P.O. Box 390
Tyler, TX 75710
592-1661

Nacogdoches

Population - 33,300 **Elevation - 283'**
Area Code - 936 **County - Nacogdoches**

ACCOMMODATIONS
Best Western - Northpark Inn, 4809 N.W. Stallings (US 59 North) / 560-1906 / 72 rooms / $$
EconoLodge, 2020 N.W. Stallings Drive / 569-0880 / 68 rooms / $$
Holiday Inn - Nacogdoches, 3400 South Street / (800-) HOLIDAY / 106 rooms / $$

BED AND BREAKFAST
Llano Grande Plantation Bed and Breakfast, Route 4, Box 9400 / 569-1249 / 3 rooms / $$
Stag Leap Retreat, Route 3, Box 1267 FM 2782 - off Hwy. 7 West / 560-9511 / 4 rooms / $$

RESTAURANTS
Butcher's Boy's Meats and Delicatessen, 603 North Street / 560-1137 / $
La Hacienda, 1411 North Street / 564-6450 / $
Blank and Company, 201½ East Main Street / 560-0776 / $

SPORTING GOODS STORES
Wal-Mart, 4810 North Street / 560-6969

HOSPITALS
Nacogdoches Medical Center, 4920 Northeast Stallings Drive / 936-569-9481

FOR MORE INFORMATION
Nacogdoches Convention and Visitors Bureau
P.O. Box 631918
Nacogdoches, TX 75963
564-7351

Lufkin

Population - 33,979   **Elevation - 328'**
Area Code - 936   **County - Angelina**

ACCOMMODATIONS
La Quinta Inn, 2119 South First / 800-531-5900 / 106 rooms / $$
Best Western Expo Inn, 4200 North Medford Drive / 632-7300 / $$
Holiday Inn, 4306 South First Street / 639-3333 / $$

RESTAURANTS
Cafe Del Rio, 1901 South First Street / 639-4471 / $

SPORTING GOOD STORES
Massey and Brown, 124 Shelley / 561-7613
Tri Lakes Tackle and Outdoor, 2208 E. Denman Ave. / 637-7119

FOR MORE INFORMATION
Lufkin Convention and Visitors Bureau
P.O. Box 1606
Lufkin, TX 75901
634-6305

FLYFISHING CLUBS IN PINEYWOODS REGION
East Texas Flyfishers
P.O. Box 5971
Longview, Texas 75608
Pineywoods Flyfishers
P.O. Box 153651
Lufkin, Texas 75904

REGION 4

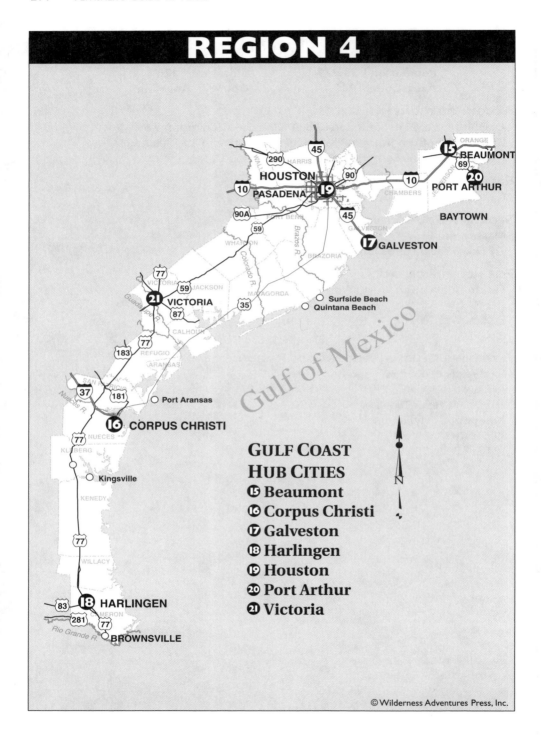

GULF COAST
HUB CITIES
⓯ Beaumont
⓰ Corpus Christi
⓱ Galveston
⓲ Harlingen
⓳ Houston
⓴ Port Arthur
㉑ Victoria

© Wilderness Adventures Press, Inc.

Gulf Coast

Fisheries are shaded by plants as diverse as cypress trees and Sabal palms ; wildlife varies from alligators to ocelots. Flyfishers have a shot at feisty "swamp bass" under the moss draped oaks and cypresses of the Sabine River on the border with Louisiana.

There are also sunfish in freshwater ponds within earshot of the Gulf surf, and alligator gars roll like tarpon in Rio Grande Valley resacas.

This region runs along the entire 367-mile gulf coast from the Louisiana border to Mexico and among the many unique fly fishing destinations here are the lakes in Brazos Bend State Park, where anglers can view the rich bird life, keep an eye out for alligators and cast to sunfish from oak-shaded trails. Lake Corpus Christi offers a dramatic South Texas brush country setting and abundant largemouth. Coleto Creek Reservoir near Goliad is a favorite of flyfishers and Sheldon Reservoir's bayous and bucket mouth bass offer a taste of Okeechobee only 13 miles from Houston.

Cities in the region include Orange, Port Arthur, Houston, Galveston, Victoria, Corpus Christi, Harlingen and Brownsville.

RIVERS

SABINE RIVER

The small southernmost stretch of the Sabine River flows through Orange County forming a boundary with Louisiana along refinery docks and old shipbuilding plants until it joins Sabine Lake, a large marine estuary. On the upper end of this stretch, the Sabine offers flyfishers shoreline fishing for river largemouth, called marsh bass, as well as bowfin along the main river and off the main flow in a variety of bayous and oxbow lakes. Down toward the refinery docks along the main channel, flyfishers often can find top water striped bass action.

The Sabine is a powerful river affected by strong currents during normal flow and upstream rainfall and runoff. It is best fished from powerboats, including john-boats, flats skiffs and bay boats, launched from area marinas. Striped bass are present in the Sabine River, the result of earlier stocking programs by Texas Parks and Wildlife Department South of the IH 10 bridge, and around Livingston Island, and in the deep water around the shipbuilding operations on the river. "A lot of these stripers also come down the river from Toledo Bend Lake, where they are often caught in the tailrace," says Sabine River fly fishing guide Chuck Uzzle.

The action for these river stripers usually begins in the late summer and extends into the winter months. Fish up to 36 pounds have been caught in this area. Uzzle says the stripers often will bunch up to chase shad on the surface, offering flyfishers exciting topwater action. Occasionally, they will also school up with spotted sea trout that have moved up the river into this brackish water environment to chase baitfish.

Uzzle has encountered stripers in the 10- to 15-pound range around Livingston Island. These stripers will hold near heavy structure such as parts of sunken ships and pier pilings, requiring fly rodders to use stout leaders and heavy rod pressure to turn them after the strike.

Another area that attracts stripers downstream from Livingston Island is the mouth of a bayou outflow called Burton's Ditch. Stripers will gather here at the mouth of this outflow as water moves off the marshes. These are river stripers but this is a saltwater and freshwater transition zone and the stripers often move down-river toward Sabine Lake, a marine estuary, to feed on shrimp being washed out of the marshes. When the conditions are right, the stripers can be seen smashing shrimp and finfish on the surface near the outflow. Uzzle has taken stripers in the 6- to 10 pounds range using an 8 weight rod and working Clousers and other streamer patterns just below the surface during these feeding frenzies. He chooses a 12 pound Flourocarbon tippet for this kind of action.

Sabine River

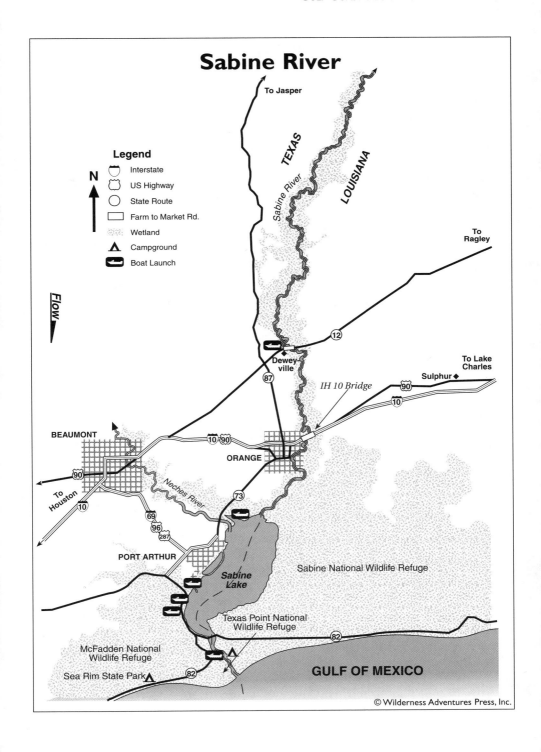

Legend

N

Interstate
US Highway
State Route
Farm to Market Rd.
Wetland
Campground
Boat Launch

Flow

To Jasper

TEXAS

LOUISIANA

Sabine River

To Ragley

12

Dewey-ville

87

IH 10 Bridge

To Lake Charles

Sulphur ◆

90

10

BEAUMONT

10 90

ORANGE

To Houston

10

90

Neches River

73

69

96

287

PORT ARTHUR

Sabine Lake

Sabine National Wildlife Refuge

Texas Point National Wildlife Refuge

82

McFadden National Wildlife Refuge

Sea Rim State Park

82

GULF OF MEXICO

© Wilderness Adventures Press, Inc.

SAN BERNARD RIVER

Flyfishers can cast the riverbanks and flooded timber for largemouth, sunfish, crappie, channel catfish and spotted gar.

From US 59 at Kendleton, the Sand Bernard River runs south and forms the boundary between Wharton and Fort Bend Counties until in flows into Brazoria County and heads to the Gulf of Mexico. As it approaches the gulf from Texas FM 2004 in Brazoria County, it begins to take on coastal characteristics becoming a broad waterway. It is accessible as a freshwater fishery between US 59 and Lake Jackson. Because of heavy overgrowth and intermittent flows, the San Bernard is best accessed from county and city parks and selected bridge crossings.

Bates Allen Park in Kendleton provides good access to the San Bernard. Located at 630 Charlie Roberst Road in Kendleton, this park provides canoe and kayak access to largemouth and sunfish under a scenic canopy of cypress trees. The park has a boat launch ramp, restrooms, picnic tables and grills. To get to the park proceed south from Houston on US 59 to Kendleton. At Kendleton, turn left at the flashing caution light onto Lum and proceed about one block to Charlie Roberts Lane. Turn right on Charlie Roberts Lane and follow it to the park.

The Texas FM 2611 Bridge crossing also provides great access to the river. Located just north of the San Bernard National Wildlife Refuge, this bridge crossing has adequate parking and a Texas Parks and Wildlife launching ramp. This is a good put-in for launching a canoe, kayak or johnboat. Both upstream and downstream areas are good for both largemouth and sunfish. The fish will be holding along the grassy shorelines and around boat docks.

COLORADO RIVER

The stretch of the Colorado River that runs through the Gulf Coast Region begins north of Wharton in Wharton County and runs southward through Matagorda to the Gulf of Mexico near the town of Matagorda. There are a number of access points at bridge crossings and city parks that offer opportunities for floats or shoreline fly fishing in the immediate area. Depending on flow levels and water clarity these lightly fished stretches of river near the launch sites can offer surprisingly good small bass and sunfish action.

The Texas (FM) 960 Crossing in Glen Flora

Located north of Wharton, this bridge crossing provides walk-in access to the river from the highway right-of-way. A dirt track leads from Texas (FM) 960 to the water's edge. The banks are steep at this access making it difficult to launch or take-out a canoe with heavy gear.

The Wharton Riverfront Park, operated by the city, offers a canoe launching pier, picnic sites, restrooms and a pavilion. It is located off Loop 183 and Texas (FM) 60 within the Wharton city limits. The Lower Colorado River Authority (LCRA) advises that the 10-mile float from Glen Flora to Wharton Riverfront Park is a manageable day trip. The 25-mile stretch from Garwood to Glen Flora is not recommended as

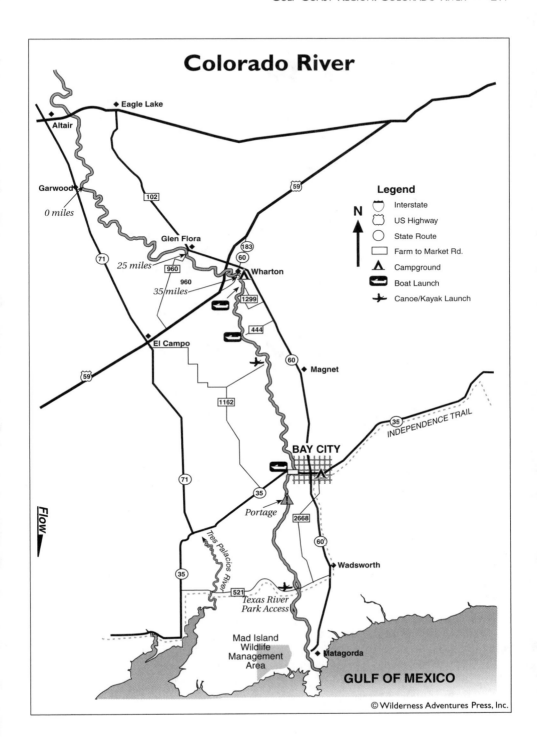

Colorado River

Eagle Lake

Altair

Garwood

0 miles

102

Glen Flora

71

25 miles

960

960

35 miles

Wharton

183
60

1299

El Campo

444

59

60 ◆ Magnet

1162

35 INDEPENDENCE TRAIL

BAY CITY

71

35

Portage

2668

60

Tres Palacios River

35

Wadsworth

521

Texas River
Park Access

Flow

Mad Island
Wildlife
Management
Area

Matagorda

GULF OF MEXICO

Legend

N

🔲 Interstate

🔲 US Highway

⭕ State Route

🔲 Farm to Market Rd.

▲ Campground

⬭ Boat Launch

✈ Canoe/Kayak Launch

© Wilderness Adventures Press, Inc.

Flyfishers taking a break on the Colorado River.

a day trip. The LCRA notes that there are fewer natural campsites available in this stretch due to a limited number of gravel bars and islands. LCRA advises that there are no major hazards on this stretch of the Colorado although boaters should be watchful for shallow areas and snags during periods of low water.

Wharton to Bay City

David S. Hall Boat Ramp- Four miles downstream from the Wharton Riverfront Park is a public access to the Colorado River at the David S. Hall Boat Ramp, operated by the Texas Parks and Wildlife Department. The ramp is south of Wharton off Texas (FM) 1299. Heading south on 1299, turn right on Nelson Road and travel approximately three quarter of a mile to Pecan Valley. This is a good launch point for small johnboats, canoes or kayaks but parking is at a premium.

Lane City Dam Portage Easement

Five miles below the David S. Hall Boat Ramp is the Lane City Dam Portage Easement on the west bank of the river (approximately 2 miles upstream from the County Road 444 (Hollywood Road) access point. This easement operated by the Lower Colorado River Authority (LCRA) is designed to allow safe and legal portage around the Lane City Dam. The LCRA advises that this portage site is accessible only by water and no camping or picnicking is permitted there.

County Road 444 (Hollywood Road) access

Located at the end of County Road 444, four miles east of Texas (FM) 1162, this access on a dirt road is best reached in a four-wheel-drive vehicle and is suitable for launching a canoe or kayak. For an update on this access and current river conditions, contact the Lower Colorado River Authority at (800-) 776-5272 ext. 3366.

Texas 35 Bridge Crossing in Bay City

Access to the Colorado River is available here at a public launch ramp in the highway right-of-way beneath the bridge one mile west of Bay City just off Texas 35. This is a good access point for fishing the shorelines in the immediate area. For longer floats downstream toward the Gulf, boaters should put-in below the Bay City Dam at the Riverside Park access south of Bay City.

Bay City to the Gulf of Mexico

Bay City Dam Portage Site - Located one mile south of the Texas 35 bridge crossing access in Bay City, this portage site is on the east bank (river left). It is maintained by the Lower Colorado River Authority as a safe and legal portage around the Bay City Dam. The Bay City low water dam just downstream from the portage site is considered a serious hazard. This launch ramp provides access to a good stretch of fly fishing along shorelines and boat docks in the immediate vicinity.

Riverside Park, Bay City

Located about 1.5 miles off Texas (FM) 2668, this access offers a boat ramp, camping facilities and a day use area.

Texas (FM) 521 River Park Access

Located four miles west of Wadsworth on 521, this is a 13-acre park facility developed by the Lower Colorado River Authority (LCRA) and operated by Matagorda County. There is a picnic site and a ramp for launching canoes, kayaks and johnboats. The LCRA says the distances between these access points can be floated comfortably in one day but the Bay City Dam and Intracoastal Waterway should be avoided by small, non-motorized craft.

NAVIDAD RIVER

US 59 Crossing at Edna

An improved launch ramp on US 59 east of Edna provides access to the upper portion of Lake Texana. This launch ramp gives access to thick mats of floating vegetation that provide excellent habitat for largemouth. Coffee-colored water is the rule on this waterway and dark deer hair bugs and leech patterns are a wise choice. The lake also holds white bass and sunfish. Texas Parks and Wildlife fisheries officials caution boaters and anglers to be on the alert for alligators on this waterway.

ARANSAS RIVER

US 77 Bridge at Sinton

Flyfishers can access the Aransas River east of Sinton at the US 77 Bridge. There is no ramp here but small boats, canoes and kayaks can be launched. The river holds largemouth and sunfish. Texas Parks and Wildlife fisheries officials caution boaters and anglers to be on the alert for alligators on this waterway.

Texas (FM) 629 at Woodsboro

Another access point on the Aransas River is at an improved launch ramp located south of Woodsboro on Texas (FM) 629. This ramp provides access for boaters at the boundary between freshwater inflows and a saltwater estuary at the upper portion of Mission Bay. Rockport fly fishing guide Ethan Wells says this remote section of river can offer sight-casting opportunities for a mixed bag of species including largemouth bass, catfish and redfish present in this brackish water.

FRIO RIVER

An improved launch ramp located in the James Dougherty Wildlife Management Area east of Tilden provides fishing access to a stretch of the Frio River near the upper portion of choke Canyon Reservoir. Largemouth bass, sunfish and white bass are among the species available.

Texas Parks and Wildlife fisheries officials caution boaters and anglers to be on the alert for alligators on this waterway.

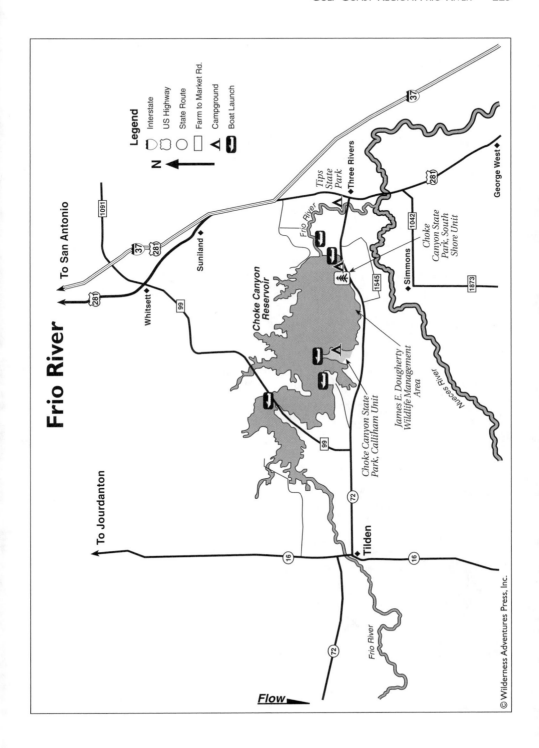

Frio River

To San Antonio

To Jourdanton

Choke Canyon Reservoir

Choke Canyon State Park, Calliham Unit

James E. Dougherty Wildlife Management Area

Choke Canyon State Park, South Shore Unit

Nueces River

Frio River

Tips State Park

Three Rivers

George West

Suniland

Whitsett

Simmons

Tilden

Flow

Legend

Interstate
US Highway
State Route
Farm to Market Rd.
Campground
Boat Launch

N

GUADALUPE RIVER

Private launch ramps are available for launch small boats, canoes or kayaks on the Guadalupe River at the Texas 35 Bridge crossing near Tivoli. This southernmost stretch of the Guadalupe offers largemouth, catfish, sunfish, alligator gar and redfish action near the saltwater boundary at the upper portion of San Antonio Bay. The waterway maintains its river characteristics in the vicinity of the launch ramp and flyfishers can prospect this a brackish water fishery for a mixed bag of fresh and saltwater species. Texas Parks and Wildlife fisheries officials caution boaters and anglers to be on the alert for alligators on this waterway.

NUECES RIVER

Hazel Bazemore County Park

A 77-acre park on a hillside lined with mesquite and hackberry that slopes down to the Nueces River bottom, the Hazel Bazemore County Park offers an intriguing sample of the birds, animals, plants and diverse landscape of South Texas ranch country. Trails lead through thick brush and grasslands and there is a shaded picnic area and pond. A blind for bird-watchers and photographers overlooks the 2-acre pond that attracts waterfowl and wading birds. Fishing for largemouth bass and sunfish is allowed along the tree-shaded banks along the river.

This is one of the limited accesses to the Nueces in the South Texas region where these smaller waterways traverse large private ranch lands. These small waterways can offer exciting light tackle fly fishing for small bass and sunfish.

The Gulf Coast region will give you some glimpses of wildlife (such as this armadillo) as well as great flyfishing.

Guadalupe River

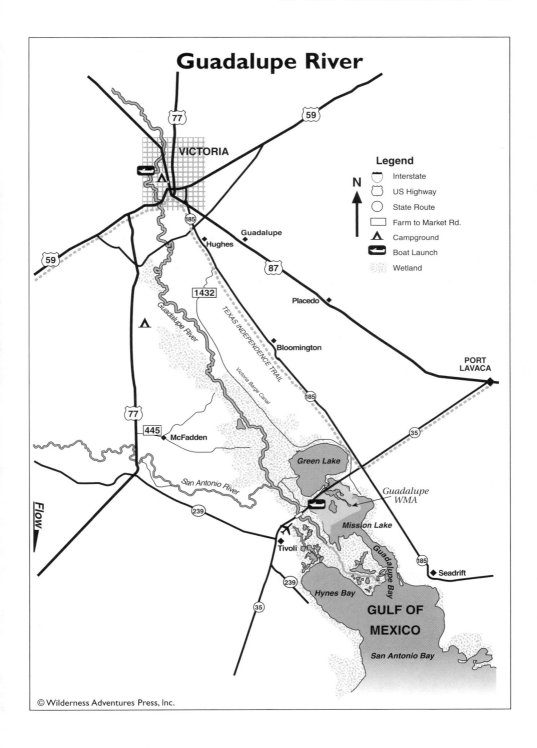

Legend

N

- Interstate
- US Highway
- State Route
- Farm to Market Rd.
- ▲ Campground
- Boat Launch
- Wetland

VICTORIA

77

59

185

Guadalupe

Hughes

1432

87

Placedo

TEXAS INDEPENDENCE TRAIL

Bloomington

59

Guadalupe River

Victoria Barge Canal

185

PORT LAVACA

77

445

McFadden

San Antonio River

Green Lake

35

239

Guadalupe WMA

Mission Lake

Guadalupe Bay

185

Seadrift

Tivoli

Flow

239

Hynes Bay

GULF OF MEXICO

35

San Antonio Bay

© Wilderness Adventures Press, Inc.

LAKES

TAYLOR BAYOU COMPLEX
(Including J.D. Murphree Wildlife Management Area and Big Hill Bayou)

Taylor Bayou is a freshwater marsh located west of Port Arthur off Texas 73. It offers flyfishers a wild and natural setting with rich bird life, alligators and a thriving population of Florida-strain largemouth. Public launch ramps are located under the Texas 73 bridge on the lower section of the bayou and there is access for a fee at commercial fish camps near the community of Labelle on the upper end of the bayou.

The Taylor Bayou system is one of the few natural freshwater swamp habitats open to public access in the state. South of the Texas 73 bridge, Taylor bayou is joined by Big Hill Bayou, which runs through the Texas Parks and wildlife Department's J.D. Murphree Wildlife Management Area. Fishing on Big Hill Bayou is allowed from the Monday following the close of the general duck season until October 31. Fishing is permitted from 30 minutes before sunrise until 30 minutes after sunset. Fishing on Big Hill Bayou is generally for largemouth bass.

For additional information on these waterways, contact:

Texas Parks and Wildlife Department
10 Parks & Wildlife Drive
Port Arthur, TX 77640
(409) 739-2551

EAST BAY BAYOU

Access to freshwater fishing is permitted at the 30,000-acre Anahuac National Wildlife Refuge at East Bay Bayou. Flyfishers can cast from the banks of the bayou, the wooden bridge or launch non-motorized boats on the bayou. Species present include largemouth, crappie, gar, bowfin and channel catfish. The extensive bayou system offers flyfishers ambush style bank fishing while enjoying the rich animal and wildlife within the refuge.

The refuge is located southeast of Houston on the north shoreline of East Galveston Bay. Take exit 812 off I-10 near the town of Hankamer and proceed south for 12.5 miles on Texas (FM) 61 and Texas (FM) 562. Turn left at the intersection of 562 and Texas (FM) 1985 and proceed 4.2 miles on 1985 to the refuge entrance, then go 3.0 miles to the check-in station. The refuge can also be reached from Texas 87 on the Bolivar Peninsula. At High Island, take Texas 124 north, then turn left on Texas (FM) 1985 and follow the signs to the refuge entrance.

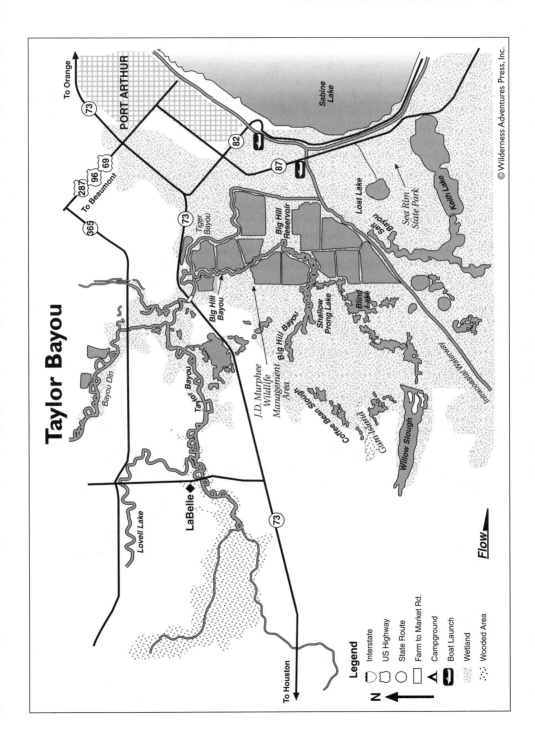

Taylor Bayou

Legend

Interstate
US Highway
State Route
Farm to Market Rd.
Campground
Boat Launch
Wetland
Wooded Area

N

Flow

To Orange

PORT ARTHUR

Sabine Lake

To Beaumont

Lost Lake

Sea Rim State Park

Keith Lake

Salt Bayou

Tiger Bayou

Big Hill Reservoir

Big Hill Bayou

J.D. Murphee Wildlife Management Area

Big Hill Bayou

Shallow Prong Lake

Blind Lake

Intracoastal Waterway

Coffee Bean Slough

Gum Island

Willow Slough

Bayou Din

Taylor Bayou

LaBelle

Lovell Lake

To Houston

© Wilderness Adventures Press, Inc.

SPRING CREEK

Located at 20634 Kenswick Dr. in the community of Humble in Harris County, the 225-acre Jesse H. Jones County Park offers bank-fishing access to Spring Creek. This stretch of water along about 25 acres of park property produces good hybrid bass fishing and white bass during winter spawning runs. Angler can use park for put-in and take-out point for floats but only bank fishing is allowed along park property because of park opening and closing hours.

The park is open 8 a.m. to 7 p.m., except December and January (8 a.m. to 5 p.m.), and February (8 a.m. to 6 p.m.). There is no fee for admittance or fishing in the park. For additional information, contact the park at (281) 446-8588.

SHELDON RESERVOIR

This 1,200-acre lake is marked by heavy vegetation and shoreline cover and located only 20 miles from the heart of Houston, produces double digit Florida-strain largemouth. The Everglades-like appearance of this shallow, swampy, alligator infested waterway with flooded timber and thick fields of water lotus and hydrilla offers flyfishers a wilderness habitat, perfect for bass bugging.

While flyfishers can fish the lake from johnboats, canoes and kayaks during part of the year, it is one of the best lakes in the region for "big game" hunting from the bank. Largemouth to 14 pounds have been taken by anglers casting from the bank, which is the only legal way to fish the lake during the early portion of the annual spawning season. The lake serves as a waterfowl wintering area and boats are banned from the lake from November 1 through the end of February. From March 1 to October 31, boats powered by outboards up to 10 h.p. or boats with larger engines

Heavy lily pad cover provides habitat for largemouths at Sheldon Reservoir near Houston.

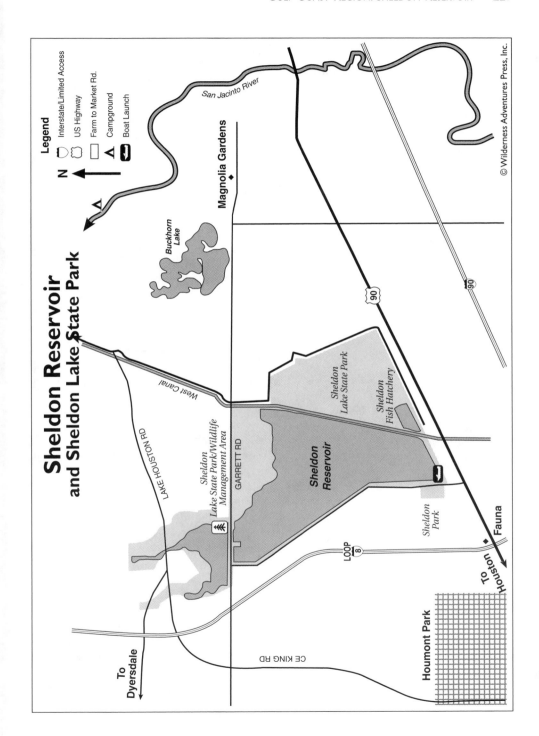

Sheldon Reservoir
and Sheldon Lake State Park

Legend
Interstate/Limited Access
US Highway
Farm to Market Rd.
Campground
Boat Launch

N

San Jacinto River

Magnolia Gardens

Buckhorn
Lake

West Canal

LAKE HOUSTON RD

Sheldon
Lake State Park/Wildlife
Management Area

GARRETT RD

Sheldon
Reservoir

Sheldon
Lake State Park

Sheldon
Fish Hatchery

90

90

Sheldon
Park

To Fauna

LOOP
8

To
Houston

To
Dyersdale

CE KING RD

Houmont Park

© Wilderness Adventures Press, Inc.

Angler working the shoreline at Sheldon Reservoir near Houston.

that use trolling motors only are allowed on the lake. Due to the broad shoulders of the resident alligator population, wade fishing and dangling feet from float tubes is not considered a healthy pursuit on this lake. Other wildlife present in the recreation area include deer, raccoons, mink, and opossum. Bald eagles are also present part of the year.

Sheldon Reservoir, part of Sheldon State Recreation Area, is located northeast of Houston off US 90, about seven miles east of Interstate 610 (Loop 610). The reservoir extends 2.5 miles from US 90 to Garrett Road along Pineland Road. There is a fishing and parking area on the north side of the lake, where car top boats can be launched and there are four T-head fishing piers, three along Pineland Road and one on the south side of the lake. There is ample parking at a launch ramp on the south side of the lake.

The Sheldon Lake Environmental Education Center offers fishing clinics, nature walks, and wetland studies to organized groups on a prearranged basis. Urban biologists educate the public on various aspects of native plants, wildlife viewing as well as staging fishing clinics. The Texas Parks and Wildlife staff provides fishing instruction including information on state fishing rules and regulations, conservation issues, and sportsmanship, followed by fishing in nearby ponds.

For additional information on lake conditions and activities at the environmental education center, contact the Sheldon State Recreation Area at (713) 456-9350.

Sheldon Lake Reservoir State Park

The shallow lake and marshland is designed primarily for fishing and viewing shorebirds and waterfowl. Migratory waterfowl make a stop here during the fall and winter. About 800 acres of the 1,200 acre waterway lake provide a permanent habitat for the lake's population of Florida-strain largemouth, crappie and sunfish, while another 400 acres serves as marshland. There are excellent bank fishing opportunities at the lake as well as launch points for canoes and kayaks. The lake is choked with water lotus and hydrilla during the warmer months. The open spots along the edges of the heavy vegetation make intriguing targets for well placed bass bugs that can attract fish well over 10 pounds in this lake. Outboards are restricted to 10 h.p. or less. The park is open year around to bank fishing but boats are not allowed on the lake from November 1 to February 28 to protect waterfowl. The park is located on the northeast side of Houston off US 90. For more information, contact park officials at (713) 456-9350.

Warning sign posted at Sheldon Reservoir.

LAKE HOUSTON

Located on the San Jacinto River, 18 miles from Houston, this 12,240-acre reservoir is stocked with Florida-strain largemouth, striped bass, hybrid striped bass, crappie and sunfish. Marked by sandy shoals and clay bottoms, the typically sandy brown water can be a challenge for flyfishers trying to sight-cast to fish.

LAKE TEXANA

Located on the Navidad River in Jackson County near Edna and Ganado, this 11,000-acre lake is located off US 59 about 25 miles east of Victoria. The north end of the lake crosses US 59 and Texas 172 at Ganado. The lake is stocked with Florida-strain largemouth and striped bass. There are feeder creeks, standing timber and inviting shorelines with heavy vegetation throughout the lake but the perpetual coffee-colored water makes this a scenic but challenging destination for flyfishers.

Lake Texana State Park

Located on the shores of 11,000-acre Lake Texana, this 575 acre park offers piers, launch ramps and campsites for anglers interested in sampling the fishing on this relatively shallow reservoir. Shorelines with standing timber as well as the small creeks which feed into the lake provide the best opportunities for flyfishers.

Lake Texana State Park is located in Jackson County between the towns of Edna and Ganado off US 59. Traveling north on US 59, take Texas 111 about six miles east of Edna. Traveling south on US 59, take Texas 172 south to Texas 111 and travel west to the park entrance.

The park has 141 campsites including 55 tent sites with water and 86 sites with  back-in parking with water and electricity. There are also 70 picnic sites with tables, grills and drinking water. There is a double boat ramp, three fishing piers (two lighted) and one jetty. For additional information, contact Lake Texana State Park at (512) 782-5718.

Angler with a nice striped bass from a Texas lake.

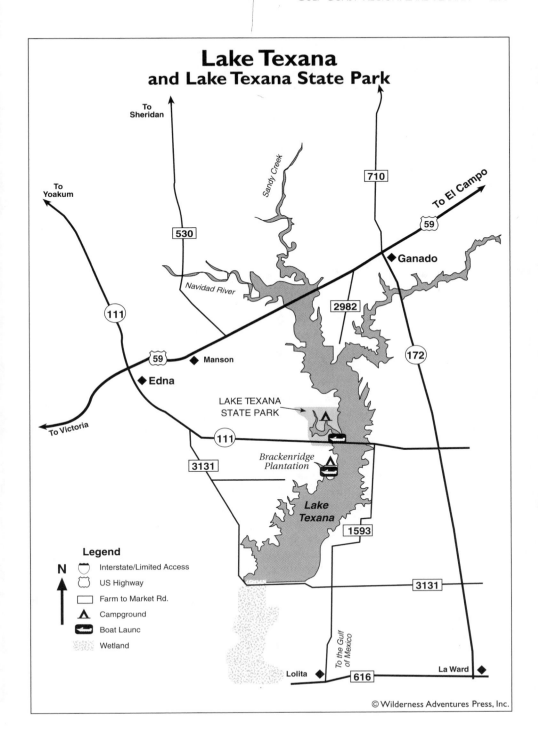

Lake Texana
and Lake Texana State Park

To
Sheridan

To
Yoakum

Sandy Creek

710

To El Campo

530

59

Ganado

Navidad River

2982

111

59

Manson

172

Edna

LAKE TEXANA
STATE PARK

To Victoria

111

*Brackenridge
Plantation*

3131

*Lake
Texana*

1593

Legend

N

Interstate/Limited Access

US Highway

Farm to Market Rd.

Campground

Boat Launc

Wetland

3131

To the Gulf
of Mexico

Lolita

616

La Ward

© Wilderness Adventures Press, Inc.

COLETO CREEK RESERVOIR

Fed by the Guadalupe River, this attractive 3,100-acre lake is located off US 59 between Goliad and Victoria. The lake is fed by a number of small creeks and has a mix of excellent game fish habitat including submerged vegetation, stumps and flooded timber, creek mouths, sloughs and coves. Flyfishers can wade shorelines around park areas or fish the lake from kayaks, canoes and johnboats. Primary quarries for flyfishers are Florida-strain largemouth, hybrid striped bass, white crappie and coppernose bluegill. There also have been experimental plantings of Nile perch and peacock bass over the years. Non-game fish including common carp, smallmouth buffalo, freshwater drum, alligator gar, spotted gar and shortnose gar will occasionally strike a fly at Coleto Creek.

The lake has an abundant largemouth population. A 1994 electro shocking survey conducted by Texas Parks and Wildlife Department fisheries biologists recorded a catch rate of 195 bass per hour on the lake, one of the highest in the region. Recent studies have indicated a high percentage of Florida-strain largemouth bass gene influence in the bass population. In Texas, the average largemouth bass reaches legal size (14 inches) in three years. Bass in Coleto Creek Reservoir reach 14 inches in two years, reports the Texas Parks and Wildlife Department. Wilford Korth, chief ranger on Coleto Creek, says it is not uncommon for anglers to catch-and-release 200 bass in a day's fishing during the spring. Prime areas to find largemouth are around piers, submerged vegetation, flooded timber and brush.

Since 1982, the Texas Parks and Wildlife Department has stocked as many as 30,000 hybrid stripers in the lake annually. The best fishing for this species is in the winter when hot water is discharged from the power plant. When the hybrids are on the surface the action can be non-stop," Korth says. "I personally have caught and released up to 50 in an hour," he says.

Coleto Creek is also home to an abundant white crappie population, with spawning periods in March and April being the peak fishing period for this species. White crappie weighing in excess of 1.5 pounds have been taken from the lake. During the peak spring months, fly rodders should target fish in shallow water, often less than a foot deep, where they have moved to build nests. During the hottest and coolest months, look for crappie suspended in deeper water over structure such as old road beds, timber along creek channels, or along the face of the dam.

There is a daily fee of $6 per vehicle for entry to Coleto Creek Reservoir and Park. The recreation area includes a boat ramp, campsites, RV hook-ups, picnic tables and a 200-foot lighted fishing pier. A cooling reservoir for a power generating plant, the park and lake is operated by the Guadalupe-Blanco River Authority. For information on current lake conditions call (361)575-6366 or visit the park's website at www.coletocreekpark.com.The fishery is managed by the Texas Parks and Wildlife Department.

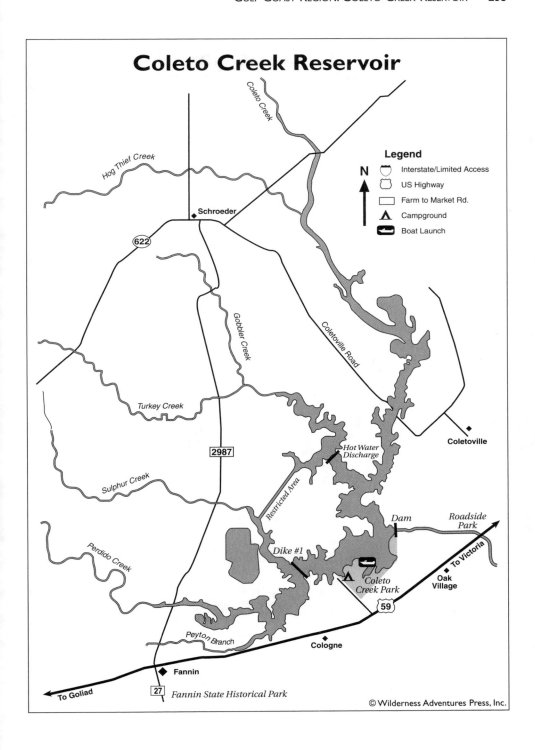

Coleto Creek Reservoir

Coleto Creek

Hog Thief Creek

Legend

N

Interstate/Limited Access

US Highway

Farm to Market Rd.

△ Campground

Boat Launch

Schroeder

622

Gobbler Creek

Coletoville Road

Turkey Creek

2987

Coletoville

Sulphur Creek

Hot Water Discharge

Restricted Area

Dam

Roadside Park

Perdido Creek

Dike #1

Coleto Creek Park

To Victoria

Oak Village

59

Peyton Branch

Cologne

Fannin

27 Fannin State Historical Park

To Goliad

© Wilderness Adventures Press, Inc.

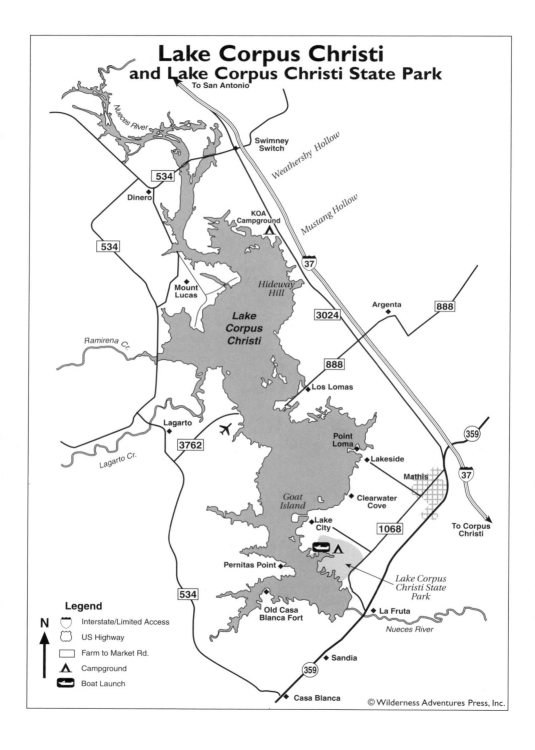

Lake Corpus Christi
and Lake Corpus Christi State Park

To San Antonio

Nueces River

Swimney
Switch

Weathersby Hollow

534

Dinero

KOA
Campground

Mustang Hollow

37

Mount
Lucas

Hideway
Hill

Lake
Corpus
Christi

Argenta

888

3024

Ramirena Cr.

888

Los Lomas

Lagarto

3762

Lagarto Cr.

Point
Loma

359

Lakeside

Mathis

37

Goat
Island

Clearwater
Cove

Lake
City

1068

To Corpus
Christi

Pernitas Point

Lake Corpus
Christi State
Park

534

Legend

N

Interstate/Limited Access

US Highway

Farm to Market Rd.

Campground

Boat Launch

Old Casa
Blanca Fort

La Fruta

Nueces River

Sandia

359

Casa Blanca

© Wilderness Adventures Press, Inc.

LAKE CORPUS CHRISTI

Located on the Nueces River, this 21,900-acre lake in the heart of Texas brush country extends into parts of Live Oak, Jim Wells and San Patricio counties. Located 20 miles northwest of Corpus Christi, it can be reached off US 37 at Mathis. This relatively shallow reservoir - average depth 13 feet - undergoes seasonal water level fluctuations. It is stocked with Florida-strain largemouth, striped bass, hybrid striped bass and white bass.

While this shallow lake is subject to strong south winds off the Gulf of Mexico and off color water conditions, there are a number of protected coves and shorelines that offer opportunities for flyfishers.

During dry years when the water level drops, extensive areas of native brush and willow trees spring up providing excellent cover for fish and wildlife when the lake level rises. The coves have a variety of aquatic plants including native stargrass, bulrush, pondweeds and water primrose that provide excellent habitat for largemouth. There are also a number of river channels and backwater areas on the upper section of the lake that concentrate game fish.

Largemouth bass spawn from February through May on this lake and often during this period can be found in shallow water near flooded timber and aquatic vegetation. Boat docks located near deeper water are excellent structures for flyfishers to prospect and are often overlooked by other anglers on the lake. During the fall months, the bass move into shallower water to feed aggressively before the winter dormant period. This is a good time to fish for largemouth in the backwater channels and oxbows of the upstream portion of the reservoir, say Texas Parks and Wildlife fisheries officials.

Lake Corpus Christi also has a good population of white crappie and black crappie, with the former being the most abundant. Crappie in excess of two pounds have been caught in the lake. Look for the crappie action to turn on any time between February and April. Parks and Wildlife officials say the ideal scenario for targeting crappie would be after several consecutive days of warm weather and strong southerly winds motivate the large adult fish to move into protected coves to seek spawning sites. During the summer months, crappie move into deeper water often near creek channels. During this time of year, flyfishers target crappie with lead-eyed Clousers around the state park fishing piers and the Alice water intake, which are located near deep-water drop-offs.

Texas Parks and Wildlife Department reports that there is an abundant population of sunfish in the lake including bluegill, longear, warmouth and redear.

There are excellent camping, boat launch and picnicking facilities at Lake Corpus Christi State Park.

Lake Corpus Christi State Park

Located in San Patricio County, six miles southwest of the town of Mathis on Texas (FM) 1068, Lake Corpus Christi State Park offers access to a number of inviting shorelines and coves ideal for fly fishing.

With roadways and shorelines lined with mesquite as well as a generous sprinkling of huisache, Spanish daggers, yuccas, black brush acacia and prickly pear, this brush country park offers a dramatic setting for bass fishing. White-tailed deer, gray fox, javelina, raccoons and rabbits are spotted in the park as well as the 300 bird species that visit during different seasons.

Lake Corpus Christi, a relatively shallow lake (average depth 13 feet) is stocked with Florida-strain largemouth, hybrid striped bass and striped bass. The striped bass often can be spotted in schools chasing baitfish around the flooded timber. Lakeside facilities include two lighted fishing piers and two boat ramps. Situated on the southeast corner of the 21,900-acre lake, the 288-acre park has a large number of campsites with showers. For more information about lake conditions and park facilities contact park officials at (512) 547-2635.

South Texas Resaca.

RESACAS AND AGRICULTURAL DRAINAGES

There are a number of oxbow lakes, old river channels, in the Lower Rio Grande Valley from Harlingen to Brownsville. Some of them provide public access and the opportunity to fly fish for largemouth, sunfish, Rio Grande perch, carp, alligator gar and spotted gar.

Located on Texas 77 (business route) between San Benito and Harlingen (Turn right at the O.C. Tire Store), there is a canal that extends along the road for several miles offering good access for bank fishing.

East of San Benito along Nelson Road which runs off Texas (FM) 510, there are a number of resacas that come to an end at the roadside. These are places where flyfishers can fish from the bank or launch a canoe or kayak.

LOS INDIOS

Harlingen fly fishing guide Rick Hartman recommends one of the drainages on Rangerville Road near the small community of Los Indios in Cameron County south of Harlingen. A canal-like drainage used for agriculture irrigation, it holds good numbers of Florida-strain largemouth in the pound to two pound range. It is accessible by canoe or kayak and for bank fishing. Hartman recommends poppers late in the day or streamer imitations that mimic coppernose bluegill, one of the main forage fish in the drainage.

A large number of resacas in Cameron County near the Bayview community north of Brownsville, accessible along County Roads 2480, 3069 and 510, are excellent for fly fishing, Hartman says. These resacas have heavy vegetation and overhanging brush that provides excellent habitat for largemouth as well as coppernose bluegill, redear and longear sunfish. The resacas also hold some Rio Grande perch. The resacas are also excellent for viewing some of the birds and wildlife native to the valley including chachalacas, kingfishers, kiskadees and cardinals. Early morning fishing in the spring and fall months offers the best fly fishing on these South Texas resacas, Hartman says.

Resaca near San Benito, Texas.

STATE PARK WATERS

Lake Houston State Park

Located a half hour's drive from Houston and situated between the East San Jacinto River on the East and Caney Creek and Peach Creek on the west, Lake Houston State Park provides flyfishers with access to a number of creeks and rivers. Despite its name, the park does not provide boat access to Lake Houston, but the slow flowing creeks in the park hold largemouth and sunfish.

The park, which covers almost 5,000 acres, is open year around and there are a small number of walk-in tent campsites with showers. For additional information on park facilities, call (713) 354-6881.

Galveston Island State Park

Known primarily as a saltwater fly fishing destination, Galveston Island State Park also has three freshwater ponds that hold a good population of largemouth and sunfish. These ponds are best fished from the bank or from a float tube. Water levels on the ponds vary with rainfall but the largest of the three offers excellent fly fishing action. Anglers can find lots of action by wading along the channels and casting Wolly Buggers or poppers along the edges of submerged vegetation. The scenic little ponds attract a rich variety of bird life including roseate spoonbills, Louisiana herons, yellow-crowned night herons and black-necked stilts. Alligators also are present in the ponds.

The park, which has 170 campsites and provides access both to the Gulf of Mexico beachfront and Galveston Bay estuaries, is located on Termini Road (Texas (FM) 3005) east of downtown Galveston toward San Luis Pass. Flyfishers interested in fishing the freshwater lakes can obtain the combination to the locked gate on the north side of Texas (FM) 3005 near the park entrance. The $3 per person fee for entering the park properties covers fishing on the freshwater ponds.

Freshwater lake at Galveston Island State Park with roseate spoonbills on the wing.

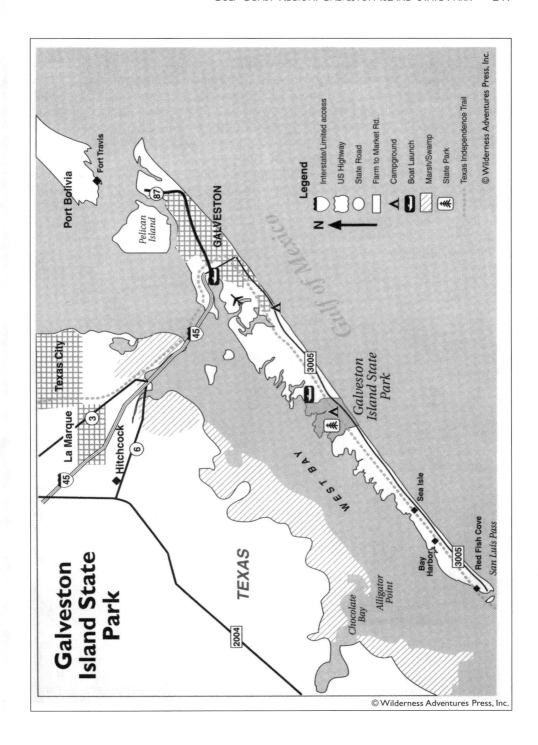

Galveston
Island State
Park

TEXAS

Port Bolivia

Fort Travis

Pelican
Island

GALVESTON

Texas City

La Marque

Hitchcock

Gulf of Mexico

Galveston
Island State
Park

WEST BAY

Chocolate
Bay

Alligator
Point

Bay
Harbor

Sea Isle

Red Fish Cove

San Luis Pass

N

Legend

Interstate/Limited access
US Highway
State Road
Farm to Market Rd.
Campground
Boat Launch
Marsh/Swamp
State Park
Texas Independence Trail

© Wilderness Adventures Press, Inc.

BRAZOS BEND STATE PARK

Located southwest of Houston off US 59 near the communities of Rosenberg and Richmond, Brazos Bend State Park offers bank fishing at a number of lakes. Due possibly to the large alligator population, swimming and boating are not allowed on the lakes but there are several fishing piers and a number of scenic trails that provide openings for well placed roll casts to bedding sunfish and cruising largemouth. This park, located less than an hour's drive from Houston, offers a wild and scenic setting for fly fishing as well as for viewing wildlife and birds.

To reach Brazos Bend State Park from Houston, take US 59 south toward Rosenberg and after crossing the Brazos River Bridge, take the Crabb River Road exit. From the Crabb River Road exit, turn left on Texas (FM) 2759 and travel south about two miles until it connects with Texas (FM) 762. Continue south on 762 for 14 miles to the park entrance. The fee for entering the park is $3 per person and there are 120 picnic sites. A visitor's center is open on weekends with interpretive programs on park wildlife.

Outdoor visitors to Brazos Bend State Park will find an observation tower and platforms for wildlife observation and photography of more than 270 species of birds; 21 species of reptiles and amphibians, including American alligator and 23 species of mammals including bobcat, white-tailed deer, raccoon, gray fox, and javelina (pictured above).

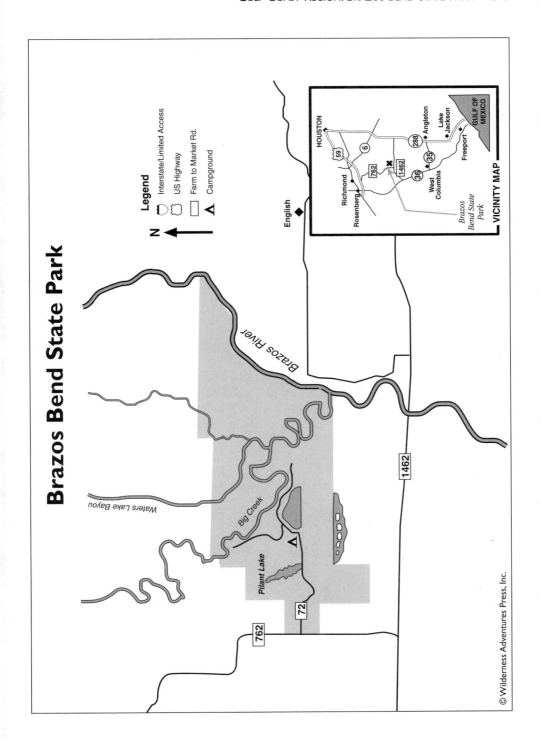

Brazos Bend State Park

Legend

- Interstate/Limited Access
- US Highway
- Farm to Market Rd.
- Campground

N

Brazos River

Waters Lake Bayou

Big Creek

Pilant Lake

762

72

1462

English

VICINITY MAP

HOUSTON

Richmond

Rosenberg

59

6

762

1462

36

288

35

Angleton

Lake Jackson

Freeport

West Columbia

GULF OF MEXICO

Brazos Bend State Park

© Wilderness Adventures Press, Inc.

URBAN OPTIONS
HOUSTON
Houston Bayous and Drainages

Grass carp and several other freshwater species make their homes along the 500 miles of drainage channels and bayous that snake through the city of Houston. Some are overgrown with wild vegetation while others are bordered with groomed lawns with park benches. The six primary bayous that help drain Houston are Buffalo, Brays, White Oak, Greens, Simms, and Hunting.

One of the popular urban fly fishing sites in Houston is Brays Bayou near the intersection of Stella Link and South Braeswood. During low-water periods, most of the moving water is confined to the channels in the middle of the bayous. But at the Stella Link and Braeswood location, the channel flows into a deeper hole where rocks have been washed downstream and provide shade and protection for the carp population. Several culverts drain into the basin, delivering nutrients that sustain this urban fishery.

In the bayou drainages of Houston, grass carp have proven to be strong fighters that will test the drag on a top-of-the-line reel. They push big wakes as they feed in shallow water and bear a strong resemblance to saltwater redfish. Flyfishers can find them sipping insects off the surface or waving their broad tails in the air while they root for food on the bottom.

The grass carp are easily spooked and offer challenging sight-casting practice. Depending on the mood of the fish on a particular day, presentations can require an "in your face" saltwater-flats approach or a carefully dead-drifted dry fly in the slow-moving current. Sloppy casting or unnecessary movement will cause the bigger grass carp to explode in churning boils.

Mark Marmon guides flyfishers on inner-city fly fishing adventures in Houston. Trips can include a visit to Brays Bayou, the Lakes of Post Oak, and the ponds near the Astrodome. Contact Marmon in Houston at Metro Anglers (713) 666-8868.

PRIVATE WATERS
BIERI LAKES

Located 40 miles south of Houston outside Angleton in Brazoria County, this managed fishery offers guided trips for Florida-strain largemouth and Florida / northern (native) hybrid largemouth on three lakes ranging in size from 40- to 125-acres. The scenic, heavily wooded lakes also hold crappie, bluegill and catfish. Flyfishers can prospect for largemouth around a variety of habitat such as scattered timber, brush piles, stumps and boat Houses. The lakes also have several small islands, which form underwater points, drop offs, and deep channels between the islands. Anglers have access to skiffs with electric motors. Fishing is catch and release only for bass. The fee is $150 a person per day (two person minimum). Weekend packages and lodging are also available. For more information, call (979) 848-8181.

THE LAKES OF DANBURY

A one-time rice farm and cattle ranch run by the Zwahr family, The Lakes of Danbury is one of the state's oldest and largest privately managed bass fisheries and is a model for a host of other fee-fishing waters springing up across Texas. Danbury's 11 fishing lakes host Florida-strain largemouth, as well as hybrid stripers and coppernose bluegills.

Danbury's fisheries managers say that during the spring and fall anglers often catch 60 to 70 bass, averaging from two to four pounds, in a day's fishing. Some of the lakes are designed to offer anglers a chance at big numbers of medium-sized fish while other lakes are known for the few, the proud and the heavyweight. The top-end bass at Danbury can weight in at 17 pounds or more. Danbury fisheries managers say it is not uncommon to catch 10 pound largemouth on some of the lakes.

Like wary bass on most lakes, the bigger fish on these managed waters don't routinely hang out in places where it's easy to cast a fly. The well-placed popper under an overhanging branch, tight to a stickup, is much more likely to provoke a response than a safe throw two feet from the bank.

Lakes of Danbury is located about 40 miles south of Houston near Angleton off Texas 35. The fee of $250 per day includes an optional boat and guide. Flyfishers also may walk the banks and sight-cast to fish. For more information, call 800-460-8414.

Flyfisherman casting from the bank of a ranch pond in South Texas.

Gulf Coast Hub Cities
Beaumont

Population -116,875   **Elevation - 32'**
Area Code - 409   **County - Jefferson**

ACCOMMODATIONS
Beaumont Hilton, 2355 IH-10 South / 842-3600 / 283 rooms / $69 -$134
Best Western - Jefferson Inn, 1610 IH - 10 South / 800-528-1234 / 120 Rooms / $54 - $75
Holiday Inn - Beaumont Plaza, 3950 IH-10 South at Walden Road / 842-5995 / 253 rooms / $69 - $125
La Quinta Inn - Beaumont, 220 IH-10 North / 800-531-5900 / 122 rooms / $49 - $99

CAMPGROUNDS
East Lucas RV Park, Tent and RV sites available / 2590 East Lucas Drive Beaumont, TX / 899-9209 Information / d.Sorenson@worldnet.att.net www.wastlucasrvpark.com

RESTAURANTS
Patillo's BBQ, 2775 Washington / 832-2572 / $
Robert's Fajitas and Tamales, 6096 College / 866 3503 / $
Texas Pig Stand, 612 Washington / 835 5753 / Open 24 hours / $

SPORTING GOODS
Academy Sports, 6250 Eastex / 898-1569
Oshman's, 166 Gateway / 832-7781
Outdoor Outfitter, 3803 Calder / 833-0716

CAMPING
Tyrell Park, take Walden Road off I-10 (exit 848) to Tyrell Park Road / 838-3648 / 46 camper and RV sites
East Lucas RV Park, 2590 E. Lucas Dr., 1.4 miles off US 69N / 899 9209 / RV sites and tend camping

FOR MORE INFORMATION
Beaumont Convention and Visitors Bureau
801 Main
Beaumont, TX
880-3750

Port Arthur

Population - 57,709   **Area Code - 409**
County - Jefferson

ACCOMMODATIONS

Holiday Inn - Park Central, 2929 Jimmy Johnson Boulevard / 724-5000 /
164 rooms / $62 - 84
Best Western - Airport Inn, 200 Memorial Hwy. 69, Nederland / 727 1631 /
115 rooms / $46 - 63

BED AND BREAKFAST

Aurora Bed and Breakfast, 141 Woodworth Boulevard / 983 4205 / five bedrooms
/ $75 - $95

RESTAURANTS

Esther's Seafood and Oyster Bar, 9902½ Rainbow Drive (Texas 87 at the Rainbow
Bridge) / 962-6268
Dorothy's Front Porch, Homes road off US 69 and Beauxart Gardens Road
between Port Arthur and Beaumont / 722-1472
Larry's French Market and Cajun Cafeteria, Texas Farm Road 366, Groves /
962-3381

SPORTING GOODS

Fish-er Hunt, 3001 Hwy 73 / 736-1884

Flyfishers casting shoreline on Sabine River near Orange.

Houston

Population - 1,879,912 **Elevation - 55'**
Area Code - 713 **County - Harris**
(unless otherwise noted)

ACCOMMODATIONS

Days Inn - Houston, Hobby Airport, 1505 College ave / I-45 / 946-5900 /
124 rooms / $$
Comfort Suites-Near the Galleria, 6221 Richmond Avenue / 787-0004 / 62 rooms
/ $$$
Crowne Plaza - Houston / Galleria, 2222 West Loop South / 800-327-6213 /
476 rooms / $$
Holiday Inn Astrodome, 8111 Kirby Drive / 790-1900 / 235 rooms / $$$
Holiday Inn - Intercontinental Airport, 15222 JFK Blvd. / 415 rooms / $$$
Holiday Inn - NASA, 1300 NASA Road 1 / (281) 333-2500 / 223 rooms / $$
La Quinta Inn - Hobby Airport, 9902 Gulf Freeway / 800-531-5900 / 130 rooms /
$$
La Quinta Inn and Suites - Bush Intercontinental Airport, 15510 JFK Boulevard /
132 rooms / $$$
Holiday Inn Select - Greenway Plaza, 2712 Southwest Freeway / 523 8448 /
355 rooms / $$$

BED AND BREAKFAST

Angel Arbor Bed and Breakfast Inn, 848 Heights Blvd. / 800-722-8788 / 5 rooms /
$$$
Patrician Bed and Breakfast Inn, 1200 Southmore Blvd. / 800-553-5797 / 6 rooms
/ $$$

CAMPGROUNDS

Houston Central KOA, 1620 Peachleaf Houston, TX / 800-562-2132 Reservations /
281-442-3700 Information / www.koa.com
Houston East KOA, 11810 I-10 East Baytown, TX / 800-562-3418 Reservations /
281-383-3618 Information / www.koa.com
Houston West KOA: 35303 Cooper Rd. Brookshire, TX. / 1-800-562-5417 /
Reservations 1-281-375-5678 / Information www.koa.com

RESTAURANTS

The Moose Cafe, 1340 West Gray / 520-9696 / $
Good Company Texas Bar-B-Que, 5109 Kirby (also at 8911 Katy Freeway) / 522-
2530 / $
Ragin' Cajun, 4302 Richmond / 621-6602 / Open Monday through Saturday for
lunch and dinner / $
Trebeard's, 315 Travis (also at 1117 Texas and 1100 Louisiana) / 229-8248 / open
11 p.m. to 2 p.m. Monday through Thursday and Friday also open 5 p.m. to
9 p.m. / $
Good Company Texas Seafood, 2621 Westpark / 523-7154 / open daily for lunch
and dinner / $

Fly Shops and Guide Services
Angler's Edge, 1141-5 Uptown Park Blvd. / 993-0208
Bass Pro Shop, 500 Katy Mills Circle #145, Katy / 281-644-2200
Canoesport, 5808 S. Rice Ave. / 660-7000
Cut Rate Sporting Goods Inc., 10551 Telephone Road (Near Hobby Airport) / 827-7762
Flywater Outfitters - Cut Rate Sporting Goods Inc., 8933 Katy Freeway / 827-7762
Orvis Houston, 5848 Westheimer Rd / 713-783-2111
Westbank Angler, 5000 Westheimer / 961-3474
Tackle Hut, 216 W. Little York Rd #C / 713-694-8008

Sporting Goods Stores
Academy Sports-
    565 Uvalde / 713-453-8366
    10375 N. Freeway / 281-445-9838
    12700 N.W. Freeway / 713-895-7395
    13150 Breton Ridge Street / 281-894-5858
    10414 Guld Freeway / 713-944-7511
    8236 S. Gessner / 713-271-1679
    8723 Katy Freeway / 713-465-9565
    2404 S.W. Freeway / 713-520-1795
    1450 Westheimer / 281-870-0105
Oshman's-
    1200 McKinney Ave. / 713-650-8240
    2131 South Post Oak Blvd / 713-622-4940
    8625 F.M. 1960 West / 281-807-9020
    975 Gessner / 713-467-1155

Airports
William P. Hobby Airport, 643-4597 / Southwest Airlines: 800-435-9792 / American Airlines / American Eagle: 800-433-7300 / Delta: 800-221-1212 / Continental Airlines: 800-525-0280
George Bush Intercontinental Airport / 281-230-3100 / Aeromexico: 800-237-6630 / Air Canada: 800-776-3000 / Airfrance: 800-237-2747 / America West / 800-235-9292 / American Airlines: 800-433-7300 / Atlantic Southeast Airlines (Delta): 800-282-3424 / Aviasca: 266-6653 / British Airways: 800-247-9297 / Continental Airlines: 800-525-0280 / Delta: 800-221-1212 / KLM Royal Dutch Airlines: 800-374-7747:Lufthansa German Airline: 800-645-3880 / Southwest Airlines 800-435-9792 / Sun Country Airlines: 800-359-5786 / TACA International Airlines:800-535-8780 / United Airlines: 800-241-6522 / US Air: 800-428-4822

For More Information
Houston Convention and Visitors Bureau
801 Congress
Houston, Texas
227-3100

Galveston

Population - 64,519	**Elevation - 20'**
Area Code - 409	**County - Galveston**

ACCOMMODATIONS

Flagship Hotel, 2501 Seawall Boulevard / (409) 762-9000 / $$

La Quinta Inn - Galveston, 1402 Seawall Boulevard / (800-) 531-5900 / 118 rooms / $$ to $$$

Motel 6, 7404 Avenue J / 800-4MOTEL6 / 114 rooms / $ to $$

BED AND BREAKFAST

Stacia Leigh BandB aboard the Chryseis, Pier 22 at Harborside Drive / shipboard lodging on a 120-foot schooner / (409) 750-8858 / $$$.

The Queen Anne Bed and Breakfast Inn, 1915 Sealy / (409) 763-7088 / $$ to $$$

RESTAURANTS

Mosquito Cafe, 628 14th Street / (409) 763-1010 / $

Cafe Michaelburger, 8826 Seawall Boulevard / (409) 740-3639 / closed Monday and Tuesday / $

Queen's Bar-B-Que, 3428 Avenue S. / (409) 762-3151 / $

Slices, 2113 Post office / gourmet deli sandwiches, pizzas, take-out lunches / 766-1779 / $$

SPORTING GOODS

Bayou Fishing Pier, 8227 Teichman Road / 740-9990

Galveston Bait & Tackle, 9301 Broadway / 740-1185

Islands Custom Tackle, 6608 Stewart Road / 744-1054

Smitty's Bait & Tackle, 7805 Broadway Street / 744-7705

FOR MORE INFORMATION

Galveston Island Chamber of Commerce
621 Moody Avenue
Suite 300
Galveston TX 77550
(409) 763-5326

Victoria

Population - 63,824
Area Code - 361

Elevation - 93'
County - Victoria

ACCOMMODATIONS
Best Western, 2605 Houston Hwy. / 578-9911
Holiday Inn, 2705 Houston Hwy. / 575-0251
Ramada Inn, 3901 Houston Hwy. / 578-2723
La Quinta Inn, 7603 N. Navarro St. / 572-3585

BED AND BREAKFAST
Friendly Oaks Bed and Breakfast, 210 East Juan Linn Street / 575-0000 / 4 rooms
/ $$

RESTAURANTS
Ramsey's, 1403 N. Navarro / 572-3287
Luby's, Victoria Mall / 572-3287

SPORTING GOODS
Wal-Mart, 9002 N. Navarro / 573-0041 / open 24 hours
Victoria All Sports, 1902 Houston Hwy. / 575-0655 / Monday through Saturday 8
a.m to 6 p.m.
K-Mart, 3601 N. Navarro / 572-8211 / Open 24 hours
Tackle Box, 3305 N. Ben Jordan St. / 575 8700 / Monday through Saturday 9 a.m.
to 7 p.m.

GUIDES
Tom's Tackle and Guide Service / 888-436-2533 / half day and full day trips
Bill's Guide Service / 713-541-2322 / half day and full day trips

Flyfisher wading at Coleto Creek State Park near Victoria.

Corpus Christi

Population - 275,924   Elevation - 35'
Area Code - 361   County - Nueces

ACCOMMODATIONS

Omni Bayfront Hotel, 900 North Shoreline Boulevard / 887-1600 / 474 rooms / $$$

Best Western - Corpus Christi Inn, 11217 IH-37 / 241-6675 / 141 rooms / $$

La Quinta Inn - South, 6225 South Padre Island Drive / 800-531-5900 / 129 rooms

BED AND BREAKFAST

Clubhouse B and B, 211 Indiana / 887-7514 / 2 rooms / $$

Smith Place, 420 Grant Place / 853-1222 / $$

CAMPING

Hatch RV Park, 3101 Up River Road / 800-332-4509

Colonia del Ray RV Park, Tent and RV sites available / 1717 Waldron Rd. Corpus Christi, TX / 937-2435 Local / 800.580.2435 Toll free / coloniadelray@gocampingamerica.com

Padre Palms, Tent and RV sites available / 131 Skipper Lane Corpus Christi, TX. 361-937-2125 Local / 800-552-6250 Toll Free / padrepalms@gocampingamerica.com

RESTAURANTS

Water Street Seafood Company, 309 North Water / 882-8684 / $

Snoopy's Pier, Intracoastal Waterway at JFK Bridge / $

FLY SHOPS AND GUIDE SERVICES

Gruene Outfitters of Corpus Christi, 1233 Airline Road / 994-8361 / Full service guide shop, guide services recommended / instructions in casting

SPORTING GOODS

Academy Sports, 4914 South Padre Island / 361-992-9022

Oshman's, 5858-46 South Padre Island / 361-993-0832

AIRPORTS

Corpus Christi International Airport / 289-2675 / American Airlines / American Eagle: 800-433-7300 / Atlantic Southeast Airlines (Delta) 800-282-3424 / Continental Airlines: 800-525-0280 / Southwest Airlines: 800-435-9792

FOR MORE INFORMATION

Corpus Christi Area Convention and Tourist Bureau
1823 North Chaparral
P.O. Box 659
Corpus Christi, TX 78403
561-2000

Harlingen

Population - 59,686   **Elevation - 36'**
Area Code - 956   **County - Cameron**

ACCOMMODATIONS

Best Western - Harlingen Inn, 6779 West Expressway 83 / 800-425-7080 /
103 Rooms / $$

La Quinta Inn - Harlingen, 1002 South Expressway / 800-531-5900 / 130 rooms /
$$

CAMPGROUNDS

Sundance RV Village, Tent and RV sites available / 6101 W Business 83 / 423-8314
/ Reservations: sundanceht@aol.com

RESTAURANTS

Applebee's Neighborhood Grill and Bar, 1519 West Harrison Street / 425-5544 / $
Lone Star Restaurant, 4210 West Business 83 / 423-8002 / $

SPORTING GOODS STORES

Hook, Line and Sinker, 2704 S. 77 Sunshinestrip / 956-428-6473

FOR MORE INFORMATION

Harlingen Chamber of Commerce / Convention and Visitors Bureau
311 East Tyler
Harlingen, TX 78550
425-3870

FLY FISHING CLUBS IN REGION 4

Gulf Coast Flyrodders
Victoria
Texas Flyfishers
P.O. Box 571134
Houston TX 77257
Laguna Madre Flyfishers
P.O. Box 2729
South Padre Island, TX 78597

LODGING PRICE KEY

$	=	$30 - $50 per night
$$	=	$50 - $70 per night
$$$	=	$70 per night and up

RESTAURANT PRICE KEY

$	=	$10 and under per meal
$$	=	$10 - $20 per meal
$$$	=	$20 and up

REGION 5

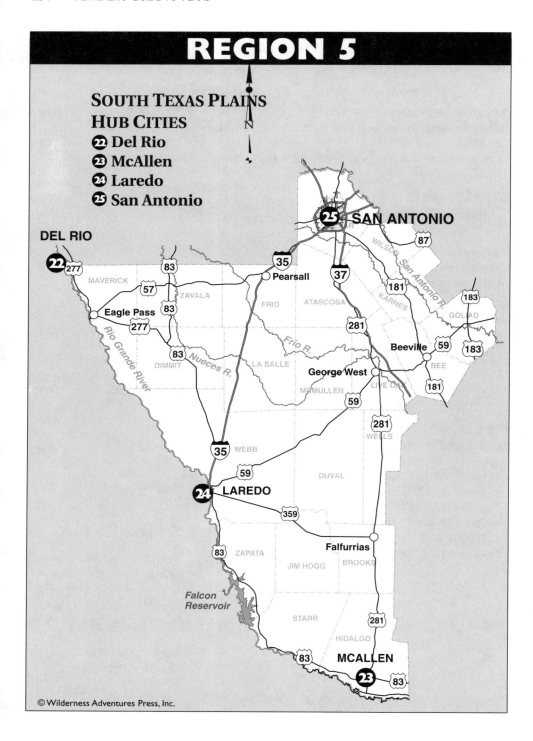

SOUTH TEXAS PLAINS
HUB CITIES
㉒ Del Rio
㉓ McAllen
㉔ Laredo
㉕ San Antonio

© Wilderness Adventures Press, Inc.

South Texas Plains

REGION 5

PANHANDLE PLAINS

PRAIRIES & LAKES

BIG BEND COUNTRY

HILL COUNTRY

PINEY WOODS

SOUTH TEXAS PLAINS

GULF COAST

From the edge of the Hill Country in south-central Texas, this region stretches south-ward from San Antonio through brush and mesquite plains to the sabal palm groves and subtropical environment of the Lower Rio Grande Valley.

In the dense grassland and mesquite of the "Wild Horse Desert" highly skilled Mexican cowboys, called vaqueros, once herded wild Texas Longhorns. Today, their descendants still use those skills on modern Texas cattle ranches, where oil exploration, deer, dove and quail hunting also contribute to the annual income. Rivers that run through the region forming reservoirs and offering angling opportunities include the Rio Grande, Frio and Nueces. Choke Canyon Lake and Falcon Reservoir offer spectacular wildlife viewing and some of the best bass fishing in the state.

The most prevalent fisheries in this semi-arid region of the state are manmade lakes with earthen dams, called "tanks" that are found on almost all South Texas ranches. Designed to provide water for livestock, many of these lakes are stocked with voracious largemouth. A number of these ranches allow flyfishers to sample the action on these lakes for a fee.

Major cities including, San Antonio, Laredo and McAllen, reflect the region's rich Hispanic heritage.

RIVERS
RIO GRANDE RIVER

Falcon Dam to Roma

Fly fishing in one of the most remote, wild and scenic waterways in the South Texas Plains region is available to adventurous anglers along some 40 small islands located in the Rio Grande River between Falcon Dam and Roma. Often referred to as the "Lost Islands of the Rio Grande," ownership of these islands is divided evenly between the United States and Mexico. Half of the islands are on the US side of the river while the other half are on the Mexican side of the river.

The islands, shoreline vegetation, and flooded timber provide ideal habitat for a variety of fish species including largemouth, sunfish and grass carp.

Float trips from Falcon Dam to Roma, a 20 mile stretch, can take a full day and anyone attempting the float should obtain information on releases from the dam. Canoeists and kayakers should be experienced enough to handle swift currents on short notice. Prevailing south winds off the Gulf can present a different problem for paddlers, creating headwinds that make paddling particularly arduous over the 20-mile distance. Shorter trips between Falcon Dam and the small communities of Salineno or Santa Margarita offer more fishing time and less paddling. Townspeople are cooperative in watching over vehicles for the shuttle runs to put-ins.

Smuggling activity is a fact of life on this vast and remote border country. Fortunately, smugglers are nocturnal by trade and not the least bit sociable. On day float trips, the recommended way to sample this intriguing fishery, anglers are much more likely to come into contact with the Border Patrol and US Customs officials patrolling the waterway.

The Rio Grande provides ideal habitat for a variety of fish, including this sunfish.

NUECES RIVER

US 59 Bridge Crossing at George West

While the red clay and sandy soils of the South Texas Ranch country rovers give the Nueces a totally different look here than on the clear flowing limestone ledges of the Hill Country, flyfishers prospecting along the shoreline vegetation can find good largemouth and sunfish action on the stretch of river near this crossing.

A launch ramp at this bridge crossing provides access to a stretch of shoreline that also holds white bass and channel catfish.

FRIO RIVER

Several short stretches of the Frio River downstream from Choke Canyon Reservoir offer flyfishers opportunities for wade fishing and short float trips. Flyfishers can catch largemouth, white bass, sunfish, carp, and catfish.

Three Rivers

There is public access to the Frio River at Tips Park, which is located near the Texas 72 Bridge at Three Rivers. Anglers can wade fishing downstream or use the park for a take-out point for about a 3 mile float from the dam on Choke Canyon Reservoir. There is a small dam and waterfall at the park that creates a deep pool that holds largemouth and sunfish. Boaters and anglers are advised to be on the alert for alligators on this waterway. The small, tree-shaded park has picnic tables and RV campgrounds. For more information contact park staff at (361)786-4324.

Tilden

A launch ramp in the community of Tilden provides access to the Frio River and upper end of Choke Canyon Reservoir. This stretch of the Frio can provide excellent largemouth action for flyfishers. Anglers should be advised that they would be sharing the waterway with alligators. Before setting out on a float, check conditions and water levels with Texas Parks and Wildlife Department office at Mathis (361) 547-7225.

Small dam and waterfall on Frio River in Tips Park, Three Rivers, Texas

LAKES

LAKE CALAVERAS

Located in Bexar County just south of San Antonio on Interstate 37, 3,450-acre Lake Calaveras lies on Chupaderas and Calaveras creeks. The lake is one of the most heavily stocked in the state. In addition to a population of Florida-strain largemouth, crappie, sunfish, striped bass and hybrid striped bass, the lake also is home to red drum, or redfish, which enjoy rapid growth rates but do not reproduce in the freshwater environment. Month old, quarter- to one-inch long redfish fingerlings are planted in the lake and reportedly are now growing to between 17- to 21-inches in their first year. The Texas Parks and Wildlife Department also has experimented with stockings of corvina in the lake.

Largemouth exceeding 10 pounds and red drum of more than 20 pounds have been landed in the lake. With almost an eleven-month growing season, the lake has an abundance of forage fish, including gizzard shad, threadfin shad and tilapia.

Lake Calaveras fishing guide Jeff Snyder says there are a number of options available to flyfishers at the lake. He says flyfishers should time their visits to the lake based on the periods in which the lake's population of striped bass, hybrid striped bass and freshwater redfish are most active. "There are times when there is a good topwater bite with our hybrid stripers in the spring," he says. He says it also is productive to cast -weighted streamers up in the shallows when the striped bass are spawning in the spring.

Lake Calaveras is normally clear enough to offer opportunities for anglers using artificial lures and flies, Snyder says. He notes water clarity at Calaveras and Braunig can be affected by algae blooms during the warmer months, so flyfishers should consider these factors when planning a trip. Water visibility is better at Calaveras than at Braunig, Snyder says, because Calaveras has better water circulation than at Braunig, a smaller lake. The striper action begins to emerge in the last part of January through the first part of February. As the water temperature starts to stabilize in the upper 60s to the low 70s, the striper activity picks up significantly, Snyder says. At this time of year, the fish are normally holding at depths of 15 to 20 feet.

When the water temperature moves up to the mid 70 degree mark, the fish start moving on to shallower structure. This is when stripers will hold on structure between about 18 feet to 8 feet and "roamers" will begin working up into the shallows into water depths of 5 to 18 feet. The average depth to find spawning fish is from 5 to 10 feet, Snyder says. Once the water temperature starts warming up, the striper action tapers off and they become more dormant, Snyder says. An excellent technique for all anglers on Calaveras, including flyfishers, is to locate fish on electronic fish finders and then put the flies in front of them. Snyder says the introduction of talapia in the lake as a means of controlling vegetation not only accomplished that goal by virtually eliminating all vegetation in the lake, but also has created an abundance of forage fish. The lack of cover has held back the growth of the largemouth population because the fry no longer can use the vegetation to hide from predators. Snyder says there is a good sunfish population in the lake and that Texas Parks and Wildlife biologists have found bluegills up to a pound in their sampling efforts.

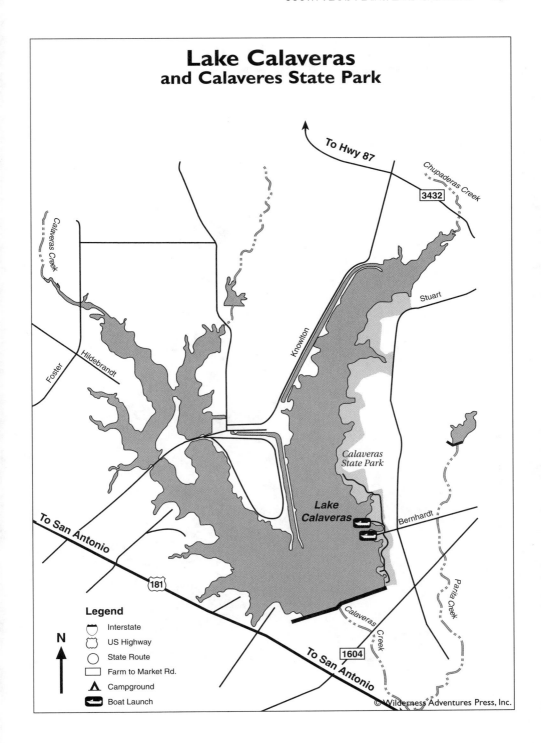

Lake Calaveras
and Calaveres State Park

To Hwy 87

Chupaderas Creek

3432

Calaveras Creek

Stuart

Foster

Hildebrandt

Knowlton

Calaveras
State Park

To San Antonio

Lake
Calaveras

Bernhardt

Parita Creek

181

Calaveras Creek

To San Antonio

1604

Legend

N

Interstate
US Highway
State Route
Farm to Market Rd.
Campground
Boat Launch

©Wilderness Adventures Press, Inc.

LAKE BRAUNIG

Located in Bexar County south of San Antonio of Interstate 37, Lake Braunig is a 1,350-acre, heavily stocked power plant lake that holds Florida-strain largemouth, crappie, and hybrid striped bass. The lake also offers one of the largest fisheries for red drum in a freshwater environment in the state.

Don't be surprised by what takes your fly in this lake. The long growing period and large forage fish population in the lake have prompted Texas Parks and Wildlife biologists to experiment over the years with stockings of Nile perch, tarpon, corvina and spotted sea trout.

Flyfisher shows off a beautiful crappie from a South Texas lake.

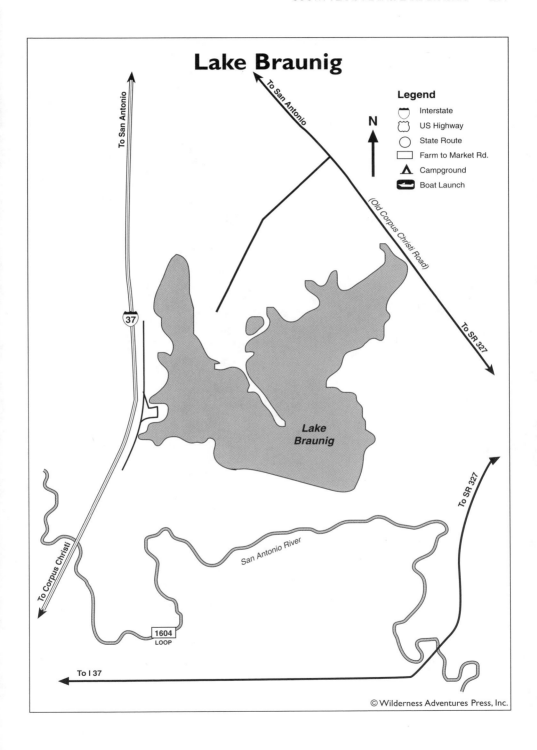

Lake Braunig

To San Antonio

To San Antonio

(Old Corpus Christi Road)

To SR 327

Legend

- Interstate
- US Highway
- State Route
- Farm to Market Rd.
- ▲ Campground
- Boat Launch

N

37

Lake
Braunig

To Corpus Christi

To SR 327

San Antonio River

1604
LOOP

To I 37

© Wilderness Adventures Press, Inc.

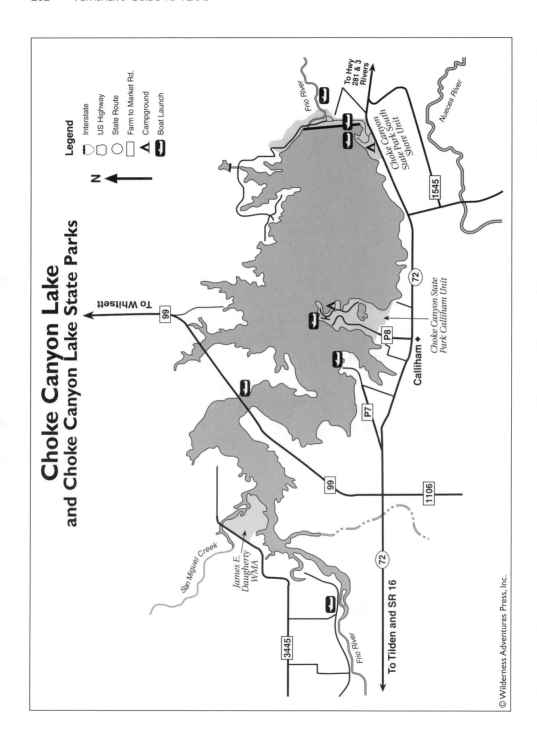

Choke Canyon Lake
and Choke Canyon Lake State Parks

Legend
- Interstate
- US Highway
- State Route
- Farm to Market Rd.
- ▲ Campground
- Boat Launch

N

To Whitsett

To Hwy 281 & 3 Rivers

Frio River

Nueces River

Choke Canyon State Park South Shore Unit

1545

72

P8

Choke Canyon State Park Calliham Unit

Calliham ◆

P7

99

1106

San Miguel Creek

James E. Daugherty WMA

3445

Frio River

72

To Tilden and SR 16

© Wilderness Adventures Press, Inc.

CHOKE CANYON LAKE

Located on the Frio River west of Three Rivers off Texas 72 in McMullen and Live Oak counties, this 26,000-acre lake in the heart of South Texas brush country offers excellent largemouth action for flyfishers that target the lake's protected shorelines, coves and edges of heavy submerged vegetation. In addition to Florida-strain largemouth, there are abundant stripers and white bass in the lake. Coppernose bluegill round out the offerings targeted by fly rodders. The shores and parks on this lake offer a glimpse of a wide range of wildlife including, large population of whitetail deer, wild turkey, quail, javelina, and American alligator.

One of the pleasant dilemmas at Choke Canyon is that so much water and structure looks so attractive for fishing that often it is hard to decide where to start fishing. There are many areas near launch ramps that, with a little scouting, can be extremely productive. Due to the hefty largemouth and heavy cover, veteran flyfishers on Choke Canyon recommend short, stout leaders and fly rods in the 8- to 10-weight range when doing battle near brush and timber. Many of the techniques used on Lake Fork (See Pineywoods Region) will apply at Choke Canyon.

Veteran Choke Canyon anglers note that largemouth congregate around stands of hydrilla during the summer months. Dropping deer hair and hard-bodied poppers with industrial strength weed guards through the holes in the floating mats can draw explosive strikes from wide-bodied bass.

Launch ramp at Choke Canyon State Park, South Shore Unit.

From October through December, flyfishers can enjoy excellent topwater action on the lake, sometimes all day long. Some of the largest bass are caught at Choke Canyon during the winter and early spring. Flyfishers are very much in the ball game on this South Texas Lake from December through April because bass will often move up into shallow areas close to gullies and drop-offs. Even on days when the air temperature drops into the 30s, bass on this lake can be found in water two feet deep.

There are extensive camping and boat launch facilities as well as shore fishing access at two units of Choke Canyon State Park.

In addition to launch ramps and bank fishing access to the lake at the two units of Choke Canyon State Park, there is also a launch ramp on the north end of the lake off Texas (FM) 99 that provides access to some of the prime nearby coves and shorelines suitable for fly fishing from kayaks and canoes. There also are launch ramps available on the south side of the lake at the Bracken Boat Ramp off Texas 72 near Tilden and at the Mason Point Boat Ramp, four miles off Texas 72 on Park Road 7.

Choke Canyon State Park

Entrances to the two units of the 1,485-acre Choke Canyon State Park are located about 10 miles apart on the shores of 26,000-acre Choke Canyon Reservoir just off Texas 72, east of US 281 and the town of Three Rivers. The two units, South Shore and Calliham, are located within a 38,000-acre wildlife management area, and offer, in addition to the fishing for largemouth, striped bass, white bass and sunfish, exceptional wildlife viewing and birding opportunities.

In recent years flyfishers have found excellent largemouth action along protected shorelines and in the many coves that are an attractive feature of this otherwise intimidating reservoir. Flyfishers use canoes, kayaks and other small watercraft to prospect around the flooded timber and aquatic vegetation. There are open patches of water among heavy growths of hydrilla that provide undisturbed habitat for largemouth and prime ambush sites for well placed poppers. The coves often hold some of the lake's clearest water, which can vary, depending on wind conditions, from downright murky to clear brackish. The entrance to the South Shore Unit at Choke Canyon State Park is 4.2 miles west of Three Rivers on Texas 72. For additional information contact the park at (361) 786-3538.

In addition to boat ramp, camping and picnicking facilities and shore fishing access, the Calliham Unit also has a 90-acre catch-and-release only lake for bass that is ideal for bank fishing. For additional information on lake conditions and park facilities, contact the Calliham Unit office at (512) 786 3868.

Coves at Choke Canyon State Park, South Shore Unit.

Certified scale station, South Shore Unit.

Alligator at launch ramp, South Shore Unit.

LAKE CASA BLANCA

Lake Casa Blanca, a relatively shallow lake, is located on a flat plain surrounded by brush country just west of Laredo on US 59 next to the Laredo Airport. The lake was impounded in 1946, and was one of the early sites of experimental stockings of redfish. It also received one infusion of walleyes in the 1970s. The 1,100-acre lake, which has an average depth of 12 feet, has heavy shoreline vegetation, which serves as excellent habitat for largemouth as well as sunfish, white and black crappie, and catfish.

The lake can attract recreational boating and water-skiing activity during the summer months and is best fished early and late during this period or during the fall and early spring when anglers usually have the lake to themselves.

The 371 acres that surround the lake are part of Lake Casa Blanca State Park and offer shoreline fishing and boat launch access to the lake.

Lake Casa Blanca International Park

Located in Webb County near Laredo off US 59, the 371-acre Lake Casa Blanca State Park offers access to the 1,100-acre lake. In addition to a boat ramp, the park offers campsites with partial hookups and showers. For more information, contact park officials at (210) 725-3826.

Wildlife species which have been noted in the park include jackrabbit, ground squirrel, cottontail, deer, and javelina.

Lake Casa Blanca
and Lake Casa Blanca State Park

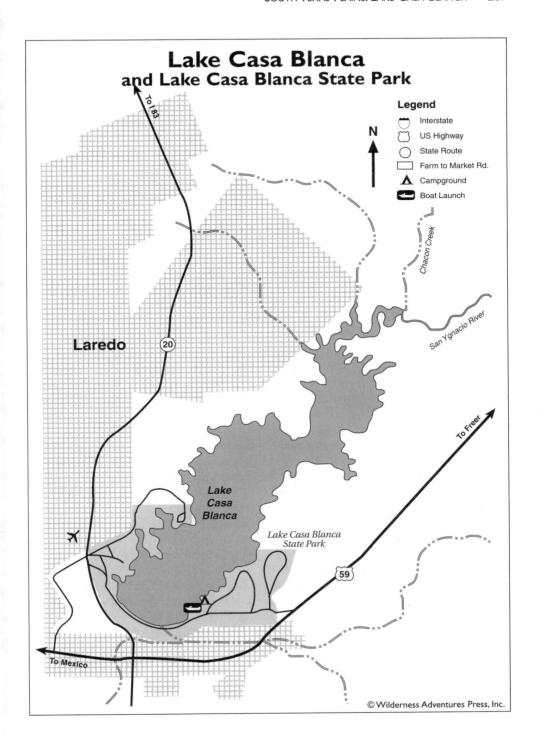

Legend

N

- Interstate
- US Highway
- State Route
- Farm to Market Rd.
- ▲ Campground
- Boat Launch

To I 83

Chacon Creek

San Ygnacio River

Laredo

20

To Freer

Lake
Casa
Blanca

Lake Casa Blanca
State Park

59

To Mexico

© Wilderness Adventures Press, Inc.

FALCON LAKE

Falcon Lake lies on the Rio Grande River, 75 miles south of Laredo off US 83. This 78,300-acre lake, the second largest in the state, was built jointly by the United States and Mexico for irrigation, hydroelectric power generation, and recreation. Demands on this reservoir create frequent changes in lake levels. Droughts also can severely affect lake levels and fishing conditions. Under prime conditions, the average depth is 31 feet. Water clarity varies with the clearest water most often found on shorelines protected from the wind.

In addition to Florida-strain and native-northern largemouth, the lake also has been stocked over the years with hybrid striped bass, striped bass, smallmouth, walleye and sunfish.

Harlingen fly fishing guide Rick Hartman says Lake Falcon offers excellent spring and fall fly fishing options along a variety of features, including flooded timber, shorelines, and along the rocks around the dam. The submerged willow and huisache offer many shaded, shallow flats where largemouth are frequently found on Falcon.

Hartman says a five-mile stretch of coves and shorelines at Falcon State Park offers flyfishers "every variation of terrain that you can imagine," along with excellent largemouth action for big fish and a good numbers of smaller fish.

The lake has been known for its consistent year-round shallow water fishing for largemouth even during the hottest months of the year. Veteran anglers on Lake Falcon say there apparently is no thermocline on Falcon. Fish are caught in 20 feet of water as well as in 2 feet of water and apparently there is enough oxygen to support feeding activity at a variety of depths throughout the year.

Falcon State Park

Located on the east shore of Falcon Lake, the 573-acre Falcon State Park offers access to explosive fly fishing for largemouth as well as excellent wildlife viewing. The brush country surrounding the lake, which includes thickets of mesquite, huisache, palo verde, and ebony, is home to many subtropical plant and animal species found only in far South Texas and Mexico. Chachalaca, a pheasant-like bird with a piercing call, is native to the area as well as the green jay, ringed kingfisher, and groove-billed ani. Once part of the range of the jaguar, the thick brush of this Rio Grande Valley area provides some of the last remaining habitat in the United States for two other rare cats, the ocelot and the jaguarundi.

The park launch ramp provides access to excellent shoreline fly fishing. There are a large number of campsites with partial and full hookups for RVs and showers. The park is extremely popular in the winter and reservations are recommended. For more information contact Falcon State Park, P.O. Box 2, Falcon Heights TX 78545, (210) 848-5327.

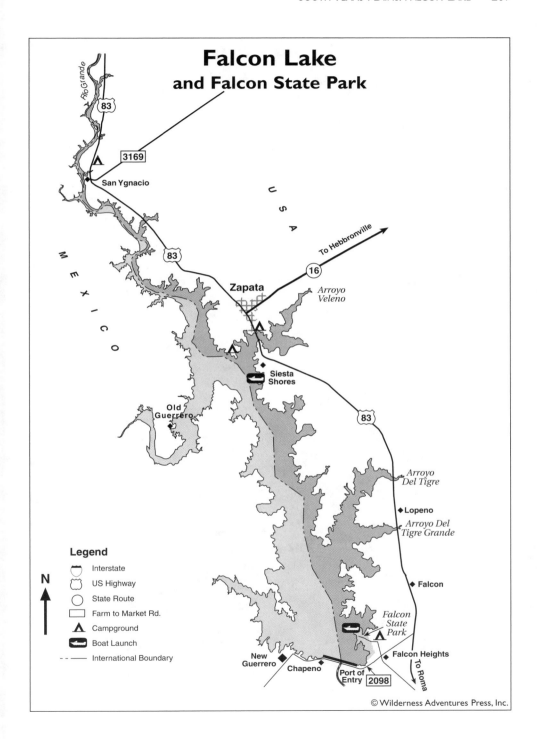

Falcon Lake
and Falcon State Park

Rio Grande

83

3169

San Ygnacio

U S A

83

To Hebbronville

16

Zapata

Arroyo
Veleno

Siesta
Shores

Old
Guerrero

M E X I C O

83

Arroyo
Del Tigre

Lopeno

Arroyo Del
Tigre Grande

Falcon

Falcon
State
Park

New
Guerrero

Chapeno

Port of
Entry

2098

Falcon Heights

To Roma

Legend

N

⬡ Interstate
⬡ US Highway
◯ State Route
▢ Farm to Market Rd.
▲ Campground
⬓ Boat Launch
‑ ‑ ‑ International Boundary

© Wilderness Adventures Press, Inc.

STATE PARK WATERS

Goliad State Historical Park

This 187-acre park south of Goliad off US 183 offers access for launching canoes and kayaks and fishing on the San Antonio River.

Species in the river include largemouth, green sunfish, warmouth, and Rio Grande perch.

There are campsites and screened shelters available in the park. The imposing reconstructed white church of Mission Espiritu Santo de Zuniga built by the Spanish in 1722 is located in the park. The Mission was established by the Spaniards near Matagorda Bay to serve the Karankawa Indians. For more information on the park, contact Goliad State Historical Park, P.O. Box 727, Goliad, TX 77963 (361) 645-3405.

Church of Mission Espiritu Santo de Zuniga.

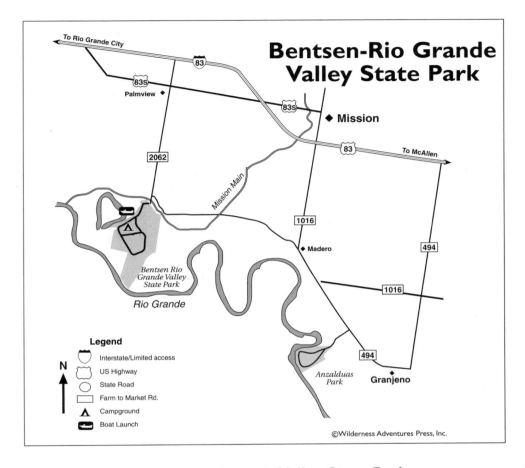

Bentsen-Rio Grande Valley State Park

The Bentsen-Rio Grande Valley State Park not only offers flyfishers a chance to sample the fishing in a Resaca, an old, cut-off river channel common in this border area of Texas, but also to view some of the tropical bird species found no where else in the United States, including the green jay, Altamira oriole, white-tipped dove and groove-billed ani. There is a concrete boat ramp as well as bank fishing access to the 60-acre resaca from the picnic area. The small waterway, which holds largemouth and sunfish, is surrounded by lush stands of cattails and other shoreline vegetation.

The 588-acre park is adjacent to the Rio Grande River near the city of Mission. To reach the park, take US 83 west of Mission to the small community of Palmview, turn south on Texas (FM) 2062 and travel 3.5 miles to the park entrance. The fee for entering the park is $2 per person per day. Campsites and hot showers are also available for an additional fee. For additional information, contact the park staff at (956) 585-1107.

URBAN OPTIONS

SAN ANTONIO

Brackenridge Park

Brackenridge Park, located in the heart of San Antonio, offers a tranquil setting for fly fishing on feeder creeks of the San Antonio River. Sunfish, Rio Grande perch and a few small largemouth provide the fun under stately oaks and pecans in the scenic park area near the San Antonio Zoo.

To get to Brackenridge Park, take US 281 north to the Mulberry exit and follow the signs to the zoo. There is a stretch of river across from the zoo next to the city's old waterworks building that has parking and easy access along the rock walkways. This is a picnic area that can get crowded on some weekends during the summer but is usually uncrowded during the early morning hours. Other stretches of the creek that border the nearby Brackenridge Park Golf Course offer a little more solitude.

PRIVATE WATERS

A number of ranches in the South Texas Plains region offer fishing for a fee on lakes stocked with largemouth. These private waters are carefully managed to provide high quality fishing in relative solitude for those flyfishers willing to pay for the privilege. Most fee-fishing operations charge in a range of $100 to $275 per day and some provide food and lodging. What all of these fisheries have in common are careful management of fish populations, ample stocking of forage fish, and rigid control of vegetation and water quality. Some of them also have fisheries biologists in residence.

777 Ranch

Located outside Hondo in Medina County, 32 miles west of San Antonio, the 777 Ranch offers guided catch-and-release fishing on more than 30 ponds and lakes. The daily fee includes guided fishing plus breakfast, lunch and dinner. Anglers also have a chance to see the native white-tailed deer as well as some 50 different animal species from five continents that live on the ranch. For more information contact the ranch at (830) 426-3476.

Guajillo Ranch

Located near D'Hanis, 50 miles west of San Antonio, the Guajillo's 100-acre lake holds Florida-strain largemouth up to 15 pounds. Besides explosive largemouth action, flyfishers can walk along the banks on the Guajillo Ranch lake and spot cast to large sunfish. For more information, contact the ranch at (210) 824-0025.

Hilltop Fish and Game Ranch

Located 35 miles south of San Antonio in Atascosa County near Pleasanton, Hilltop's offerings include guided catch-and-release fishing for largemouth from 3 to 7 pounds. For additional information, contact the ranch at (210) 569-5555.

Southwest Safaris 74 Ranch

Located in Cambellton, 50 miles south of San Antonio, this ranch offers flyfishers a number of lakes from 5 to 30 acres in size stocked with largemouth and sunfish. The daily fee includes guided catch-and-release bass fishing and breakfast lunch and dinner. For more information contact the ranch at (210) 579-4808.

Sandy Oaks Ranch

Located 35 miles south of San Antonio near Devine, Shady Oaks Ranch offers guided fly fishing on stock tanks and lakes on the ranch and at neighboring ranches. Flyfishers can walk the banks, wade or fish from a canoe for largemouth and sunfish.

To get to Sandy Oaks Ranch, take Interstate 35 south of San Antonio to Devine. Just south of Devine, take exit 121 and turn left (south) on the access road and travel about a half-mile to the ranch entrance. For additional information, contact Foard Houston at Sandy Oaks Ranch (830) 665-3202.

Callahan Ranch

Located on Interstate 35 in Webb County, 27 miles north of Laredo, the 80,000-acre Callahan Ranch offers fishing for largemouth in some 40 stock tanks up to 80 acres in size. For additional information, contact the ranch at (800) 535-8098.

Flyfisher in kickboat on small ranch stock tank in South Texas.

BORDER CROSSINGS

Lake Vicente Guerrero

Located northeast of Ciudad Victoria in northern Mexico, Lake Vicente Guerrero has had a reputation dating back to the early 1970s as one of the best destinations for largemouth bass fishing in North America. Anglers using conventional tackle routinely landed 100 or more fish per day. Like many large reservoirs, the fishery was affected by commercial and recreational fishing pressure as well as seasonal changes in water levels, which in turn affected the quality of the fishing.

In more recent years, while bass fishing on the lake has been upstaged by other newer and highly publicized bass fishing lakes in Mexico, Guerrero has reestablished itself as a quality fishery that holds giant largemouth in spectacular surroundings. Florida-strain largemouth have been introduced in the lake, and local wardens more strictly enforce bag limits. Many of the American outfitters who operate hunting and fishing lodges on the lake actively promote catch and release. The lake still attracts a steady stream of American anglers who make the 200- mile drive and trailer their boats from border crossings in McAllen and Brownsville. Flyfishers on Lake Guerrero have an endless variety of features to prospect, such as river bottoms, fields of flooded timber, heavy shoreline vegetation and the clear depths and rocky points around the lake's many small islands. While the fishing can be good year- round on Guerrero, the spring and fall cycle can bring spectacular topwater action when the giant female bass are moving in the shallows.

One of the lodges that offers an excellent fishing package, including guided fly fishing, on Lake Guerrero is Hacienda Las Palmas (formerly No Le Hace Hacienda). The lodge is surrounded by palm trees on a hillside overlooking a river access to the lake. Three and four night fishing packages are available and transportation can be arranged from the Texas border. For more information, contact Sports Resorts International, P.O. Box 79467, Houston, TX 77279, or call (800) 285-1803.

South Texas Plains Hub Cities
San Antonio

Population - 1,131,786	Elevation - 701'
Area Code - 210	County - Bexar

ACCOMMODATIONS

Hilton Palacio Del Rio, 200 S. Alamo St. / 800-HILTONS / 481 rooms / $$$
Marriott Riverwalk, 711 E. Riverwalk / 800-648-4462 / 511 rooms / $$$
Holiday Inn Riverwalk, 217 N. St. Mary's St. / 800-445-8475 / 313 rooms / $$$
La Quinta Inn Convention Center, 1001 E. Commerce St. / 800-531-5900 / 192
    rooms / $$.
La Quinta Inn Airport West, 219 Northeast Loop 410 / 342-4291 / $$$

BED AND BREAKFASTS

A. Beckmann Inn and Carriage House, 222 E. Guenther St. / 800-945-1449 /
    5 rooms / $$$
A. Blansett Barn Guest House, 206 Madison / 800-221-1412 / 2 rooms / $$$
Brackenridge House Bed-and-Breakfast, 230 Madison Street / 271-3442 / $$$
The Inn at Craig Place, 117 west Craig Place / 2 rooms / 736-1017 / $$$

CAMPGROUNDS

Alamo KOA, RV Sites, cabins and tent sites / 602 Gembler Rd. / 800-563-7783
    Reservations / 224-9296 Information / akoasa@aol.com www.koa.com
Tejas Valley Inc. RV park & Campground Tent and RV sites available / 13080
    Potranco Rd. / 679-7715 / 800-729-7275 Toll Free / tejasrv@aol.com

RESTAURANTS

Casa Rio, 430 East Commerce Street / 225-6718 / $
Kangaroo Court, River Walk downtown / 224-6821 / $
La Fonda, 2415 North Main Avenue / 733-0621 / $
Mi Tierra Cafe and Bakery, 218 Produce Row / open 24 hours / 225-1262 / $
The Original Mexican Restaurant, 528 River Walk / 224-9951 / $
La Fogata, 2427 Vance Jackson / 340-1337 / Tex Mex including tacos Nortenos,
    queso flameado and steak tampiquena / open Monday through Thursday, 11
    a.m. to 10 p.m., Friday 11 a.m. to 11 p.m., Saturday 7:30 a.m. to 11:30 p.m.,
    Sunday 8 a.m. to 10 p.m. / $ to $$

FLY SHOPS AND GUIDE SERVICES

Hill CountryOutfitters, The Northwoods Shopping Center, 18030 Hwy. 281 North
    / 491-4416 / www.hillcountryoutfitters.com
Tackle Box Outfitters / 821 5806
One Shot Outfitters, 1870 Stone Oak Parkway / 402-5344
    / www.oneshotoutdoors.com

SPORTING GOODS STORES

Oshman's, La Plaza Del Norte, 125 N.W. Loop 410 / 341-1244
Academy Sports, 2727 N.E. Loop 410 at Perrin-Beitel / 590-0500

Academy Sports, 755 N.W. Loop 410 / 523-5191
Academy Sports, 165 S. W. Military Drive / 927-0509
Northwest Tackle Center, 6812 Bandera Road #126 / 512-681-0009
Good Sports, 9861 I-H 10 West / 694-0881
One Shot Outdoors, Inc., 18720 Stone Oak Parkway, Suite 105 / 210-402-5344

AIRPORTS

San Antonio International Airport, 207-3450 / America West: 800-235-9292 /
American Airlines: 800-433-7300 / Continental Airlines: 800-525-0280 / Delta:
800-221-1212 / KLM Royal Dutch Airlines: 800-374-7747 / Mexicana Airlines:
800-531-7921 / Northwest Airlines: 800-225-2525 / Southwest Airlines: 800-435-
9792 / Trans World Airlines: 800-221-2000 / United Airlines: 800-241-6522

FOR MORE INFORMATION

San Antonio Convention and Visitors Bureau
P.O. Box 2277
San Antonio, TX 78298
270 8700

The Alamo in San Antonio.

Del Rio

Population - 34,931   **Elevation - 948'**
Area Code - 830   **County - Valverde**

ACCOMMODATIONS
Del Rio Motor Lodge, 1300 Avenue F / 775-2486 / $$
Best Western Inn of Del Rio, 810 Avenue F / 775-7511 / $$
Ramada Inn, 2101 Avenue F / 775-1511 / $$

BED AND BREAKFAST
1890 House Bed and Breakfast Inn, 609 Griner Street / 775-8061 / $$$
La Mansion Del Rio, 123 Hudson Street / 768-1100 / $$$

CAMPGROUNDS
American Campground / Tent and RV sites available / 12 Cabins also available / HCR 3 Box 44 Highway 90 West Del Rio, TX / 210-775-6484 Local / 1-800-525-3386 Toll Free / amercamp@delrio.com

SPORTING GOODS STORES
Wal-Mart, 2401 Ave. F / 800-774-4593

CAMPING
Yucca Trailer Village, US 90 on way to Lake Amistad / 775-6707
Fisherman's Headquarters, US 90 at US 277 / 774-4172

RESTAURANTS
Memo's, 804 E. Loyosa / 775-8104 / Open Monday through Saturday for lunch and dinner, Sunday for dinner only / $
Las Cazuelas, 1912 Avenue F / 768-0272 / Open 24 hours / $

FOR MORE INFORMATION
Del Rio Chamber of Commerce
1915 Avenue F
Del Rio, TX 78840
775 3551

Laredo

LODGING PRICE KEY		
$	=	$30 - $50 per night
$$	=	$50 - $70 per night
$$$	=	$70 per night and up

RESTAURANT PRICE KEY		
$	=	$10 and under per meal
$$	=	$10 - $20 per meal
$$$	=	$20 and up

Population 189,021   **Elevation - 100'**
Area Code - 956   **County - Webb**

ACCOMMODATIONS
Best Western - Fiesta Inn, 5240 San Bernardo / 723-3603 / 152 rooms / $$$
La Quinta Inn - Laredo, 3610 Santa Ursula / 800-531-5900 / 152 rooms / $$
Motel 6 - North, 5920 San Bernardo Ave. / 800-4 MOTEL6 / 109 rooms / $$

RESTAURANTS
Charlie's Corona of Laredo, 3902 San Bernardo Ave. / 725-8227
Las Asadas, Interstate 35 North at Del Mar Boulevard / 726-1822
La Reynera Bakery and Restaurant, 1819 San Bernardo / 722-6641 / $

SPORTING GOODS STORES
Arnold Distributing, 4520 San Bernardo / 956-223-2066
Border Sporting Goods, 5219 Maher Ave. / 210-722-1007

AIRPORTS
Laredo International Airport, 795 2000 / American Airlines-American Eagle:
800-433-7300 / Continental Airlines: 800-525-0280

FOR MORE INFORMATION
**Laredo Convention
and Visitors Bureau**
501 San Augustine
Laredo, TX 77573
795 2200

*Small dam and waterfall
on the Frio River, Tips
Park in Three Rivers,
Texas.*

McAllen

Population 105,919
Area Code - 956

Elevation - 122'
County - Hidalgo

ACCOMMODATIONS
Courtyard by Marriott, 2131 South 10th Street / 888-668-7808 / 110 rooms / $$$
Best Western - Rose Garden Inn and Suites, 300 E. Expressway / 630-3333 /
    92 rooms / $$
Drury Inn and Suites, 612 West Expressway 83 / 687-5100 / $$$

RESTAURANTS
O España, 701 N. Main / 618-5242 / open daily for lunch and dinner / $
Casa del Taco, 1100 Houston / 631-8193 / $
Alonso's Escorial, 4501 N. 10th / 686-1160 / open daily for lunch and dinner / $

FLY SHOPS AND GUIDE SERVICES
Rio Grande Outfitters, 905 Dove Avenue / 800-294-0104
Bud's Fly Shop, 5509 N. Ware Rd / 800-294-0104

SPORTING GOODS STORES
Academy Sports and Outdoors, 100 South Second Street at Business 83 and 2nd
    Street / 686-1742

AIRPORTS
McAllen-Miller International Airport, 682 9101 / American Airlines:800-433-7300
    / Continental Airlines: 800-525-0280
Trans World Airlines:800-221-2000

FOR MORE INFORMATION
McAllen Chamber of Commerce / Convention and Visitors Bureau
P.O. Box 790
McAllen, TX 78505
682 2871

FLYFISHING CLUBS
Alamo Flyfishers
P.O. Box 291034
San Antonio, TX 78229

REGION 6

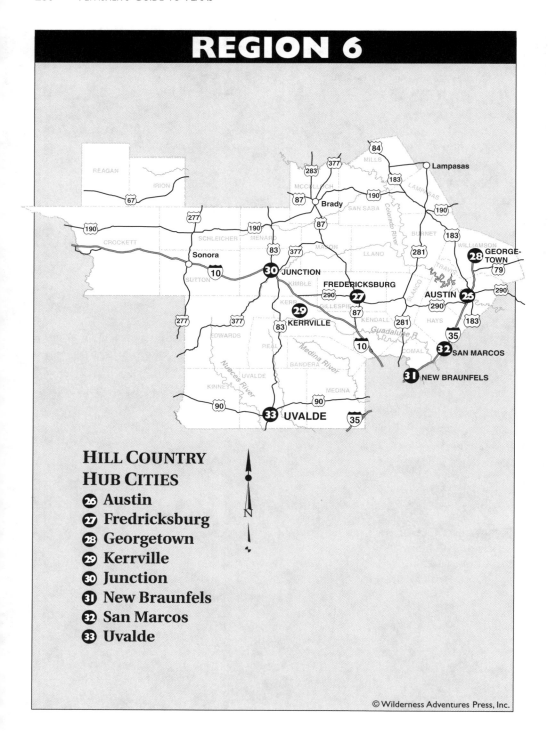

HILL COUNTRY HUB CITIES

- **26** Austin
- **27** Fredricksburg
- **28** Georgetown
- **29** Kerrville
- **30** Junction
- **31** New Braunfels
- **32** San Marcos
- **33** Uvalde

© Wilderness Adventures Press, Inc.

Hill Country

REGION 6

"The places where I love most to encounter them-fishermen as well as fish-are those crystal-clear, spring-fed Texas streams. Those clean, beautiful little sycamore-lined streams in the hills of Texas-streams untouched except by the hand of a man who fishes."

Written by renowned Texas outdoor writer Hart Stillwell in 1947, the same observations could be made today about fly fishing on many stretches of the Hill Country streams in Texas.

Rising at the Balcones Escarpment, the juniper-and-oak-blanketed Hill Country spreads westward across the Edwards Plateau. This region of dramatic scenery and picturesque, spring-fed rivers offers cascading whitewater streams and deep blue lakes. Austin, Fredericksburg, Johnson City, Junction, New Braunfels, and San Marcos are among the communities in the region.

The waters in this region offer flyfishers the unique opportunity to catch Guadalupe bass and Rio Grande perch, two feisty Texas native species that are found in the Hill County region. Their range is restricted to the clean-running, spring-fed pools of the Rio Grande drainage, which includes the Llano, Guadalupe, San Marcos and Colorado rivers. Rio Grande perch also are found in the Highland Lakes west of Austin and in Lake Georgetown. The region is also the location of the southernmost trout fishery in the United States. The Hill Country offers flyfishers a number of state parks, many of which provide wade fishing and canoe, kayak and float tube access in scenic settings on streams and lakes.

Planning a float trip during periods of adequate flows between public access points often is a practical way to fish sections of many Hill Country rivers. There are also many access points at public bridge and low water crossings and at state parks, where flyfishers can wade stretches of river or launch small watercraft. On some Hill Country rivers heavy recreational use by tubers during the summer months has increased the possibility of confrontations with private landowners over trespass issues. Anglers using these waterways should be careful in selecting public access points and respect private property laws at all times.

RIVERS

COLORADO RIVER

The Colorado River upstream from Lake Buchanan is one of the state's top destinations for white bass action during the spring run and it attracts large numbers of anglers. Flyfishers can take part in the action by floating the 16 mile stretch from the put-in at the Highway 190 crossing between San Saba and Lometa to the Flat Rock take-out just west of the community of Bend. The second take-out is at Sulphur Springs Camp at the 24.0 mile point. There is a nominal charge for taking out at Flat Rock and Sulphur Springs Camp.

White bass (Roccus chrysops)

White bass (*Roccus chrysops*)

Known locally as sand bass in Texas, the white bass is a member of the temperate bass family Percichthyidae. Coloration is dark along the back, silvery on the sides, and white on the underbelly. The sides are streaked lengthwise with several broken, dusky lines. The average size of white bass is a pound or less but in some Texas waters 2 pound fish are not unusual but considered large for the species. Specimens have been caught in Texas waters exceeding five pounds. The life expectancy of white bass is about four years, which is one reason they exhibit modest growth. The white bass prefers the open waters of the state's large reservoirs but moves into tributary waters of streams and creeks to spawn. Most spawning activity takes place from February into April at water temperatures from about 58 to 62 degrees. White bass are "free spawners" and do not build or guard nests. The males travel first into the tributary streams during the spawning period and spawning activity takes place mostly at night in shallow, running water or along sand bars and beaches where the wind creates water movement. A female white bass is capable of laying more than a half-million eggs. The male fish fertilizes the eggs and they drift and sink until they come to rest on some stream feature such as a rock or log. Young of the year grow to about eight inches. The principal food of white bass is the gizzard and threadfin shad, and they will readily take a fly. On lakes, they are known for schooling up in large numbers to chase shad to the surface and going on feeding sprees especially early and late in the day during the summer months. The white bass is prized by anglers in Texas as a food fish.

Poppers and streamer flies that match with baitfish targeted by white bass on Texas lakes.

Colorado River

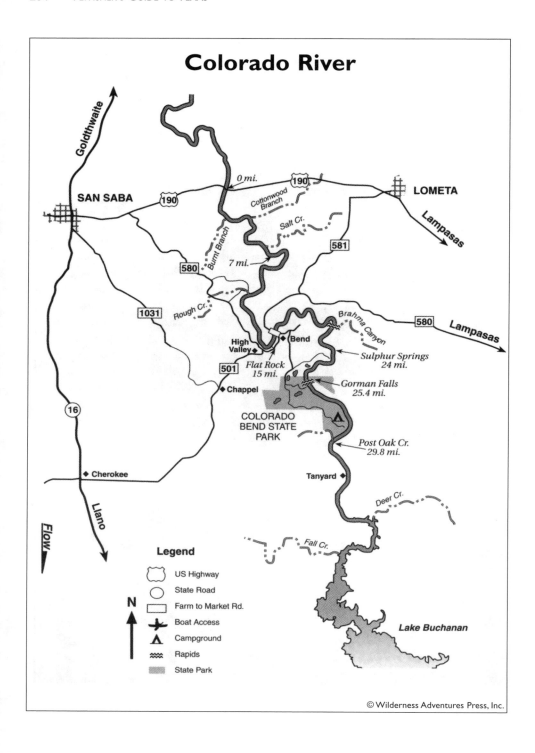

Goldthwaite

SAN SABA

190

0 mi.

190

LOMETA

Cottonwood Branch

Salt Cr.

Lampasas

Burnt Branch

7 mi.

580

581

1031

Rough Cr.

Brahma Canyon

580

Lampasas

High Valley

Bend

501

Flat Rock 15 mi.

Sulphur Springs 24 mi.

Chappel

Gorman Falls 25.4 mi.

16

COLORADO BEND STATE PARK

Post Oak Cr. 29.8 mi.

Cherokee

Tanyard

Deer Cr.

Llano

Flow

Fall Cr.

Legend

- US Highway
- State Road
- Farm to Market Rd.
- Boat Access
- Campground
- Rapids
- State Park

N

Lake Buchanan

© Wilderness Adventures Press, Inc.

Peak fishing action usually takes place from mid-February to mid-April. In addition to white bass, this stretch of the Colorado is also known for good numbers of striped bass and hybrid striped bass.

Wade fishing access to the Colorado River is available at Colorado Bend State Park, south of and for a fee at private ranches upstream from the park.

Fly fishing guide Charlie Cypert calls this stretch of the Colorado River the state's number one hot spot for white bass during the spring spawning run. He says the best fishing areas can be reached by traveling west from Lampasas on Texas 580 to Bend, where there are several excellent options including the state park, Sulphur Springs Camp and Barefoot Ranch.

Cypert says that the white bass action at each location depends on the fluctuations in water levels on Lake Buchanan downstream. If the lake is at a low level, Cypert recommends flyfishers try the state park. But if the lake is at normal levels, he recommends fishing one of the ranches upstream from the park. Most of the water on this stretch of the Colorado is wadable, Cypert says. Flyfishers can expect action from striped bass as well as white bass during the spring run.

White bass with a fly.

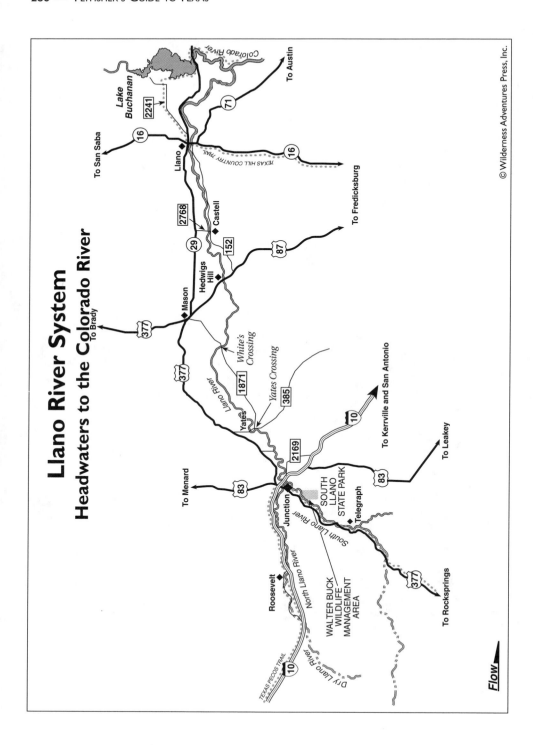

Llano River System
Headwaters to the Colorado River

© Wilderness Adventures Press, Inc.

LLANO RIVER SYSTEM

For many city-dwelling Texas flyfishers, the Llano River System is like having a Livingston, Montana, or Last Chance, Idaho, just a few hours down the road. The free-flowing, spring-fed rivers and creeks around Junction are warm water habitats, but they have the look and feel of mountain streams.

The riffles and runs, boulder-strewn pools, and gravel bars along the Llano River don't hold westslope cutthroats or wild rainbows, but they are home to Guadalupe bass and Rio Grande perch, native Texas fish that live in fast water and take flies fished wet or dry. Added to the mix are redbreast, or "yellow-belly" sunfish, and largemouth-transplants that also thrive in the area's clear, fast-moving rivers and streams.

The South Llano, one of the most scenic rivers in Texas, rises from springs in northern Edwards County and flows northward for 20 miles as a clear, narrow stream. The Llano's North Fork begins just east of Sonora and flows west to Junction. The South Fork is a user-friendly stream, less than 50 yards wide in many places, that are marked by small rapids and long deep pools. Although hefty largemouth up to eight pounds or more are caught in the Llano, 4-to-6-weight fly rods match up best with the small but feisty Guadalupes, Rio Grande perch, and sunfish that make up the majority of the fish population.

Flyfisher casting on South Llano River.   *Redbreast or "yellowbelly" sunfish.*

Guadalupe bass.

The Llano River System seems to have been designed with flyfishers in mind. For the most part, it is not heavily traveled and is far enough away from major urban centers to cut down on the tubing and rafting traffic that can overrun other Hill Country rivers like the Guadalupe during the summer months.

While a midsummer trip is a welcome break from a south Texas summer, veteran Llano flyfishers say the best fishing is in the spring and fall months. Normal flow on the Llano River is 300 to 400 cubic feet of water per second (cfs), enough for a comfortable float. Canoes and kayaks are the recommended transport. The shallow riffles and rapids make float tubes impractical. There are many small rapids and falls on the Llano, but none that are considered dangerous. Inexperienced paddlers should approach them cautiously, however.

Kayak and canoe outfitter Bruce Gillan of Houston says beginners can have pleasant day floats that end with all equipment intact if they take the time to stow fly rods before navigating the stretches of faster water and do not overload their craft.

Flyfishers do not need to embark on long floats on the Llano. A stretch between low-water crossings advertised as a three-hour float can easily turn into five or six hours on the river as anglers stop to thoroughly fish the entire attractive, fish-holding habitat.

Guadalupe Bass

The Guadalupe bass, the Lone Star State's official fish, is found nowhere else but the Texas Hill Country. The Guadalupe was long thought to be a subspecies of the spotted bass, but in 1955, after a scientific study, it was declared a distinct species. These fish are not large-most weigh less than a pound-but they have adapted well to the clear, shallow, fast-flowing streams. In this setting, they behave a lot like trout or smallmouth bass, holding in the wash behind submerged rocks, along the edges between eddies and currents, and in the shade of overhanging branches and undercut banks. One way to identify Guadalupe bass which can be confused with pint-size largemouth is to look for the broken lateral stripe and the rows of stripes on the whitish belly area.

The Guadalupe bass, (Micropterus treculi), lives only in streams of the Edwards Plateau region of central Texas. These streams include the San Antonio, Guadalupe, Llano, Colorado and Brazos river systems. In 1973, Texas Parks and Wildlife Department introduced it into the headwaters of the Nueces River as well. These stream adapted fish do not reach a large size; the state record is only 3 pounds, 11 ounces, yet it is an extremely popular Hill Country game fish because of its feisty nature and penchant for scenic, clear-running streams.

Even though the Guadalupe bass has a distinctive black, diamond-shaped pattern along its sides and rows of spots that form stripes on its belly, this fish was originally described in the 1870s as a strain of largemouth bass. Much later, it was reclassified as a form of spotted bass. In the early 1950s, Dr. Clark Hubbs of the University of Texas found Guadalupe bass and spotted bass living together in several streams. This proved that the Guadalupe bass was a distinct species.

Like other black bass, the Guadalupe bass eats fish, crayfish, and insect larvae and builds nests for spawning in early spring. It is, however, specialized for flowing streams, while the largemouth bass thrives in deep, still pools. After millions of years of adapting to its stream environment, the Guadalupe bass is at a disadvantage in modern-day reservoirs.

The Texas Parks and Wildlife Department has developed a Guadalupe bass refuge at Lost Maples State Natural Area. This location has habitat similar to the natural environment of the bass and provides security for protection of the species. The Guadalupe bass was stocked at the park in Spring 1988.

Rio Grande Perch

The Rio Grande perch (Cichlasoma cyanoguttatum) *is another Texas original that prefers fast flowing, spring-fed rivers and scenic surroundings like the Llano River. Rio Grande perch compete with the Llano's Guadalupes for well-presented flies. With colored bars of light gray and bluish-black, and specks of silver, turquoise, and blue, the Rio Grande is a handsome fish. One thing that Rio Grandes have in common with sunfish in the Llano is that they are not shy about feeding during the hottest part of the day. They are bullish fighters that can put a healthy bend in a 4- or 5-weight rod.*

The Rio Grande system was the species' primary habitat, making it the northernmost member of the cichlid family. The fish is related to the peacock bass of the Amazon Basin as well as 600 other freshwater cichlids spread across North and South America and Africa.

Writing in the 1940s, renowned Texas angling author Hart Stillwell, in his book Hunting and Fishing in Texas, *made the case that the Rio Grande cichlid was the most active of all the "perch" in taking an artificial lure. In those days, the Rio Grande also was called the Guinea perch because its coloration resembled that of a guinea fowl.*

With its vivid coloration, the Rio Grande perch often can be spotted in the clear water of Hill Country streams from a good distance.

Stillwell wrote that the species provided some of the best fishing he had ever experienced using a "tiny fly and spinner combination." He also gave them high marks as sport fish because of their strength and aggressive nature.

Rio Grandes coexist with bass, bluegills, redears and other members of the sunfish family and grow to an average size of about a half-pound, although specimens up to two pounds have been reported. The Rio Grande's diet includes small fish, insects and crayfish as well as the eggs of other fish and it will take a variety of fly patterns.

Rio Grande Perch.

Effective fly patterns for all the Llano River System species run the gamut from damselfly nymphs and Woolly Buggers to popping bugs and hopper patterns. Closer Deep Minnows tied on size 2 hooks (and smaller), fished around the edges of the fast water, will draw strikes from the Guadalupes. Free-drifted nymphs work well, as do streamers and minnow patterns fished across current with fast, erratic strips. The Accardo Voo Doo Diver, a popping bug with a wobbling action, will attract a lot of exciting topwater strikes when fished at dusk up against the bank.

For sunfish action on the Llano and other Hill Country rivers, fly fishing guide Bill Waldron uses a 7½ foot 3-weight rod that will roll cast smoothly and throw a tight overhead loop. On open water in the wind, he prefers a fast action 5-weight rod.

Allison Park, located off US 10 and Texas (FM) 3130, 26 miles northwest of Roosevelt in Sutton Co. The park provides access for float trips down the North Fork of the Llano.

The North Fork of the Llano runs into the town of Junction where it joins the South Llano to form the Llano River. A low water crossing on the North Llano at Texas FM 270 off US 10 about three miles from downtown Junction provides good access for wade fishing. This area has the advantage of being very lightly fished.

The South Llano River rises from springs in northern Edwards County and flows northward to join the North Llano River at Junction. Typical of Hill Country streams, its 20-mile course is a series of shallow riffles, small rapids and long, deep pools. While none of the rapids are particularly hazardous and all are in relatively shallow water, care should be taken when negotiating them, particularly by paddlers with limited experience. Anglers should always scout rapids and low bridge underpasses, and when in doubt, line canoes and kayaks through these features. The South Llano is ideal for flyfishers. In fact, it is difficult to make good time on a float because there are so many runs, gravel bars and pools that are worth prospecting for the resident population of Guadalupe bass, largemouth, Rio Grande perch and yellow-belly sunfish.

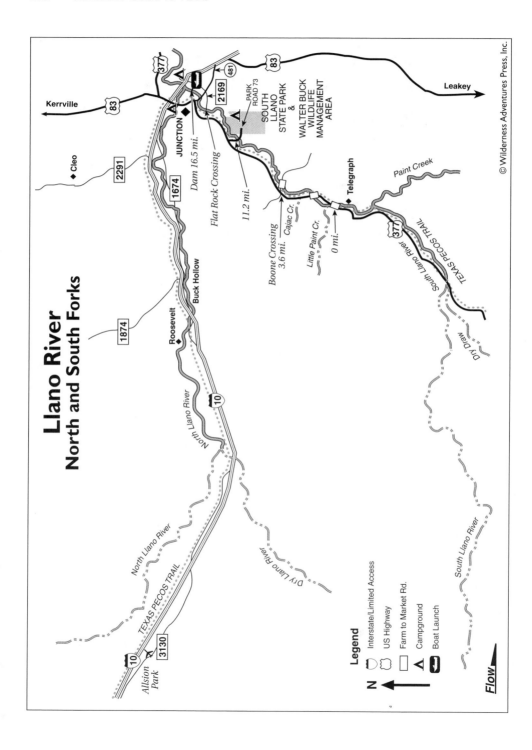

Llano River
North and South Forks

Legend

Interstate/Limited Access
US Highway
Farm to Market Rd.
Campground
Boat Launch

N

Flow

Access Points For Floating Or Wading The South Llano River:

US 377 Crossing

A low water highway crossing known as Flat Rock Crossing.

US 377 Crossing

A low water crossing located 11 miles southwest of Junction. This is an excellent put-in for short floats either to the next low water crossing or to lodges and rental cabins downstream. The waterfall area and pools at this crossing hold good numbers of sunfish and Rio Grande perch. There is also wade fishing and bank fishing access for a short stretch of river downstream around exposed gravel bars.

US 377, South Llano State Park and Buck's Wildlife Management Area.

Located 4.4 miles southwest of Junction on US 377, there is a small oxbow lake in the park but it requires a small boat, float tube, kayak or canoe to fish effectively. The scenic stretch of the South Llano that runs along the park holds good numbers of Guadalupe bass and other species but it is heavily fished by park visitors during the summer months. There is a day use fee at the park.

LLANO RIVER MAINSTEM

Junction City Park

Located near the US 10 Bridge in Junction, City Park at river mile 15.25 offers many bank and wade fishing options accessible by a number of gravel roads. There is a prospect for Guadalupe bass around edges of riffles and runs, in channels, and at heads of deeper pools. Closer Deep Minnow flies in hook sizes 8 to 1, as well as weighted nymphs, work well on this stretch of river.

In planning trips to this area, flyfishers should check to see if any recent rains have created high water and off color conditions. One of the many charms of the Llano River System is the opportunity to fish its clear, spring-fed waters. This area of the Llano south of Mason, which has mud banks, takes longer to clear than the South Llano and trips are best scheduled to avoid periods of high, muddy water.

Local anglers recommend wade fishing the stretch of Llano River that runs below the dam in the community of Llano rather than floating it because there are limited take-out points downstream.

Llano River fly fishing guide Constance Whiston says this stretch holds good numbers of Guadalupe bass and sunfish especially in the islands area around Morgan Shady Park, just above the dam. She recommends driving down to the parking lot and wade fishing the area around the low water crossing. "I have seen largemouth in excess of six pounds in the section above the crossing as well as a lot of Guadalupe bass and a few Rio Grande perch," Whiston says. A productive feature for flyfishers is a deep hole below the dam that will hold Guadalupe bass, sunfish and catfish. Whiston recommends weighted nymphs and Woolly Buggers fished with floating

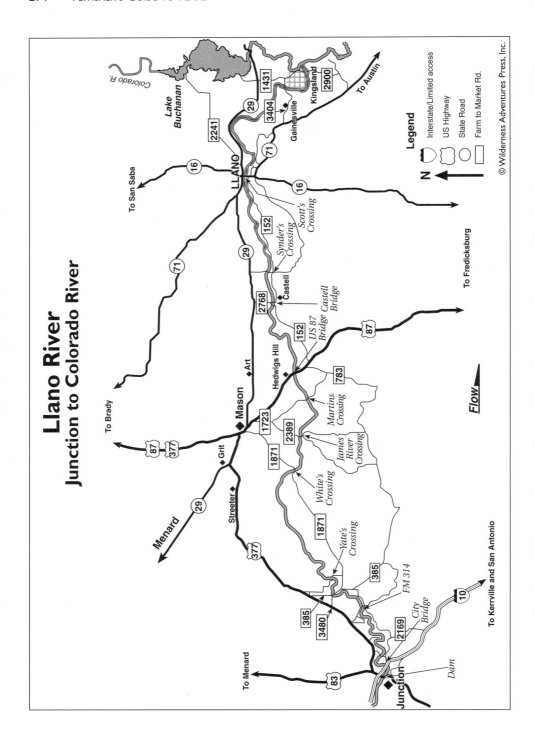

Llano River
Junction to Colorado River

lines and 9 foot leaders or with sinking lines. "You can put a canoe or kayak in at this point," Whiston says, "but it requires carrying down a steep embankment."

Whiston says the City Park is an excellent put-in for a two day, 16-mile float trip down to the County Road 314 crossing. The float includes scenic Hill Country settings and excellent fly fishing opportunities. There is about a 4 foot high waterfall on the stretch that will require boaters to line canoes over. Whiston says the base of the waterfall holds a number of fish and is worth prospecting.

River Crossing on Texas (FM) 314.

This crossing is located off Texas 377, about 12 miles east of Junction. There are dramatic rock formations near this stretch of river, which is an access point for walk-in wade fishing.

Texas (FM) 385

This access, called Yates Crossing, is located off US 377 south of the London community. Locals consider this a good access for wadefising, but a difficult float from here downstream to the Texas (FM) 1871 crossing because of the rocky features and shallow stretches.

Texas (FM) 1871

Known as White's Crossing at river mile 59.25, this access is located about 8 miles southwest of Mason and is considered a good take-out and put-in for float trips. (Anglers taking float trips downstream should be aware of a stretch of whitewater two miles downriver at Soldier's Crossing that is best avoided by portaging.)

Fly fishing guide Constance Whiston calls this stretch of river downstream from Texas (FM) 1871 to the Texas (FM) 1723 crossing one of the most diverse, scenic and beautiful in the Hill Country, with deep pools that hold hefty largemouth. Flyfishers can find fish holding along cliff faces and in canyons, as well as along stretches of shallow water with riffles, runs and gravel bars.

This crossing is a good walk-in wade fishing access or put-in for floating down to the "James River Crossing" at Texas (FM) 2389, 4.5 miles downriver. Whiston says flyfishers also can walk in here to wade upstream or use a canoe, kayak or kickboat to travel a short distance downstream where there is a deep hole that holds good numbers of Guadalupe bass. This is a remote location where it is probably best to arrange a drop off with a shuttle service rather than leave a car overnight.

Texas (FM) 2389

Called the James River Crossing, this access at the 63.75 mile mark is located about 8 miles south of Mason where Texas 2389 branches off Texas (FM) 1723 and runs south.

This is where the   and the Llano River meet and is a popular area with flyfishers. A large island upstream offers opportunities for bank and wade fishing as well as camping.

Whiston says she has taken bass up to 5 pounds in the deeper holes along this stretch using Woolly Bugger and leech patterns.

Flyfishers making floats from this access to the next crossing at Texas (FM) 1723 will travel through scenic bluffs which are one of most beautiful features on the river.

Flyfisher casting from gravel bar, South Llano River.

Downstream from this canyon stretch there is deeper, slower moving water where topwater bugs are extremely effective in the spring and summer, Whiston says.

Texas (FM) 1723

Known locally as the Martin's Crossing, the access is located about 8 miles south of Mason. It offers a take-out point after the six-mile float from the Texas (FM) 2389 crossing.

For information on parking, river flows and camping in this area, contact Homer Martin at (915) 347-6852 (see Private Waters section, Homer Martin Ranch.) Whiston recommends poppers, streamers, tarantula patterns and micro jigs on this stretch of river.

US 87 Crossing

This bridge crossing 10 miles south of Mason offers access on the southeast side of the bridge. It offers a put-in for the 8 mile, day-long float to the next crossing at Texas (FM) 2768 near Castell. Whiston notes that there is good wade fishing upstream from the bridge but flyfishers should wade carefully because footing can be challenging along some of the rocky, submerged channels. The float to Castell frequently offers steady largemouth and Guadalupe bass action.

Texas (FM) 2768 Crossing

This bridge crossing at river mile 82 is located in the Castell community, Llano County. It offers a put-in for one or two day floats to Scott's Crossing nine miles downstream. Wade fishing is excellent at this crossing, according to Whiston. She says this also is a good put-in for a float trip to County Road 103, which is 4.5 miles downstream. Whiston advises boaters to be on the lookout for a large boulder that is situated in the middle of the river on this stretch. Flyfishers on float trips should survey the river conditions upstream of the boulder before trying to navigate past it. A portage around it might be the prudent choice. Whiston says the last quarter mile of this stretch is shallow and flyfishers should pack light to avoid having to get out and drag their boats over this last section.

County Road 103 Crossing

Known locally as Snyder's Crossing, this access is located about 4½ miles east of the Castell community off Texas (FM) 152. Whiston says this crossing offers excellent wade fishing access with deep holes upriver.

County Road 102 Crossing

Known as Scott's Crossing, this access point is located at river mile 91 between Castell and Llano off Texas (RR) 152. Whiston says this access also offers excellent wade fishing opportunities. Stretches of shallow water downstream make this a less favorable put-in for a float trip.

City Lake, Llano

Access for small watercraft, kayaks, canoes and float tubes is available here. With a nearby golf course, city park, RV park and rodeo area, this access draws a crowd on weekends and is best fished on weekdays early and late. There is good topwater action here in the spring and fall.

Texas 16, Llano

This bridge crossing in Llano offers access to the river on the southeast side of the bridge. Whiston says she has always found the best action below the City Lake Dam where the deep holes hold good numbers of fish. For many anglers, some of the best fishing is right in town, near the city park just below the Days Inn. "There are gravel bars and you can walk in and fish for about two miles," says Bill Waldron, a Hill Country fly fishing guide.

South Llano River State Park

This park is located five miles south of Junction in Kimble County off US 377 on Park Road 73.

The Llano River runs along park boundaries for about two miles and the park waters offer flyfishers a chance at Guadalupe bass, catfish, Rio Grande perch and a variety of sunfish. A two-acre spring-fed lake also offers catch and release fishing for largemouth.

Wild turkeys frequent the park all year and in the winter, congregate there to roost. Some of the park's bottomland is closed during the winter to protect the turkey roost.

Camping facilities are available in the park. It is located next to the Walter Buck Wildlife Management Area, which offers hiking and wildlife observation.

The park is open year-round and has campsites with water and electricity as well as day use facilities. For information contact South Llano River State Park, HC-15, Box 224, Junction, TX 76849.

Flyfisher wading South Llano River.

Flyfisher with channel cat-fish, South Llano River.

Flyfisher with Rio Grande perch, South Llano River.

Flyfisher casting into pool at low water crossing on South Llano River.

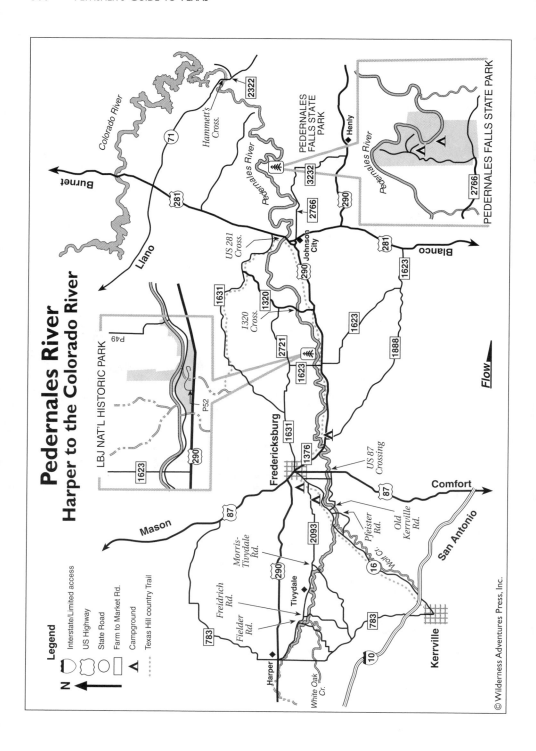

Pedernales River
Harper to the Colorado River

PEDERNALES FALLS STATE PARK

PEDERNALES FALLS STATE PARK

Colorado River

Burnet

Llano

Mason

Comfort

San Antonio

Blanco

Flow

LBJ NAT'L HISTORIC PARK

Johnson City

Fredericksburg

Kerrville

Harper

Tivydale

Henly

Hammett's Cross.

US 281 Cross.

1320 Cross.

US 87 Crossing

Pedernales River

White Oak Cr.

Wolf Cr.

Morris-Tivydale Rd.

Friedrich Rd.

Fielder Rd.

Pfeister Rd.

Old Kerrville Rd.

P49

P52

Legend
- Interstate/Limited access
- US Highway
- State Road
- Farm to Market Rd.
- Campground
- Texas Hill country Trail

N

© Wilderness Adventures Press, Inc.

PEDERNALES RIVER

This small river flows east from its headwaters near the community of Harper in Gillespie County. Good fly fishing can be found by hiking along the back trails of Pedernales River State Park according to Bill Waldron. He recommends hiking into the primitive area of the park, which connects with about a five mile trail that provides access to the river. Overnight camping is prohibited in this area because of the risk of flash flooding. The Pedernales holds good numbers of largemouth and Guadalupe bass as well as a variety of sunfish. The average Guadalupe will run under a pound. Largemouth also run small, which is typical in Hill Country streams but occasionally the deeper holes can produce fish in the 3 to 5 pound range.

Access points on the Pedernales

Fielder Road off Texas (FM) 2093

Located about 6 miles east of the Harper community. Best to ask permission from landowners for access here.

Flyfisher landing sunfish in pool along Hill Country stream.

Friedrich Road Crossing

Located off Texas (FM) 2093 about 7 miles east of Harper, also requires permission from landowners to access.

Morris-Tivydale Road Crossing

Located about 16 miles east of Harper off Texas (FM) 2093. Receives some activity from locals. Wade fishing access upstream and downstream.

Pfeister Road Crossing

Located 2 miles downstream from the SH 16 crossing.

Center Point Road Crossing

Located off SH 16 southwest of Fredericksburg. This stretch of river must be floated due to posted signs.

Old Kerrville Road Crossing

Old Kerrville Road leaves SH 16 and intersects River Road. There is access to wade fishing and the downstream stretch is good for float tubes or canoe. This is also the launch site for a two mile float to the US 87 crossing.

US 87 Crossing

Located south of Fredericksburg on River Road, this crossing provides good access to the river from several points along the road.

Lyndon B. Johnson State Park and National Park

Several small lakes with dams in the parks offer float tube and small watercraft options for flyfishers. This stretch is stocked with rainbow trout during the winter months.

Texas (FM) 1320 Crossing (north of US 290)

This crossing provides access for wade fishing upstream and downstream.

US 281 Crossing (north of Johnson City)

A small lake formed by a dam near Johnson City. Walk-in access is on the southwest side of highway.

Pedernales Falls State Park

The park offers wade fishing and bank fishing in a scenic setting and is a good launch site for downstream floats.

Hammett's crossing

Located on a dirt road off Texas 71 in Travis County.

Texas 71 Crossing

Access is limited at this crossing due to a lack of parking, but anglers can get to the river for white bass fishing at the Milton Reimer Ranch located off Texas 71. Turn left off Texas 71 on Hamilton Pool Road and proceed about 2 miles past Bee Caves Road.

Lyndon B. Johnson State Park

Located on the Pedernales River next to the LBJ Ranch National Historic Site, park waters offer excellent fly fishing for smallmouth, Guadalupe and largemouth bass, crappie, channel catfish and a variety of sunfish. Three low water dams widen the Pedernales in the park and there are some holes as deep as 12 feet. There is access for bank fishing and wadefishing and float tubes and small watercraft are allowed.

The park has no camping facilities but a variety of motels and bed and breakfasts are available in the nearby towns of Stonewall, Fredericksburg and Johnson City. For information contact park officials at (210) 644-2252.

Pedernales Falls State Park

Located in Blanco County, nine miles east of Johnson City on Texas (FM) 2766, or 32 miles west of Austin on US 290, then north on Texas (FM) 3232 for six miles, the park offers access to fishing on stretches of the Pedernales River which flow over tilted stair steps of layered limestone ledges into deep, clear pools. The park is a favorite stop for tourists and hikers but receives very little fishing pressure.

Flyfishers, who wade the waters downstream from the popular falls area, can find excellent action for Guadalupe bass, sunfish and channel cats. About five miles of river run through the scenic park, offering plenty of solitude for the adventurous fly fisher. Pedernales Falls is one of the most popular parks for camping in the state. For information, contact park officials at (210) 868-7304.

Channel catfish and fly reel.

CIBOLO CREEK

Located in the town of Boerne on Texas 46 (East River Road) off Interstate 10, Cibolo Creek has an abundant population of sunfish, largemouth and Rio Grande perch.

There is wade fishing access along the creek in the scenic Boerne City Park located next to the Kendall County Fairgrounds. Flyfishers should use long leaders or clear stillwater fly lines in the clear creek water in the park because fish are extremely wary. Fly fishing is excellent along the creek under a shaded canopy of cypresses. The 70-acre park includes the Cibolo Wilderness Trail and Nature Center.

Flyfishers also can bank fish along the creek by parking along Texas 46, which heads east from Boerne to New Braunfels. The creek also can be accessed for wading and fly fishing at the 70-acre Cibolo Wilderness Trail and Nature Center, a Boerne city park. No admission is charged at the park but donations are accepted. The scenic stretch of creek in the little park is shaded with cypress trees, with largemouth, sunfish and Rio Grande perch holding in small pockets and holes and along the gravel bars in the clear running stream.

The park attracts heavy use on weekends but the creek is a lightly fished jewel. For information contact the Cibolo Nature Center (830) 249-4616.

Flyfisher in float tube on Hill Country creek.

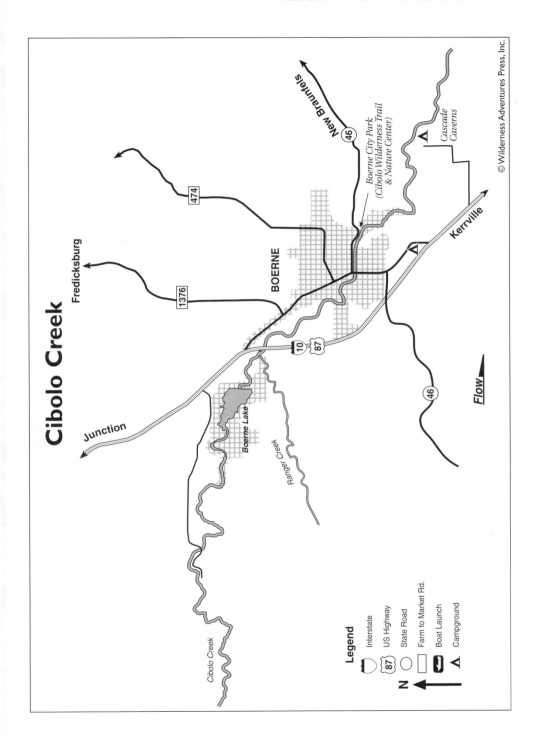

Cibolo Creek

Fredericksburg

Junction

BOERNE

Boerne Lake

Ranger Creek

Cibolo Creek

New Braunfels

474

1376

10 87

46

46

Boerne City Park
(Cibolo Wilderness Trail
& Nature Center)

Cascade
Caverns

Kerrville

Flow

© Wilderness Adventures Press, Inc.

Legend

Interstate

87 US Highway

State Road

Farm to Market Rd.

Boat Launch

Campground

N

BLANCO RIVER

The Blanco River flows through Kendall and Hays counties through the town of Blanco and into the San Marcos River just south east of San Marcos. It is a scenic, spring fed, clear-running river that holds largemouth, smallmouth, Guadalupe bass, Guadalupe / smallmouth hybrids and sunfish including redear, redbreast and blue-gill. Access can be difficult on the upper reaches because of the many private homes along its banks but there are a number of public access points that allow for wade fishing or float trips. Landowners along the river have constructed many small dams along some stretches of the river to create deep pools for swimming and fishing.

To reach wade fishing and float tube access points on sections of the Blanco take Texas (FM) 2325 southeast of Blanco to County Roads 405 and 406. Another section with good access points is southeast of Wimberly. From Texas 12, take Texas (FM) 3237 and turn right on County Road 173 and left on County Road 314, which crosses the river several times.

Blanco Community

Located on the south side of the town of Blanco is the 105-acre Blanco State Park. There is bank fishing and canoe and kayak put-in and take-out access from the park. In addition to being a good stopping point for shore lunches on floats down the Blanco, Hill Country fly fisher Rod Viator says this stretch of water can be good for largemouth and Guadalupe bass, sunfish and trout during the winter months. He recommends Madam X and small olive damsel nymph patterns fished deep.

Upriver from the Blanco community along several county roads that run off Texas 1888 are a number of low water crossings that provide wade fishing access to the Blanco River. Deep holes make this a good stretch to launch a kickboat, kayak or float tube. The deeper holes attract swimmers during the summer months but the fishing still can be good just upstream from the activity, which is usually centered near the low water bridges.

West of the Town of Blanco

County Road 104 Crossing

This low water bridge crossing is another good access point for wade fishing or fishing from a float tube or kickboat on the river. Travel west of Blanco to County Road 104, which runs south off Texas (FM) 1623.

Texas (FM) 1888 Crossings

There are also low water bridge crossings that run off county roads from Texas (FM) 1888 west of Blanco. A number of these are popular swimming holes during the warmer months but a good strategy is to use a float tube or kickboat and move upstream from the activity to find good fishing. Anglers seeking access to the Blanco outside of Blanco State Park should be particularly careful in avoiding trespassing on private land.

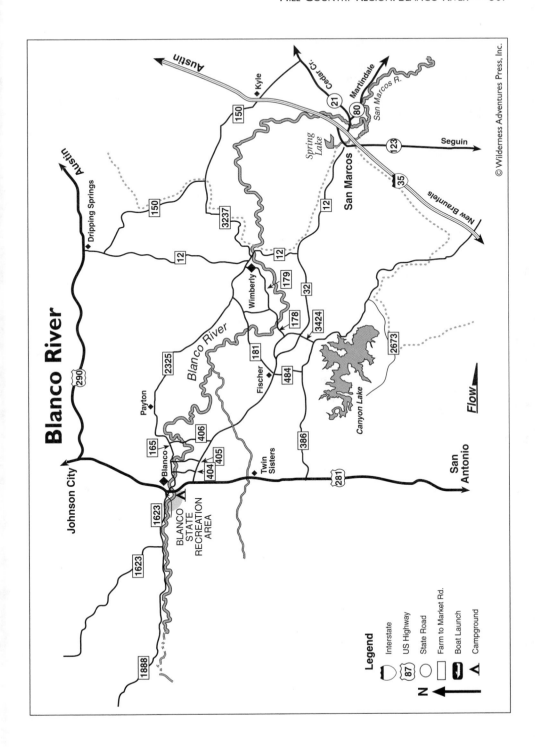

© Wilderness Adventures Press, Inc.

Blanco River

Legend

Interstate
US Highway
State Road
Farm to Market Rd.
Boat Launch
Campground

East of the Town of Blanco

County Road 405 and 406 Crossings
To reach wade fishing and float tube access points on sections of the Blanco take Texas (FM) 165 east of Blanco to County Roads 405 and 406.

County Road 407 Crossing
Fly fishing Guide Bill Waldron says there is good access to the Blanco from the low water crossing on County Road 407 off Texas 165 east of Blanco. Further down-stream, starting below the County Road 407 crossing, access becomes more difficult on the Blanco. Posted signs are much in evidence along this stretch. Floating the Blanco as it runs along County Road 407 can also be difficult because of numerous small dams that have been built by ranchers. One will certainly see many "posted" and "no parking" signs on the stretch of river downstream from County Road 407 off of Texas (FM) 165. Opportunities for floats on the river also can be adversely affected by drought conditions on the river, according to Waldron.

County Road 314 Crossing
Another section with good access points is southeast of Wimberley. Take Texas 12 south from Wimberley then turn east onto County Road 314 and travel back northeast to the crossing.

Dudley Johnson Park
Located near the Kyle community near Interstate 35, the park offers access for flyfishers in kickboats, kayaks, canoes and float tubes to a small lake formed on the Blanco River. This is one of the better areas for largemouth on this stretch of the Blanco.

Interstate 35 Bridge to Convergence with San Marcos River
San Marcos fly fisher Jim Darnell says this stretch of the Blanco River holds good numbers of sizable redbreast or "yellow-belly" sunfish "that just love to hit a popping bug." In addition, there are some large redear sunfish, known locally as "shellcrack-ers" that hold down deep along the limestone walls. Bluegill, sunfish, largemouth and smallmouth/Guadalupe bass hybrids can also be caught in the Blanco. High water is usually not a problem on this stretch of the Blanco, Darnell says, but periods of drought can lower water levels significantly enough to restrict float trips.

Another good put-in for a float on this stretch of the Blanco is at the Texas 80 Bridge Crossing on the road that goes south from San Marcos to Martindale and Luling. Darnell says he normally puts in here and fishes downstream through an area called Green Valley.

Hill Country fly fisher Rod Viator says the crossing under the Interstate 35 Bridge northeast of San Marcos offers parking and provides easy access to the river. A good stretch of the river can be fished from this access without having to organize a shuttle and downstream pick up, Jolly says. He recommends taking the channel with the faster water to the right of the rock dam at the Cape Road Bridge portage and then paddling back upstream to the put-in in the slower moving channel.

Blanco State Park

Blanco State Park is located on the Blanco River, just blocks south of downtown Blanco, which is about 50 miles west of Austin and 50 miles north of San Antonio. Flyfishers can wade the clear, spring-fed waters for largemouth, a variety of sunfish including redear and bluegills, Rio Grande perch, Guadalupe Bass and channel catfish.

The park waters also provide an excellent winter fishery for rainbows. Up to 8,000 trout are stocked in one of the lakes each winter.

The park offers access to quality year-round fly fishing, due in large part to a series of low-water dams that create deep holes and widen the river. The park offers a variety of bank fishing since the entire shoreline is accessible. Watercraft is allowed but only those that can be carried by hand to the shoreline. Power is restricted to electric trolling motors.

For information on camping facilities, contact park officials at (210) 833-4333.

Bluegill sunfish.

SAN MARCOS RIVER

The San Marcos River starts in town at Spring Lake near Southwest Texas University. Access is limited in that area because back casts can interfere with college students going and coming from class. The spring fed river is crystal clear and is known for its consistent flow rates and lush streamside vegetation that includes elephant ears and water hyacinths.

Clear intermediate sinking fly lines and light leaders combined with stealthy approaches will pay dividends on the San Marcos.

Thompson's Island to Martindale

There is an access point for flyfishers on River Road in San Marcos called Thompson's Island, a city park. This is a good spot to put in a canoe or kayak for a float downriver toward Martindale. This stretch is lightly fished and runs clear and deep, holding good numbers of bass and large sunfish. San Marcos fly fisher Scott Williams says he has seen some of the biggest Rio Grande perch in the Hill Country on this stretch of the San Marcos. The presence of many deep holes and steep banks make the San Marcos River better suited for float fishing than wading. Major access points are southeast of San Marcos on farm-to-market roads off Highway 80. Among good access points are on FM 1979 west of Martindale, on FM 1977 near Staples, and on FM 20 west of Fentress. In San Marcos there are a number of access points on public streets in San Marcos in addition to a boat ramp at the San Marcos City Park.

Flyfisher at small dam on San Marcos River.

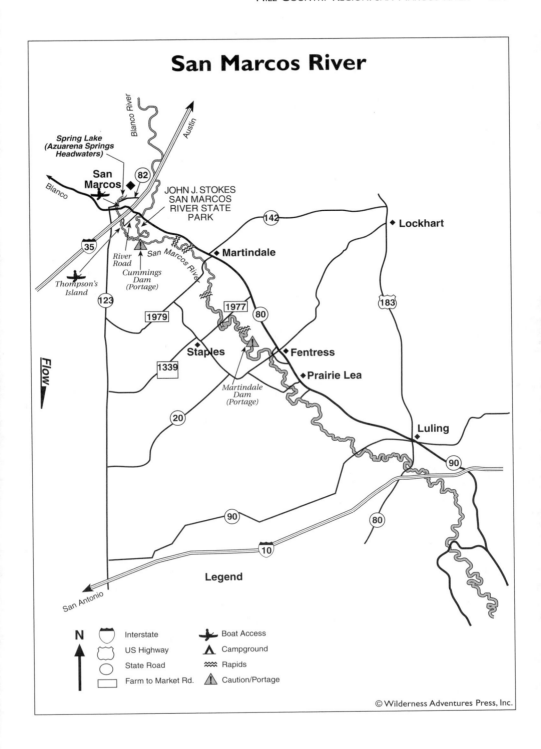

San Marcos River

Blanco River

Austin

Spring Lake
(Azuarena Springs
Headwaters)

San Marcos

Blanco

82

JOHN J. STOKES
SAN MARCOS
RIVER STATE
PARK

142

♦ Lockhart

35

River
Road

San Marcos River

♦ Martindale

Cummings
Dam
(Portage)

Thompson's
Island

123

1979

1977

80

183

Staples

♦ Fentress

1339

♦ Prairie Lea

Martindale
Dam
(Portage)

20

Luling ♦

90

Flow

90

80

10

San Antonio

Legend

N

- Interstate
- US Highway
- State Road
- Farm to Market Rd.

- Boat Access
- Campground
- Rapids
- Caution/Portage

© Wilderness Adventures Press, Inc.

County Road 101 Crossing

This crossing located south of San Marcos between Guadalupe and Caldwell counties between Texas (FM) 621 and Texas 80 offers walk-in access to the river.

To float the upper part of the San Marcos River, flyfishers with kayaks, canoes, or johnboats can put-in at the headwaters in downtown San Marcos and fish downstream under Interstate 35. Another approach is to skip that downtown stretch and put-in at Thompson Island or near the Interstate 35 crossing, and fish the stretch downstream from San Marcos. Veteran San Marcos River angler Jim Darnell points out that the river at this point remains a constant 72 degrees coming up out of springs.

The San Marcos River and the Blanco River intersect several miles below the town of San Marcos. This stretch from Thompson Island to the point where the San Marcos River meets the Blanco River provides " a nice, slow half day of fishing," Darnell says.

Largemouth, smallmouth, Guadalupe bass, redear, redbreast and bluegill sunfish are caught at the intersection of the San Marcos and Blanco Rivers.

Darnell notes that in the summer the water in the Blanco will be much warmer than the spring-fed flow in the San Marcos. Because of this, the San Marcos provides a much cooler environment for fishing in the heat of the summer.

On the stretch of the San Marcos River below intersection with the Blanco River, flyfishers will come to Cummings Dam, which will require a portage. Below the dam, it is less than a half-mile to the West Hill Crossing Bridge.

Martindale to Staples

This stretch of the San Marcos offers a slower flow. Fly fishing can be good on this stretch but water is not as clear as it is on the upper stretches of the San Marcos.

Hill Country flyfisher Ken Jolly notes that the Martindale Dam has a 10-foot drop requiring a portage on the right. There are two trails and a park as well as a low water bridge, which provide access to the river downstream from the dam. Look for the portage trail on the right side of the low water bridge facing downstream.

Texas (FM) 1977 Crossing

This crossing in the Staples community provides an excellent access point to the river, says Jolly. Downstream from the access is Staples Dam, which requires a portage on right.

Prairie Lea Community

There are two crossings on county and farm roads off Texas 80 on either side of the Prairie Lea community that offer about a 3 mile stretch to float and fish. Jolly recommends taking the River Road from Texas 80 just north of Prairie Lea to the "T" intersection. Turn right to get to the upstream crossing at a wooden bridge, or turn left to the downstream crossing. The downstream part of this two to three hour float offers the best fishing, according to Jolly.

John J. Stokes San Marcos River State Park

This small, 5.5-acre undeveloped park is located on the San Marcos River east of Interstate 35 in San Marcos. Set in a lush woodland along the banks of the river, it is not far downstream from the headwaters of the San Marcos River where it emerges from the Edwards Aquifer at Azuarena Springs in the center of town. This is a good access point for bank fishing and for launching a canoe, kayak or float tube to prospect for largemouth, Guadalupe bass, Rio Grande perch and sunfish on the San Marcos River.

Flyfisher fishing from bridge on San Marcos River.

GUADALUPE RIVER SYSTEM

The Guadalupe River makes about a 250-mile journey from its north and south branch beginnings in the west-central part of Kerr County near the Hunt community to the Texas coast. Born of spring-fed streams, its two prongs combine near Ingram and it runs eastward through the Texas Hill Country. Near New Braunfels it turns southeast and follows a course across the Coastal Plain until it empties into San Antonio Bay where it forms one of the state's major estuaries.

As the Guadalupe flows through the Hill Country region of the state, the river offers flyfishers a variety of walk-in wade fishing options as well as adventurous float trips. At its upper end, there is access to the river at several scenic state parks and community lakes.

Waterfall in Guadalupe River State Park.

Scene on stretch of Guadalupe River at Guadalupe State Park.

There are no rapids of any magnitude on the two forks of the Guadalupe or on the main river above Kerrville. A number of summer camps for youths are located in this area and recreational activity on the water and vehicle traffic on the roads picks up substantially during the summer months.

The Guadalupe River is more suited to floating than wading in normal flow, but it offers walk-in wade fishing access at many points, including Kerrville State Park, Guadalupe River State Park above Canyon Lake and crossings along the River Road between Sattler and Gruene. It is best fished on weekdays in the summer and early fall due to large weekend crowds of recreational canoeists and float tubers.

For information on Guadalupe River flows, contact the Corps of Engineers in Fort Worth at (817) 332-8611.

Upper Guadalupe River North and South Forks

Near its headwaters, there are several low water bridge crossings with limited roadside parking along Texas 39 near the Hunt and Ingram communities. The pools around these low water crossings can be accessed from the roadside and hold good numbers of Guadalupe bass, sunfish and carp. This is also a good stretch of the Guadalupe from which to launch a float by kayak or canoe down short sections of the river between crossings.

There are summer homes along the north and south forks of the Guadalupe River as well as several lodges that provide river access for a fee. The Guadalupe River has been determined to be navigable up to the Mo-Ranch property on the north fork and up to the Southfork Ranch on the south fork of the river. Wade fishers and boaters have a legal right to fish the Guadalupe River but also must recognize and respect the property rights of landowners and always avoid trespassing on private property. It is not productive to argue over access rights with landowners. Disputes can be reported to the Texas Parks and Wildlife Department Enforcement Division (512) 912-7062 or the Kerr County Sheriff's Office (512) 912-7062.

Upper Guadalupe River, North Fork

The following entry points for fly fishing access to the North Fork of the Guadalupe, starting along Texas (FM) 1340 at the Kerr Wildlife Management Area, are recommended by veteran Guadalupe guide and outfitter Bob Miller, owner of Pico Outdoor Company in Kerrville. For current information on fishing, flow conditions; canoe rentals and shuttles contact Pico Outdoor Company at (830) 895-4348 or 800-256-5873.

Kerr Wildlife Management Area

The North Fork of the Guadalupe begins at springs in the wildlife management area where there are two access points to the river. This is a prime area for sunfish and small bass action. The Kerr Wildlife Management Area is located off Texas (FM) 1340 west of the Hunt community in Kerr County.

Rock Bottom Road

This road off Texas (FM) 1340 west of Hunt leads to a low water crossing that runs along the upper limits of the Mo-Ranch property and the Mo-Ranch campground.

Mo-Ranch Entrance

The Mo-Ranch off Texas (FM) 1340 west of Hunt provides access to the river for day use and camping facilities for a fee. The day use fee includes use of canoes on the property. Miller reports good wade fishing upstream and downstream for sunfish and surprisingly hefty largemouth holding in the clear water. A stealthy approach, and light, clear, intermediate fly lines with long fluorocarbon leaders are recommended.

Guadalupe River
North and South Forks (Headwaters)

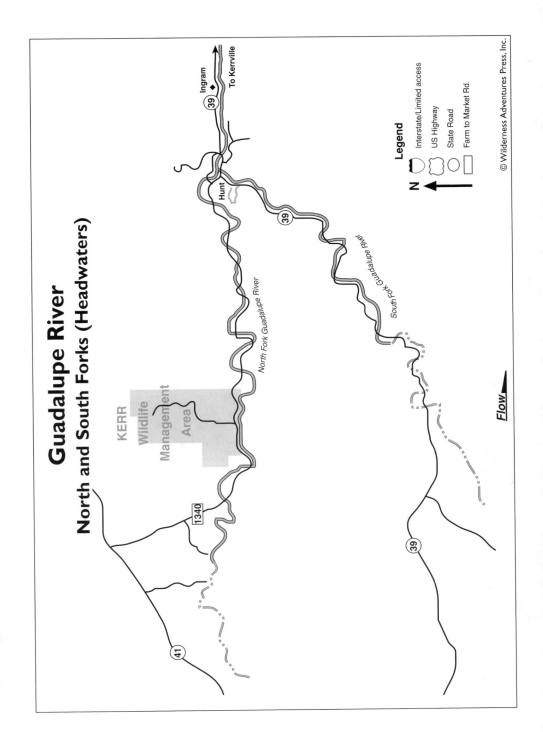

Ingram
To Kerrville
39
Hunt
39
North Fork Guadalupe River
South Fork Guadalupe River
KERR
Wildlife
Management
Area
1340
41

Legend

Interstate/Limited access
US Highway
State Road
Farm to Market Rd.

N

Flow

© Wilderness Adventures Press, Inc.

Old Road Bed Crossing

Off-road parking is available at this crossing off Texas (FM) 1340 west of Hunt. It provides access to a good stretch of river that holds bass and sunfish. Downstream, wade fishers will find the upper end of Wooden Dam pool.

Wooden Dam Crossing

Miller advises flyfishers to fish this scenic stretch of river out of a float tube or canoe and to put-in on the right side of the dam. Features include a long, deep pool along the bluff. Parking is available in the old road bed.

Sunshine River Ranch Crossing

This crossing provides access to slow moving section of the river.

Bear Creek Crossing

Flyfishers can prospect a pool formed by a small dam on the upstream side of this crossing.

Camp Waldemar

Miller advises that this is another good put-in for a canoe or float tube trek downstream.

Flyfisher with brown trout, Guadalupe River.

River Bend Low Water Crossing

This crossing is another good put-in and take-out point.

River Bend B and B

This is another good put-in and take-out point for floating short stretches between crossings.

Camp Stewart

Miller says this summer camp sometimes make available river access and cottages during the fall.

Stonehenge Low Water Crossing

This entry point provides access to good wade fishing upstream and downstream, Miller says. Flyfishers should look for the long pool downstream formed by a wooden dam.

Upper Guadalupe River, South Fork

Lynxhaven Lodge

Beginning in Southwest Kerr County off Texas 39, there are a number of entry points to the South Fork of the Guadalupe, starting with four crossings that can be accessed by guests at Lynxhaven Guest Lodge. In addition to cabins, Lynxhaven offers parking and day use access to the river for a fee. There are a number of deep holes along this stretch of the river that offer excellent fly fishing opportunities. For information contact the lodge at (830) 238-4931 or (713) 228-5911.

Sixth Crossing

This crossing provides public access to a shallow stretch of river. Wade fishers should look for fish holding in deeper pockets and holes.

Cedar Stone B & B

Guests at this bed and breakfast have easy access to about quarter mile stretch of river. Day use access is also offered for a fee.

Seago Road Low Water Crossing

Located downstream from the Heart of the Hills Conference Center, this is a good put-in for floats, downstream to Camp Flaming Arrow on the main branch of the Guadalupe.

Camp Flaming Arrow Low Water Crossing

This is a good put-in for a day-long canoe or kayak float trip downstream to Picnic Table Crossing (Shumaker's Crossing). Canoe rentals and day use access are available at the camp for a fee.

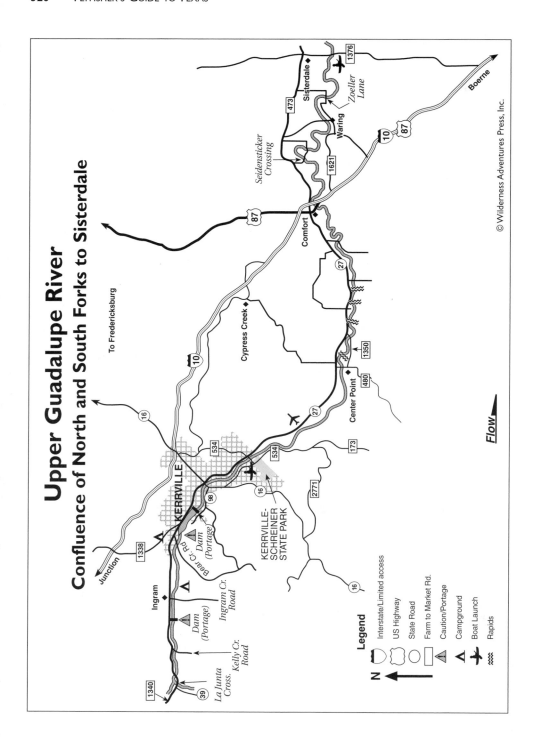

Upper Guadalupe River
Confluence of North and South Forks to Sisterdale

© Wilderness Adventures Press, Inc.

Flyfisher releasing brown trout, Guadalupe River.

Casa Bonita Lodges

Guests at rental these rental cabins have access to the river in a stretch that is best fished out of a canoe, kayak or small watercraft.

Upper Guadalupe River, Main Branch

La Junta Crossing

This access is near the first South Fork crossing, located near the junction of Texas 39 and Texas (FM) 1340. Miller advises that this is a good stretch of fishable water downstream to the junction with the North Fork of the Guadalupe. Upstream, there is a shallow stretch and some deeper water at a dam.

Picnic Table Crossing

Also called Shumaker's Crossing, a good put-in for a downstream float. Miller cautions anglers about steel beams on the right side of the channel.

Waltonia Crossing

This low water bridge entry point is suitable for launching a canoe, kayak, or johnboat, Miller says. He notes that there is a long, deep pool that holds fish upstream from this crossing. Downstream it is wadable for about a half mile.

Camp Rio Vista

Miller recommends this crossing as a good put-in for a float downstream to the Ingram Lake Boat Ramp.

Ingram Lake Boat Ramp

This is the last public boat ramp on the Upper Guadalupe. This ramp provides canoe and kayak access to the river upstream. Miller says flyfishers can prospect excellent fish-holding features on the lake, including lily pads and a nearby island.

Ingram Dam

The dam is accessible from Cade Loop Road.

Cade Loop Road

From this crossing upstream to Ingram Dam, there is a wadable stretch of river that holds good numbers of Guadalupe bass, Miller says. The downstream stretch is also wadable but can be slippery.

Johnson Creek Bridge

Walk-in access is on the right. This is also a good access point for float tube fishing to the mouth of Johnson Creek and downstream to the Guadalupe.

Old Ingram Loop

Access is on the east side of the entrance. Anglers can park on Ingram Loop Road near the intersection of Indian Creek Road and walk to the river. This entry point offers good wadefishing down to Ingram City Park.

Ingram City Park to Harper Road in Kerrville

Ingram City Park: Look for this access to the river across the street from the Phillips 66 Station. Miller advises that there is good wade fishing along this stretch of river.

River View Road

This access is located on a river campground and there is a small fee for entry. There is a sizeable pool that can be waded or fished from a float tube.

Guadalupe River RV Resort

RV park guests have good wade fishing access to river.

Arcadia Loop / Bear Creek Road

Located three quarters of a mile off the east entrance of Arcadia Loop, this low water crossing provides wade fishing access upstream. Float tubes or kayaks can also can be launched here for downstream floats.

UGRA Launch Ramp

Located across from a Texaco station, this entry point provides good access for launching a canoe or float tube to fish the upper end of the small lake.

Knapp Road Launch Ramp, Kerrville

Located just past Chili's Restaurant, this entry point provides kayak, canoe or float tube access to the middle of the lake.

Harper Road to Kerrville-Schreiner State Park

Louise Hays Park, Kerrville

This day use park near downtown Kerrville offers bank and wade fishing access to the Guadalupe River in a scenic and tranquil setting. Largemouth, Guadalupe bass, smallmouth and sunfish can be caught along this stretch of river. To get to the park, take Texas 16 to the Guadalupe River Bridge and turn west onto Spur 98. Follow Spur 98 to the entrance of the park. The park, which includes picnic tables and barbecue pits, is open from 7:30 a.m. to 11 p.m. For more information contact the park at (830) 257-8000.

G. Street Bridge, Kerrville

This is a good put-in to wade fishing or start a float downstream to Flat Rock Lake. To get to this entry point in downtown Kerrville, turn left at G Street at the traffic light by Dr. Pepper warehouse.

Kerrville-Schreiner State Park

Located on Texas 173 on the southeast side of this park provides access to a section of the Guadalupe that offers flyfishers shots at largemouth, smallmouth, Guadalupe bass, and sunfish as well as stocked rainbow trout during the winter months. The river is the most popular destination in the 517-acre park, attracting crowds of swimmers and canoeists during the summer months. As on most stretches of the Guadalupe River near urban and camp centers, early morning and late afternoon sessions are the most productive for flyfishers working shorelines and rock ledges out of float tubes, kayaks or other small watercraft.

Flat Rock Lake

To get to this lake from Kerrville-Schreiner State Park, turn right on Loop 534 and look for the road on the right that leads to a low water bridge. Miller says this low water bridge crossing is a good put-in for float trips downriver as well as a good take-out point for floats starting at the G Street Bridge in Kerrville. In addition to native species, the lake is stocked with rainbow trout during the winter months.

To get to the county park from the low water bridge, turn right on River Side Drive, which runs along Flat Rock Lake. Flyfishers can fish the lake after launching kayaks and canoes from the boat ramp in the county park.

Kerrville to Comfort

The stretch of the Guadalupe River beginning below the dam on Flat Rock Lake in Kerrville parallels Texas 27, offering floats down the 21-mile stretch to Comfort. There are take-out and put-ins about halfway to Comfort at the low water bridge near the community of Center Point. Houston fly fisher Greg Berlocher, a former Guadalupe River canoe guide, says this stretch between Kerrville and Comfort offers a good two day float with stops for fishing. Species along this stretch include largemouth, smallmouth, spotted bass, Guadalupe bass, Rio Grande perch, channel catfish and carp. This is a scenic stretch of the Guadalupe that includes limestone-walled canyons, maiden hair ferns along the banks, and sharp elbow turns in the river with frequent deep pools and pockets that hold game fish. Berlocher recommends prospecting for bass and sunfish in the deep pool around the low water bridge near Center Point. Drive in fishing is also available to flyfishers at the low water crossing near Center Point. Lily pads and rocky outcrops are among the fish-holding features in the wide pool created by the low water bridge. "You can fish that one pool for a couple of hours in crystal clear water," Berlocher says.

Brink's Crossing

Located between Kerrville and Center Point on a road that runs between Texas 173 and Texas 27, this is a good access for floats downstream. There is a rocky expanse that affords adequate off-road parking.

Flyfisher wadefishing for trout on the Guadalupe River.

Texas 480 Crossing, Center Point

This entry point offers a put-in for a four mile float to the Roane Road Crossing.

Texas (FM) 1350 Crossing, Center Point

This crossing, located about 2 miles southeast of Center Point in Kerr County, offers a put-in for a 1.9 mile float to the Roane Road Crossing. There is parking available along the roadside.

Roane Road Crossing

A take-out point for short floats from the Center Point community and a put-in for floats up to 12 miles downstream to the Seidensticker Crossing south of Comfort.

Lane Valley Road Crossing

This access offers a 17-mile float to the Waring community with several low water crossings, an old millrace, and a ledge en route.

Mill Road Crossing

Located on a road off Texas 27 just north of Comfort, this crossing offers walk-in access to the river down the old paved road. Anglers putting in here should be mindful of swift currents in this curve of the river than can stackup debris near the put-in.

Texas (FM) 473

This access is located along the road 3 miles east of Interstate 10 near Comfort in Kendall County. It provides access to wade fishing and serves as a launch point for canoes or kayaks.

Seidensticker Crossing

This low water crossing on a dirt road located south of Texas (FM) 473 provides access to wade fishing on the river above and below the crossing and or for floats downstream to Waring.

Waring Community Area

Zoeller Lane, Waring Community

This entry point is located six miles downstream from Comfort. The crossing north of Zoeller Lane provides access for wade fishing as well as a launch point for a float downstream to Zoeller Crossing.

Zoeller Crossing

Reached by traveling east on Zoeller Lane in Waring, this crossing provides access to wade fishing, and also serves as a launch point for floats downriver.

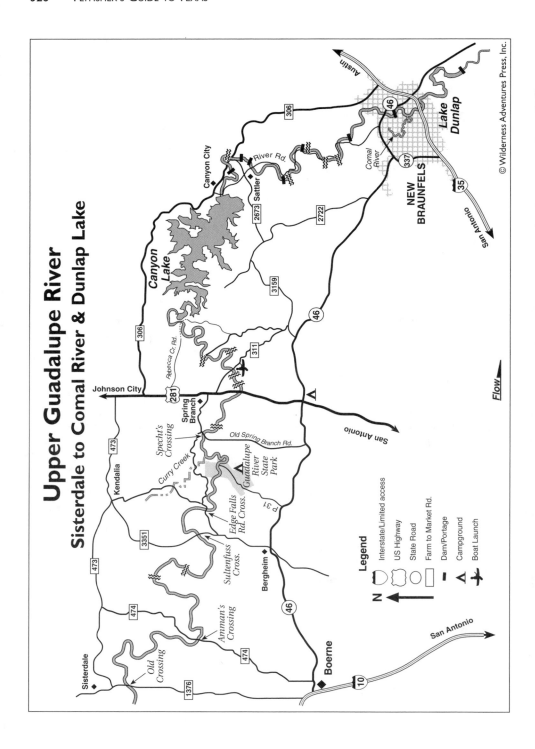

Upper Guadalupe River
Sisterdale to Comal River & Dunlap Lake

© Wilderness Adventures Press, Inc.

Austin

306

Canyon City

River Rd.

Sattler

2673

2722

Comal River

306

46

337

NEW BRAUNFELS

Lake Dunlap

35

San Antonio

3159

Canyon Lake

Rebecca Cr. Rd.

46

311

281

Johnson City

Spring Branch

Specht's Crossing

Old Spring Branch Rd.

San Antonio

Curry Creek

473

Kendalia

Guadalupe River State Park

Edge Falls Rd. Cross.

P. 31

Sultenfuss Cross.

3351

473

Bergheim

Amman's Crossing

474

Old Crossing

474

46

Boerne

Sisterdale

1376

10

San Antonio

Legend

Interstate/Limited access
US Highway
State Road
Farm to Market Rd.
Dam/Portage
Campground
Boat Launch

N

Flow

Sisterdale to Spring Branch

Texas (FM) 1376, Sisterdale

This crossing is located south of Sisterdale. A good put-in and take out site for canoes or kayaks as well as wadefishing in the immediate area.

Texas (FM) 474 (Ammans Crossing)

This crossing is located north of Boerne. There is launch site for canoes and kayaks on the west side of the bridge for floats to Bergheim Campground on Texas (FM) 3351.

Sultenfus Crossing / Bergheim Campground

Located on Texas (FM) 3351, this entry point is located five miles north of Bergheim. This facility provides camping, canoe rentals, shuttle service and access to the river. There is also public access below a nearby dam. For information call (210) 336-2235. (Texas 3351 is a new name for this road, previously it was designated Texas 3160 and still appears that way on some maps).

Downstream floats will cover a scenic stretch of 23 river miles that includes some rapids and springs. This float offers flyfishers a shot at big sunfish and Rio Grande perch.

For information on river conditions, canoe rentals and shuttle services contact the Bergheim Campgrounds and Canoe Livery on Texas (FM) 3351, between US 281 and Boerne off Texas 46 (830) 336-2235.

Float tubes can be a successful way to fish the Guadalupe River.

Edge Falls Road Crossing on Texas (FM) 3351 (formerly Texas 3160)

This crossing, located on Edge Falls Road just over three quarters of a mile south of the Bergheim Campground, is a good launch site for floats to Guadalupe River State Park.

Guadalupe River State Park

Located on Texas (SH) 46 between Boerne and US 281, Guadalupe River State Park offers access to the river for flyfishing. Hill Country fly fishing guide Bill Waldron notes that fishing is restricted at the swimming area at the drive-up area along the Guadalupe River, but flyfishers can hike upstream and downstream and find excellent wade fishing opportunities. Guadalupe bass, sunfish and largemouth are available and white bass come into the river along this stretch in the early spring.

Anglers who put-in at the park for downstream floats should be aware that three miles below the park is a low water crossing near Curry Creek that can be hazardous

Specht's Crossing

Comal County is developing a park called Specht's Crossing at this crossing on Old Spring Branch Road east of Guadalupe River State Park. It will have camping facilities and will provide good access to the river. Anglers will be able to float the scenic stretch from Specht's Crossing to Rebecca Creek Crossing. This access also serves as a take out point for a float from Guadalupe River State Park. Anglers can extend their trip by spending the night at the county park, then floating downriver to Rebecca Creek..

Spring Branch Area

Texas 46 Crossing

Located 3.25 miles west of US 281 in Comal County, this entry point is a good put-in and take-out access for float trips and wade fishing. This access attracts a lot of local angler activity.

Texas (FM) 311

This crossing located east of Spring Branch provides access to the river on the west side of the bridge.

Canyon Lake on the Guadalupe

This 8,240-acre lake is considered one of the most scenic in the state. Beginning at its tail waters below the dam and stretching for about 15 miles downriver is a productive area for rainbow and brown trout, the southernmost trout fishery in the United States. See page 362 and 363 for map and description.

Flyfisher with son fishing on the Guadalupe River below Canyon Dam.

Discussing the finer points of flyfishing at a bridge crossing on the Guadalupe River.

Guadalupe River rainbow.

Brown trout.

THE GUADALUPE RIVER TROUT FISHERY

State Parks and Wildlife Department stockings of rainbow trout are concentrated a few miles below Canyon Dam because the water coming from under the dam is cold on a year round basis. In the summer, the water warms up and approaches the maximum temperature that the trout can tolerate. Trout cannot survive when the water temperatures move up into the 75-77 degree range. After about 71 degrees their quality of life begins to go down. Upper 60s and low 70s are acceptable in the upper range. The temperature in this stretch is determined by flow levels from the dam during the summer months. The more flow, the faster the water runs down the river and the more cold water habitat is created. If the flow is reduced, the water warms up a lot quicker and the habitat is reduced.

Riverfront property and habitat on the Guadalupe suffered from severe flooding in 1998, when 22 inches of rain fell over a 24 hour period. It caused the Guadalupe to rise 30 vertical feet over a seven mile stretch of river.

It was called a 500 year flood (which means there was only a one in five hundred chance that a flood of that magnitude would happen in a given year) and was the worst flood ever documented on this stretch of the Guadalupe.

Veteran Guadalupe River fly fishing guide Scott Graham says that on the positive side, the flood may have given the river a boost by depositing rocks in the river from the nearby hills rather than just scouring the bottom, which is typical in high water situations in the Hill Country.

The flooding was unique in that it occurred primarily from runoff into the river downstream from the dam with the lake receiving relatively little impact, Graham says.

Despite the significant impact of the flood, veteran Guadalupe guides and anglers say the fishery has bounced back strongly. "I was amazed at the amount of fish that made it through the flood," Graham says. "I was utterly surprised to see hatches coming off the river within two weeks of the flood."

While a number of factors make this stretch of the Guadalupe a prime winter trout fishery, Graham says the fishing also can be excellent in the summer if there are favorable stream flows and cool water temperatures. "Some of the tricks on fishing the river in the summer time include being on the water at five-thirty in the morning and fishing until about nine or ten o'clock when the canoeists start coming downriver," Graham says. "Then you can come back in the evening and fish from about six-thirty to nine-thirty."

Wade fishing is safe and accessible on the Guadalupe at flows of 300 cfs (cubic feet per second) and less. The limestone and cobble bottom of the Guadalupe is typical of many streams in the Texas Hill Country. There are flat areas and also trenches several feet deep. Felt sole wading boots are recommended and spikes are even better, Graham says. Flyfishers should always be deliberate in their wading, even during lower flow periods, because many spills occur when anglers get too comfortable.

Graham says anglers should not attempt to wade the river at flows in excess of 400 cfs. Wading at 400 cfs should only be attempted by anglers who are fit and use a wading staff and felt sole waders, he says.

Wadefishers should be aware that there are many in-stream springs that feed into the Guadalupe downstream of the flow monitoring stations. These raise the flow above the levels being released from the dam.

For information on current and future river flows, contact the Army Corps of Engineers at (800) 964-3342. In flow, out flow and lake levels can be obtained. The Guadalupe River Trout Unlimited Chapter advises that if the in flow is significant and the lake level is higher than 909 feet above mean sea level, then anglers can be fairly certain that the out flow in the Guadalupe will continue to be high. Generally, the Corps of Engineers will try to match the outflow with the inflow to maintain the level once it is at 909 feet.

The Corps of Engineers controls water releases at lake levels of 909 feet above mean sea level and higher. Below 909 feet, the flow is controlled by the Guadalupe Blanco River Authority (GBRA) to meet downstream contracts for water.

In modern times, trout stockings, underwritten by a San Antonio brewery, were first launched on the Guadalupe River in 1969.

TPWD has conducted spring stockings of up to 50,000 rainbows in the river as part of the states regular put and take program. Graham says stocked trout on the Guadalupe have exhibited a growth rate in the wild that is comparable to the growth rate in the hatchery. "Given the chance with the appropriate summer flow rates, a guaranteed minimal flow, this river quality-wise will rival the San Juan River in New

Mexico," Graham says. "If we have the consistent flows in the summer time, the water temperature will always be in the prime feeding range. It will never get down in the 30s, which would slow down the metabolism of the fish." He says water temperatures in the low 50s to the mid 60s is the ideal level for the Guadalupe trout fishery.

Since the flood, a lot of the shading on the river was lost, so there is now more radiant heating from the sun in the summer.

Brown trout, which also have been stocked in the Guadalupe by the Guadalupe River Trout Unlimited Chapter, have also done well. "We put brown trout in our stocking programs and we have gone a whole season without hearing of any of them caught," says Graham.

Since Canyon Lake is a flood control lake, high level releases of water-5000 cfs-could create a prolonged scouring effect on the river and have an adverse effect on insect life, Graham says.

What has really jump-started the fishery is that its solid limestone, alkaline bottom promotes bug and algae life on the river. "It is typical of tailraces, the bugs are small and you have your blue-winged olives and tricos," Graham says. In addition there are green drakes, brown drakes, and hexagenia. Graham says caddis predominate, but aquatic moths that look very similar to the caddis are also present. "But as far as the fly pattern, a fish is not going to be able to tell the difference between the caddis and the moths," Graham says. In addition to the insect life, minnows and crawfish are also a part of the trout diet on the Guadalupe.

Rainbow trout.

Caddis, midge and mayfly hatches are plentiful enough to feed hungry trout on the Guadalupe, and flyfishers that pick the right time and spot can enjoy a taste of Texas style dry fly fishing. But, like on most trout streams, flyfishers will have a much higher success ratio getting down on the bottom in the cracks and crevices with nymphs and streamers. A productive technique on the Guadalupe is to make a cross-stream cast, let it swing downstream and strip it back into the current. The strike most often comes from these aggressive hatchery fish just as the fly swings into the current.

Free drifting weighted Woolly Buggers, Flashback Hare's Ears and other streamer and nymph patterns in the grooves and troughs that parallel the banks is a productive strategy on the Guadalupe. A San Juan worm with a Glo Bug dropper is a good way to get the attention of one of the wide-shouldered Missouri rainbows holding in one of the channel grooves. To find these fish-holding features, look for the strips of darker green water running parallel with the bank.

Two of Bill Waldron's favorite patterns for the Guadalupe are the Guadalupe Green, a caddis imitation tied with an olive maribou tail and dubbed maribou body with a hackle collar and gold dumbbell eyes. He also favors a grey caddis emerger pattern tied on a No. 16 hook. An effective nymphing technique on the Guadalupe, Waldron says, is to use a weighted line and a strike indicator with a small tandem rig with the top fly a size 16 and the bottom fly a No. 22 or No. 24 (a hair's ear as a dropper tied directly to the hook of the other flyworks well). Dead drift the nymphs by casting upstream and allowing them to swing downstream with the rod tip high, a "high sticking" technique. He recommends a small split shot that will get the fly down to bounce on the bottom. "If you are not hanging up occasionally, you are not deep enough," Waldron says. When the stocked fish become a little more wary and begin to feed on some of the small scuds in the river, dry fly patterns including Adams and Elk Hair Caddis are effective on the river, Waldron says. He usually fishes the Guadalupe with an 8½ foot rod matched to a 5-weight line.

Trout, at home in the cooler water nearest the dam, are found for 15 miles downriver. Graham says the reason this tailrace works as opposed to other tailraces in Texas is that it is a bottom-feed reservoir. There is no spillway. The water comes through a tube from the bottom of the lake so it is always cold and very sterile and void of oxygen. Oxygenators on the dam on the downstream side mix oxygen in the water and it goes through the weirs and the riffles and the oxygen levels are very high for the trout.

Ideally, trout need 6-8 parts per million of dissolved oxygen and the Guadalupe River below the dam has shown levels around 10 parts per million. "We have a highly oxygenated stream," Graham says.

On other tail water fisheries, including the one below Possum Kingdom, there are some mineral deficiencies, Graham says. The research from Parks and Wildlife has indicated that the trout typically will not live year round in other tail waters so they are managed as put and take fisheries.

Inconsistent water releases at the dam, creating drought-like conditions at times and flood-like conditions at other times, are an obstacle to the development of a superior trout fishery on the Guadalupe, Graham says.

Striped bass are another detriment to the trout fishery in the Guadalupe below Canyon Dam. These fish are released in the river during periods of flooding. They hold in the bottom of Canyon Lake where the water is cooler and get sucked through the tube, finding themselves in the river with a whole lot of rainbow trout to eat.

Shocking surveys find some shad forage fish in the striper diet but rainbows are the main course, biologists say. The last two state record stripers came out of the Guadalupe River.

Although there is a partial natural reproduction chain in effect for rainbows on the Guadalupe, Graham says he doesn't think it will be a self-sustaining stream because of poaching and the heavy utilization of the put and take fishery on some areas of the river. "I think there will always have to be supplemental stocking on this stretch of the Guadalupe," Graham says.

There are a few warm water species - sunfish and bass- that hang around in the colder water in the 15-mile stretch of river immediately below the dam, but most of these species head farther downriver below the community of Gruene in their search for warmer water.

Canyon Dam has been in place for 36 years and there have never been any supplemental stockings of bass and sunfish, Graham says. "Typically, you don't get those species in that deep water where the tube is. In addition, the growth rate for those warm water species would be slow in the colder water, on a par with Canada."

Graham says fishing pressure and catch and keep practices have had an impact on these warm water species. There are also some smallmouth in the Guadalupe, but TPWD no longer stocks smallmouth in Texas streams after concerns that they would hybridize with the native Guadalupe bass.

Access To Trout Fishing on the Guadalupe

Access to trout fishing on this stretch of the Guadalupe below Canyon Dam is broken down into three categories: Free public areas, fee access at private campgrounds, and riverfront leases overseen by the Guadalupe River Trout Unlimited Chapter.

Canyon Dam to New Braunfels

There is access to the river at a number of local businesses along River Road from Texas 306. The outfitters and canoe shuttles that are open in the winter all post signs in view along the River Road advertising access to the river for a fee. The standard rate for access at these operations is about $5 per person.

Canyon Dam

The river below Canyon Dam is stocked with rainbows by the state. From below Canyon Dam to Texas 306 is a catch and keep area, subject to the five fish per day bag limit and is open to any type of tackle, bait and lure. From the river crossing at Texas 306 to the Second Crossing on River Road is designated the Trophy Trout Regulation Zone on the Guadalupe.

The Corps of Engineers Park below the dam offers good wade fishing access to about a half-mile stretch of wade fishing. Stream flows of about 300 cubic feet per second (cfs) or less are ideal for wading. A release of 600 cfs or more can be extremely hazardous. The 10 mile stretch of river that begins here has been managed for a number of years as a trout fishery and holds good numbers of hatchery raised rainbows as well as stocked brown trout and golden trout.

The Trophy Trout Regulation Zone

This zone on the Guadalupe River extends from the easternmost bridge crossing on Texas 306 to the 2nd bridge crossing on River Road. Anglers may keep one rainbow or brown trout 18 inches or longer per day. Trout less than 18 inches must be immediately released. There are no restrictions on bait type, but only trout caught on artificial lures may be kept. The Texas Parks and Wildlife Department enforces the Trophy Trout Regulation Zone and posts the following notice along that stretch of the Guadalupe River: This section of the Guadalupe is managed under an experimental fishing regulation with the intent of creating a trophy trout fishery. Studies conducted by the Inland Fisheries Division of the Texas Parks and Wildlife Department indicate this section of the river has the potential for a year-round trout fishery. This unique opportunity is possible due to the cold water discharge from Canyon Reservoir. Over summer survival and natural reproduction of trout have been documented in this section of the river. TPWD studies have also concluded the food supply for trout is excellent, with trout growing at approximately ½ inch per month. Texas Parks and Wildlife Department Fisheries Biologists are evaluating this experimental regulation.

Maricopa Riverside Lodge

This lodge is located west of the Texas 306 Bridge at about the 2.5 river mile mark and offers access to the river for its guests. Call (210) 964-3731 for more information.

Whitewater Sports Campground and Canoe Livery

This facility is located on Texas 306 near the Horseshoe Falls community at river mile 4 below Canyon Dam on the Guadalupe River. It is open in the winter months and is adjacent to a state stocking site for rainbow trout. For a fee, Whitewater Sports offers wade fishing and bank fishing for flyfishers and is also an excellent put-in for floats downriver. The Whitewater Sports Campground area is in the put-and-take zone on the river. The trophy zone begins just downriver from Whitewater Sports after the 306 Bridge.

Texas 306 Bridge

Anglers can also use the roadside right-of-way at the Texas 306 Bridge near the Horseshoe Falls community at river mile 3 (across from Whitewater Sports) to launch downstream floats.

Rio Raft Company

This river raft and tubing outfitter is located on River Road at the Fourth Bridge Crossing at about the 5.5 mile mark below Canyon Dam. This is a good take-out point for float tube, canoe, and kayak trips downstream from Whitewater Sports Campground. There is a fee charged for put-in and take-out services and for wade fishing access to the river. This is an excellent stretch of water for wade fishing with a variety of deep holes and limestone seams to prospect.

Little Ponderosa Outfitters

Located on River Road at about the 7.5 mile mark below Canyon Dam, this facility provides access to stretches of the river administered by the Guadalupe River Trout Unlimited chapter.

Guadalupe River Trout Unlimited (GRTU) Release Program

Guadalupe River Trout Unlimited (GRTU) also provides access to prime fly fishing waters on the Guadalupe River through a lease access program offered to its members. GRTU is an affiliate of Trout Unlimited, a national organization dedicated to the preservation of cold water fisheries. As part of its goal to maintain a permanent and growing trout population in the Guadalupe, GRTU is active in stocking the Guadalupe River with rainbow and brown trout at selected sites several times each year.

GRTU supporting members can enroll in the lease access program, which allows catch and release fishing on GRTU-leased lands. The lease access season normally runs from late October through April. Participants must attend a one-hour lease access orientation. Lease access memberships are priced at $85 per year and are renewed each November. For additional information, contact Scott Graham at (512) 847-6222.

L and L Campground

Access at this location is controlled by the Guadalupe River Trout Unlimited chapter during winter months and is open to the public during summer for bass and sunfish.

Camp Beans

A popular campground and another Texas Parks and Wildlife Department rainbow trout stocking point, Camp Beans is located along River Road near the Third Bridge Crossing at river mile 10. There is free access to this stretch of river for walk-in fishing or those anglers fishing from canoes, kayaks, float tubes or other non-motorized craft. Camp Beans is located among towering bluffs and has traditionally been a popular area with fly anglers because of its excellent trout habitat and wading water.

The Camp Beans section of the river is located in the special trout regulation zone, where an 18-inch minimum size and one trout per day bag limit is in effect. Trout that are harvested in this area must be caught on an artificial lure or fly. The property is open to bait fishermen but any fish caught with bait must be released.

The entrance to Camp Beans is about a quarter of a mile north of the Third Bridge Crossing on the River Road. Camping is available at the site for a fee.

Sign on tree giving notice of trophy trout waters on Guadalupe River.

Guadalupe River rainbow.

Third Bridge Crossing on the River Road

This crossing is located at the 10.5 river mile below Canyon Dam. Access to the river is available here for a fee at The Cliffs. Mountain Breeze Campground, located just downriver from the Third Bridge Crossing, also provides access to the river for a fee.

The Mountain Breeze Facility

Located on River Road at the 11.5 river mile below Canyon Dam, Mountain Breeze is open during the winter months providing day access to the river for a fee.

River Road Camp Rentals

Located just downstream from the Second Bridge Crossing at river mile 14, this facility offers access to the river for flyfishers for a fee.

Riverbank Outfitters and Krause's Riverbank Grill

These facilities are located on River Road at the 14.5 river mile, just upstream from the First Bridge Crossing.

First Bridge Crossing

This crossing is located along River Road (Texas 306) just below river mile 15. Texas Parks and Wildlife Department recently opened up free access to anglers on both sides of the river at Camp Hueco, located at the First Bridge Crossing. "This 32-acre campground contains a beautiful stretch of water that has some great habitat for trout," says Steve Magnelia, Texas Parks and Wildlife fisheries biologist. The department also has added this stretch of the Guadalupe to its trout stocking program. The Camp Hueco stretch of the river is in an area that allows the harvest of five trout per day with no minimum size restriction.

Gruene to New Braunfels

This stretch of river beginning at Hueco Springs holds smallmouth and sunfish. It attracts heavy recreational use by tubers and rafters during summer months.

Gruene

This stretch of the Guadalupe near the historic community of Gruene is known for holding hefty redbreast sunfish.

New Braunfels

There are several parks in New Braunfels where flyfishers can launch kayaks or canoes to fish this stretch, which is fished by very few anglers.

For fly fishing stretches of the Guadalupe River downstream from Gruene and New Braunfels, see Lakes and Plains region.

Guadalupe River at Lake Dunlap

Located off US 35 in New Braunfels, Lake Dunlap is formed by the Guadalupe River. It offers flyfishers excellent sunfish and bass action. There is a public launch ramp here and it is ideal for launching a johnboat, canoe, kayak, or kickboat. There are also areas to wade fishing above the dam. There is bass boat and jet ski activity on the lake at times but flyfishers can find fishable areas around the lake.

Kerrville Schreiner State Park

Located in Kerr County, three miles southeast of Kerrville on Texas 173, Kerrville-Schreiner State Park is located along the Guadalupe River and offers flyfishers opportunities for largemouth, smallmouth, Guadalupe bass, sunfish and crappie.

A narrow lake formed by a low-water dam on the Guadalupe River offers opportunities for fly fishing in the park. Called Flat Rock Lake by locals, it holds largemouth, sunfish and channel catfish. Flyfishers can prospect from the bank or launch kayaks, canoes or float tubes. Park reservations are recommended for overnight stays. For information on camping facilities, call (210) 563-2342 or (512) 389-8900.

The park is located on Texas 173 at its intersection with Loop 534. From Interstate 10, take Texas 16 south to Loop 534, turn left (south) on Loop 534 and follow it to Texas 173. Turn east on Texas 173 and travel half a mile to the park entrance. The entrance fee is $3 per person. The park closes at 10 p.m. except for overnight guests.

Guadalupe River State Park

Located in Comal and Kendall counties, 30 miles north of downtown San Antonio, 13 miles east of Boerne on Texas 46, or eight miles west of US 281 on Texas 46, then three miles on Park Road 31, the park offers excellent wade fishing for Guadalupe bass and sunfish. Flyfishers can wade stretches of the river or use float tubes for fishing some of the deeper holes.

There is excellent fly fishing in Guadalupe River State Park upstream or downstream from the swimming area where fishing is prohibited. There are a number of trails that provide access to about five miles of river upstream and downstream. During spring white bass are added to the largemouth, sunfish, spotted bass and Guadalupe bass that can be taken in the river.

Guadalupe River scene.

COMAL RIVER

Called the "Shortest River in the World" the Comal runs only about 1.5 miles from its headwaters in Landa Park through the Schlitterbahn Water Park in New Braunfels. The water temperature of the spring-fed river holds steadily in the upper in a range from the lower 50s to the upper 60s. It is best to fly fish this stretch during the cooler months because there is so much recreational activity during the warmer months. The extremely clear water offers sight casting to the Comal's population of largemouth, Rio Grande perch and sunfish.

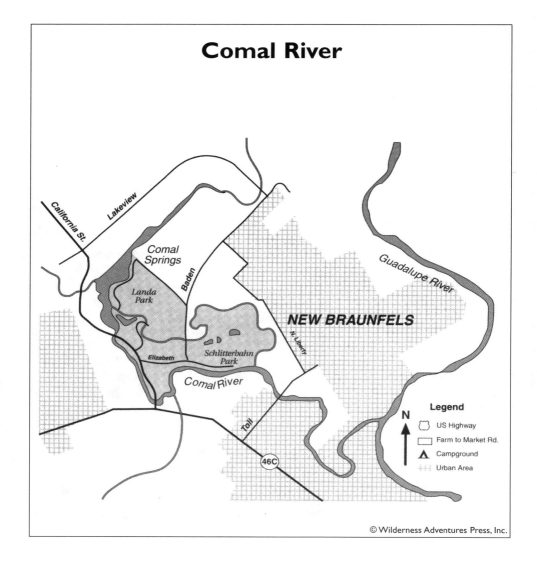

Comal River

California St.

Lakeview

Comal Springs

Baden

Landa Park

Guadalupe River

NEW BRAUNFELS

N. Liberty

Elizabeth

Schlitterbahn Park

Comal River

Toll

46C

Legend

N

US Highway

Farm to Market Rd.

Campground

Urban Area

© Wilderness Adventures Press, Inc.

SABINAL RIVER

The Sabinal is a small river that offers excellent fishing for largemouth, Guadalupe bass and sunfish. It flows south into Uvalde County from its headwaters in western Bandera County. There are low water crossings at bridges along Texas 1987 at the communities of Vanderpool and Utopia, which provide wade fishing access to some of the deeper holes on the river. "There are some nice pockets of fish in these stretches," says fly fisher Scott Williams of nearby Medina.

Lost Maples State Natural Area

The park offers some fly fishing opportunities for sunfish and small bass but it is a fairly shallow stretch of the Sabinal River. Hill Country fly fishing guide Bill Waldron says the waters of the Sabinal River that are easily accessed in Los Maples State natural area hold mostly small sunfish and a few Guadalupe bass, but the best fishing in the park requires about a mile and a half hike on back trails to the backpacking area where the Sabinal forms a small pond. This park also draws crowds during the summer months when the backpacking area is used by scout groups. The best time to fish the park is in the fall (after Labor Day) or during the early spring. Rainbow trout are also stocked in the park during the winter months. A good guideline for finding solitude on Hill Country rivers is to fish when the water is warm enough to make the fish active but cool enough to hold down the numbers of swimmers and tubers.

Deer hair bass fly with fly reel.

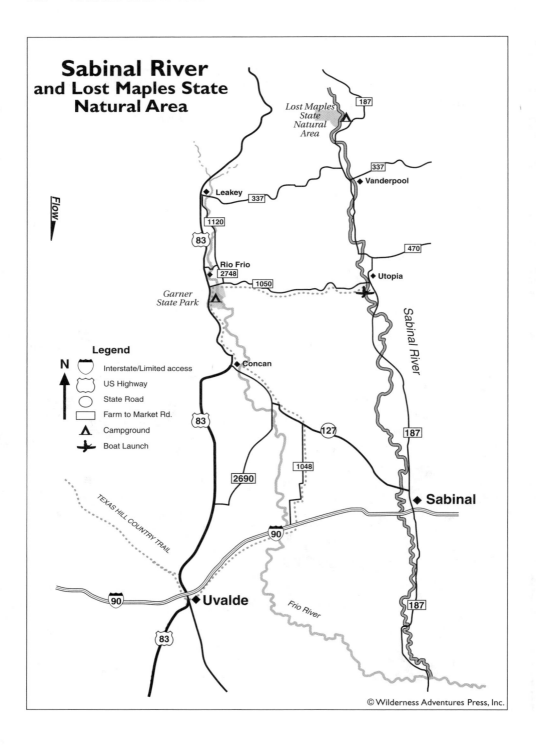

Sabinal River
and Lost Maples State Natural Area

Lost Maples State Natural Area

187

337

Vanderpool

Leakey

337

1120

83

470

Rio Frio
2748

1050

Utopia

Garner State Park

Sabinal River

Legend

N

Interstate/Limited access

US Highway

State Road

Farm to Market Rd.

Campground

Boat Launch

Concan

83

127

187

1048

2690

TEXAS HILL COUNTRY TRAIL

Sabinal

90

90

Uvalde

Frio River

83

187

Flow

© Wilderness Adventures Press, Inc.

Other Access Points to the Sabinal River

Vanderpool and Utopia Communities

There are several good access points for flyfishers along Texas 187 between Vanderpool and Sabinal.

Texas (FM) 187

This access to the Sabinal is located about 1½ miles below the intersection of Texas (RR) 337 and Texas (RR) 187.

Texas (FM) 187 Crossing

This entry point provides access to the Sabinal four miles downriver from the crossing listed above. A deep pool upstream make this good for fishing, but it is also a popular swimming hole for local residents.

Texas (FM) 1050 Crossing off Texas (RR) 187

This entry point to the Sabinal is at a crossing in Utopia where the river is dammed and accessible with float tubes, kayaks or canoes. The pool below the dam is accessible for wade fishing.

Texas (FM) 187 Crossing

Access is somewhat limited at this crossing located South of Utopia. Utopia on the River, a nearby bed and breakfast, offers access to a stretch of river for guests.

Texas (FM) 187 Crossing

This is a second crossing on this farm road located a little farther south of Utopia. A section of river is accessible to waders about a quarter mile upstream from the crossing.

US 90 Crossing

This entry point is located west of Sabinal and offers access for wade fishing downstream.

Texas (FM) 187 Crossing

This access is located about 15 miles south of Sabinal. Look for a deep pool upstream from the crossing, as well as wade fishing opportunities downstream.

FRIO RIVER

The Frio River begins in Real County and flows south into Uvalde County. The predominant species include bluegill and green sunfish, with good numbers of Guadalupe bass and largemouth.

Hill Country guide Bill Waldron says hefty largemouth are often spotted in the clear waters of the Frio. "You can see them and they can see you," Waldron warns. The stretch of river that runs along Texas 83 between the Rio Frio and Concan communities is one of the most scenic and beautiful in the state. This section runs through Garner State Park. The park gets large crowds during the summer months but Waldron recommends trying the deep pools in the park. The larger fish are very wary and longer leaders and clear fly lines are a must for success here as well as on other stretches of this clear, flowing river.

An excellent area to wade fishing inside Garner State Park is the area starting just below the dam.

There are several bridges that cross the Frio in Leakey that provide good access points for fly fishing. Neal's at Concan offers cabins and access to the river. Waders are important equipment on this river because it runs cold year around. The river is similar to the Medina and Sabinal in holding abundant stocks of Guadalupes, largemouth and sunfish.

Leakey to Vanderpool

A good access point for the Frio River can be found off of Texas (FM) 337 between Leakey and Vanderpool, and several others can be found from farm-to-market roads off US 83 south of Leakey, including Texas (FM) 1120 and Texas (FM) 1050.

Texas (FM) 337 Crossing

This crossing is located in Real County one mile east of Leakey. Flyfishers can launch canoes or kayaks here for floats downstream. Pools near the bridge hold sunfish and can be fished from canoes or kayaks but local landowners discourage wade fishing in this area.

Texas (FM) 1120 Crossing

This entry point located south of Leakey is a good put-in or take-out point for floating 2- to 3-mile stretches of the river, but a number of riverfront homes are present in this stretch.

Texas (FM) 1120 Crossing

Located west of the Rio Frio community, this is a good launch site for 2-mile float downstream to the Texas (FM) 1050 crossing.

Texas (FM) 1050

Located in Uvalde County on the road to Utopia community, this crossing offers a take-out point for floats launched at upstream crossings as well as access to wade fishing downstream.

Frio River

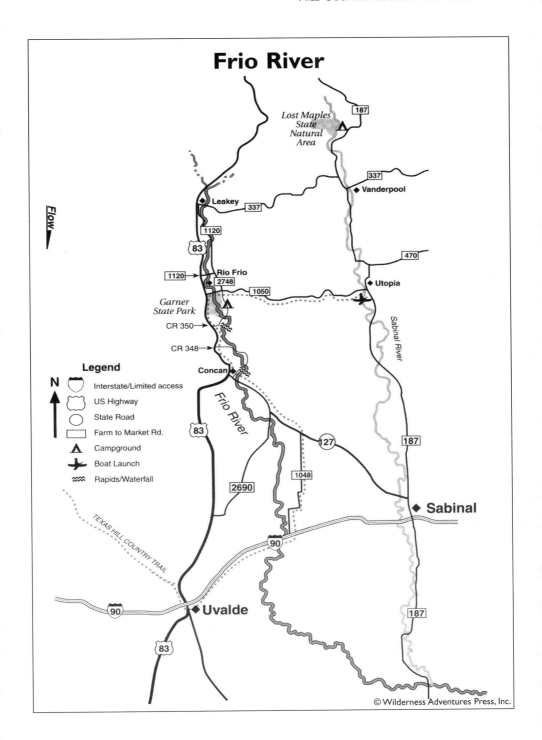

187

Lost Maples
State
Natural
Area

Flow

337

♦ Vanderpool

♦ Leakey   337

1120

470

83

1120 →   Rio Frio
         2748   1050   ♦ Utopia

Garner
State Park

CR 350 →

CR 348 →

Sabinal River

Legend

N

Concan ♦

Frio River

⬭ Interstate/Limited access

⬡ US Highway

◯ State Road

▭ Farm to Market Rd.

▲ Campground

➤ Boat Launch

〰 Rapids/Waterfall

83

127   187

1048

2690   ♦ Sabinal

TEXAS HILL COUNTRY TRAIL

90

90   ♦ Uvalde

83   187

© Wilderness Adventures Press, Inc.

Garner State Park Access

The Frio River downstream from the park offers canoeists and kayakers deep pools and excellent fishing for bass and sunfish when park is not overcrowded with summer visitors.Garner State Park draws big crowds of vacationers during the summer months but Hill Country fly fishing guide Bill Waldron says the deep pool behind the main pavilion holds numbers of hefty largemouth that are very wary in the clear spring-fed river. He recommends using one of the clear, intermediate fly lines and longer leaders for these fish.

Flyfishers can have better luck enticing strikes from less wary largemouth, Guadalupe bass and Rio Grande perch by wade fishing the Frio downstream from the dam in Garner Park, Waldron says.

Rio Frio to Concan

The stretch of river that runs from the community of Rio Frio to Concan is excellent fly fishing water, according to Waldron. There are a number of low water crossings that provide access to the river along US 83.

Mager's Crossing

This crossing is located south of Garner State Park on a dirt road off Texas (FM) 1050.

County Road 348 Crossing

Called the Cliff Seven Crossing by locals, it is located on 348 as it runs east off US 83. It is a good put-in and take-out for floats and offers good wade fishing upstream. The crossing offers a launch point for the four mile float downriver to Concan , a stretch that will require portages at two small dams.

Texas 127 at Concan community

This crossing is popular take-out point for recreational tubers and canoeists.

Texas (FM) 2690

Located off Texas 127 about five miles southeast of Concan, this crossing offers access to wade fishing upriver.

Garner State Park

Garner State Park is located on the Frio River near Concan in Uvalde County, 31 miles north of Uvalde on US 83 or 9 miles south of Leakey. The park provides bank fishing and wade fishing access to the river where flyfishers can sight cast to largemouth, Guadalupe bass and sunfish. Long leaders and soft presentations are necessary to the wary game fish in this clear flowing river.

One of the most scenic parks in the Hill Country, with cypresses lining the river banks at the foot of rocky bluffs, Garner State Park draws large crowds throughout the summer as well as on weekends in the spring and fall.

Despite the frequent crowds in the park and tubing and swimming activity on the river, Hill Country fly fishing guide Bill Waldron says there are less traveled and more productive stretches of the Frio to wade fishing only a short walk upstream from the dam. A deep pool behind the large park pavilion is home to some hefty largemouth and is a good choice at first light.

The park has a large campground, picnic facilities and a seasonal park store operation with paddleboat rentals. Book reservations well in advance for camping in the park. For additional information, contact the park at (210) 232-6132.

To get to the park, take US 83 north from Uvalde, turn east on FM 1050, travel a half-mile to Park Road 29 and proceed to the entrance.

Wadefishing in Hill Country.

The Nueces fishes well for sunfish, bass, and perch.

NUECES RIVER

The Nueces River, an outstanding fly fishing destination for Guadalupe bass on its upper stretches, begins in Edwards County and flows about 300 miles to Nueces Bay on the Gulf of Mexico near Corpus Christi. After Texas won its independence from Mexico in 1836, the Republic of Texas and Mexico both claimed the territory between the Nueces and the Rio Grande River. The Treaty of Guadalupe Hidalgo settled the dispute in 1848, which fixed the international boundary at the Rio Grande River.

The river begins above the community of Vance, but better access points are to the south because of higher flow. Species common to the river include native large-mouth, long ear sunfish, Guadalupe bass, yellow-belly sunfish, bluegill, sunfish, rock bass, green sunfish, and Rio Grande perch.

Vance Community Access

The Nueces River forms an east-west boundary between Real and Edwards counties near the community of Vance. A quarter-mile below Vance is a walk-in access point, and about three quarter of a mile upstream there is a deep pool that can hold good numbers of bass and sunfish.

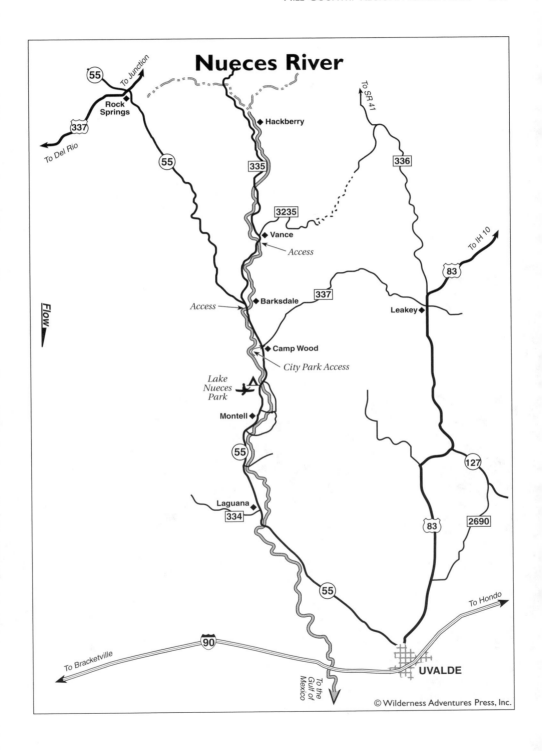

Nueces River

55

To Junction

Rock
Springs

337

To Del Rio

55

337

Hackberry

335

To SR 41

336

3235

Vance

Access

To IH 10

83

Access

Barksdale

337

Leakey

Camp Wood

City Park Access

Lake
Nueces
Park

Montell

55

127

Laguana

334

83

2690

55

To Hondo

Flow

90

To Bracketville

To the
Gulf of
Mexico

UVALDE

© Wilderness Adventures Press, Inc.

Texas 55 Crossing near Barksdale

To get to this entry point, take the road leading east from Barksdale to the river crossing. There is a wadable area downstream and a large hole upstream that can be fished from a float tube.

Texas 55 South of Barksdale

This entry point also leads to a deep pool upstream that can be fished from a float tube.

Texas 55 Crossing at Camp Wood

This crossing is located west of the city park at Camp Wood. Turn west at the First State Bank of Uvalde onto the road that leads to the river. The road runs along a sizeable stretch of the Nueces, providing ample access for bank or wade fishing. This access is very close to the center of town so it attracts a lot of local use.

Texas 55 at Lake Nueces

This access to the Nueces and a small lake is located in Uvalde County about three miles below Camp Wood at West Cooksy Park. A kickboat, canoe, kayak or float tube is required for fishing the lake. The park, located in a live oak-shaded grove, provides a good base camp for short floats between low water bridges in the area. There are 42 campsites, restrooms and showers. Those with full RV hook-

Nueces River panorama north of Uvalde.

ups rent for $15; sites with water and electricity for RVs or tent sites rent for $10. For more information, contact the park at (830) 597-3223.

County Roads 412 and 414 at Montell

The County Road 412 crossing is a gravel-banked, low water bridge crossing. The river is directed through drainage pipes at the crossing. A float tube is recommended for the stretch of river above these crossings.

County Road 410 Crossing south of Montell

Also located off Texas 55, this is a gravel-banked road crossing that allows access to wade fishing upstream and down. This is a good launch point for floats.

This county road leads to the Friday Ranch, a working cattle, goat, and sheep operation, which offers anglers several lodges and fishing and camping packages as well as access to two miles of the Nueces River. For information on rates, contact the Friday Ranch at P.O. Box 1, Uvalde, TX 78802, (830) 597-3257.

County Road 408 Crossing

Located off Texas 55, this low water bridge offers an excellent option for walk-in wade fishing in pools and runs upstream and downstream. It is also a good launch for downstream floats between low water crossings.

Texas 55 Crossing, 19 Miles North of Uvalde

This crossing provides a wadable stretch of river downstream but is heavily used by local anglers.

MEDINA RIVER

The Medina River System begins near the Bandera Community of Medina where the West Prong of the Medina meets the main branch. It flows southeast through the town of Bandera to Medina Lake. It is a lightly fished waterway that runs crystal clear with scenic shorelines and stretches shaded by a canopy of cypress trees. Anglers frequently will see whitetail deer moving across the river as well as wild turkeys, javelina and wild hogs. A flood in 1978 deposited a number of fallen trees in the river that provide excellent habitat for the bass and sunfish. It holds good numbers of Guadalupe bass, largemouth, Rio Grande perch and bluegill. Medina River fly fisher Scott Williams says the Medina offers sight casting in crystal clear pools. While some of the largemouth can run up into the 5 pounds range, most of the action comes from the smaller Guadalupe bass and redear and redbreast sunfish. For the most exciting sport, he recommends 4- and 5-weight fly rods with weight forward, floating lines. Williams says the Medina even offers flyfishers the opportunity to experiment with extremely light tackle, down to 1 weight fly rods. On the upper sections, the river is only about 25 feet across at it's widest, and a roll cast is an effective approach. "On the Medina, you will see a group of bluegill by the bank, and you can cast right on top of them and you will get one every time," Williams says.

North Prong Medina River

Brewington Creek Area

There are several access points on river crossings north of Medina on Texas 2107 in the vicinity of Brewington Creek. Wade fishing is good downstream from Brewington Creek, or anglers can launch a canoe or kayak and fish upstream in deeper holes and d in pockets at the bottom of the rapids.

Williams says the Guadalupes and sunfish are not that selective on this stretch and Woolly Buggers, size 10 and up, in olive or purple with a little flashabou in the tail are effective. Closer Deep Minnows bumped along the bottom also get a lot of attention. For topwater action most poppers, as well as a Dave's Hopper or Dave's Cricket, will work well. "In the warmer months it is really not hard to catch fish in the Medina," Williams says. "They hit anything you throw out there." The Rio Grande perch are a little more selective, so take a selection of the classic nymph patterns to entice a strike from these members of the cichlid family.

West Prong Medina River

Texas 16 Bridge and Camp Bandina to Peaceful Valley Ranch, Bandera

The first access heading south from Medina is a high bridge crossing that is a good wade fishing access point or put-in for about a 4-hour float downstream to Camp Bandina, a church camp that also offers a launch point for a downstream float toward Peaceful Valley and Bandera. Williams says this stretch of the Medina offers excellent fly fishing for bass and sunfish. It has a number of feeder creeks connected to upstream stock ponds that have deposited larger bass in the 4- to 5-pound class into the river.

Medina River

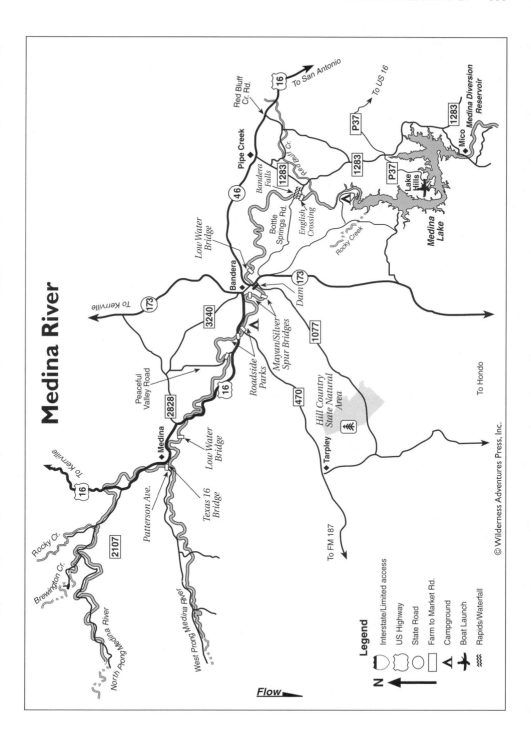

Legend

Interstate/Limited access

US Highway

State Road

Farm to Market Rd.

Campground

Boat Launch

Rapids/Waterfall

N

Flow

© Wilderness Adventures Press, Inc.

Bandera to Medina Lake

This stretch of the Medina River downstream from Bandera also holds good numbers of bass and sunfish, but it gets much more fishing pressure than the upper sections because there are a number of RV parks.

Medina to Bandera

There are two public access points off Texas 16 between Bandera and Medina, and one off FM 470 near the intersection of Texas 16 just north of Bandera.

Downstream from Medina Lake

A private camp just below the dam is the best access point below the lake.

FM 2107 Crossing

Anglers report that this stretch offers large pools but they are difficult to wade fishing and there are also access problems due to private development along the banks.

Rocky Creek Crossing

A large pool is located upstream from this access.

Texas 16 Crossing

Located about 4.5 miles north of Medina, this crossing is used primarily as a take-out point for floats from launches at Rocky Creek Crossing about 4 miles upriver. Just south of this crossing is the Baxter Ranch, which offers access to the river for a nominal fee.

Moffett Park - Located one mile downstream from the railroad crossing on Texas 337. Turn west toward the river on Patterson Street and cross the bridge. Parking is available and anglers can wade upstream or downstream from the park. A good put-in location for floats downriver.

Texas 16 Crossing

This access is located about 2.75 miles southeast of the Medina community and is recommended as a take-out point only.

Peaceful Valley Ranch Road

This crossing is recommended as a take-out or launch site only.

Texas 16 Crossing

This crossing, located three miles west of Bandera, offers good access for wade-fishing and serves as a put-in for floats downstream. There is a large pool a short distance downstream.

Texas (FM) 470 Crossing near Tarpley
This crossing provides access to the river downstream. Three miles below this crossing is the Bandera Beverage Barn, which is a good take-out point. The area immediately downriver from this crossing is considered hazardous for floats.

Bandera City Park
This park offers good access to the river for a nominal entry fee. It is a good put-in for floats along the remote stretch of river to Bandera Falls ten miles downstream. The park attracts a lot of visitors on weekends.

Ruede Ranch
Located near the Pipe Creek community. Travel southeast on Texas (FM) 1283 toward Medina Lake, cross the Red Bluff Creek bridge and then turn right on Red Bluff Ranch Road, the first road after crossing the bridge. Then take a left at the fork in the road and look for signs indicating the road to the river.

Landmark Inn State Historical Park
Located in Castroville about 39 miles west of San Antonio via US.90, this small 4.7-acre park offers fishing access on the Medina River. The landscaped grounds are open for day use, and there is a stately inn dating back to the mid-1800-s when it was a stopping point for travelers on the busy San Antonio-El Paso road. Rooms at the historic inn are available year-round from Wednesday through Sunday night and daily during March.

For additional information, contact the park at (210) 931-2133.

LAKES

LAKE BUCHANAN

Located near Llano in Llano and Burnet counties, 23,060-acre Lake Buchanan is the northernmost of a string of six impoundments on the Colorado River known as the Highland Lakes. In recent years the lake attracts most anglers for its striped bass and white bass fishing, but it also holds Florida-strain and native northern large-mouth, Guadalupe bass, walleye, crappie and sunfish. Features along the lake's 124 miles of shoreline include sand bars, limestone ledges and mud flats rimmed with mesquite, cedar and oak.

Tail water fishing below Buchanan Dam can be reached by exiting Texas 29 at the blue generator/turbine LCRA Hydro sign east of the LCRA administration building on the south side of the lake next to the dam.

There are a number of private fishing camps and marinas around the lake. Inks Lake State Park, located just south of the dam provides picnic and camping facilities.

View of Lake Buchanan, an exceptional striped bass fishery.

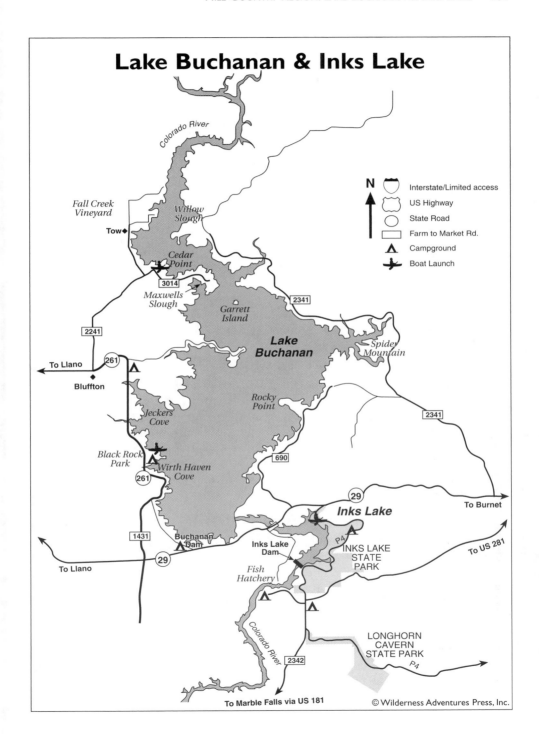

Lake Buchanan & Inks Lake

Colorado River

Fall Creek
Vineyard

Willow
Slough

Tow◆

Cedar
Point

3014

Maxwells
Slough

Garrett
Island

2341

Lake
Buchanan

Spider
Mountain

2241

To Llano ◄

261

Bluffton

Jeckers
Cove

Rocky
Point

2341

Black Rock
Park

Wirth Haven
Cove

261

690

29

Inks Lake

To Burnet

1431

Buchanan
Dam

Inks Lake
Dam

INKS LAKE
STATE
PARK

To US 281

29

To Llano

Fish
Hatchery

LONGHORN
CAVERN
STATE PARK

Colorado River

2342

P4

To Marble Falls via US 181

© Wilderness Adventures Press, Inc.

Legend:
- Interstate/Limited access
- US Highway
- State Road
- Farm to Market Rd.
- ⩓ Campground
- Boat Launch

N

For more information on lake levels and fishing conditions, contact the Lower Colorado River Authority at 800-776-5272.

INKS LAKE

This 803-acre lake on the Colorado River in Llano County lies just below Lake Buchanan, and similarly is a prime destination for striped bass fishing. It also holds good numbers of Florida-strain and native-northern largemouth, Guadalupe bass, hybrid striped bass, crappie and sunfish. Over the years, thanks to the close proximity of state and federal fish hatcheries, Inks Lake has become a test lake for small stockings of Coho salmon, northern pike and muskellunge.

Flyfishers should target schooling or cruising striped bass in open water or largemouth and Guadalupe bass holding along the rocky shallows.

Tail water fishing below Inks Lake Dam can be reached by exiting on County Road 301 on the south side of Inks Lake just before crossing the Texas 29 bridge. Proceed about a mile and exit left at the Shady Oaks RV Park sign and continue for about a half mile.

There is boat and bank fishing access and camping facilities at Inks Lake State Park, which lies along one-third of the lake's shoreline. For additional information on lake levels and fishing conditions, contact the Texas Parks and Wildlife Department at (512) 353-0072.

Inks Lake State Park

Located in Burnet County, nine miles west of Burnet off Texas 29 on Park Road 4, Inks Lake State Park offers fly fishing for largemouth and sunfish as well as striped bass and white bass. White-tailed deer roam the campgrounds and raccoons can often be seen scrounging for food. The Devil's Waterhole, a large deep pool with many shaded pockets that hold small bass and sunfish is located in the park.

Kerr Wildlife Management Area - Located in Kerr County near Hunt, there are two designated bank fishing sections in the management area that provide access to the North Fork of the Guadalupe River.

LAKE LYNDON B. JOHNSON

Formerly known as Granite Shoals Lake, this 6,375-acre lake etched in steep hills and granite domes is one of the most scenic in the chain of six Highland Lakes.

While this lake has a good population of largemouth, including Florida-strain and native-northern, smallmouth, striped bass, hybrid striped bass and sunfish, it also gets a sizable turnout of water skiers and recreational boaters. Flyfishers can beat the crowds by getting out early and prospecting around the many rocky points with minnow patterns and lead-eye Clousers in white and chartreuse fished with intermediate or full-sink lines.

Recreational areas that provide boat and bank fishing access are reached by traveling south from the community of Kingsland on Texas (FM) 1431 to the west side of the lake.

Excellent white bass fishing, including some wade fishing access, is available below Wirtz Dam on Lake Lyndon B. Johnson, located midway between Granite Shoals and Marble Falls on Texas 143. Exit south at the Alvin Wirtz Dam sign.

LAKE MARBLE FALLS

Part of this 780-acre impoundment on the Colorado River, just downstream from Lake Lyndon B. Johnson, is within the community of Marble Falls in Burnet County. The lake is stocked with largemouth and smallmouth bass, hybrid striped bass, white crappie and sunfish.

Two city parks along the lake provide picnic grounds and boat launches and there are privately operated tackle shops and bait camps.

Tail water fishing below the Max Starke Dam on Lake Marble Falls can be reached on Texas 281. Exit east at the sign for the dam and bear right to the parking area. This is a private access area and there is a nominal parking fee.

For more information about current lake conditions, contact the Texas Parks and Wildlife Department at (512) 353-0072.

LAKE TRAVIS

This 18,930-acre reservoir on the Colorado River just above Austin winds through the scenic Texas Hill Country for 65 miles. The lake offers 270 miles of shoreline for fishing, but it is also heavily developed as a resort getaway and utilized by recreational boaters and skiers. The lake is stocked with a variety of game fish and has produced Guadalupe bass weighing more than 3.5 pounds, striped bass exceeding 30 pounds and white bass of more than 3 pounds.

Anglers on Lake Travis key on the rocky points, which provide the primary fish habitat on the lake. Flyfishers should look for striped bass schooling and chasing live bait in the shallows during warmer months.

Tail water fishing below Mansfield Dam on Lake Travis can be reached from the north side of the bridge on Texas 620 near the dam by exiting at the sign for the low water bridge.

LAKE AUSTIN

This 1,830-acre lake on the Colorado River begins within the Austin city limits and runs about 20 miles north to Marshal Ford Dam and Lake Travis. In addition to a good population of largemouth and sunfish, the lake has been stocked over the years with striped bass, hybrid striped bass, northern pike and walleye. Striped bass in excess of 40 pounds have been taken on the lake.

Flyfishers have a number of features to prospect, including creek mouths and shoreline vegetation. Over the years, Lake Austin has provided exceptional sunfish action around boat docks.

Tail water fishing below Tom Miller Dam on Lake Austin can be reached from Red Bud Trail off Lake Austin Boulevard.

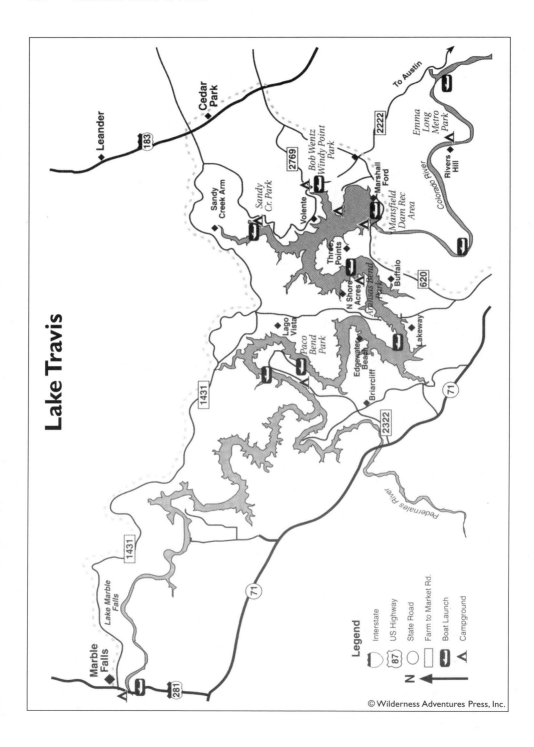

Lake Travis

Leander

Cedar Park

183

To Austin

2222

Emma Long Metro Park

Colorado River

Rivers Hill

Sandy Creek Arm

Sandy Cr. Park

2769

Bob Wentz Windy Point Park

Volente

Marshall Ford

Mansfield Dam Rec Area

Three Points

Buffalo

620

N Shore Acres

Arkansas Bend Park

Lago Vista

Paco Bend Park

Edgewater Beach

Briarcliff

Lakeway

71

2322

Pedernales River

1431

1431

71

Lake Marble Falls

Marble Falls

281

Legend

Interstate

87 US Highway

State Road

Farm to Market Rd.

Boat Launch

Campground

N

© Wilderness Adventures Press, Inc.

Lake Austin & Town Lake

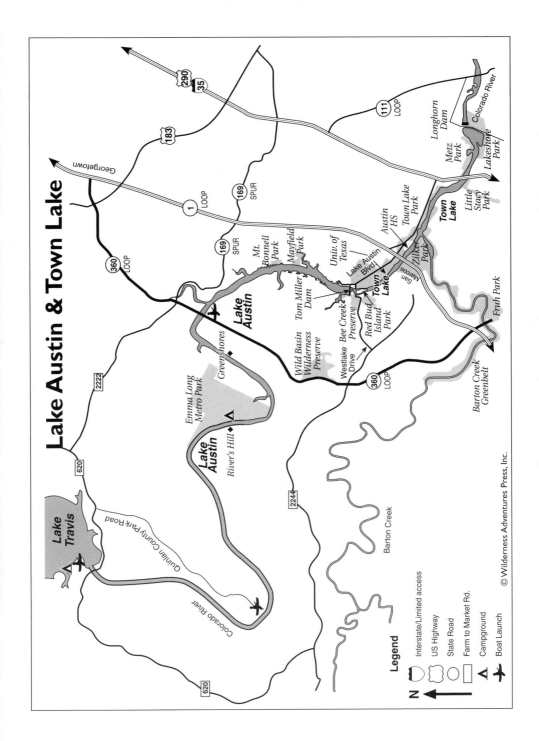

Legend

Interstate/Limited access
US Highway
State Road
Farm to Market Rd.
Campground
Boat Launch

N

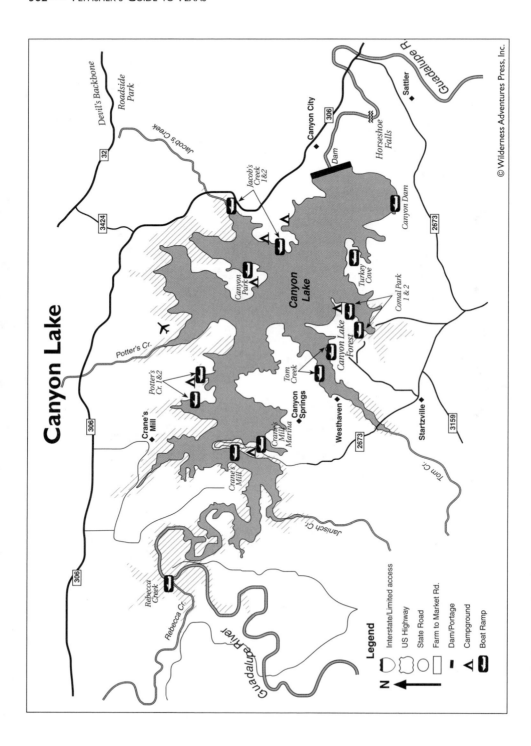

Canyon Lake

© Wilderness Adventures Press, Inc.

Legend

Interstate/Limited access

US Highway

State Road

Farm to Market Rd.

Dam/Portage

Campground

Boat Ramp

N

LAKE DUNLAP

Lake Dunlap (see map page 325), a wide area of the Guadalupe River on the southeast side of New Braunfels offers flyfishers high quality angling for sunfish. Boat access is available under the Interstate 35 Bridge in New Braunfels.

CANYON LAKE

Located off Texas (FM) 306 on the Guadalupe River 15 miles west of New Braunfels in Comal County, this very clear, very deep Hill Country lake holds Florida-strain largemouth, smallmouth, striped bass, white bass and sunfish with a few walleye thrown in. The clear water along steep, rocky ledges offers sightcasting opportunities to wary game fish. Skillful presentations and light fluorocarbon leaders will pay dividends on this 8,240-acre impoundment.

In addition to the lake itself, creeks and tributaries that flow into Canyon Lake are known to produce excellent white bass action. Off Texas 306 past the lake, turn south on Eagle Rock Drive and continue as it turns into Tanglewood Trail. Proceed 2.3 miles and take the first road on the right, and proceed past "Chapel in the Cove" to the Rebecca Creek boat ramp. There are a number of areas upstream worth prospecting during the winter and early spring white bass runs, including creek mouths and high spots in the river.

On the main lake, areas near the dam and around the island near Comal Park can also be good for white bass during the summer months.

For additional information about lake conditions, contact the US Army Corps of Engineers at (830) 964-3341 or the Texas Parks and Wildlife Department at (512) 353-0072.

STATE PARK WATERS

Colorado Bend State Park

Located in San Saba County near the community of Bend, the park can be reached from Lampasas on Texas (FM) 580 West or from San Saba by taking 190 East to Texas (FM) 580 East, then continuing ten miles on an unpaved road to park headquarters. Hidden away in the park is Gorman Falls, which is sustained by a spring-fed stream that cascades over a cliff lining the Colorado River Canyon. Spring is a good time for flyfishers to take part in the white bass run on the river. Hybrid striped bass, largemouth, sunfish and crappie are also present in park waters.

This is an excellent winter fishery with peak action often occurring from mid-February to mid-April. Park waters are accessible to bank and wade fishing in the narrower and shallower sections or from boats in the deeper sections. Boaters should seek information from park officials on the best places to float the river since the Colorado is narrow and rocky in many places.

For information on camping in the park, contact park officials at (915) 628-3240.

McKinney Falls State Park

Located in Travis County, two miles west of US 183 on McKinney Falls Parkway, McKinney Falls offers a quiet, natural retreat from the bustle of Austin. Pools below the two main waterfalls hold largemouth, Guadalupe bass, catfish and sunfish. Wade fishing is possible on shallower stretches of the creek. Austin fly fisher Dr. Larry McKinney, senior director for aquatic resources with the Texas Parks and Wildlife Department (whose headquarters are near McKinney Falls State Park) has caught several good-sized bass out of streams in the area. Onion Creek feeds into McKinney Falls and also offers good fly fishing opportunities. These small creeks and streams need adequate rainfall to reach flow levels, but they can provide excellent fly fishing opportunities and have very little angling pressure.

Lost Maples State Natural Area

Located five miles north of Vanderpool off Texas 187 in Bandera County, Lost Maples offers flyfishers two spring-fed ponds in a beautiful setting among bigtooth maple trees. Species present include largemouth and Guadalupe bass. The park waters on the Sabinal River and Can Creek have been designated a genetic refuge for Guadalupe bass. The river was stocked with Guadalupes to maintain a fishery with pure-strain fish since the species has hybridized with smallmouth in other Hill Country waters. A catch and release regulation is enforced in the park on Guadalupes and largemouth.

Hill Country fly fishing guide Bill Waldron recommends that flyfishers hike along the trails about a mile into the backpacking area of the park where they can find larger fish in the Sabinal River its feeder creeks. The park attracts heavy visitor traffic during the summer months, but late spring and fall is an ideal time for fly fishing in this scenic park.

Hill Country State Natural Area

Located 10 miles west of Bandera off Texas 173 and Texas (FM) 1077, Hill Country State natural area offers fly fishing in West Verde Creek for largemouth, sunfish and channel catfish. The holes and pockets of this lightly fished creek offer excellent wade fishing for sunfish.

The spring-fed creek winds for more than six miles through the park. Park officials say the best fishing is in the fall and winter months. For information call (512) 796-4413.

URBAN OPTIONS
Austin
TOWN LAKE

This Colorado River impoundment (see Town Lake map on page 359) running through downtown Austin is only blocks from the state Capitol and offers superb fly fishing for sunfish, white bass, black bass and striped bass. Anglers can access shorelines or use canoes and kayaks on the lake. A city ordinance prohibits gasoline-motor boats. This regulation, as well as directives indicating that some fish in the lake possess unsafe levels of chlordane and DDT, has greatly reduced fishing pressure and made Town Lake one of the most attractive catch and release fly fishing destinations in the state.

The lake has produced the state record redear, an incredible 2.99 pound fish, and the state record warmouth at 1.3 pounds.

There are a number of put-ins for launching a canoe or kayak on Town Lake, including one at Austin High School near Tom Miller Dam, Festival Beach, behind the Holiday Inn at Interstate 35 or at the Youth Hostel on the south end of the lake. Austin fly fisher Constance Whiston says she likes to fish the south side of the lake and around Red Bud Island near Tom Miller Dam. There are some rocky areas where the bass spawn. The colder the water, the deeper you want to fish the fly, she says.

Town Lake in Austin.

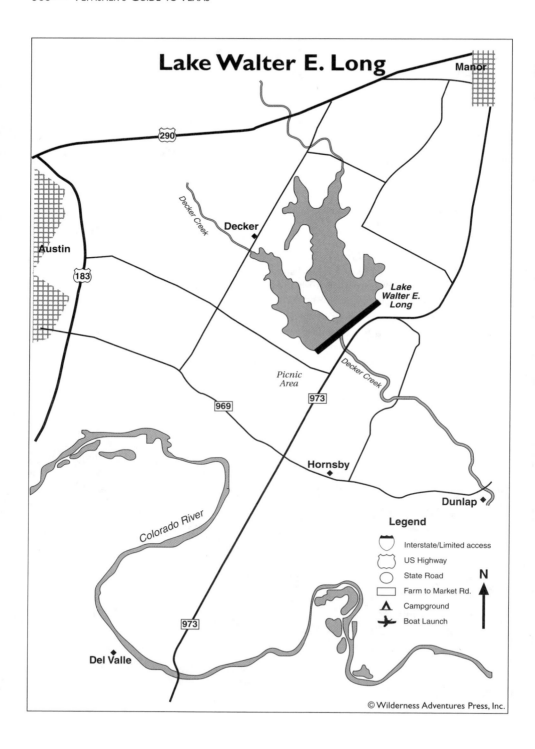

Lake Walter E. Long

Manor

290

Decker Creek

Decker

Austin

183

Lake
Walter E.
Long

Decker Creek

Picnic
Area

969

973

Hornsby

Dunlap

Colorado River

973

Del Valle

Legend

Interstate/Limited access
US Highway
State Road
Farm to Market Rd.
Campground
Boat Launch

N

© Wilderness Adventures Press, Inc.

Mike Verduin of Dallas, a nationally known Texas fly tier and skilled fly fisher, won several of the highly competitive sunfish tournaments once held on Town Lake. He says the hardest thing in that tournament was to try not to catch a bass. "A big Hexegenia hatch comes off right about the first of June when they had the tournament. And the bass sit under there and suck those things down and get gorged."

Between Tom Miller Dam and Longhorn Dam, Town Lake provides a varied habitat for game fish, including cliff faces and moss banks. The weekends attract heavy boating activity on the lake, and like most urban fisheries, weekdays are the best times to fish.

Verduin recommends using traditional damsel fly and dragon fly nymphs on size 14 hooks, as well as anything that imitates a small crawfish because the mud bugs spawn in that area. A size 10 Woolly Bugger is also an excellent choice, Verduin says. He notes that one of the best stretches of Town Lake to fish is by the Elephant Ear plants by Austin High School.

LAKE WALTER E. LONG

Located on the east side of Austin, 1,210-acre Lake Walter E. Long is known for its population of largemouth and hybrid striped bass. Largemouth in excess of 12 pounds and hybrid striped bass weighing more than 8 pounds have been taken in the lake.

Bulrush and cattails along the shorelines provide cover for game fish and the lake can be fished from power boats as well as canoes, kayaks and other small watercraft. There is also good bank access on city park property, where there are picnic facilities and boat ramps.

For additional information, contact the park at (512) 926-5230.

PRIVATE WATERS

Rio Bonito Ranch

Located 20 miles south of Junction, The Rio Bonito Ranch offers meals and lodging in a stately 1930s-era, hacienda-style ranch house along with catch and release fishing for largemouth, bluegill, longear, redear, and green sunfish in two creeks. The handsome, two-story ranch House is situated on a high bluff overlooking a lake fed by the creeks. A second lake on the property is also open to fly fishing.

For information, contact Rio Bonito Ranch at 800-864-4303.

Rio Bonito ranch house near Junction.

Hill Country Hub Cities
Austin

Population - 487,944   **Elevation - 550'**
Area Code - 512   **County - Travis**

ACCOMMODATIONS

Best Western - Executive Inn, 1851 North IH-35, Round Rock / 225-3222 /
70 rooms / $$ to $$$
Comfort Inn, 700 Delmar Avenue / 302-5576 / 73 rooms / $ to $$
Days Inn - University / Downtown, 3105 North IH-35 / 60 rooms / $$
La Quinta Inn and Suites - Airport, 7625 East Ben White Blvd. / 142 rooms /
$$ to $$$
Ramada Ltd. - Airport, 5526 North IH-35 / 800-880-0709 / 140 rooms / $ to $$

BED AND BREAKFASTS

Country Cottage, 2008 Travis Heights Boulevard / 479-0073 / 2 rooms / $$$
Woodburn House Bed and Breakfast, 4401 Avenue D / 888-690-9763 / 5 rooms /
$$$
Wildflower Inn, 1200 West 22½ Street / 4 rooms / $$$

CAMPGROUND

Austin Lone Start RV Resort, Cabins as well as tent and RV sites available / 7009 S.
IH-35 / 444-6322 Information / 1-800-284-0206 Reservations /
austinlonestar@gocampingamerica.com

RESTAURANTS

Art's Rib House, 2330 South Lama Boulevard / 442-8283
Cafe' Mozart, 2414 Exposition Blvd / Austrian cuisine / take-out / Lunch or dinner
/ 479-6660
Holiday House, 5201 Airport Boulevard / 452-3136
El Gallo Restaurant, 2910 South Congress Avenue / 444-2205 / 444-6696
La Posada Restaurant, 6800 West Gate Boulevard / 444-2631
Madam Nadalini's Restaurant & Cafe, 3663 Bee Caves Road / Dressy or casual /
Stunning, contemporary dining room. Milanese dishes prepared fresh / Smoke
free premises / 328-4858
Taco Xpress, 2529 S Lamar Blvd / 444-0261 / Virtually always a crowd at this little
hot spot serving up some of the best Tacos and Tex-Mex in Austin
Texas Land & Cattle Steak House, 6007 North Interstate 35 / 451-6555

FLY SHOPS AND GUIDE SERVICES

Austin Angler, 312½ Congress Avenue / 472-4553 / www.Austinangler.com
Orvis Austin, The Arboretum Crossing, 9333 Research Boulevard / 231-1645
Austin Outfitters, 2901 Capital of Texas Highway / 329-6061

SPORTING GOODS STORES

Austin Outdoor Gear and Guidance, 3411 North IH 35 / 473-2644 / www. Austinoutdoors.com

Academy Sports and Outdoors, 4103 North Interregional Highway / 453-7261

Academy Sports,11150 Research Blvd / 512-343-8800

Academy Sports, 6601 Burnett Road / 512-451-6408

Academy Sports, 801 E. William Cannon Drive / 512-444-9573

Academy Sports, 4970 West US Hwy 290 / 512-899-3401

KC's Outdoors, 6800 W. Hwy 290

Oshman's, 2525 W. Anderson Lane, Suite 600 / 512-459-6541

Second Seasons Outdoors, 4402 N. Lamar / 512-302-4327

HOSPITALS

Brackenridge Hospital, 601 E. 15th Street / 324-7000

AIRPORTS

Bergstrom International Airport / 530-6510 / America West: 800-235-9292 / American Airlines: 800-433-7300 / Continental Airlines / 800-433-7300 / Delta: 800-221-1212 / Northwest Airlines: 800-225-2525 / Southwest Airlines: 800-221-2000 / United Airlines 800-241-6522.

FOR MORE INFORMATION

Greater Austin
Chamber of Commerce
P.O. Box 1967
Austin, TX 78767
478-9383

Flyfishers taking an afternoon break at a Hill Country ranch.

Georgetown

Population - 16,752   **Elevation - 750'**
Area Code - 512   **County - Williamson**

ACCOMMODATIONS
Comfort Inn, 1005 Leander Road / 863-7504 / dogs are welcome for $5 fee /
    $60 to $70
Days Inn, 209 N. Interstate 35 / 863-5572 / $44 to $56

BED AND BREAKFASTS
Clabourne House, 912 Forest Street / 930-3934

CAMPING
Cedar Breaks Park, located west of Georgetown off Texas (FM)
2338 / 930-5253 / free entry / open 6 a.m. to 10 p.m.
Jim Hogg Park, located northwest of Georgetown off Texas (FM) 2338 / free entry /
    open 6 a.m. to 10 p.m.

RESTAURANTS
Cianfrani Coffee Company, 715 Main Street / 869-7030 / Coffee and pastries
Courthouse Cafe and Creamery, 805 South Austin Avenue / 863-9755

FLYSHOPS AND GUIDES
For nearest fly shops see Austin

FOR MORE INFORMATION
Georgetown Convention and Visitors Bureau
P.O. Box 409
Georgetown, TX 78627-0409
800-436 8696 www.georgetown.org

LODGING PRICE KEY

$	=	$30 - $50 per night
$$	=	$50 - $70 per night
$$$	=	$70 per night and up

RESTAURANT PRICE KEY

$	=	$10 and under per meal
$$	=	$10 - $20 per meal
$$$	=	$20 and up

Junction

Population - 2,681   **Elevation - 1,710'**
Area Code - 915   **County - Kimble**

ACCOMMODATIONS

Goodman Cabins - Located on the South Llano River on a scenic hillside with pecan groves ten miles south of Junction on US 377, Goodman Cabins / 446-3870 / offers canoe shuttle service.

Fox Hollow Cabins - Located nine miles south of Junction on US 377 / 446-3055 / two furnished cabins with kitchens / 45 to 55.

Days Inn, Junction, Located near the Llano River and City Park in Junction / 446-3055.

Homer Martin Ranch, Located 55 miles east of Junction and 10 miles south of Mason, this working cattle ranch on the main section of the Llano River has eight cabins and a lodge. There is access for wade fishing and the owners will arrange shuttles for day long float trips.

BED AND BREAKFASTS

Sunny Williams Bed and Breakfast, Junction. Also offers canoe shuttle service for flyfishers in the Junction area / 915-446-2112.

Rio Bonito Ranch, Located 20 miles south of Junction, the Rio Bonito Ranch offers meals, lodging and catch-and-release fishing for largemouth bass and sunfish on several small lakes and creeks.

Willow Creek Ranch, Located on the Llano River, south of the small community of Art, which is about 8.0 miles east of Mason on Texas 87. Turn south in Art on Lower Willow Creek Road and proceed for about 7.0 miles. Bear right and look for the sign to the ranch. Owners Kay and Dennis Evans live in the smaller House behind the big ranch House. There is a guest cottage and lodge on the property and access to a quarter of a mile of the Llano River. For more information write Willow Creek Ranch, P.O. Box 1599, Mason TX 76856 / 915-347-6781 or 888-281-7242 / e-mail: willowcr@hctc.net.

CAMPING

South Llano River State Park, Located 3.5 miles south of Junction off US 377.

Morgan Shady Park, Located near Junction Courthouse where Sixth Street dead ends at the city park. Open from March 1 to September 15, campground offers camping on the river in pecan groves / 915-446 2580.

KOA Campground, Located on the north side of Junction on the North Llano River / 2145 Main Street / 800-562-7506 Reservations / 915-446-3138 Information / jctkoa@ktc.com www.koa.com

CANOE AND KAYAK RENTAL

Llano River Canoes, A canoe shuttle and rental service operated out of Goodman Cabins on US 377, ten miles south of Junction. Among float trips offered is a scenic stretch on South Llano River from low water crossing near Telegraph to Goodman Cabins / 915-446-3192 / e-mail: chkgood@ktc.com

South Llano River Canoes, Located on US 377, 1 mile south of South Llano State Park / 915-446-2220.

RESTAURANTS

Come'n Git It, 2341 North Main Street / 446-4357

Lum's,2031 North Main Street / 446-3541 / barbecue and deli sandwiches

VISITOR INFORMATION

Kimble County Chamber of Commerce
402 Main
Junction, TX 76849
446-3190
Kimblecocofc@satl.net

Car with kayaks at cabins on Llano River near Junction.

Uvalde

Population - 15,304
Area Code - 830

Elevation - 913'
County - Uvalde

ACCOMMODATIONS
Holiday Inn, 920 East Main St / 512-278-4511 / $
Continental Inn, East Main / 278-5671 / $$
Amber Sky, East Hwy 90 / 278-5602

BED AND BREAKFAST
Casa de Leona Bed and Breakfast, 1149 Pearsall, Highway 140 / 278-8550 /
   located on Leona River

RESTAURANTS
Jerry's Restaurant, 539 West Main / 278-7556 / $
Don Marcelino's, East Main Street / 278-8998 / $
Jorge's Tacos, 308 West Main Avenue / 278-4721 / $

CAMPGROUNDS
Park Chalk Bluff, located on Texas 55 about 15 miles northwest of Uvalde /
   278-5515 / Nueces River runs through the campground / cabin rentals
   $35 to $65, campsites with water and electricity hookups $15 / daily entrance
   fee is $3 per person.
Wes Cooksy Park, located three miles south of Camp Wood on Texas 55, about 30
   miles north of Uvalde / 597-3223 / 42 campsites / sites with full hookups rent
   for $15, those with water and electricity rent to $10.

SPORTING GOODS STORES
Wal-Mart, 2340 E. Main / 830-278-6221

FOR MORE INFORMATION
Uvalde Convention and Visitors bureau
300 East Main
Uvalde, TX 78801
278-4115

Fredericksburg

Population - 7,745   Elevation - 1,743'
Area Code - 830   County - Gillespie

ACCOMMODATIONS
Fredericksburg Lodge, 512 E. Main / 997-6568
Best Western, 312 East Hwy Street / 992-2929
Comfort Inn, 908 South Adams St / 997-9811
Days Inn, 808 South Adams St / 997-1086

BED AND BREAKFAST
Gastehaus Schmidt, 231 West Main Street / 997-5612

CAMPGROUNDS
Fredericksburg KOA, Cabins as well as tent and RV sites available / 5681 US 290 / 997-4796 Information / www.koa.com

RESTAURANTS
Altdorf Restaurant, 301 West Main / 997-7865 / open every day except Tuesday. Closed in February / serves American-Mexican-German menu for lunch and dinner / $-$$

FLY SHOPS AND GUIDES
Hill Country Outfitters, 109 East Main Street / 997-3761

CAMPGROUNDS
Lady Bird Johnson Municipal Park, located three miles south of Fredricksburg on Texas 16 / 997-4202 / liveoak shaded campground in 340-acre park with creek running through it / hookup sites $13, tent sites $6 / Park office hours 7 a.m. to 11 p.m.

FOR MORE INFORMATION
Fredericksburg Chamber of Commerce
106 North Adams
Fredericksburg TX 78624
997-6523

Kerrville

Population - 21,992   **Elevation - 1,645'**
Area Code - 830   **County -Kerr**

ACCOMMODATIONS
Holiday Inn Y.O. Ranch Hotel, 2033 Sidney Baker / 200 rooms / 257-4440 / $$
Hillcrest Inn, 1508 Sidney Baker / 800-221-0251 / $
Best Western Sunday House Inn / 2124 Sidney Baker / 896-1336 / 97 rooms / $$

BED AND BREAKFASTS
Marianne's Country Bed and Breakfast, Route 1, Box 527, Center Point / 3 rooms / 634-7489
River Run Bed and Breakfast, 120 Francisco Lemos Street / 6 Rooms / 896-5402 / www.riverrunbb.com

CAMPGROUNDS
Kerrville KOA, Cabins as well as tent and RV sites available / 2950 Goat Creek Rd. / 800-562-1665 Reservations / 895-1665 Information / kervlkoa@ktc.com www.koa.com
Buckhorn Lake Resort, Tent and RV sites available / I-10 Exit 501. 4071 Goat Creek Rd. / 800-568-6458 Toll Free / 895-0007 Local / buckhorn@ktc.com

FLY SHOPS AND GUIDE SERVICES
Pico Outdoor Company, 1600 Harper Road / Kerrville / 895-4348 / www.pico-outdoor.com

SPORTING GOODS STORES
Champion Fishing Company, 624 Clay St. / 210-896-3474
Killen Tackle, 1319 E. Veterans Mem Drive / 817-634-2020
Oshman's, 2100 South W.S. Young / 254-699-4741

FOR MORE INFORMATION
Kerrville Convention and Visitors Bureau
2108 Sidney Baker
Kerrville, TX 78028
792-3535
www.ktc.net / kerrcvb

San Marcos

Population 40,411
Area Code - 512

Elevation - 58'
County - Hays

ACCOMMODATIONS
Best Western, 108 IH-35 North / 754-7557 / 50 rooms / $ to $$
Best Western - San Marcos, 917 North IH-35 / 800-528-1234 / 51 rooms / $ to $$
La Quinta Inn - San Marcos, 800-531-5900 / 116 rooms / $ to $$
Shoney's Inn, 817 IH-35 North / 50 rooms / $ to $$

RESTAURANTS
Bubba's Bar-B-Q, 119 East Hutchinson Street / 392-6111 / ribs, brisket, sliced and chopped barbecue sandwiches / $
Grins Restaurant, 802 North LBJ Drive / 396-0909 / $
Fuschak's Pit Bar-B-Q, 920 State 80 / 353-2712 / $
Peppers at the Falls, 100 Sessom Drive / 396-5255 / $

CAMPGROUNDS
Shady Grove, Texas (FM) 1919 crossing / 357-6113
Pecan Park Retreat, on the San Marcos River / 392-6171
Plum Creek RV Park: Tent and RV sites available / 24800 IH 35 South (Exit 210) Kyle, TX / 396-8300 Information / Reservations camp@plumcreekrv.com

RIVER OUTFITTERS, CANOE RENTALS AND SHUTTLES
T.G. Canoe Livery, 402 Pecan Park Drive / 353-3946
Pecan Park Retreat, on the San Marcos River / 392-6171

SPORTING GOODS STORES
Wal-Mart, 1015 Hwy 80 / 512-353-0617

FOR MORE INFORMATION
San Marcos Chamber of Commerce / Convention and Visitors Bureau
P.O. Box 2310
San Marcos, TX 78667
393-5900
www.sanmarcostexas.com

New Braunfels

Population - 37,855   **Elevation - 720'**
Area Code - 830   **County - Comal**

ACCOMMODATIONS

Maricopa Riverside Lodge, Texas 306 and the Guadalupe River / 18 rooms / 964-3600 or 800-460-8891

Best Western Inn and Suites, 1493 IH-35 North / 800-528-1234 / 60 rooms / $ to $$$

Comal Inn, 424 Comal Avenue / 629-6060 / 2 rooms / $$$

Edelweiss Inn, 1063IH-35 North / 629-6967 / 40 rooms / $ to $$$

Holiday Inn, 1051 IH-35 East / 625-8017 / 140 rooms / $$ to $$$

RESTAURANTS

The Gristmill Restaurant, 1287 Gruene Road / 625-5722 / located in old cotton gin overlooking the Guadalupe River / chicken fried steak, rib eyes, hamburgers and chicken among specialties / $ to $$

Naegelin's Bakery, 129 South Seguin Avenue / located in the heart of downtown New Braunfels / pastries, coffee, tea and hot chocolate / $

Krause's Cafe, 148 S. Castell / 625-7581 / German-American food including sausages and sauerkraut / closed first three weeks in September / $

BED AND BREAKFASTS

Prince Solms Inn, 295 East San Antonio St., New Braunfels / 625-9169, 800-625-9169 / $$$

Gruene Mansion Inn, 1275 Gruene Road / 629-2641 / 28 rooms / $$$

Historic Kuebler-Waldrip Haus Bed and Breakfast, 1620 Hueco Springs Loop / 800-299-8372 / 10 rooms / $$ to $$$

CAMPGROUND

Landa RV & Campground: Tent and RV sites available . 565 North Market / 625-1244 Information / Reservations landarv@hotmail.com www.landarv.com

RIVER OUTFITTERS, CANOE RENTALS AND GUIDES

River Raft Company, Gruene / 625-2800

Rockin' 'R' River Rides, Gruene / 629-9999

Maricopa River Rides, Texas 306 and the Guadalupe River / 964-3600, 800-460-8891

Gruene River Company, 1404 Gruene Road, New Braunfels, Guadalupe River at Gruene Crossing / 625-2800

Bezdek's Rentals, 7308 River Road / 964-2244

FLY SHOPS AND GUIDES

Gruene Outfitters, 1629 Hunter Road / 625-4440

SPORTING GOODS STORES

Academy Sports and Outdoors, 2727 N.E. Loop 410 at Military Drive, San Antonio
/ 523-5191

FOR MORE INFORMATION

New Braunfels Convention and Visitors Bureau
P.O. Box 311417
New Braunfels, TX 78131
625-2385

FLYFISHING CLUBS IN HILL COUNTRY REGION

Austin Flyfishers
P.O. Box 10504
Austin, Texas 78766
(512) 918-1832

Central Texas Flyfishers
P.O. Box 1564
San Marcos, TX 78667

Flyfishing at park on San Marcos river in downtown San Marcos.

REGION 7

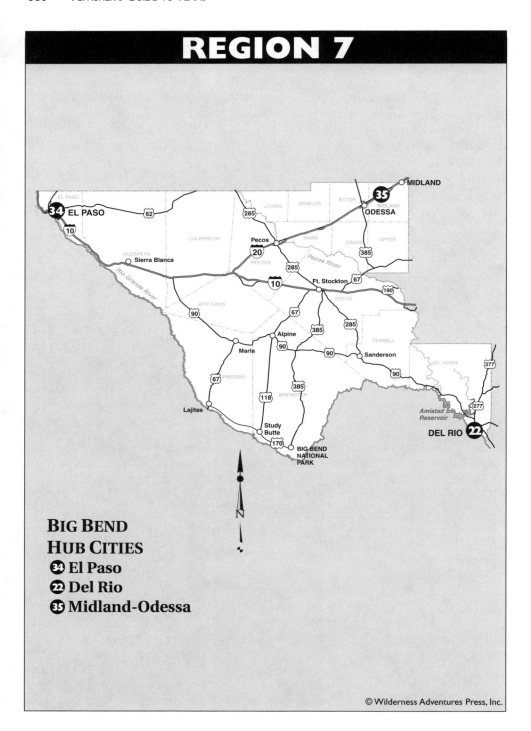

BIG BEND
HUB CITIES
34 El Paso
22 Del Rio
35 Midland-Odessa

© Wilderness Adventures Press, Inc.

Big Bend Country

REGION 7

PANHANDLE PLAINS

PRAIRIES & LAKES

PINEY WOODS

BIG BEND COUNTRY

HILL COUNTRY

GULF COAST

SOUTH TEXAS PLAINS

Located west of the Pecos River, the Big Bend Country Region - also called the "Trans-Pecos" - holds the largest state park, largest county, deepest canyons, and the only mountains in the state.

A big and broad area, several of its counties are the size of New England states. Except for El Paso and its environs, the region has remained,lightly populated, living up to the name, el despoblado, unpopulated land, that Spanish explorers gave it. Its colorful history is identified with the Apache and the Tigua, Judge Roy Bean and Pancho Villa. The Rio Grande, one of the longest rivers in North America bounds the region along its western and southern flanks.

Most of the region lies within the Chihuahuan Desert and the lower elevations in the region usually receive less than 10 inches of rain annually, allowing only sparse, hardy vegetation to grow.

Despite the meager annual rainfall and the considerable distances between fisheries, the region is the home of some of the most beautiful spring-fed waters in the state. Balmorhea Lake in Reeves County is an oasis of bird life and McKittrick Creek is a refuge for the only reproducing population of rainbow trout in the state. In addition to its rugged landscape and pristine spring-fed waters, the Devils River north of Del Rio offers flyfishers a robust smallmouth bass population.

RIVERS

McKITTRICK CREEK

Located within the boundaries of Guadalupe Mountains National Park, this sce-nic creek bathed in dappled sunlight and shaded in an over story of oaks and maples has the distinction of being the home of the "wildest" and possibly the only native trout in Texas waters. McKittrick Creek supports the only reproducing population of trout in the state. And while it is too fragile to be open to angling, the fish are there to be marveled at along with an intriguing story about their origins.

McKittrick Canyon and the Guadalupe Mountains are the only area of the state believed to have once supported a native population of Rio Grande cutthroat trout. The Rio Grande cutthroat (*Oncorhynchus clarki virginalis*), also called "Apache trout" for the early human inhabitants of the region, is the southernmost subspecies of cut-throat trout and still maintains a tenuous existence in New Mexico.

While the range and habitat would have been supportive to Rio Grande cut-throat in McKittrick Canyon, the mystery is complicated by the lack of any mention of the cutthroats in early railroad surveys or Calvary records dating back to the 1840s. Similar records of areas only 20 miles to the north in New Mexico document the pres-ence of the fish.

El Capitan in Guadalupe National Park.

McKittrick Creek

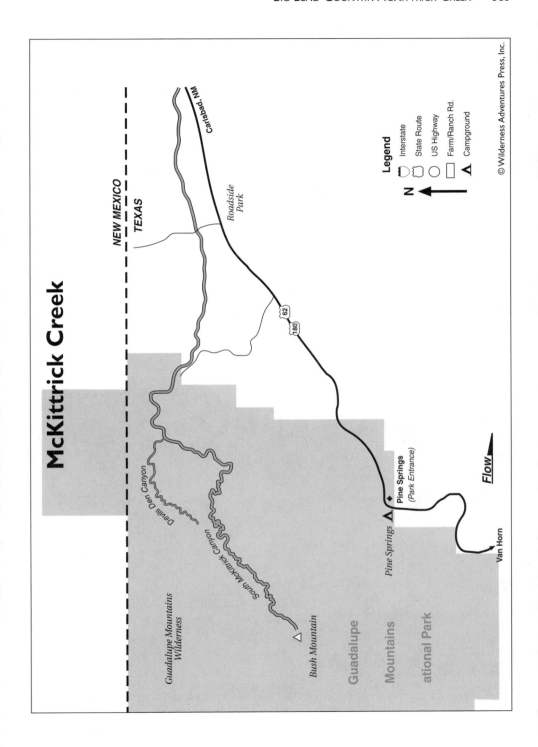

NEW MEXICO

TEXAS

Carlsbad, NM

Roadside Park

62
180

Guadalupe Mountains Wilderness

Devils Den Canyon

South McKittrick Canyon

Bush Mountain

Pine Springs
(Park Entrance)

Pine Springs

Guadalupe

Mountains

ational Park

Van Horn

Flow

N

Legend

⬡ Interstate
⬭ State Route
◯ US Highway
▭ Farm/Ranch Rd.
△ Campground

© Wilderness Adventures Press, Inc.

"But that doesn't totally exclude the possibility of cutthroats being here," according to Fred Armstrong, Natural Resources Program Manger at the park. "When we look at geographic distribution and historic distribution, the Rio Grande was probably present in these canyons if there was a perennial water source." The fish taken from McKittrick Creek for study by fisheries biologists are rainbow trout that have been traced to stockings in the late 1920s by ranchers and the Texas Game and Oyster Commission. But Armstrong notes that the canyon stream may have once held native cutthroat trout. The creek is within the distribution area of a native species of cutthroat trout present during presettlement periods.

Armstrong says park officials are currently working with researchers at Colorado State University to determine whether any of the existing rainbows in McKittrick Creek possess genes from cutthroat trout, which might confirm that a native species first inhabited the stream. The problem with that approach is that rainbows are susceptible to such a degree of cross breeding in the hatchery environment that even evidence of cutthroat DNA might not nail down an undisputed link to McKittrick Canyon cutthroats.

The populations of rainbow trout that now thrive in the 2.5 mile open-water stretch of the creek come with their own mystery and historical significance.

According to oral histories, the first foreman on the ranch that would later become the park is credited with releasing trout in the creek back in the 1920s. Other ranchers who settled in the area a decade later reported that the trout were present when they arrived.

Flyfishers can enjoy the beauty of the Guadalupe Mountains National Park and watch the rainbows rise on the creek.

Armstrong says there is only sketchy information about the stockings by pioneer ranchers in the 1920s. Questions also remain about where the fish came from. There is the possibility, Armstrong says, that a state hatchery truck en route between scheduled stockings at other waters might just dropped some fish in the creek in a handshake deal with local ranchers during the same period. Whatever the scenario, those fish adapted well to their new environment. "There are no records of any stockings since then so the fish that were planted were able to take to the creek and they have self-perpetuated," Armstrong says.

Based on the unique history of the fishery, park biologists are forced to wrestle with two different approaches, Armstrong says. One of those is whether the "exotic" rainbows should be removed to provide a habitat for the endangered Rio Grande cutthroat. The other is whether the rainbows should receive the same consideration afforded any native trout since they are not only self-perpetuating but also unique to the human history of the area. "So it is a darned if you do, and darned if you don't situation," Armstrong says. "Because if we maintain the current trout population, we are in the purest sense violating the purpose of a national park to not manage for an exotic species. But (the rainbows) have a connection with an eminent figure with the establishment and story of the park."

Flyfishers can enjoy the beauty of the Guadalupe Mountains National Park and watch the rainbows rise on the creek from the vantage point of the McKittrick Canyon Trail, which crosses the creek at two different locations. But don't even think about casting a dry fly to one of these trout. No fishing is allowed. Besides observing the trout of McKittrick Canyon, there are many other attractions in the 86,416-acre park. Between the desert below and the highlands above, McKittrick Canyon has a mix of life that is part desert, part canyon, woodland, and forest. Bigtooth maple, Texas walnut, velvet ash, gray oak, and choke cherry trees grow along McKittrick Creek. Elk range throughout the high country and down into the canyons and lower slopes of the Guadalupe Mountains. An estimated 50 to 70 elk inhabit the park. Other wildlife in the park includes coyotes, porcupines, gray foxes, mule deer, and mountain lions.

Moderate temperatures and protection from the sun and wind provided by the high cliffs create a lushness that is rare in this part of Texas. In late October and early November the foliage turns to brilliant reds, yellows, and oranges.

There are more than 80 miles of trails, ranging in difficulty from easy to strenuous. The trails are rocky and often steep and rugged.

The Headquarters Visitor Center at Pine Springs has natural history exhibits and slide shows. There are no lodging facilities in the park but two front-country campgrounds have tent and RV sites, water and restrooms. There are also 10 backcountry campgrounds. Camping permits are required and may be obtained at the Headquarters Visitor Center. For additional information, contact the park at (915) 828-3251.

Guadalupe Mountains National Park is located in Pine Springs, 110 miles east of El Paso via US 62/180 or 65 miles north of Van Horn on Texas 54.

Smallmouth bass (Micropterus dolomieui)

A book published in 1971 by the Texas Parks and Wildlife Department on freshwater fishes of Texas listed 35 species in state waters but the smallmouth bass was not among them. About the same time that the book was published, smallmouth bass were being introduced into Texas lakes and streams. Today there are a number of excellent smallmouth fisheries in Texas and smallmouth in excess of 7 pounds have been caught in Texas lakes. Lakes Meredith, Whitney and Texoma are among the leading lake habitats and the Devils River in West Texas is considered one of the premier smallmouth fisheries in the country.

Smallmouth bass (Micropterus dolomieui) *introduced in Texas in the early 1970s can trace their roots to broodstock from Arkansas and Tennessee. Like smallmouth in other states, they seem to thrive where there are rocky shorelines, gravel bars and clear, cool water. Their average size in Texas is one to two pounds in reservoirs and less than a pound in streams. A principal food source for the smallmouth is the crayfish and flyfishers rely on a number of effective fly patterns that imitate or simulate the freshwater crustacean to take Texas smallmouth. The vertical barring on the sides of the smallmouth and its brownish, green color differentiate it from the Guadalupe and spotted bass, which are similar in appearance and sometimes found in the same waters.*

Like the spotted bass, smallmouth are most active in the spring and fall. Smallmouth spawn in water temperatures that range from the high 50- to the mid-60 degrees F. and prefer to build their nests in deeper water.

DEVILS RIVER

Located about a 90-minute drive from Del Rio, Devils River is a sparkling oasis of life in the rocky, dry, desert country of West Texas. In recent years, tales of its population of smallmouths have reached almost folklore status in Texas. One of the big reasons for this is that there are lots of fish and not many anglers fishing for them on the Devils. These bronzebacks thrive in one of the most enchantingly beautiful, yet maddeningly inaccessible rivers in the Southwest. Working to protect and conserve the river's natural state while overseeing a prudent level of access to the fishing is the Texas Parks and Wildlife Department, which administers the Devils River State Natural Area. The river is bordered by large private ranches, the owners of which enforce their property rights vigorously. No vehicles are allowed along the river except those operated by licensed outfitters taking out or launching float trips. Day use of the state natural area is limited to within the boundaries of the park, and overnight camping is permitted only for groups embarked on a float down the river.

Despite the difficulties faced, a growing number of intrepid anglers and seasoned outfitters are willing to suffer the bruises and rock rash of boulder-strewn portages and low-flow stretches for a shot at exceptional smallmouth fishing.

Baker's Crossing (on Highway 163) to Rough Canyon Recreation Area, where the river meets Amistad Reservoir, is a 48-mile stretch of the river that offers the best fishing opportunities. For the most complete tour of the river, canoeists and kayakers can put-in at a private riverside campground at Baker's Crossing and proceed down the river about 15 miles to the state natural area. Float trip parties are allowed to camp there overnight and continue down the river the next day. A second night's stop is available at Dandridge Falls in the Blue Sage Subdivision at the 25-mile point, leaving the option of paddling the final lengthy stretch to the Rough Canyon Marina and Recreational Area on Amistad Reservoir.

The 15-mile upper section of the river from Baker's Crossing to the state natural area has the lowest flow levels and will test the endurance of most paddlers. An ideal time to float the river is March through May when water levels are normally highest. A flow of 250 cubic feet per second (cfs) is the minimum for canoeing the river, with 300 to 360 cfs the ideal. The lower section of the river, from the natural area to Amistad Reservoir, is somewhat easier to manage because numerous springs add water to the river and raise its level, so there are fewer portages for canoeists to negotiate.

Full sinking and sink-tip fly lines matched to 6-weight to 8-weight fly rods are ideal for fishing the deep holes and heavy currents of the Devils River. Most of the larger fish hold along the rocks in the deepest holes. Flyfishers will need an 8 to 10-pound test tippet to counter abrasion from the many submerged rocks. The long, deep pools, grassy flats, and idyllic spring creeks along the state natural area provide some of the most attractive smallmouth habitat on the river.

Craig Kautsch, owner of Main Street Outfitters in Fort Worth and a veteran of several Devils River float trips says the trip down the river can be demanding.

Devils River

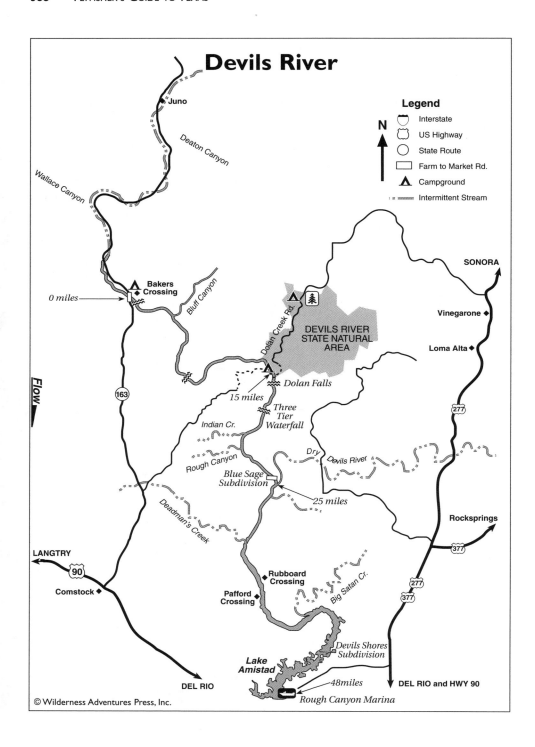

Juno

Deaton Canyon

Wallace Canyon

Legend

N

Interstate

US Highway

State Route

Farm to Market Rd.

Campground

Intermittent Stream

SONORA

Bakers
Crossing

0 miles

Bluff Canyon

Vinegarone

Dolan Creek Rd.

DEVILS RIVER
STATE NATURAL
AREA

Loma Alta

Flow

163

Dolan Falls

15 miles

Three
Tier
Waterfall

Indian Cr.

Dry Devils River

277

Rough Canyon

Blue Sage
Subdivision

25 miles

Deadman's Creek

Rocksprings

377

LANGTRY

90

Rubboard
Crossing

277

377

Comstock

Pafford
Crossing

Big Satan Cr.

Devils Shores
Subdivision

Lake
Amistad

48 miles

DEL RIO and HWY 90

DEL RIO

Rough Canyon Marina

© Wilderness Adventures Press, Inc.

"If you are not in shape, it can be difficult float," Kautsch says."The river looks like it is four different rivers when you do the whole float."

While a float can mean a lot of hard work and dragging canoes over shallow areas, it often is a rewarding angling experience. Kautsch says he has caught small-mouth up to 3½ pounds using intermediate and full-sink lines. Among the bonuses is great wildlife viewing, including the possible sightings of the painted bunting and crested caracara.

Kautsch says he uses river guide Gerald Bailey, Devils River Outfitters (1-800-7-DEVILS) for put-in and take-out services. He says his groups park their vehicles at Baker's Crossing, spend the night there and put-in the next morning for a three day float that allows lots of time for fishing. Overnight camping is done on islands in the river bed and not on private ranch property along the shorelines.

Devils River State Natural Area

The 19,989-acre Devils River State Natural Area is located 65 miles north of Del Rio. Take Texas 277 north out of Del Rio for 43 miles, then turn left at Dolan Creek Road and travel 22 miles on the county-maintained dirt road to the park headquarters.

Public access to the state natural area is carefully controlled to retain the natural beauty of the waterway while respecting the privacy of the neighboring landowners. The riverside section of the natural area is open for walk-in day use, but it was intentionally designed to be a considerable trek. With a one day permit, visitors can drive the 3½ miles to a parking area and gate then walk 1½ miles down a gravel road to the river. Float tubes or other light watercraft are allowed on the river, but they must be carried in, and carried out at the end of the day.

There is limited primitive camping and bunkhouse space available. Reservations can be made by contacting the Texas Parks and Wildlife Department in Austin at (512) 389-8900. A permit is required for all persons entering the natural area for day use or overnight camping.

Permits may be obtained for backcountry campsites at the park headquarters between 8 a.m. and 5 p.m.

For additional information, contact the Devils River State Natural Area at (210) 224-8774 or Texas Parks and Wildlife Department at (512) 389-8900.

LAKES

RED BLUFF RESERVOIR

Located on the Pecos River along the border with New Mexico east of Guadalupe Mountains National Park, Red Bluff Lake is stocked with Florida-strain and native-northern largemouth, striped bass, hybrid striped bass, white and black crappie, black drum, and red drum.

Surrounded by arid, desert country, the 11,700-acre lake holds clear water but little in the way of fish-holding structure except bottom features. This, coupled with frequent fluctuations in water levels, make this lake a difficult prospect for anglers. To get to the lake, take US 285 north at Pecos and travel 43 miles to the Orla community. The lake is 5 miles north of Orla off of US 285. There are unimproved launch ramps at the north and south end of the lake.

BALMORHEA LAKE

Located on Sandia Creek in Reeves County, this 573-acre lake is stocked with largemouth, crappie, sunfish and channel catfish. This oasis in the heart of the Chihuahuan Desert offers flyfishers bank and boat fishing access. Canoes, kayaks and other small watercraft are ideal for fishing the lake and a 10 m.p.h. speed limit is enforced on boats with outboard motors. The lake, whose features include grassy as well as rocky shorelines, also attracts a wide variety of bird life, from loons, pelicans and geese to painted buntings and red- winged blackbirds.

There are RV camping and launch ramp facilities available at the lake. For additional information, contact the Balmorhea Fishing Resort at (915) 375 2308. The park is located 3 miles east of Balmorhea in Reeves County.

Balmorhea State Park

Located about 6 miles from Lake Balmorhea in the desert flatlands on the north side of the Davis Mountains in Reeves County, the 46-acre Balmorhea State Park is the site of San Solomon Spring, the largest artesian springs in the area. The desert spring holds sunfish and catfish but no fishing is allowed in the park due to the presence of two other endangered species, the Comanche Springs pupfish and the Pecos mosquito fish. The spring boils up in the sandy bottom of a 1.75 acre, 30-foot deep pool, whose clear, cold waters are attract swimmers and divers. The park has motel units and a small campground with partial hookups and showers. Reservations are recommended. For additional information, contact Balmorhea State Park at (915) 375-2370. The park is located just south of Interstate 10 near Balmorhea.

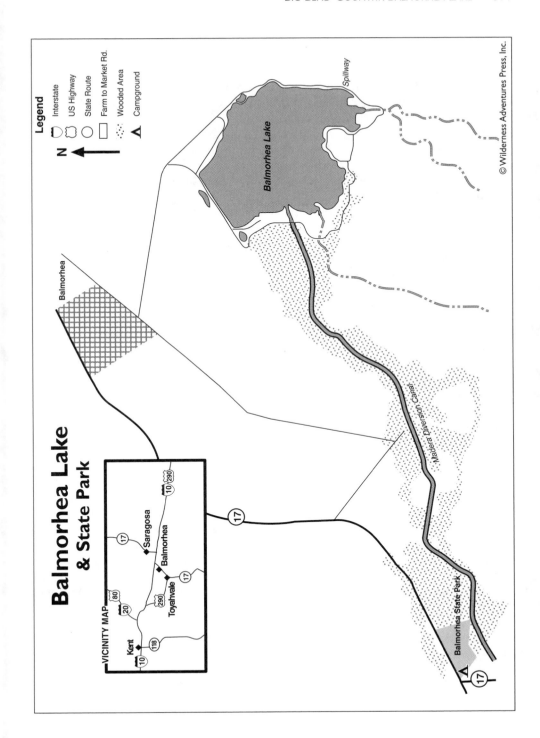

Balmorhea Lake & State Park

Legend

- Interstate
- US Highway
- State Route
- Farm to Market Rd.
- Wooded Area
- Campground

N

Balmorhea

Balmorhea Lake

Spillway

Madera Diversion Canal

Balmorhea State Park

17

VICINITY MAP

10 / 290

17 Saragosa

Balmorhea

80

290 Toyahvale 17

20

Kent

118

10

© Wilderness Adventures Press, Inc.

LAKE AMISTAD

Located on the Rio Grande River along the Texas-Mexico border, 13 miles north-west of Del Rio, Lake Amistad, which covers almost 65,000 acres at its normal level, lies along steep limestone canyons and holds an abundant population of Florida-strain and native-northern largemouth, striped bass, hybrid striped bass, channel catfish, smallmouth bass, white crappie and sunfish. In the 1970s, Texas Parks and Wildlife fisheries specialists also experimented with stockings of walleye, northern pike, and muskie.

The lake offers a variety of options for all anglers including flyfishers. Amistad supports a showcase smallmouth fishery that extends upstream from the Devils River, a tributary on its northern end. Largemouth in excess of 15 pounds and striped bass in the 40 pound class have been taken in the lake. When the largemouth move into shallow water during the spring months, local anglers recommend targeting them with deer hair and hard-bodied bass bugs on the inside of grass lines. Amistad's abundant hydrilla beds are also excellent places for flyfishers to find largemouth action.

Boats can be launched at Amistad only from designated ramps. There are a num-ber of commercial marinas located on the lake provide lodging and RV camping sites and the National Park Service also provides boat ramps, primitive campgrounds, pic-nic areas, marinas and day use facilities. There is a fee for boat launch and camping services. Three major ramps are the Diablo East ramp, 10 miles from Del Rio, Rough Canyon ramp, 23 miles from Del Rio, and Pecos ramp 44 miles from Del Rio. There are unimproved launch ramps at the north and south end of the lake.

Texas and Mexico fishing licenses are required in their respective water. For addi-tional information, contact the superintendent, Amistad National recreation Area at (830) 775-7491 or the Texas Parks and Wildlife Department at (210) 349-2174.

STATE PARK WATERS

Big Bend Ranch State Park

For the fly fisher determined to cast a fly on one of the more remote and beau-tiful stretches of the Rio Grande River in the heart of the Chihuahuan Desert, the 269,714-acre Big Bend Ranch State Park offers that singular opportunity. Fishing is permitted at a few locations along the river and flyfishers are virtually guaranteed a level of solitude not found on many western rivers. The tradeoff, according to park rangers, is that the species available are limited to gar, carp, and blue catfish. Trotline and jug fishing for catfish and gar, popular pastimes on other stretches of the Rio Grande, are prohibited in the park. Flyfishers and other rod and reel anglers must possess a valid fishing license and activity permit.

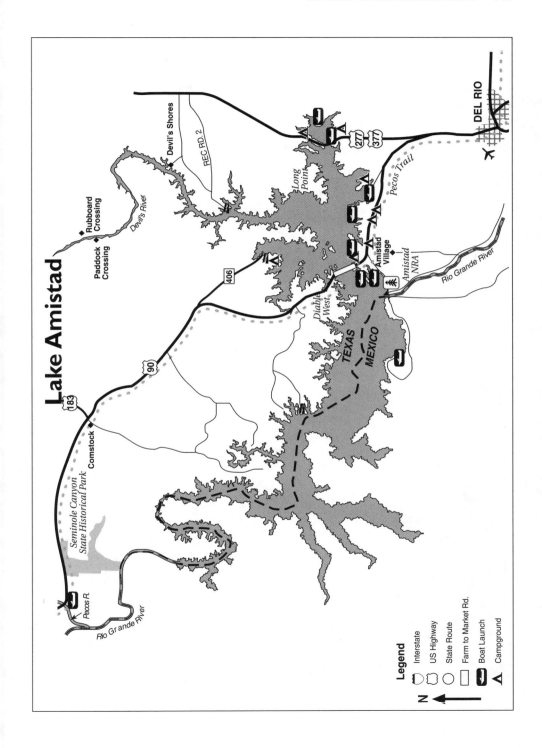

Lake Amistad

DEL RIO

Devil's Shores

REC RD. 2

Rubboard
Crossing

Paddock
Crossing

Devil's River

Long Point

Pecos Trail

277
377

Amistad
Village

Amistad
NRA

Rio Grande River

406

Diablo
West

TEXAS

MEXICO

183

90

Seminole Canyon
State Historical Park

Comstock

Pecos R.

Rio Grande River

Legend

Interstate
US Highway
State Route
Farm to Market Rd.
Boat Launch
Campground

N

In this remote corner of West Texas, the Rio Grande flows through sheer-walled Colorado Canyon, forming the southern boundary of the park. Texas (FM) 170 that follows the river is considered one of the most spectacular drives in the state.

Other popular activities in the park include hiking and backpacking along trails ranging in length from 1.5 miles to more than 20 miles.

Primitive car campsites with composting toilets are available along the river. There is no water or hookups. There is also primitive backcountry camping available for backpackers. Group accommodations with meals are available at the former ranch headquarters by reservation. For additional information, contact the park at (915) 229 3416.

URBAN OPTIONS

Ascarate Park

Ascarate Park in El Paso includes a 44-acre lake that is stocked with largemouth, sunfish and catfish and rainbow trout during the winter months. The pond yielded a 9.87 pound largemouth in 1988.

For additional information, contact the park at (915) 772-3941.

Rio Grande River.

Big Bend Country Hub Cities
El Paso

Population - 609,518   Elevation - 3,762'
Area Code - 915   County - El Paso

ACCOMMODATIONS
Holiday Inn Airport Hotel, 6655 Gateway West / 800-882-6411 / 206 rooms / $$
La Quinta Inn - Cielo Vista, 9125 Gateway West / 800-531-5900 / 115 rooms /
    $ to $$
Quality Inn, 6201 Gateway West / 778-6611 / 306 rooms / $ to $$
Motel 6 Central, 4800 Gateway Boulevard / 800-4MOTEL6 / 200 rooms / $

RESTAURANTS
Bill Parks Bar-B-Que, 3130 Gateway East / 542-0960 / open Monday through
    Saturday for lunch and dinner / $
Avila's, 10600 Montana / 598-3333 / open daily for lunch and dinner / $
Forti's Mexican Elder, 321 Chelsea / 772-0066 / open daily for lunch and dinner /
    $

SPORTING GOODS STORES
Big 5, 735 Mesa Hills / 915-585-8414
Trouster Flys, 609 Spring Crest / 915-585-3661

AIRPORTS
El Paso International Airport / 772-4271 / Aerolitoral: 1-800-237-6639 / America
    West: 1-800-235-9292 / American Airlines: 1-800-433-7300 / Continental
    Airlines: 1-800-525-0280 / Delta: 1-800-221-1212 / Frontier: 1-800-432-1359:
    Southwest: 1-800-435-9792

FOR MORE INFORMATION
Greater El Paso Civic, Convention, and Tourism Department
One Civic Center Plaza
El Paso, TX 79901
534-0600

Midland - Odessa

Population - 194,719 (combined)   **Elevation - 2,891'**
Area Code - 915   **County - Midland &Ector**

ACCOMMODATIONS

Best Western - Garden Oasis, 110 West IH-20, Odessa / 877-574-9231 / 118 rooms
/ $$

La Quinta Inn - Odessa, 5001 East Highway 80, Odessa / 800-531-5900 /
122 rooms / $$

Claydesta Inn, 4108 North Big Spring, Midland / 800-365-3222 / 115 rooms / $$

Ramada Inn, Midland Airport, 100 Airport Plaza Drive / 561-8000 / 96 rooms /
$ to $$

CAMPGROUND

Midessa Oil Patch RV Park: Tent and RV sites available / 4220 South County Road
1290 / 563-2368 campoilcountry@aol.com

RESTAURANTS

Wall Street Bar and Grill, 115 East Wall Street, Midland / 684-8686 / Open Monday
through Saturday for lunch and dinner, Sunday for brunch only / $

Dona Anita's, 305 West Florida, Midland / 683-6727 / $

The Barn Door, 2140 Grant Street, Odessa / 337-4142 / open Monday through
Saturday for lunch and dinner

SPORTING GOODS STORES

H&E Sports, 410 N.Main St. / 915-682-2473

AIRPORTS

Midland International Airport / 560-2200 / American Airlines / American Eagle:
800-433-7300 / America West: 800-235-9292 / Continental Airlines:
800-525-0280 / Southwest Airlines: 800-435-9792

FOR MORE INFORMATION

Midland Chamber of Commerce / Convention and Visitors Bureau
109 South Main
Midland, TX 79702
683-3391

Odessa Chamber of Commerce
700 North Grant Street
Suite 200
Odessa, TX 79761
332-9111

Del Rio

Population - 34,931
Area Code - 830

Elevation - 948'
County - Val Verde

ACCOMMODATIONS

Best Western - Inn of Del Rio, 810 Avenue F / 800-336-3537 / 62 rooms / $

Ramada Inn, 2101 Avenue F and Highway 90 West / 800-228-2828 / 155 rooms / $$

Laguna Diablo Resort, Lake Amistad

La Quinta Inn - Del Rio, 2005 Avenue F / 800-531-5900 / 100 rooms / $$

BED AND BREAKFAST

Villa Del Rio, 123 Hudson Drive / 768-1100 / 5 rooms / $$ to $$$

1890 House Bed and Breakfast Inn, 609 Griner Street / 775-8061 / 5 rooms / $$ to $$$

RESTAURANTS

Cripple Creek Saloon, US 90 West at US 277 / 775-0153 / Open Monday through Saturday for dinner / $

Memo's, 804 East Loysoya / 775-8104 / Open Monday through Saturday for lunch and dinner, Sunday for dinner only / $

Crosby's Restaurant and Bar, Avenida Hidalgo 195, Ciudad Acuna, Mexico / 2-20-20 / $

FLY SHOPS AND GUIDE SERVICES

Gerald Bailey, Devils River Outfitters / float trip guide and put-in and take-out services on the Devils River / 1-800-7DEVILS

FOR MORE INFORMATION

Del Rio Chamber of Commerce
1915 Avenue F
Del Rio, TX 78840
775-3551

Rio Grande River.

Big Bend National Park.

Texas Fly Patterns

A colorful and deadly collection of battle tested fly patterns - both classic and modern - grace the fly boxes of Texas flyfishers. These run the gamut from streamers, hair and hard-bodied bugs, terrestrials, dry flies and nymphs to tiny lipped plugs and plastic worms with tandem hooks, beads and spinners.

The following is a list of the personal favorites of some of the most savvy freshwater flyfishers in the state.

TOPWATER POPPERS, HAIR BUGS, DIVERS AND TERRESTRIALS

Target species: Largemouth, Guadalupe bass, Kentucky spotted bass, sunfish

Verduin's Ball Joint Fly

The creation of Mike Verduin of Lewisville, considered one of the most innovative fly tiers in Texas, this unique combination of a rounded spun deer hair head and jointed streamer tail give this fly an action that bass find hard to resist.

To tie the tail, place a No. 12 sewing needle in the vise with the point extending forward. Form a ¼ inch loop in a piece of 20 pounds coated wire leader material, and tie it to the point of the needle. Draw it snug but not tight and wrap thread about ¼ inch back from the loop. Trim the tag ends of the leader material and coat the wraps with epoxy. Tie in splayed hackles, wrap schlappen collar and whip finish. Slide the completed tail assembly off the needle and allow it to dry.

To tie the body, place the hook in the vise and tie in a section of 20 pounds coated wire leader for the weed guard. Thread a length of the coated wire material through the tail assembly and form another ¼ inch loop. Anchor it with thread wraps on top of the weed guard above the hook barb making the connection with the jointed tail. Spin or stack deer hair for the head and trim it in a rounded ball shape. Tie in the weed guard at the hook eye and add doll's eyes to the rounded head.

Hook:	No. 6 Mustad 8300 bronze
Weedguard:	20 pounds coated wire leader
Thread:	Size A
Tail:	Four splayed hackles with a schlappen collar
Body:	Spun or stacked deer hair, trimmed into rounded ball

Accardo's Miss Prissy

Whether purchased off the shelf at a K-Mart or from a dusty back road grocery store, this popular floater with hard body, rubber legs and full hackle tail will draw strikes whether fished like a bug or a plug.

Bob's Baby Doll Muddler

Austin fly fisher Billy Trimble calls his adaptation of the Robert McCurdy Baby Doll Muddler "the single most effective pattern for bass that he has ever fished." He uses the fly on Texas rivers and lakes including one of his favorite waters, the San Saba River. In the original pattern, McCurdy uses marabou blood feathers for the tail and dubbing for the gills. Trimble says he substitutes fake fur for the tail because it is tougher than the marabou, which sunfish can tear off. He also uses red hackle feathers for the gills.

When trimming the head, Trimble says he chooses to give the bug a higher profile than that of the original pattern.

Thread:	Flymaster +
Hook:	Mustad 3366
Tail:	Marabou or Fake Fur with flash
Gills:	Red hackle or dubbing
Collar:	Natural deer hair
Head:	White deer hair
Eyes:	Doll eyes

Baby Doll Muddler

For those who also want to try the original Bob's Baby Doll, select a Mustad No. 3366 in size 1/0 or 2, **(1)** wrap about $1/3$ of the hook shank with black monocord, reverse and wrap back to the starting point. **(2)** Slip mylar tubing over the eye and extend the ends to the hook bend. Wrap thread around the ends leaving about ¼ inch extending. Whip finish and tie off. **(3)** Tie in a clump of white marabou on the underside of the hook. **(4)** Tie in a clump of black marabou equal to about 1½ to 2 lengths of the hook shank and cement the feather ends. **(5)** Tie in red hackle, make two turns with thread and tie off. **(6)** Trim a clump of deer hair so the tips will extend back no farther than the hook point with the butts half as long as the tips. Tie in and flair around the hook shank. (7) Tie in two more clumps of deer hair, tie off and cement. Trim the head so it is flat on the sides. Attach doll eyes with shoe goo or similar product.

Hook:	Mustad 3366 (or a Mustad Stinger hook) in size 1/0 or 2
Weed guard:	15 pounds hard monofilament
Thread:	Black monocord
Body:	$^1/_8$ inch pearlescent mylar tubing, white blood marabou, black blood marabou, red hackle, white deer body hair
Eyes:	$^5/_{16}$ inch to $^3/_8$ inch doll eyes

Hula Popper Fly

A classic bug whose consistent, boiling action, tough finish and rubber skirt cause many a largemouth to commit suicide in self defense.

Hula Popper

Dahlberg Diver

All the right contours on this deer hair classic make it the first choice around floating vegetation, flooded timber and other favorite largemouth haunts. Popular colors range from brown and black to chartreuse and purple. Experienced bass-buggers recommend greasing all deer hair bugs with a paste floatant before a day on the water. And after fishing a deer hair fly, always let it dry before putting it back in the fly box.

Dahlberg Divers

Near Nuff Frog

Created by Dave Whitlock and interpreted by Texas master fly tier Billy Munn, this deer hair amphibian has proven it will turn-on bucketmouth largemouth from here to Possum Kingdom.

Accardo Voo Doo Diver

This popping bug with a wobbling action will get the undivided attention of largemouth and sunfish when fished up against the banks of Texas rivers and lakes especially around dawn and dusk.

*Accardo Voo
Do Diver*

STREAMERS, LEECHES, AND MINNOW PATTERNS

Target species: Striped bass, white bass, hybrid striped bass, largemouth, Guadalupe bass, Kentucky spotted bass, sunfish

Cypert Mylar Minnow

Created by Lake Whitney fly fishing guide and fly designer Charlie Cypert, this flashy, durable minnow pattern has proven to be one of the most effective flies for white bass, smallmouth, striped bass and largemouth on lakes and streams throughout the state. Tied on a 34011 Mustad in sizes 6 through 4, it comes in gray, chartreuse, black, white and other colors to match the local forage fish. It is available from Charlie Cypert's Waterbugs, Inc., Aquilla, TX (254) 694-3422.

*Cypert
Mylar
Minnow*

Guadalupe Green

Designed and adapted by Hill Country fly fishing guide Bill Waldron, this Woolly Bugger imitator is effective on a variety of Texas species including Llano River Guadalupe bass and Guadalupe River rainbows.

Hook:	No. 12 Orvis dry fly hook
Head:	¹/₈ gold beadhead
Thread:	No. 6 black
Tail:	olive marabou
Body:	Wrap full shank with lead wire and overwrap with fine grade dubbing hackle.

Guadalupe Green

Hart Ghost Minnow

Tied by Brazos River fly fishing guide and outfitter Richard Hart, the Ghost Minnow is a sparsely tied attractor pattern with a beadhead that is deadly for largemouth, white bass, Kentucky spotted bass and other species on Texas rivers.

Gambill's EHR Fly

This streamer pattern created by East Texas fly fishing guide Brian Gambill, has proven itself on Red River and Brazos River stripers as well Lake Fork and Lake Monticello largemouth. The fly gets its name from the egg yarn, hackle and rabbit materials used to tie it that give it a tantalizing action in the water. The combination of cone-shaped head, rabbit tail, oversized hackle and flat belly causes the fly to "come alive in the water," Gambill says. An all-white fly seems to out fish other colors in Texas waters.

Hook:	1/0 Eagle Claw 253
Thread:	6/0 or 3/0 Flymaster
Tail:	Three inch rabbit strip
Body:	Rabbit, egg yarn and webby soft hackle collar
Eyes:	Solid red (Trim red post eyes and glue with Zap-A-Gap)

Seaducer

Fort Worth fly fisher Brian Camp has success with striped bass on the tail water stretches of the Brazos and Red rivers with a simple but effective Seaducer pattern tied with gray hackle and a few strands of Flashabou. This classic bass and saltwater pattern has a tantalizing swimming action in the fast water and can be dead-drifted around the deep holes downstream on these rivers, Camp says.

Woolly Bugger

Simply one of the most deadly patterns ever invented for freshwater species. Try black, olive and brown colors with a touch of flash material in hook sizes 4 though 10. Works equally well in clear running streams of the Hill Country and in tannin-stained ponds and reservoirs of the Prairies and Lakes and Pineywoods regions.

Woodruff '57 Chevy Bugger

This Woolly Bugger adaptation by East Texas fly fishing guide Robert Woodruff is one of his favorite subsurface patterns for Lake Fork largemouth.

Hook:	Mustad 9762 in size 4 or 6
Tail:	Gray marabou and pearl Krystal Flash
Body:	Silver-tinsel chenille
Hackle:	Light blue dun

Clouser Deep Minnow

The pattern that works on all species in all waters likewise is extremely effective in Texas waters for largemouth, striped bass, white bass, hybrid striped bass, smallmouth, Guadalupe bass, the list goes on and on.

Bendbacks

An often overlooked pattern because of its simplicity, this deadly effective, pioneer warm water pattern is tied on an inverted hook and will go virtually anywhere that bass and sunfish live without snagging. Start with a basic black chenille body with matching marabou tail. Add a matching deer hair wing with a few strands of flash material.

Woodruff Swamp Rabbit

Another Robert Woodruff pattern proven effective on Lake Fork largemouth.

Hook:	2/0 Mustad 3366
Head:	Red rabbit strip
Eyes:	1/36 lead dumbbell eyes
Tail:	Wapsi Fly Tail

Hellgrammite

Hellgrammite patterns match food sources on many Texas rivers. Austin fly fishing guide Joey Lin uses the fly for Kentucky spotted bass in the fast water of Hill Country streams. The trick, Lin says, is to resist stripping the fly in too soon. The pattern can be extremely effective if allowed to sink in the current so the fish can pick it up.

Blanton's Tropical Punch

An effective saltwater pattern tied with red and orange hackle with bead-chain eyes and orange or red chenille head. Lake Fork fly fishing guide Robert Woodruff says this brightly-colored streamer will work on largemouth when shad and sunfish patterns "are not doing the trick."

Marabou Leech

Dallas fly fisher Charles Ducote likes to use a orange beadhead marabou leech pattern when fishing small waters like the 300-acre lake at Purtis Creek State Park.

Nix's Shine-a-bou Shad

A deadly baitfish pattern originated by master fly tier Jimmy Nix of Texas and Costa Rica, this fly is a proven producer on Texas reservoirs and tail water fisheries.

Hook:	3366 size 6 - 2/0
Weed guard:	30 pounds monofilament
Thread:	3/0 monocord, gray and red rod winding thread
Body:	Gray Antron (#27 Wapsi)
Wing: and	Gray marabou topped with pearl and silver Krystal Flash peacock herl: an overlay of gray mallard flank forms the sides.
Throat:	Red marabou
Head:	Gray deer hair, spun and trimmed
Eyes:	Solid eyes from Wapsi or lead eyes

Muddler Minnow

Wally Van Zandt, a veteran fly fisher and fly tier from Austin, often chooses a muddler minnow tied on a No. 8 hook when he fishes Texas rivers including the San Gabriel in Williamson County, one of his favorite waters. To be most effective, Van Zandt says he spins the deer hair tightly at the head and sometimes adds a foam body to cause the fly to float when cast downstream and stripped back into the current.

SUNFISH PATTERNS

Target species: Bluegill, redear, warmouth, longear, redbreast and hybrid sunfish

Petrie's Bluegill Bug

Tied by Houston angler and fly tier Mark Petrie, this little fly with a chenille body, rubber legs and bead eyes is a killer on largemouth, white bass, and crappie. The pattern is available in Houston area fly shops.

Hook:	Orvis 1524
Head:	5/32 bead
Body:	Ice chenille (medium) in black and olive
Legs / Tail:	Round rubber

Petrie's Baby Craw

A similar fly to the Bluegill Bug, but tied on an inverted hook with lead wire wrapped around the full shank, it is a deadly pattern when hopped along the bottom of Texas streams and ponds.

Hook:	Orvis 1524
Body:	.025 lead wire around full shank overwrapped with ice chenille in black, olive or brown
Wing:	Calf tail

Other effective sunfish patterns:

Adams, humpys, hopper imitations, in size 12 to 18, Gold Ribbed Hare's Ear, black ants, woolly worms, and sponge spiders (yellow and black) in size 10 to 12.

DRY FLY, NYMPH AND TERRESTRIAL PATTERNS

Target species: Largemouth, white bass, sunfish, and carp.

Dave's Hopper

As they say, this Dave Whitlock classic is so realistic it could jump out of your hand. Extremely effective on Texas streams, lakes and farm ponds for largemouth as well as the whole lineup of sunfish species.

Dave's Hopper

EFFECTIVE TEXAS TROUT PATTERNS (GUADALUPE AND BRAZOS RIVERS)

Target species: Rainbow, brown trout, golden trout

Jeff's Soft Hackle Casual Dress

Adapted from a Polly Rosborough creation by Dallas flyfisher and tier Jeffrey Hines, this weighted fly is a proven killer on the Brazos River below Possum Kingdom Dam and the Blue River in Oklahoma. Can be dead-drifted behind a strike indicator. Pattern can also be tied without weight and fished as an emerger.

This fly, in size 8 to 10, is also effective on largemouth, smallmouth, sunfish and catfish in lakes and ponds.

Hook:	Tiemco 2312 or Mustad 9672 in size 10 to 16
Thread:	Black 8/0 Pac thread or 6/0 Flymaster
Tail:	Dark brown tuft of muskrat fur with guard hairs left in and tied short
Body:	First, wrap five turns of lead wire in a diameter equal to the hook wire. Wrap wire under the thorax. Over wrap wire and hook shank with mixed muskrat fur twisted into a dubbing loop. Underwing: One or two strands of pearl Krystal Flash or a slender holographic tinsel tied on each side of abdomen.
Hackle:	One and a half to two turns of gray partridge body feather
Collar:	Black ostrich herl
Head:	Tying thread

Waldron's Guadalupe Green

(See Streamers, Leeches, and Minnow Patterns)

Other effective Texas stream patterns include weighted Woolly Buggers, flashback hare's ear, gray caddis emergers, and pheasant tail, red squirrel and stone nymphs.

A San Juan worm with a Glo Bug dropper or other tandem rigs with the top fly a size 16 and the bottom fly a size 22 or 24 is an effective system on these tail water fisheries.

MISCELLANEOUS, UNCONVENTIONAL AND SPECIAL SITUATION FLY PATTERNS

Target species: Largemouth, white bass, sunfish, crappie

Calcasieu Pig Boat

A rubber-hackled fly created by Louisiana flyfisher Tom Nixon, this Cajun-country classic is an excellent choice for largemouth on slow moving rivers and large reservoirs in Texas.

Hook:	1 to 2/0 regular
Head:	Tied in black thread built up into large head
Eyes:	Yellow with red pupils
Body:	Heavy black chenille with black saddle hackvle wound over it. The hackle is tied in near the butts at the bend of the hook.
Skirt:	56 strands of regular size black rubber thread tied evenly around the hook and extending past the hook about one inch.

Midjit Crawler

Made by the Creme Lure Co. of Tyler, Texas, this "mini-worm" pattern also comes with leader assembly, tandem single hooks, beads and spinner (propeller) blade. Each package includes a spare 3 inch worm imitation. This multi-media contraption with many moving parts is fun to fish and will draw savage strikes when dropped around weed beds and submerged brush piles.

Target species: Grass carp, German carp

Marmon Coffee Bean Beetle

An extremely effective pattern on grass carp in the bayous of Houston. Created by urban fly fishing guide Mark Marmon, the Coffee Bean Beetle starts with a selection of a coffee bean. A Costa Rica, Antiqua, or Guatemala bean will add style but any old coffee bean will do. Lay the bean upside down on a sticky tack surface such as double-stick masking tape. Enlarge the natural seam on the bean with a small hacksaw blade. Wrap the hook with thread and apply an adhesive such as Hard As Nails on the thread place the hook in the seam of the bean. Apply epoxy to seal the seam.

Hook:	No. 12 dry fly hook, short shank
Body:	Coffee bean
Thread:	Black or brown
Coating:	Epoxy

Target species: Bowfin

Any gaudy streamer or Deceiver pattern, preferably one that the angler is willing to sacrifice to a shredding machine.

Conservation and Catch & Release

Conservation practices, including catch and release of game fish, are encouraged and widely practiced by flyfishers, tournament bass anglers, guides and fly fishing associations in Texas. A conservation ethic based on the recognition that gamefish populations and the environments that support them are fragile and finite resources is a long time tradition in Texas both in freshwater and saltwater.

In 1955 the Port Aransas Rod & Reel Club instituted a program of tagging and releasing saltwater gamefish, particularly tarpon and billfish, as a way to aid in research and promote conservation in sportfishing. The tradition that began in the marine environment has carried over in more recent years to the state's lakes and rivers. To promote healthy fisheries through sound management, The Texas Parks and Wildlife Department, with support from the state's anglers, has instituted length and bag limits for largemouth bass on most of the state's public waters.

In 1986, a statewide 14-inch minimum length limit and five-fish daily bag limit was established. Texas became a leader in experimenting with higher minimum length limits and protected length, or "slot" limits on selected lakes and reservoirs. The slot-length limit in place on the highly productive but heavily fished Lake Fork, for example, requires anglers to release any largemouth bass measuring more than 16 inches and less than 23 inches in length. The regulation is designed to allow harvest of small and large bass, while protecting the species most prolific breeders. Anglers are allowed to keep one bass measuring 23 inches or more but despite this rule, the practice of killing any large bass on the lake is discouraged with friendly but firm reminders at the docks and cleaning tables on the value of returning the quality breeder gamefish back to the lake.

The Texas Parks and Wildlife Department also has experimented with catch and release only lakes with positive results. At present there are three lakes-Purtis Creek, Gibbons Creek Reservoir and Lake Raven in Huntsville State Park-that require that all bass be released. The exception is that any bass 22 inches or greater may be retained alive in a live well, weighed at a lakeside weigh station and then immediately released or donated to the state's SharelunkerProgram, a state operated research and spawning program.

Texas Parks and Wildlife fisheries biologist Richard Ott said the department was a little hesitant about introducing catch and release fishing on any Texas lake. "We weren't sure anglers would accept it," he said. "But Purtis Creek has proven that anglers have been more than willing to practice it."

Following its opening in 1988, Purtis Creek, a relatively small lake at 355-acres, experienced extremely heavy fishing pressure as much as ten times the level at other Texas lakes. When anglers sensed that the fishing pressure was causing a decline in the fish population through hooking mortality, they backed off, reducing the catch rate at the lake. Since then the lake has maintained a reputation for producing black bass in quality and quantity. Bass in excess of 13 pounds have been weighed at the lake and flyfishers have a realistic chance to land a double digit largemouth during the prime spring and fall fishing seasons.

In addition to conservation measures, fisheries officials say another important reason for the high quality bass fishing now enjoyed by anglers in Texas lakes was the decision in the early 1970s to stock Florida-strain largemouth, a subspecies of large-mouth bass native to the Sunshine state. The premise was that the faster-growing Florida-strain bass would thrive in the large reservoirs which were being created by dams on many of the state's rivers, the home of the feisty but slower growing native northern largemouth.

It did not take long after the introduction of the Florida-strain largemouth and the enforcement of size and bag limits to see the positive effects on the fishery. The 13.5 pound state record for largemouth, which had stood for 37 years, was broken by a 14.1 pound Florida-strain largemouth in 1980. Largemouth exceeding 13 pounds have now been caught in more than 50 Texas reservoirs and today it takes a bass weighing more than 15.15 pounds to rank among the state's top 50 biggest bass.

In addition to a goal of maintaining quality bass fishing for freshwater anglers throughout the state, the Texas Parks and Wildlife Department makes no bones about its desire to play a role in producing a world record bass from Texas waters. To claim that distinction, a Texas angler will have to catch a largemouth that exceeds the 22 pound 4 ounce fish caught in Georgia in 1932.

Operation World Record, a TPWD Inland Fisheries initiative started in 1998, is attempting to determine if fast growth and maximum size are traits in largemouth bass that are inherited and can be amplified through a selective breeding program. TPWD's ShareLunker Program, which collects live bass weighing 13 pounds or more from anglers, has been a successful part of this ongoing program.

Flyfisher releasing brown trout.

Stream Etiquette

With the number of people entering our sport, I would like to share with you an inventory of ideas on stream conduct for flyfishermen to follow. Here are common questions and the answers:

- **How does a flyfisher approach another angler along a stream?**
  A section of water belongs to the angler who starts fishing it first. Until that angler moves on to new water, it's very inconsiderate to crowd. If you must approach that person, move back from the bank so you don't disturb any water upstream or down. And watch your shadow, it can spook fish like crazy.

- **Is it appropriate to ask what fly is being used?**
  Yes, but do it politely. Laws are not written saying you can't ask a fellow angler a question; just use common sense and be courteous. I always try to compliment an angler's efforts before I try to pry valuable information from him or her.

- **What should anglers bring to the stream every single time they fish?**
  Courtesy, consideration, and common sense.

Here are a few ideas to adhere to and pass along to your fellow anglers:
- An angler owns a section of water if he or she is the first person to fish it.
- It is inconsiderate to crowd another angler.
- A slow moving or stationary fisherman has the right to remain where he is. If you are moving, leave the water and quietly walk around him.
- If a fisherman is resting a pool or planning his next move, it is still his water. Don't jump in without permission.
- A fisherman working upstream has the right of way over one coming downstream.
- Always yield to another angler who has a fish on his or her line.
- Don't enter the water directly across from a person fishing the opposite bank.
- Many streams flow though private property. Recognize that access is a privilege, not a right. If unsure about access, ask the landowner. Once permission is secured, don't trample crops, disturb livestock, or leave gates open.
- Try to use visible trails and paths.
- Wade only when necessary. The aquatic food chain is fragile.
- Don't litter. Pick up discarded monofilament, cans, used strike indicators, and tippet packages, and carry them out with you to be disposed of properly.
- Familiarize yourself with local and state fishing regulations.
- Drive slowly in dusty parking lots, foregoing loud music.

Travel Checklist

Whether the plan calls for a day trip or a week-long outing, pre-trip preparation goes a long way in assuring a safe and memorable angling adventure on Texas lakes, rivers and streams. The following is a pre-trip check list for the variety of fly fishing adventures offered in Texas.

Fishing Equipment

_____ "Flyfisher's Guide to Texas"

_____ Line - Include a weight forward floating line in weight appropriate for the flies chosen and a sinking line appropriate for the waterway that will be fished.

_____ Rod and Rod Case - 9' rods are appropriate for most situations, 8 feet to 8'6" for lighter lines on more confined settings.

_____ Reel - Match to line weight with a palming rim on the spool for larger fish such as striped bass and hybrid striped bass.

_____ Extra spools for making quick changes under changing conditions.

_____ Tippet - one spool for each leader diameter.

_____ Backing - 20 pounds dacron.

_____ Fly boxes - Foam lined, clamp style or compartment. Compact for carrying in shirt pocket.

_____ Flies - Selection of sizes and types for top water and subsurface.

_____ Tools - Clamp (forceps), hook sharpener, clippers (nippers, snippers)

_____ Tackle Bag - An organized carrier for tools, fly boxes, leaders and tippet while wading, walking, or boating.

_____ Sunglasses - Polarized for spotting fish and protecting eyes. Quality lenses to reduce fatigue.

_____ Hat - Long bill overs contrast for better vision and protection from sun, wind and rain, as well as errant back casts.

_____ Other optional accessories as appropriate for time of year and waterway: Waders, sun gloves, wading staff, wading boots, sun block, split shot, fly floatant, knot book, flashlight, leader wallet, landing net, pliers, fishing jacket (foul weather), drinking water bag, magnifiers.

Shelter Equipment Check List
_____ Tent
_____ Summer bag or sheet
_____ Ground clothe and stakes
_____ Outfitter wing
_____ Tent wing
_____ Pillows
_____ Sport seats
_____ Whisk for sand

Cooking Gear Check List
_____ Matches
_____ Pot set
_____ Stove with additional fuel
_____ Kitchen tool bag
_____ Water bags
_____ Water purifier
_____ Oven or skillet
_____ Cutting board
_____ Towels
_____ Trash bags
_____ Cooler
_____ Frozen water

Boating Gear Check List
_____ Boat
_____ Sponge and bailer
_____ Paddles
_____ Skirt
_____ Anchor and rod holder
_____ Throw bag
_____ Personal Floatation Devices
_____ Inflatable life jackets
_____ Helmet and thigh straps
_____ Wheels - stern or mid
_____ Duct tape
_____ Maps and charts
_____ Map holder
_____ Seat backrest

Optional Equipment Checklist
___Paddling jacket
___Paddling pants
___Watchcap
___Sandals
___Windbreaker or vest
___Bandanna
___Gloves
___Socks

Personal Item Checklist
___Toothbrush and toothpaste
___Comb
___Hand lotion
___Deodorant
___Sportsman's soap
___Toilet paper and trowel
___Waterproof binoculars
___Camera
___Bird guide
___Hiking / wading staff
___UHF / VHF radios
___Weather radio
___Spotting scope and tripod
___Insect repellent

Clothing

____ _____
____ _____
____ _____
____ _____
____ _____
____ _____
____ _____

Source: Canoesport, Houston.

Travel Tips

By Air

There are more than 1,500 airports in Texas with Houston, Dallas-Fort Worth, El Paso, and San Antonio offering international connections as well as commuter flights. More than 15 commuter airlines serve smaller cities throughout the state with Southwest Airlines offering the most flights at highly competitive fares.

By Car

Texas has some 77,000 miles of state-maintained highways and nine interstates. Speed limits are 30 mph in urban areas unless otherwise posted (watch for 20 mph zones during school hours). Highway limits are 70 mph during daytime and 65 mph at night for passenger vehicles on numbered Texas highways outside urban areas, unless otherwise posted, and 60 mph on county roads unless otherwise posted.

Drivers and front-seat passengers in passenger vehicles are required by Texas law to wear safety belts. Texas law also requires that children under age two must be secured in an approved safety seat. Children ages two to four are required to be secured in a safety seat or safety belt.

Travelers using rental cars must be a minimum of 25 years old and hold a valid driver's license.

Texas Travel Information Centers

Motorists entering Texas from other states will find travel information centers with professionally trained travel consultants, who can provide trip planning information and literature. For visitors entering the state from Oklahoma and New Mexico, there are travel centers at Amarillo (Interstate 40 and US 287) and Anthony (Interstate 10). Other Oklahoma visitors will find travel centers at Denison (US 75), Gainesville (Interstate 35) and Wichita Falls (Interstate 44 and US 277) Travelers from Mexico can stop in at the Laredo (Interstate 35) and Rio Grande Valley centers (US 77 and US 83 at Harlingen). Arkansas travelers can get information at the Texarkana center (Interstate 30) and Louisiana visitors will find a center at Waskom (Interstate 20). There is also a center at the State Capitol in Austin.

There also are thousands of roadside rest stops maintained throughout the state by the highway department. Many of these have restrooms, drinking water, and picnic tables. Camping is not allowed at the rest stops but travelers are allowed to park and sleep in cars, vans, and RVs for up to 24 hours.

By Rail

On its Chicago to Los Angeles run, Amtrak's Texas Eagle with coach, sleeping car, lounge car and dining car services stops at Texarkana, Temple, Marshall, Longview, Taylor, Austin, Dallas, Fort Worth, Waco (McGregor),Austin, San Marcos, and San Antonio.

Texas Eagle passengers can connect in San Antonio with Amtrak's Sunset Limited service to Beaumont, Houston, Del Rio, Sanderson, Alpine (Big Bend State Park) and

El Paso. The Sunset Limited also provides coach, sleeping car, lounge car and dining car services on its New Orleans to Los Angeles run.

For current schedules and other information, contact Amtrak at (800) 872-7245.

By Bus

All the larger cities in Texas and many of the smaller communities are served by Greyhound Bus Lines.

Camping

Each of the seven Texas regions offers a variety of RV and tent campgrounds that in some cases include lake and river sites, hiking trails, stocked pond fishing, marinas and launch ramps. For a free copy of the Texas RV Travel and Camping Guide, call (800) 657-6555.

More than 120 state parks are located throughout the state, many of which provide access to fishing on lakes, rivers, streams and ponds. For information on state park camping facilities, contact the Texas Parks and Wildlife Department at (800) 792-1112 or visit their website at www.tpwd.state.tx.US.

Texas Fly Shops, Tackle Shops, Guides, Outfitters & Boat Rentals

ABILENE
Academy Sports, 3950 John Knox Dr/ 915-698-5490
Dry Creek Anglers, 3301 South 14th St/ 915-698-7801

AMARILLO
Academy Sports, LP 335 & 45th Ave/ 806-468-6314
Anchor Marine, 4217 Canyon Dr./ 806-353-9511
RiverFields, 2465 I-40 West/ 806-351-0980
Top Notch Outfitters, Inc, 2617 Wolfin Village/ 806-353-9468

ARLINGTON
Academy Sports, 100 W. Arbrook Blvd/ 817-472-9700
Oshman's, 4620 South Cooper/ 817-467-0090

AUSTIN
Academy Sports, 11150 Research Blvd/ 512-343-8800
Academy Sports, 6601 Burnet Road/ 512-451-6408
Academy Sports, 4103 N. Interregional Highway/ 512-453-7261
Academy Sports, 4970 West US Hwy 290/ 512-899-3401
Academy Sports, 801 E. William Cannon Drive/ 512-444-9573
Austin Angler, 312-1/2 Congress/ 512-472-4553
Austin Outdoor Gear and Guidance, 411 North IH 35/ 512-473-2644
KC's Outdoors, 6800 W Hwy 290/ 512-288-6001
McBride's Gun Shop, 2915 San Gabriel/
Orvis Austin, 9333 Research Blvd/ 512-231-1645
Oshman's, 2525 W. Anderson Lane, Suite 600/ 512-459-6541
Second Season Outdoors, 4402 N Lamar/ 512-302-4327
The Austin Angler, 312 1/2 Congress Av/ 512-472-4553
Travelfest, 9503 Research
Travelfest Superstores, Inc., 1214 W 6th St, Suite 210/512-479-6381
Treaty Oak, P.O. Box 50295/

BAY CITY
Denn Brothers, 4806 Ave F/ 409-245-2963

BEAUMONT
Academy Sports, 6250 Eastex Frwy/ 409-898-1569
Oshman's, 166 Gateway/ 409-832-7781
Outdoor Outfitters, 3803 Calder Ave/ 409-833-0716

BEDFORD
Hunting Headquarters, Inc., 1725 Woodhill Lane/ 817-267-3700

BROWNSVILLE
  Gordons Bait and Tackle, 7066 E 14th/ 956-831-4825
BRYAN
  Sullivan's Outfitters, 3602 Old College Rd/409-260-9831
CARROLLTON
  Fly Tier's Primer, Inc,   1236 Jeanette Way/ 214-242-0458
COLLEGE STATION
  Academy Sports, 1420 Texas Ave/ 979-696-5305
  Oshman's, 1500 Harvey Road, Suite 1000/ 409-696-0546
CONROE
  Academy Sports, 1420 W. Loop 336 N./ 936-788-1888
  Oshman's, 19075 I-45/ 936-321-2550
CORPUS CHIRSTI
  Academy Sports, 4914 South Padre Island/ 361-992-9022
  Gruene Outfitters of Corpus, 1233 Airline Road/ 361-994-8361
  Oshman's, 5858-46 South Padre Island/ 361-993-0832
DALLAS
  Academy Sports, 8050 Forest Lane/ 214-221-2284
  Fishn' World Inc., 4609 W. Lovers Lane/ 214-358-4941
  Gun and Tackle Store, 6041 Forest Lane/ 214-239-8181
  Orvis Dallas, 10720 Preston Road/ 214-265-1600
  Oshman's, 9100 N. Central Expressway, #123/ 214-363-8441
  Oshman's, 15490 Dallas Parkway/ 972-991-3533
  Pocket Sports Company, 7235 Syracuse Drive/ 214-553-0347
  Rays Hardware and Sporting Goods, 730 Singleton/ 214-747-7916
  Westbank Angler-Dallas, 370 W. Lovers Lane #320/ 214-350-4665
DEL RIO
  Wal-Mart, 2401 Ave. F/ 830-774-4593
DENISON
  Daves Ski and Tackle, 3714 N Hwy 91/ 963-465-6160
  Wal-Mart, 401 N. US Hwy 75/ 963-465-0684
DENTON
  Oshman's, 2201 South I-35, Space P-7/ 940-566-3902
EL PASO
  Big 5, 735 Mesa Hills/ 915-585-8414
  Trouster Flys, 609 Spring Crest/ 915-585-3661
FREDERICKSBURG
  Hill Country Outfitters, 109 E. Main St/ 210-997-3761
FORT WORTH
  Hendrickson Rod Co., 3825 Hollow Creek/ 817-738-1587
  Academy Sports, 6101 I-20 @ Bryant Irvin Road/ 817-346-6622

Backwoods, 3212 Camp Bowie/ 871-332-2423
Main Street Outfitters, 501 S. Main/ 817-332-4144
Oshman's, 4830 S.W. Loop 820/ 817-377-1515
Oshman's, 1250 Green Oaks Road/ 817-731-8578
Texas Outdoors, 3821 SW Blvd/ 817-731-3402

GARLAND
Fin and Feather, 354 E. I-30/ 972-226-2277
Fishermans Supply, RR 3 Box 696/ 972-226-1616
Fishing Store, 3601 4th Lane/ 214-487-6330

GEORGETOWN
Wal-Mart, S Interstate 35/ 512-863-4855

GLEN ROSE
Rough Creek Lodge, P.O. Box 2400/ 254-965-3700

GRANBURY
Brazos Flyfishers, 4412 Waples Road/ 888-200-0364

GRAPEVINE
Bass Pro Shop, 2501 Bass Pro Drive/ 972-691-5217

HARLINGEN
Hook Line and Sinker, 2704 S. 77 Sunshinestrip/ 956-428-6473

HOUSTON
Academy Sports:
   565 Uvalde/ 713-453-8366
   10375 N. Freeway/ 281-445-9838
   12700 N.W. Freeway/ 713-895-7395
   13150 Breton Ridge Street/ 281-894-5858
   10414 Gulf Freeway/ 713-944-7511
   8236 S. Gessner/ 713-271-1679
   8723 Katy Freeway/ 713-465-9565
   2404 S.W. Freeway/ 713-520-1795
   14500 Westheimer/ 281-870-0105
Angler's Edge, 1141-5 Uptown Park Blvd./ 713-993-9981
Canoesport, 5808 S. Rice Ave./ 713-660-7000
Cut Rate Fishing Tackle, 8933 Katy Fwy./ 713-827-7762
Cut Rate Sporting Goods, 10551 Telephone Road/ 713-991-5812
Orvis Houston, 5848 Westheimer Rd/713-783-2111
Oshman's, 1200 McKinney Ave/ 713-650-8240
Oshman's, 2131 South Post Oak Blvd/ 713-622-4940
Oshman's, 8625 F.M. 1960 West/ 281-807-9020
Oshman's, 975 Gessner/713-467-1155
Tackle Hut, 216 W. Little York Rd #c/ 713-694-8008
Westbank Angler-Houston, 5000 Westheimer #620/ 713-961-3474

HUMBLE
Academy Sports, 9805 FM 1960 E. Bypass/ 281-446-2013
Oshman's, 20416 Highway 59 North/ 281-446-7519

IREDELL
Rough Creek Lodge, Rt 1 Box 26l

IRVING
Oshman's, 3524 Airport Freeway West/ 972-986-1110

JASPER
Ann's Tackle Shop, 924 N Wheeler/ 409-384-7685

JUNCTION
Sonnys Canoes, 915-446-2112
Coleman's Canoes, 915-446-3540

KATY
Academy Sports, 23155 I-10 West/ 281-693-2600
Bass Pro Shop, 500 Katy Mills Circle #145/ 281-644-2200

KERRVILLE
Champion Fishing Company, 624 Clay St/ 210-896-3474
Pico Outdoor Co., 1600 Harper Rd/(800) 256-5873

KILLEEN
Killeen Tackle, 1319 E Veterans Memorial Drive/ 817-634-2020
Oshman's, 2100 South W.S. Young/ 254-699-4741

KRUM
Christie Enterprises, Rt 1 Box 285/ 817-482-3418

LAKE DALLAS
Bass House, 5014 S Stemmons Fwy/ 940-321-4747

LAKE JACKSON
Academy Sports, 120 Highway 332 W./ 979-297-8100

LAREDO
Arnold Distribution, 4520 San Bernardo/ 956-223-2066
Border Sporting Goods, 5219 Maher Ave./ 210-722-1007

LEAGUE CITY
Academy Sports, 100 Gulf Freeway/ 281-332-2839

LEWISVILLE
Oshman's, 2325 S Stemmons/ 972-315-1500

LONGVIEW
Army Navy, 209 W Tyler/ 903-753-1571

LUBBOCK
Fishermans Headquarters, 2388 509th St/ 806-793-5822
Mountain Hideaway, 4816 50th Street/ 806-762-8416
Oshman's, 7020 Quaker Avenue/ 806-792-1964
The Outdoorsman, 6602 Slide Rd./ 806-794-6666

LUFKIN
Massey and Brown, 124 Shelley Dr./ 403-561-7613
Tri Lakes Tackle and Outdoor, 2208 E. Denman Ave./ 409-637-7119

MARSHALL
Shooter Sporting Goods, 909 E. End Blvd/ 963-938-0738

MCALLEN
Academy Sports, 100 South Second St./ 956-686-1742
Bud's Fly Shop, Inc., 5509 N Ware Rd/(800) 294-0104
Rio Grande Outfitters, 905 Dove Ave./ (800) 294-0104

MESQUITE
Oshman's, 3540 Emporium Circle/ 972-686-1885

MIDLAND
H & E Sports, 410 N Main St/ 915-682-2473

RICHLAND HILLS
Oshman's, 8555 Airport Freeway/ 817-428-5512
Academy Sports, 7441 N. E. Loop 820/ 817-428-1618

NACAGDOCHES
Wal-Mart, 4810 North Street/ 936-560-6969

NEW BRAUNFELS
Gruene Outfitters, Inc., 1629 Hunter Rd/ 210-625-4440

PARIS
Wal-Mart, 3855 Lamar Ave/ 903-785-7168

PASADENA
Academy Sports, 5500 Spencer Hwy/ 281-998-1632
Marburger Sporting Goods, 4016 Strawberry Suite A/ 281-487-7773

PLANO
Academy Sports, 3305 Dallas Pkwy. Suite 301/ 972-781-2970
Academy Sports, 4045 Central Expressway
Oshman's, 701 Taylor Drive/ 972-509-1992
Anglers Retreat, 4001 Preston Road/ 972-781-1820

PORT ISABELLE
The Shop, 318 Queen Isabella Blvd. / 956-943-1785

PORT ARTHUR
Fish-er-Hunt Shop, 3001 Hwy 73/ 409-736-1884

RICHARDSON
Backwoods, 1453 West Campbell Road/ 972-671-0372
Barlows Tackle Shop, 451 N. Central Expy/ 972-231-5982
Oshman's, 501 South Plano Road/ 972-783-1598

SAN ANGELO
Field and Stream Sporting Goods, 3812 Houston Harte/ 915-944-7094

SAN ANTONIO
Academy Sports, 755 N.W. Loop 410/ 210-523-5191
Academy Sports, 2727 N.E. Loop 410/ 210-590-0500
Academy Sports, 165 S.W. Military Drive/ 210-927-0509

Good Sports, 9861 I-H 10 West/ 210-694-0881
Hill Country Outfitters, 18030 Hwy. 281 North/ 210-491-4416
Northwest Tackle Center, 6812 Bandera Road #126/ 512-681-0009
One Shot Outfitters, 1870 Stone Oak Parkway/ 210-402-5344
Tackle Box Outfitters, 6330 N New Braunfels/ 210-821-5806
Oshman's, 125 N. W. Loop 410/ 210-341-1244

SAN MARCOS
Wal-Mart, 1015 Hwy 80/ 512-353-0617

SPRING
Academy Sports, 25010 Rayford Rd/ 281-367-1010

STAFFORD
Oshman's, 12730 Fountain Lake/ 281-240-3388

SUGARLAND
Academy Sports, 16610 U.S. Highway 59/ 281-494-9696

TEMPLE
Academy Sports, 1407 Marlandwood Rd./ 254-899-1597

TOMBALL
Academy Sports, 28522 SH249/ 281-351-2506

TYLER
Backcountry, 3320 Troup Hwy #125/ 903-593-4602
Jones Creek, 3800 Cloverdale, Tyler/ 903-534-8149
Jones Creek Orvis, 2301 South Broadway #A7/ 903-526-3474
Oshman's, 4023 South Broadway/ 903-581-7888
Sportster, 4542 S. Broadway/   903-561-5505

UVALDE
Wal-Mart, 2340 E. Main/ 830-278-6221

VICTORIA
Tackle Box, 3305 N. Ben Jordan/ 361-575-8700
Victoria All Sports, 1902 Houston Hwy/ 512-537-5481

WEBSTER
Oshman's, 19801 Gulf Freeway/ 281-332-6818

WEST POINT
Tejas Outfitters, 28.5 Plum Highway/ 979-242-3411

WICHITA FALLS
Big 5, 3808 Kemp Blvd/ 940-691-3628

FLY FISHING GUIDES
Cypert's Guide Service, Inc., Charlie Cypert, P.O. Box 73, Aquilla, TX 76622, 817-694 3422.
Gerald Bailey, Devils River Outfitters, 800-7 DEVILS.
Ray Box, Gruene Outfitters, Gruene/New Braunfels, 210-625-4440.
Dan Edwards (409) 321 4602.

Bill Gambill, GandW Guide Service, Little Elm, 972-294-3202.
Grady's Fishing Charters, Lake Texoma, Bill Cashin, 903-786-8316.
Scott Graham, Wimberley, 512-847-6222, troutbum@flash.net.
Richard Hart, Granbury, 279-1169.
Jackie Headrick, Jr., Empty Pockets Fishing Guide Service, Burnet, 512-793-5127
Foard Houston, P.O. Box 641, Devine, 830-665-3202 / 210-822-5325
Richard Laird, Tackle Box Outfitters, San Antonio, 210-821-5806.
Joey Lin, Austin Angler, Austin, 512-472-4553.
Dan Lynch, B'Wana Dan's Guide Service, Lake Fork, 888-667-3591 or 972-878-0923.
Mark Marmon, Metro Anglers Guide Service, Houston, 713-666-8868.
Cliff Pleake, Mabank, 903-887-1372.
Ronnie Ray, West Point, 979-242-3411.
Jeff Snyder, Southwest Fishing Charters, San Antonio, 210-649-2435.
Silver Dollar Guide Service, Red River, 405-838-2578 or 405-838-2297
Chuck Uzzle, Orange, 409-886-5222
Bill Waldron, Hill Country Angler, Canyon Lake, TX 830-935-3281
Constance Whiston, Austin
Robert C. Woodruff, Rt. 1 Box 1697, Quitman, 903-967-2665
Marcus Rodgiguez, The Guides of Texas, San Marcos 512-396-7487
Johnny Quiroz II, The Guides of Texas, San Marcos 512-396-7487

CANOE RENTALS AND RIVER OUTFITTERS
Bezdek's Rentals, 7308 River Road, 830-964-2244
Gruene River Company, 1404 Gruene Road, New Braunfels, Guadalupe
Kerrville Kayak and Canoe Rentals, 130 West Main, Kerrville, 830-895-4348.
River at Gruene Crossing, 830-625-2800
Maricopa River Rides, Texas 306 and the Guadalupe River / 830-964-3600, 800- 460-8891
River Raft Company, Gruene, 830-625-2800
Rochelle's Canoe Rental, Graford, 817-659-3341
Rockin' 'R' River Rides, Gruene, 830-629-9999
Rock Bottom Canoe Rentals, on the Square, Mason, 915-347-6440
South Llano River Canoes, HC-15, Box 214F, Junction, 915-446-2220
Whitewater Sports, Texas (FM) 306 and Guadalupe River, New Braunfels, 830-964-3800

TEXAS PARKS AND WILDLIFE
Trout Stocking Program

A Freshwater Trout Stamp is required to take or attempt to take trout.
Statewide Regulations: No Minimum Length Limit; Daily Bag = 5 trout.
Multiple stockings are made at many locations throughout
winter and early spring.

Water	Nearest City	Quantity Stocked
Ablon Park Pond	Garland	1,133
American Legion Park Pond	Missouri City	1,830
Aquatic Park Pond	Hereford	750
Ascarate	El Paso	2,630
Bane Park Lake	Spring	2,100
Bear Creek Park	Keller	3,600
Bethany Park C	Allen	637
Blanco State Park #4	Blanco	972
Blue Hole Park Lake	Georgetown	1,700
Bob Sandlin State Park	Mt. Pleasant	950
Boykin Springs	Jasper	2,101
Buena Vista Park Lake	Waco	2,913
Buescher State Park	Smithville	1,500
Burke-Crenshaw Lake	Pasadena	2,100
Burroughs Park Pond	Tomball	2,100
C. J. Kelly Park Pond	Midland	1,415
Canyon Tailrace - Guadalupe	New Braunfels	5,011
Carrollton Sports Complex	Carrollton	1,164
Centennial Park Pond	Pearland	2,100
Central Park Pond #1	College Station	1,913
Cleburne-Hulen Park	Cleburne	1,300
Colleyville Nature-Pond 4	Colleyville	915
Comanche Trails Park	Odessa	1,804
Concho River Park	San Angelo	1,000
Doornbos Park	Nederland	500
Eisenhower Park Pond	Houston	2,163
Eldridge Park Pond	Sugarland	1,913
Elm Creek Buffalo Wallow	Abilene	618
Flower Mound Rheudasil	Flower Mound	2,578
Fort Richardson State Park	Jacksboro	1,688
Greenbriar Park	Fort Worth	1,000

Water	Nearest City	Quantity Stocked
Green Valley Comm Pond A	North Richland Hills	1,430
Guadalupe River	See Canyon Tailrace	
Hamilton Creek Park Lake	Burnet	500
Harlingen Sports Complex	Harlingen	1,073
Hearne Eastside Park Pond	Hearne	621
Higginbotham Park	Lubbock	1,125
Hurst Chisholm Park	Hurst	1,264
Jasper City Park Pond	Jasper	1,000
Kennedale City Park	Kennedale	3,328
Kidd Springs Park	Dallas	3,328
Kitty Hollow	Missouri City	1,464
Lady Bird Lake	Fredericksburg	500
Lake Corpus Christi	Mathis	1,373
Lakeside Park	Duncanville	2,391
Lamesa 9th Street Park Lake	Lamesa	830
Landa Park	New Braunfels	500
State Park	Castroville	726
Louise Hayes Park	Kerrville	1,011
Mark Holtz Lake	Arlington	1,664
Martin Road	Amarillo	1,893
Mary Jo Peckham Park	Houston	2,100
McCullough	Lubbock	1,061
Medical Center North	Amarillo	2,062
Meredith Stilling Basin	Sanford	1,215
Meridian State Park	Meridian	2,500
Monahans Perch Pond	Monahans	4,000
Nelson Park	Abilene	1,000
Northwest Park Pond	Irving	2,578
Oakes Street	San Angelo	4,875
Pampa City	Pampa City	894
Pickens	Sherman	1,539
Pittsburg City Lake	Pittsburg	1,000
Plum Lake	Wichita Falls	1,250
Possum Kingdom Tailrace	Graford	1,850
Purtis Creek SP Pond E	Eustace	779
Resoft Park Lake	Alvin	1,830
Richards Park - Upper Pond	Brady	500
Rose Park	Mansfield	800
Rusk State Park	Rusk	2,079

Water	Nearest City	Quantity Stocked
Samuell Farm Pond #4	Mesquite	1,215
San Antonio River	San Antonio	2,046
Sheldon Park Children's #1	Houston	2,100
South Llano River SP	Junction	768
Spring Lake Park	Texarkana	2,910
Springfield	Mexia	1,800
Sulphur Springs City Park	Sulphur Springs	1,614
Teague Park	Longview	2,319
Temple Lions Park Lake	Temple	1,000
Temple- Miller Pond	Temple	2,500
TFFC Casting Pond	Athens	4,000
Tom Bass III	Houston	2,100
Clear Fork Trinity River	Fort Worth	1,038
Two-Acre Lake	Canton	2,170
Tyler State Park	Tyler	2,000
Victoria	Victoria	800
W.M. Brook Park Lake	Lampasas	1,000
Waldron Park	Corpus Christi	1,294
Waterloo	Denison	1,539
W. Columbia Park Pond	West Columbia	1,500

More information about dates, regulations and detailed directions to trout stocking locations may be found by going to the Texas Parks and Wildlife Website at www.tpwd.state.tx.us.htm.

Selected Bibliography

Borger, Gary A. *Nymphing*. Harrisburg, PA: Stackpole Books, 1979.

Daniel, Steve. *Texas Whitewater*. College Station, TX: Texas A&M University Press, 1999.

Ellis, Jack. *Bassin' with a Fly Rod*. North Conway, N.H.: Mountain Pond Publishing, 1994.

————-, *The Sunfishes*. Bennington, VT: Abenaki Publishers, Inc., 1993.

Engle, Ed. *Fly Fishing the Tailwaters*. Harrisburg, PA: Stackpole Books, 1991.

Gierach, John. *Fly Fishing Small Streams*. Harrisburg, PA: Stackpole Books 1989

Graves, John. *Goodbye To A River*. New York: Alfred A. Knopf, Inc. 1960

Huser, Verne. *Rivers of Texas*. College Station TX: Texas A&M University Press, 2000.

Leavell, Lorraine. *The Original Guide to Family Fishing Holes*. Houston, TX: Baylake Publications, 2000.

Lusk, Bob (with Mark McDonald). *Raising Trophy Bass*. Boerne, TX: Firewheel Media, 2000.

Miller, George Oxford. *Texas Parks & Campgrounds*. Houston, TX: Lone Star Books, 1999.

Nolen, Ben and Bob Narramore. *Rivers and Rapids*. Garland, TX: Rivers and Rapids, 2000.

Priddy, B.L. "Bud". *Fly-Fishing the Texas Hill Country*. Barksdale, TX: W. Thomas Taylor, Inc. 1996.

Tinsley, Russell. *Fishing Texas: An Angler's Guide*. Fredericksburg, TX: Shearer Publishing, 1988.

The Dallas Morning News. *Texas Almanac 2000 - 2001*. Dallas, TX: Dallas Morning News, 2000.

Whitlock, Dave. L.L. Bean *Fly Fishing for Bass Handbook*. New York, N.Y.: Lyons & Burford, 1988

————-. *L.L. Bean Fly-Fishing Handbook*. New York, N.Y.: The Lyons Press, 1996.

Zelade, Richard. *Hill Country*. Houston, TX: Lone Star Books, 1999.

Index

Fishing Diary

The following pages will provide a space to collect your thoughts after a day on the water. The "useful symbols" are meant to aid in quickly logging key features and events, while the "notes" section allows ample room for any additional infomation. Keeping an accurate diary will take the guess work out of a repeat visit and, in turn, make you a better angler.

Good Luck!

-Wilderness Adventures Press, Inc.

Date	Water Fished	Conditions		Fish Caught
		Weather	Water	
Useful Symbols	HD-Headwater CF-Confluence MO-Mouth ↑-Upstream ↓-Downstream	S-Sunny C-Cloudy R-Rain WY-Windy	CL-Clear OC-OffColor	RB-Rainbow BN-Brown GB Guadalupe Bass RG Rio Grande Perch LB/SB- Large & Smallmouth Bass

Water Temp.	Notes (i.e. time of day, flies used, fishing pressure)	Pg. #

DAM- Damselfly CDM-Clouser Deep Minnow WB Woolly Bugger TWB Top Water Bug HOP-Grasshopper
TW-Tailwater SC-Spring Creek STK-Stocktank PW-Pocket Water CB-Cutbank RES Reservoir

Date	Water Fished	Conditions		Fish Caught
		Weather	Water	
Useful Symbols	HD-Headwater CF-Confluence MO-Mouth ↑-Upstream ↓-Downstream	S-Sunny C-Cloudy R-Rain WY-Windy	CL-Clear OC-OffColor	RB-Rainbow BN-Brown GB Guadalupe Bass RG Rio Grande Perch LB/SB- Large & Smallmouth Bass

Water Temp.	Notes (i.e. time of day, flies used, fishing pressure)	Pg. #

DAM- Damselfly CDM-Clouser Deep Minnow WB Woolly Bugger TWB Top Water Bug HOP-Grasshopper
TW-Tailwater SC-Spring Creek STK-Stocktank PW-Pocket Water CB-Cutbank RES Reservoir

Date	Water Fished	Conditions		Fish Caught
		Weather	**Water**	
Useful Symbols	HD-Headwater CF-Confluence MO-Mouth ↑-Upstream ↓-Downstream	S-Sunny C-Cloudy R-Rain WY-Windy	CL-Clear OC-OffColor	RB-Rainbow BN-Brown GB Guadalupe Bass RG Rio Grande Perch LB/SB- Large & Smallmouth Bass

Water Temp.	Notes (i.e. time of day, flies used, fishing pressure)	Pg. #

DAM- Damselfly CDM-Clouser Deep Minnow WB Woolly Bugger TWB Top Water Bug HOP-Grasshopper
TW-Tailwater SC-Spring Creek STK-Stocktank PW-Pocket Water CB-Cutbank RES Reservoir

NOTES

NOTES